North Florida

Central Florida

South Florida

Florida Wildflowers in Their Natural Communities

Plant Drawings by Rani Vajravelu

University Press of Florida
Gainesville · Tallahassee · Tampa · Boca Raton
Pensacola · Orlando · Miami · Jacksonville

Walter Kingsley Taylor

Florida Wildflowers
in Their Natural Communities

Copyright 1998 by the Board of Regents of the State of Florida
Printed in Hong Kong on acid-free paper
All rights reserved

03 02 01 00 99 98 6 5 4 3 2 1

Library of Congress Cataloging-in-Publication Data
Taylor, Walter Kingsley, 1939-
Florida wildflowers in their natural communities / Walter Kingsley Taylor;
plant drawings by Rani Vajravelu.
p. cm.
Includes bibliographical references and index.
ISBN 0-8130-1616-9 (pbk.: alk. paper)
1. Wild flowers—Florida—Identification. 2. Wild flowers—
Florida—Pictorial works. 3. Plant communities—Florida. I. Title.
QK154.T38 1998
582.13'09759—dc21 98-30220

The University Press of Florida is the scholarly publishing agency for the State
University System of Florida, comprised of Florida A & M University, Florida
Atlantic University, Florida International University, Florida State University,
University of Central Florida, University of Florida, University of North Flor-
ida, University of South Florida, and University of West Florida.

University Press of Florida
15 Northwest 15th Street
Gainesville, FL 32611
http://nersp.nerdc.ufl.edu/~upf

To Angus Kemp Gholson, Jr.

A dedicated friend of our wildflowers. A Southern gentleman who has given his time freely and shared his exceptional knowledge of these plants with thousands of folk scattered throughout the United States.

And William Ray Taylor (1942–1997),

my wonderful brother who also loved the world of nature.

Contents

Figures

Maps

Preface

Florida has the third-largest flora in the contiguous forty-eight states. Of the more than 4,000 taxa (including species, varieties, subspecies, and hybrids) of plants occurring in Florida, over 3,600 are native and naturalized flowering species. Only Texas and California have larger floras; both of these states are physically larger than Florida.

Florida's diverse flora has multiple origins. Many of the tropical plants in South Florida can be found on islands of the West Indies and the Bahamas, in South America, and across the tropical zone of the world. The same north temperate species that grow in the fields of the Midwest and the mountains of the Appalachian region also grow in Florida. Then there are plants in Florida whose relatives occur in Texas and farther west into Mexico. Lastly, there are the endemics that occur nowhere else on this Earth. Endemism, a measure of an area's richness, is high in Florida. Nearly 175 endemic flowering plant species (nearly 5 percent of the total flora) have been found growing within the physical boundaries of the state. This number is higher if the endemic subspecies are included. Families with the highest number of endemic species are the asters (Asteraceae or Compositae), beans or peas (Fabaceae or Leguminosae), grasses (Poaceae or Gramineae), spurges (Euphorbiaceae), and mints (Lamiaceae or Labiatae). The Panhandle and the northern and central peninsular areas have more endemics than does South Florida, probably because South Florida's geologic history is more recent and, therefore, less time has been available for plant development and colonization.

Florida, with its 58,560-square-mile dry land mass, has a tremendously diverse and complex assemblage of terrestrial ecological communities.

Within these communities is a rich and unique assemblage of wildflowers that one would be hard pressed to find elsewhere in the continental United States. Most of Florida's plants are wildflowers—any flowering plant growing in a natural state. Although many people view wildflowers as herbaceous and showy plants, in the strict technical sense trees, shrubs, vines, cacti, grasses, rushes, sedges, and all sorts of weeds are wildflowers.

This book is about our terrestrial wildflowers and where they live. Both common and uncommon species are included and treated in a different manner than is usually found in identification guides. Instead of identifying and learning these gems by color, by structural parts, or by family characteristics, all of which have their merits, the wildflowers are displayed according to where they commonly occur in their natural communities. Knowing the community of a given species will assist one in locating the plant.

The following major terrestrial communities found in Florida are discussed in this book: Pine Flatwoods, Sandhills (Longleaf Pine-Turkey Oak Association) and Clayhills (Upland Pine Forests), Scrubs, Temperate Hardwood Forests, Coastal Uplands, Rockland Pinelands (Pine Rocklands or Subtropical Pine Forests), Rockland Hardwood Hammocks (Tropical Hardwood Hammocks), and Ruderal Sites. The descriptions and photographs of each of these communities will help with identification and learning about the natural lands of Florida as well as the wildflowers themselves.

In this book there are individual photographs of over 450 species of wildflowers representing 110 families. Most of the wildflowers described are herbaceous, but characteristic woody-types are included. I have not emphasized any particular geographical region. There are photographs in this book taken of plants growing in the wild in nearly every county in Florida. With few exceptions all of the photographs are mine and have never been published before. I have not stressed any particular family—large or small. Included are a number of wildflowers with limited distributions in the state; some of these have never had a published photograph in a book of this type. Many of our wildflowers with restricted distributions are the endemics and are often endangered, threatened, or rare, living on the verge of extinction. These plants are a part of our heritage and need our assistance to ensure their preservation.

The purposes for writing this book are, first, to help the reader discover, learn, and enjoy our wildflowers; and second, to motivate one to become actively involved in protecting and preserving these plants and their communities. We have lost too many plants already, but we still have a lot worthy of our attention and protection. We owe preservation to the plants, to ourselves, and to future generations. These plants are part of our heritage, and each one contributes to the richness of the state's flora. I hope you have as much fun using this book in the wilds of Florida, looking for these gems, as I have had putting it together for you.

Acknowledgments

I have had the good fortune of receiving encouragement and assistance in many ways from a number of gracious people. I thank all of the following for the roles they have played in making this book a reality: Richard Aguilar, Bruce H. Anderson, Dan Austin, M. Shane Belson, Linda Berlin, Seth Blitch, Boyd Blihovde, Marjorie Bitt, Nancy Bolgar, John B. Brolmann, Mary and Jim Buckner, Julius Charba, Laura Coveney, Kelly Dashtaki, Kris Delaney, David Drylie, Cindy Dupree, Barbara Erwin, Keith Fisher, Don and Clarice Ford, Angus K. Gholson, Jr., Carolyn Griggs, David Hanf, Rick Haupalo, Alyene Hays, Joseph Holland, Richard H. Jackson, Ann Johnson, Dale Johnson, Steve Johnson, Rick Joyce, Walter Judd, Timothy Kozusko, John Lesman, David Leonard, M. J. Mazurek, Jason McWhirter, David Melton, Walter Meshaka, Raymond Miller, Jr., Mike Mingea, Jeremy Moynihan, Otto and Frieda Mueller, Katy NeSmith, Eliane M. Norman, Steve Orzell, Richard Owen, Bryan and Marsha Peacock, Dodie Pedlow, Kent Perkins, Shirley Petty, Leticia Poole, Peggy Powell, Jamie and Zack Prusak, Richard G. Reimus, Brenda Rhodes, William Robertson, Jr., Elicia Sanford, Clay Scherer, Richard Spencer, Scott Steffen, Steve Stewart, John Stiner, Eric D. Stolen, I. Jack Stout, Sid Seymour Taylor, Rani Vajravelu, Kim Van Vliet, David Vickers, Dan Ward, Tom Ward, John Weishampel, Henry O. Whittier, and Richard P. Wunderlin. Wunderlin graciously furnished me with his and Bruce Hansen's unpublished compilation, "Preliminary Checklist of the Vascular Flora of Florida with Major Synonyms: Atlas Version." The line drawings of the plants were executed by Rani Vajravelu, to whom I am grateful. Richard H. Jackson provided me with his unpublished data on flowering times from his early coastal studies at north Canaveral National Seashore, Volusia County, Florida. Dick also superbly drew the Florida map showing the physiographic features. Jeff Boutet prepared the county map, and for the distribution maps of the major habitats, Jeff used the map called Florida Land Cover by Sharon B. Arnold, Landsat Thematic Mapper Satellite (1985–1989).

I have had expert input from the following individuals, who read earlier drafts on the communities: Jim Buckner and Bob W. Simons (Pine Flat-woods, Scrubs, and Sandhills), Ann Johnson and Katy NeSmith of the Florida Natural Areas Inventory (Coastal Uplands and Temperate Hardwood Forests), and William B. Robertson, Jr. (Rockland Pinelands and Rockland Hammocks). Walter Judd and Alyene Hays reviewed the entire book and offered helpful comments. Their inputs are very much appreciated.

The following individuals permitted me to use their photographs: Dameron Black IV (dingy-flowered oncidium), Jim Buckner (woody goldenrod), Todd Campbell (Turtle Mound), David Leonard (Apalachicola River Bluffs), Richard Owen (Floodplain Forest at Florida Caverns State Park), and Dodie Pedlow (yellow meadow beauty).

I extend my gratitude to the hundreds of people who have shown their kindness and expressed their appreciation to me regarding my *Guide to Florida Wildflowers* (1992, Taylor Publishing Co., Dallas). The graciousness, enthusiasm, and support from all of the folk that I have met at meetings of various chapters of the Florida Native Plant Society, garden clubs, Florida Ornithological Society, Duval County Audubon Society, Orange Audubon Society, and the library committee at Aloma United Methodist Church, Winter Park, have been overwhelming. I thank you all.

My wife, Karin, deserves high accolades for putting up with me over the years, giving her assistance to many duties of compiling data, proofreading the script, and most of all being my companion on the long-distant trips. The sites we have shared, the people we have met, and the catfish dinners we have consumed together are wonderful memories that will be everlasting. Karin, thanks!

Ken Scott, director of the University Press of Florida, has been a source of encouragement and help from the beginning of this project. To him I am grateful. I also thank Bennie Watson, Meredith Morris-Babb, Gillian Hillis, and all of the unnamed workers at the Press who have helped make this book a reality.

Florida

Not a Paradise, but a Delicious Paradox

As any traveler touring Florida knows, the "Sunshine State," lying in the latitude where major deserts of the Earth occur and lying near the edge of the tropics, is neither desert nor tropical. It is true, however, that some similarities exist between the Florida Scrub and certain scrubby areas found in the desert region of the U.S. southwest, and that stately palms waving in the ocean's breezes of extreme southern Florida create an image of the tropics. Though certainly more temperate than tropical, Florida is like a bridge that connects the two climatic regions. No point is more than 70 miles from warm, marine waters. Waters from the Gulf of Mexico and waters from the warm, north-flowing Gulf Stream moderate extreme temperatures and prevent Florida from being a desert. Furthermore, the sand-based soils are well watered, allowing for a luxuriant, varied, and year-round growth of vegetation.

Because Florida has a relatively low physical topography and is nearly surrounded by water, its climate is mild and humid. There is a long growing period.

Seasons exist in Florida, being most pronounced in the Panhandle. Florida's springs (March–May) are warm and dry, summers (June–September) hot and wet, autumns (October, November) warm and wet to dry, and winters (December–February) cool and dry. Seasonality here does influence the vegetation. South Florida's summers are generally wetter and more humid than for other regions of the state, and its winters are milder and drier than elsewhere. Climate in southern Florida is governed more by tropical factors than by temperate ones. Key West lacks distinct wet and dry seasons, escapes below-freezing temperatures, and is the driest area in the state.

Florida is the southern extension of the Southeast Coastal Plain that begins in Virginia and terminates in Texas. Extensive pinelands and forested wetlands prevailed in the area that includes parts of present-day Virginia, North Carolina, South Carolina, Georgia, Alabama, Mississippi, Louisiana, Texas, and all of Florida. The most characteristic plant of the region was the longleaf pine (*Pinus palustris*). Harvesting of the pines has practically eliminated from the region the large, continuous tracts of former years. Longleaf pines have been replanted with fast-growing pines such as slash (*P. elliottii*) and loblolly (*P. taeda*).

Geologists tell us that Florida is the youngest of the contiguous 48 states and that Florida's origin and birth are directly tied to the ocean. Well over 95 percent of Florida's history and geological development occurred below the marine waters. It is indeed difficult to visualize and comprehend that the Florida we know today was covered by the sea in the past; in fact, the emersion happened more than once.

Through the thousands of years following its initial emergence from the watery cover, land constituting the state of Florida was greatly modified, sculptured, remodified, and resculptured. How many times the sea claimed all or part of the land, only to lose it again, is not known for certain.

Overlying the bedrock base are accumulations of different types of limestones of different geological times. Covering most of the limestone formations are one or more layers of sand, silt, clay, shell fragments, gravel, marl, and other materials.

The Ocala Limestone of the Eocene period (about 65 million years ago) is, for example, the major formation that underlies the whole peninsula. This limestone contains the main Florida aquifer from which most of the state's groundwater is derived. Another limestone feature that contains phosphate-rich beds is the Hawthorn Formation dating to Miocene times (25–30 million years ago). Soils derived from this formation support broadleaf, deciduous hardwood forests.

With time, sands accumulated forming beaches, ridges, dunes, and barrier islands. Sinkholes and lime sinks formed and continue to develop today as the limestones are dissolved and broken down by a process called solution. The type of landform of extensive limestones modified by solution is called karst. Most of the lakes today, especially those in the central peninsular area, represent former sinkholes. Florida has more lakes than almost any other state.

The Peninsula

The Peninsula is flat except for rolling hills in certain areas and an elevated north-south, 100-mile-long, sandy spine called the Central Highlands—the most distinctive feature of the Peninsula (Map 1). This ancient geological formation consists of a number of longitudinal high ridges that represent former coastal ridges and dunes of marine origin. Names of the ridges (e.g., Lake Wales Ridge, Winter Haven Ridge, and Mount Dora Ridge) reflect the names of present-day towns in Florida. Can you envision the ocean's edge reaching present-day towns such as Avon Park in Highlands County, and Lake Wales and Winter Haven in Polk County? Have you ever wondered why so much sand occurs in the interior of the Peninsula?

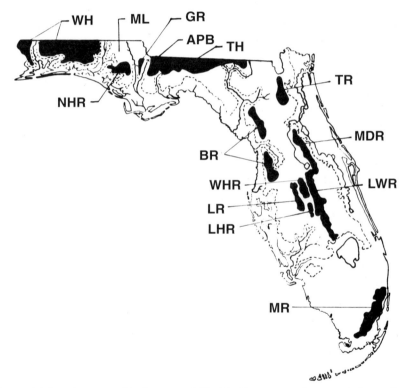

Map 1. Major physiographic features of Florida (from several sources). *Legend:* WH, Western Highlands; ML, Marianna Lowlands; NHR, New Hope Ridge; GR, Grand Ridge; APB, Apalachicola Bluffs; TH, Tallahassee Hills; TR, Trail Ridge; BR, Brooksville Ridge; MDR, Mt. Dora Ridge; LWR, Lake Wales Ridge; WHR, Winter Haven Ridge; LR, Lakeland Ridge; LHR, Lake Henry Ridge; MR, Miami Rock Ridge.

The highest measured elevation in Florida is 345 feet above mean sea level, south of Lakewood in northeast Walton County in the Panhandle. The highest elevation in the Peninsula is 325 feet at Bok Tower, in Polk County, which lies on the Lake Wales Ridge. Many plants of the Ridge are found nowhere else on the Earth.

The Panhandle

The Panhandle of Florida, geologically, is an uneven platform of layered carbonate bedrock, mainly of limestone. Much of the bedrock is of karst topography with obvious regions being the Apalachicola Bluffs and Ravines and the Marianna Lowlands (Map 1). Marianna Caverns, just north of the town of Marianna in Jackson County, are readily visible products of long-term karstic activity in that area. The flora of the Bluffs and Marianna Lowlands is rich, unique, and diverse with many species occurring nowhere else in the state. These sites are famous for their diverse and unique spring wildflowers. Soils above the rock deposits in the Panhandle are generally richer, more peaty, and more clayey than are most soils of the peninsula. Ridges like those seen in the Central Highlands of the peninsula are absent in the Panhandle.

South Florida

South Florida, the area of the peninsula generally designated south of Lake Okeechobee and including the Florida Keys, differs from the remainder of Florida in many attributes. The topography is especially flat and very low in elevation. Karstic activity is less prevalent here than in the Panhandle and peninsula. South Florida's geology also differs from that of the remainder of the state.

South Florida has been available to plant colonization for a shorter period than have most areas elsewhere in the state. The area south of Lake Okeechobee, and to a limited extent along the southern parts of the east and west coasts, supports the only luxuriant tropical flora in the continental United States. About 60 percent of the flora of South Florida is tropical. Despite having two unique physiographic provinces—the Everglades and Big Cypress Swamp—the environments of southern Florida have suffered more from human development than have those farther north. Most of the natural coastal vegetation has been wiped out and replaced with buildings and nonnative plants. South Florida today is a haven for intentionally or accidentally introduced species that have escaped into the natural environment and have consequently become serious pests. The Brazilian pepper-bush or holly (*Schinus terebinthifolius*), punk tree (*Melaleuca quinquen-ervia*), Australian pine (*Casuarina equisetifolia*), and water hyacinth (*Eich-hornia crassipes*) are textbook examples of introduced species that have become well adapted to a new area and consequently have gone out of control. Acres of land where native vegetation formerly grew have been usurped by these plant pests that continue to spread. Unfortunately, all of the above-mentioned pests have invaded central Florida.

One might conclude that present-day Florida is environmentally deso-late and that its communities are sterile and monotonous based on low topography, a latitudinal position of worldwide deserts, a recent geological history, relatively limited surface water, and the presence of nutrient-poor sands in the peninsula, sand-clays in the Panhandle, and peaty to scant soils in extreme South Florida. Therefore, species richness and endemism for both plants and animals might be expected to be low. Certainly this would be a gross error. Changes in elevation of only a few inches can have a great effect on the flora of Florida.

A number of early settlers, explorers, and even naturalists in written accounts described Florida's environment and land as sterile, desolate, and worthless. Some wrote of continuous expanses of sandy hills as being mo-notonous, strange, and sterile, with desertlike scrubs. We know these areas today as Sandhills and they are probably the most diverse terrestrial com-munities in the state. Bernard Romans, in his book originally published in 1775 and entitled *A Concise Natural History of East and West Florida,* referred to the scrub near St. Augustine as a miserable and dreary land. In 1831 John James Audubon, the famed bird artist, after visiting Bulow Ville, the largest and most successful sugar plantation along the east coast and located about fifty miles south of St. Augustine, wrote an account in which he advised people not to visit this part of Florida. In 1832 Audubon described the environs of St. Augustine as the "poorest hole in Creation."

Not all who explored and wrote about Florida in its more pristine days were as unappreciative and lacking in vision as Romans and Audubon. Charles Vignoles, a noted engineer and contemporary of Audubon, and John Kunkel Small, Florida's foremost botanist of the early 1900s, appre-ciated the white dry sands, peat-laden swamps, and rich and fertile ham-mocks of Florida.

Having spent the years of my youth roaming the rolling hills of western Kentucky, I often listened to my relatives and friends chat about their Flor-ida vacations in the 1950s. As a young boy who never took such vacations, I believed that Florida was indeed a long, long way from home, and certainly from the conversations a paradise to behold! Having now lived in Florida for more than twenty-nine years and having visited every county in Florida at least once (most counties many times), I have drastically changed my image of the state.

Florida is not a paradise, but a delicious paradox of exceptional natural diversity and richness of living organisms. In the driest of sandy scrubs there is life, and strange as it may be, that living entity may exist nowhere else. From the Florida Keys all the way to Escambia County in west Florida one can explore one of the most diverse lands in the continental United States. Go see for yourself!

Introduction

Florida's native vegetation, including the wildflowers, has been greatly modified by humans in every geographical region. The early Indians living in Florida annually burned thousands of acres of pinelands not only to increase their hunting efforts by flushing out the game but also to promote new growth of grasses and other vegetation for deer and turkeys. The long-term effects of these activities were minimal compared to man's destruction of Florida's native vegetation during the past 50 years. Never in the history of this state have the land and vegetation been raped and pillaged as they are today. No community is immune. Pristine waters were plentiful in Florida when William Bartram (1739–1823), André Michaux (1746–1802), and other naturalists explored the land in the late 1700s and early 1800s. Today many of our rivers, lakes, and creeks are polluted, laden with metals, tainted with undesirable chemicals, and unfit for human consumption.

The terrestrial communities have not escaped man's abuse, limited foresight, and lack of respect for the environment. Over half of our Pine Flatwoods are gone. The extensive forests of majestic longleaf pines (*Pinus palustris*) comprising the Sandhills of the Panhandle and north-central peninsula no longer prevail. Where the pine does exist the habitat is usually second-growth or managed pine plantations degraded by logging, turpentining, and other activities. At the time William Bartram visited Florida, longleaf pine communities covered an estimated 60 or 70 million acres throughout the lower southeastern United States, including Florida. Today, less than 10 million acres are left. Our Temperate Hardwood Forests have been fragmented beyond repair. Our fragile Coastal Uplands have felt man's abuse. Over 60 percent of Florida's upland coastal acreage has disappeared and is now occupied by commercial and residential developments. The percentage is even higher in some sections of the state. A similar fate has befallen many of the Tropical Hardwood Hammocks of South Florida. Most of the shell mounds in Florida that were built by early Indians have been hauled away as building materials for road construction. The fragile Rockland Pinelands of South Florida, whose limited distribution continues to shrink, may be the state's most endangered community. More than 95 percent of the Rockland Pinelands have been destroyed by development and fire suppression. Our scrubs have nearly vanished. Sand Pine Scrub is unique and nearly endemic to Florida, but that has not stopped the bulldozer. What took Mother Nature thousands of years to build can be uprooted by the dozer in less than one day, only to become a heap of dead trees and bushes to be burned.

Although man's past environmental record in Florida is negative, bleak, and pessimistic, there is a bright element that deserves our attention. Through the efforts of many individuals, the Florida taxpayers, the CARL program (Conservation and Recreation Lands), and conservation-minded organizations in Florida, lands representing all major communities are being purchased, set aside, and preserved by the Division of State Lands with Preservation 2000 funds for future generations to enjoy and study. Since the inception of Preservation 2000 in 1990, over 830,000 acres of natural lands have been saved in nearly every county of Florida.

These lands, together with older gifts and purchases, form the heart and soul of the Florida state park system—one of the finest in the nation. There are over 110 state parks and recreation areas that preserve and protect the natural and cultural heritage of Florida. Every geographic region of Florida is represented by one or more state parks. Excellent examples of all terrestrial communities described in this book can be seen in these publicly owned lands. Most parks encompass several community-types.

The question is often asked, "Where do I go to find a particular community or a state park?" A free booklet entitled, "Florida State Parks . . . the Real Florida," can be obtained by asking at most parks or by writing to the Department of Natural Resources, Division of Recreation and Parks, MS#535, 3900 Commonwealth Blvd., Tallahassee, Florida 32399-3000. In addition to the state park system, Florida is blessed with a large national park and several national forests, wildlife refuges, and seashores: Merritt Island National Wildlife Refuge and Canaveral National Seashore along the east coast, Gulf Islands National Seashore on Santa Rosa Island south of Pensacola, Osceola National Forest Wildlife Management Area in northeast Florida, Ocala National Forest in central Florida, Apalachicola National Forest and St. Marks National Wildlife Refuge in the Panhandle, J. N. "Ding" Darling National Wildlife Refuge near Sanibel, Everglades National Park and Big Cypress National Preserve in south Florida, Arthur R. Marshall Loxahatchee National Wildlife Refuge in southeast Florida, and Great White Heron National Wildlife Refuge and Key Deer National Wildlife Refuge in the Keys. These and other sites to visit are given in the section entitled "Places to Visit." All are exciting places to see and will make many memorable experiences for you. Enjoy!

Learning and Identifying Wildflowers

Looking for and finding an unfamiliar wildflower and then determining its identity give one a great sense of gratification and accomplishment. Some of my most memorable experiences, especially those when my wife Karin was my companion, have resulted from studying these plants. The thousands of miles driven and the countless hours I have spent seeking our wildflowers have been worth it all. There is no trip that I wish to forget. All have been real learning experiences—even those trips to the same site, because the places are never the same. Something new can be seen each time you go in the field, if only you will be observant. Wildflowers are growing treasures in the wild, waiting to be discovered and enjoyed. Let these plants become a part of you!

Studying wildflowers requires very little equipment and it is relatively inexpensive. A good 10X hand lens and ruler can be useful. The easiest way to find out what species you have found is to ask a knowledgeable person; however, this is usually not practical. For Florida and other areas of the Southeast, there are pictorial field guides that can assist you. This book and my *Guide to Florida Wildflowers* can show you photographs of over 830 species. Other source materials that can be of help are given in the reference section. No single guide is available that includes all species of wildflowers found in Florida or the Southeast. Obviously then, the more books you have at your disposal the better equipped you will be. A good library is a mark of the serious "wildflower hunter."

A person does not need formal training in botany to learn and enjoy our wildflowers. Many of the early naturalists lacked formal classroom training and there are many laymen today who are quite knowledgeable about our wildflowers but have never sat in a plant taxonomy class. I have met many of these people during the numerous presentations I have given on Florida wildflowers. This is not to say, however, that having some botanical knowledge is not useful, because it is. The zeal to learn our wildflowers is foremost.

Flower Structure

Wildflowers come in all shapes and sizes and colors. Some are woody, others herbaceous, and still others are a combination of the two. The spectrum of colors and the various shades and combinations of colors are dazzling—pink, purple, blue, yellow, orange, red, white, brown, gray, and green. The tiny flower of a weed growing in your yard can prove to be a gem when observed under magnification.

Knowing the basic flower parts and their functions, and the definitions of terms often used in descriptions and botanical keys, is essential and basic. A glossary defining the technical terms used in the species descriptions in this book is provided. For difficult species of certain grasses, sedges, asters, and a few other wildflowers, good botanical keys and the correct usage thereof are essential.

The bloom of most wildflowers is the center of focus for most observers. Based on the type of symmetry, the shape of the flower can be either regular or irregular. Regular-shaped flowers are radially symmetrical or star-shaped. Examples of this type include daisies, lilies, irises, poppies, black-berries, mallows, and phlox. Most species of our wildflowers have regular-shaped flowers. Irregular or bilateral flowers are those whose bloom can be divided into equal halves with a single, longitudinal cut. Irregular-shaped flowers are often 2-lipped (bilabiate), like that of a snapdragon. The upper lip is distinct from the lower lip. Often in our wildflowers with 2-lipped flowers, the upper lip has two fused petals and the lower lip three. Examples of irregular-shaped (bilateral) flowers include orchids, peas, beans, lobelias, violets, skullcaps, and odd-shaped types such as jack-in-the-pulpit (*Arisaema triphyllum,* photo 237).

The species descriptions in this book make use of the basic flower parts. For most of our wildflowers, learning these fundamental elements is not difficult. The bloom of most wildflowers such as the one illustrated in Figure 1 contains both male and female reproductive organs. The male organ, or stamen, consists of a filament to which is attached a terminal, pollen-producing anther. The number of stamens and their positions vary with the species. Some flowers such as the beard tongue (*Penstemon multi-florus,* photo 173) have sterile stamens called staminodes. These do not

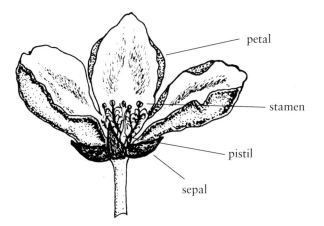

1. Flower of a spiderwort (*Tradescantia*) showing the basic structural parts.

produce pollen and they usually look different from the pollen-producing stamens.

Stamens surround the female organ, the pistil. This reproductive organ consists of a basal-located ovary, a style, and a terminal stigma that receives the pollen. The fruit is produced by the ovary. The number of pistils, styles, and stigmas varies with the species and this variation often is a family characteristic.

Surrounding the reproductive parts are the nonreproductive components, which are usually arranged in circles. The upper or inner circle comprises the petals (usually colored) and the lower or outer circle the sepals (usually green). The number of petals and sepals present, or of lobes of each part if fused, is important to determine. There is a correlation between the number of sepals and the number of petals present. If, for example, a flower has five petals there is a good chance there are five sepals. If the petals are fused then it is very likely that the sepals will be fused. The term corolla is used to designate the petals collectively, whereas the term calyx designates the sepals collectively. If the petals and sepals are not readily distinguishable, as in some lilies, the term tepal is used. The collective term for all the sepals and petals, or tepals, is the perianth. Some species such as tread softly (*Cnidoscolus stimulosus,* photo 137) lack petals but have colored sepals that resemble petals.

Because of the design and nature of this book, detailed discussions with illustrated sections on leaf structure, leaf arrangement, inflorescences, types of ovaries, family characteristics, and similar materials are omitted. Definitions of terms related to these items can be obtained from the glossary. Selected species of deciduous hardwood trees illustrating the shapes of their leaves are given in the appropriate section on communities. Additional information on the identification of trees should be obtained from guides on trees. For Florida, *Trees of Florida* (1994) by Gil Nelson, *Trees of Northern Florida* (1962) by Hurman Kurz and Robert K. Godfrey, *Trees, Shrubs, and Woody Vines of Northern Florida and Adjacent Georgia and Alabama* (1988) by Robert K. Godfrey, and *Native Trees and Shrubs of the Florida Keys* (1987) by Paul Scurlock are recommended.

Flowering Times

The flowering months that are used in this book are inclusive and largely based on nearly eight years of my own field data. Richard Jackson, who kept records for many coastal species of north Canaveral National Seashore, Volusia County, has allowed me to use his compilations. Other students of botany have shared with me their data on flowering times. No attempt has been made to visit the various herbaria in the state for flowering times. When months are not available, the season (e.g., spring, summer) is given based on information from various published sources. Because of Florida's long growing season and the impractical task of visiting every section of the state throughout all months, there will be some gaps in these data. Some plants may bloom out of their "normal" season in response to burning of the habitat.

Distributions

The distributions of species given in this book are based on my own observations, field guides, published and unpublished manuscripts and lists, inputs from knowledgeable individuals living in selected areas, and the "Atlas of Florida Vascular Plants" by Richard P. Wunderlin, Bruce F. Hansen, and Edwin L. Bridges, which can be found on the Internet (http://www.usf.edu/~isb/projects/hb-atlas.html) or by purchasing a CD-ROM from the authors. Still, the distributions for many of our wildflowers are incomplete. The absence of a species in a particular county may simply indicate that a county record has not been documented.

I have divided the state into four sections: Panhandle, North Florida, Central Florida, and South Florida. These are defined as follows: Panhandle—counties west of Madison and Taylor; North Florida—counties east of Jefferson and north of Citrus, Sumter, Lake, and Volusia; Central Florida—counties north of Charlotte, Glades, and Martin to Levy, Marion, Putnam, and Flagler; South Florida—counties south of Sarasota, De Soto, Highlands, Okeechobee, and St. Lucie.

Plant Names

The latinized scientific name or binomial (genus and species) is the most reliable name for plants. In each of the species descriptions, the scientific name and the author of the name are given. When one or more widely used common names are available for a plant, these are given along with the scientific name. Some wildflowers do not have widely accepted common names, whereas others may have a half dozen or more. Many common names for plants vary from region to region and from country to country. For this reason, common names can be confusing and unreliable.

For the scientific names in this book, I have followed for the most part the compilation "Preliminary Checklist of the Vascular Flora of Florida with Major Synonyms: Atlas Version" by Richard P. Wunderlin and Bruce Hansen. For most plants I have tried to give the most recent synonym where the scientific name has been changed. I have not included all of the synonyms because this is beyond the scope and purpose of this book. Some plants may have a dozen or more synonyms. To save space, scientific names for most plants are given in the body of the text where the name is first mentioned and not repeated throughout the text.

PART I

Florida's Major Terrestrial Communities

The terrestrial communities of Florida are diverse. Many of these have a number of shared features and they sometimes integrate; however, each community has distinct characteristics, and they can usually be readily identified.

There are communities within the boundaries of the state that are found nowhere else; Oak Scrub, Sand Pine Scrub, Rockland Pinelands, and Rockland Hardwood Hammocks are endemic or nearly so. In this section the major terrestrial communities of the state are presented in the following order: Pine Flatwoods, Sandhills (Longleaf Pine-Turkey Oak Association) and Clayhills (Upland Pine Forests), Scrubs, Temperate Hardwood Forests, Coastal Uplands, Rockland Pinelands (Pine Rocklands or Subtropical Pine Forests), Rockland Hardwood Hammocks (Tropical Hardwood Hammocks), and Ruderal Sites. The photographs of the wildflowers are arranged in this same sequence, and within each community the wildflowers are alphabetically arranged by family.

Pine Flatwoods

Piney woods, or pinelands, have been characteristic of Florida for a long time. Of the types of communities ecologists designate as piney woods, the Pine Flatwoods is the most common. In Florida, flatwoods claim about 50 percent of the land area. This percentage of coverage may have been greater in the past than now. Today extensive tracts of Pine Flatwoods can be found along the east coast from Palm Beach County northward to the Georgia border, in the southwest lowlands (Hendry, Lee, Charlotte, Sarasota, Manatee, Hardee, Hillsborough, Polk, and Pasco counties), in the central peninsular region (Sumter, Orange, and Seminole counties), in the north-central peninsular region (Alachua, Bradford, Union, Baker, and Columbia counties), and along the Gulf coast beginning with Dixie County and ending with Bay County.

As indicated by the name, the topography of Pine Flatwoods is flat (photo 1). Former names used by early naturalists and settlers for this major ecological community include pine barrens, pine flats, and low pinelands. Soils are usually acidic, sandy, and low in organic and clay contents. Drainage of flatwoods is usually poor because flatwoods are usually underlain by a relatively impermeable clay hardpan. The hardpan may impede the roots of pines from deeply penetrating the substrate. Because of the varying moisture content in the soils, Pine Flatwoods are commonly referred to as dry, mesic, or wet. Mesic flatwoods are the most prevalent.

Vegetation of Pine Flatwoods is usually three-layered (photo 1). The lowermost layer consists of a herbaceous ground cover; the middle layer, or understory, of shrubs and small trees; and an upper canopy layer of usually one but sometimes more than one species of pine trees. The pine canopy may reach over 90 feet in height and can be open or dense. Even in flatwoods with dense canopies enough light usually penetrates to the ground to allow a rich, herbaceous ground cover to develop.

The three main pine species that form the upper layer are longleaf pine (*Pinus palustris*), slash pine (*Pinus elliottii*), and pond pine (*Pinus serotina*). Based on the names of these pines, the flatwoods in Florida are commonly called Longleaf Pine Flatwoods, Slash Pine Flatwoods, and Pond Pine Flatwoods. It is not uncommon today to find stands of flatwoods with more than one species of pine trees.

Historically, longleaf pine was the signature species in Pine Flatwoods and other piney woods in Florida and in other parts of the Southeast. Mature individuals of the majestic longleaf pine attained heights of 115 feet or more and lived for several hundred years. Old growth trees have flattened crown-tops. Young longleaf pines can be identified by their white buds (photo 2). Today the faster-growing slash and loblolly (*Pinus taeda*) pines are more common in our flatwoods than longleaf. Longleaf Pine Flatwoods are found on well-drained soils. Slash Pine Flatwoods occupy soils of intermediate wetness, and Pond Pine Flatwoods occur on poorly drained soils that are wetter than those of either Longleaf Pine Flatwoods or Slash Pine Flatwoods. Standing water in the two wet-type flatwoods is temporary and seasonal, and generally occurs after hard or prolonged rains. Species diversity of wildflowers is lowest in Pond Pine Flatwoods and highest in Slash Pine Flatwoods.

The understory in Pine Flatwoods often consists of a great diversity of small or large shrubs or small trees including large or sweet gallberry (*Ilex coriacea*, photo 13), inkberry or gallberry (*I. glabra*, photo 14), saw palmetto (*Serenoa repens*, photo 1), St. Andrew's-cross (*Hypericum hypericoides*, photo 41), St. Peter's-wort (*H. tetrapetalum*, photo 42) tarflower (*Bejaria racemosa*, photo 45), dwarf huckleberry (*Gaylussacia dumosa*, photo 46), wicky (*Kalmia hirsuta*, photo 47), fetterbush or shiny lyonia (*Lyonia lucida*, photo 48), shiny blueberry (*Vaccinium myrsinites*, photo 49), beautyberry (*Callicarpa americana*, photo 96), and low-growing colonial runner oaks (*Quercus pumila* and *Q. minima*).

A rich flora of both herbaceous and low-growing woody wildflowers forms the major component of the ground layer. Most of these wildflowers also commonly grow in Sandhills, Sand Pine Scrub, and other communities. Examples include Michaux's milkweed (*Asclepias michauxii,* photo 16), Walter's aster (*Aster walteri,* photo 22), blackroot (*Pterocaulon pycnostachyum,* photo 32), scare-weed (*Baptisia simplicifolia,* photo 53), zornia or marsilea sandweed (*Zornia bracteata,* photo 55), and grass-leaved Ladies'-tresses (*Spiranthes praecox,* photo 82). Additional species will be observed in the species accounts.

Where fire has been suppressed, Pine Flatwoods often have a diminished variety of herbaceous wildflowers. Shrubby plants may reach small tree size and the ubiquitous saw palmetto may become so dense that walking through the flatwoods is difficult. Frequent fires prevent invasion of hardwoods and rejuvenate the community (photo 3).

Endemic wildflowers commonly found in the flatwoods include the widespread yellow bachelor's button (*Polygala rugelii,* photo 88) and pine-hyacinth (*Clematis baldwinii,* photo 89) of central and south Florida. Flatwood endemics of the Panhandle include Chapman's crownbeard (*Verbesina chapmanii,* photo 36), sandweed (*Hypericum exile,* photo 39), white birds-in-a-nest (*Macbridea alba,* photo 60), and Godfrey's obedient plant (*Physostegia godfreyi,* photo 61). Most of these endemics have limited distributions.

Compared with Sandhills and Scrubs, there are only a few species of endangered wildflowers characteristic of Florida's flatwoods. Examples are white squirrel-banana or beautiful pawpaw (*Deeringothamnus pulchellus,* photo 10), yellow squirrel-banana or Rugel's pawpaw (*D. rugelii,* photo 11), and Bartram's ixia (*Calydorea caelestina,* photo 59).

Man has greatly altered nearly all of the natural communities found in Florida, including Pine Flatwoods, often to the point of total elimination of some sites. Overgrazing by cattle, logging and clearing, draining, road construction, agricultural operations, turpentine-harvesting, and fire suppression are some of the assaults upon Pine Flatwoods. Most flatwoods today probably differ from presettlement stands by having a denser understory of shrubs, less herbaceous cover, and fewer fires. Suppression of fire has allowed other vegetation formations (e.g., bayheads, titi thickets, and hammocks, photo 4) to invade Pine Flatwoods.

Variations of the typical Pine Flatwoods include Cabbage Palm Flatwoods, Scrubby Flatwoods, and Dry Prairies. A brief account of these follows.

Cabbage Palm Flatwoods

Cabbage Palm Flatwoods can be seen north and west of Lake Okeechobee, from Lee to Franklin counties along the Gulf Coast, on Merritt Island in Brevard County, and in the upper St. Johns River basin east of Orlando. One site, the Tosohatchee State Reserve located 3 miles south of Christmas in Orange County, has about 2,000 acres of Cabbage Palm Flatwoods. At least one-half of the acreage is believed to be virgin.

This variant of flatwoods has a canopy of slash or pond pines and cabbage palms (*Sabal palmetto*, photo 5). The trees may become very dense. If there is little light penetration because of the dense upper and lower stories, the herbaceous layer will be sparse. In contrast, if the upper and lower stories are sparse a rich herbaceous layer may occur. Like other flatwoods, the land is flat and the poorly drained soils are of sand and marl or shell beds. Periodic fires are needed to maintain this community. In addition to the pines and palms, other plants found in Cabbage Palm Flatwoods include gallberry, saw palmetto, hairy trilisa (*Carphephorus paniculatus*, photo 24), sunflowers (*Helianthus* spp.), and various species of rushes and sedges.

Scrubby Flatwoods

Scrubby Flatwoods lack an extensive growth of pine trees; the well-spaced trees create an open canopy (photo 6). Scrubby Flatwoods are better drained and drier than either Dry Prairies or mesic Pine Flatwoods. There are ecologists who believe that Scrubby Flatwoods are ordinary flatwoods where fire has been excluded. Others view these flatwoods as intermediate and forming an ecotone between flatwoods and scrub habitats. The occurrence of wiregrass (*Aristida beyrichiana*) in Scrubby Flatwoods indicates an affinity to flatwoods. This grass is not a characteristic scrub plant. Scrubby Flatwoods, like Scrubs, have evergreen, thick-leaved oaks and shrubs; a herbaceous ground cover is sparse. In the absence of fire the vegetation can become dense.

Vegetation of Scrubby Flatwoods is a combination of mesic Pine Flatwoods and Scrubs. Oaks frequently occurring in this community include sand live or scrub live (*Quercus geminata*, photo 178), Chapman's (*Q. chapmanii*, Figure 2), myrtle (*Q. myrtifolia*, Figure 2), and small runner oaks. Other woodies include gallberry, saw palmetto (photo 1), tarflower (photo 45), dwarf huckleberry (photo 46), rusty lyonia (*Lyonia ferruginea*, photo 193), and the introduced invasive downy myrtle (*Rhodomyrtus tomentosa*, photo 73) of the southern peninsular areas. Herbs found in Scrubby Flatwoods include goldenasters (*Chrysopsis* spp.) and pennyroyal (*Piloblephis rigida*, photo 161).

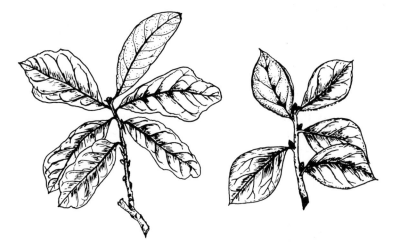

2. *Left:* Chapman's oak leaf (*Quercus chapmanii*). *Right:* Myrtle oak leaf (*Quercus myrtifolia*).

Dry Prairies

Dry Prairies are essentially treeless, grass-covered, open expanses (photo 7). Usually a rich diversity of wildflowers exists including Florida elephant's-foot (*Elephantopus elatus,* photo 28), blackroot (photo 32), pine lilies (*Lilium catesbaei,* photo 66), crow-poison (*Zigadenus densus,* photo 67), pale meadow beauty (*Rhexia mariana,* photo 71), bottlebrush three-awn (*Aristida spiciformis,* photo 83), yellow bachelor's button (*Polygala rugelii,* photo 88), pennyroyal (photo 161), and a variety of sedges and grasses. It is not uncommon for scattered patches of saw palmetto, gallberry (photo 14), shiny lyonia (photo 48), and other low-growing shrubs to occur in Dry Prairies. Many of the plants that occur here also occur in mesic Pine Flatwoods, Sandhills, Scrubby Flatwoods, and Coastal Grasslands.

Soils of Dry Prairies are acidic sands overlying an organic hardpan or clay subsoil. During the rainy season the prairies may briefly become flooded. Fires caused by lightning strikes are fairly common and necessary to maintain this community. Within Dry Prairies, Cabbage Palm Flatwoods may occur as islands as well as isolated bayheads, freshwater marshes, and cypress domes.

Many of Florida's Dry Prairies are now pastures, farm fields, or citrus groves. About 17 percent of existing acreage of Dry Prairies in Florida lies in protected conservation lands. The most extensive Dry Prairies in Florida

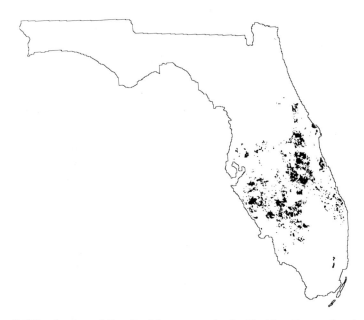

Map 2. Distribution of Dry Prairie community in Florida. (From Florida Land Cover, Sharon B. Arnold, Landsat Thematic Mapper Satellite, 1985–1989, Florida Game and Fresh Water Fish Commission, Tallahassee.)

are located north and west of Lake Okeechobee to the east bank of the Kissimmee River (Map 2). Two protected prairies in this area of Okeechobee County are the Kissimmee Prairie and the National Audubon Society's Ordway Whittell Kissimmee Prairie Sanctuary, located just east of the former. Myakka River State Park (Sarasota County), east of Sarasota, also has extensive Dry Prairies.

Sandhills (Longleaf Pine-Turkey Oak Association) and Clayhills (Upland Pine Forest)

Extensive tracts of longleaf pine once covered much of the Southeast Coastal Plain, from eastern Virginia to east Texas and down into Florida. These majestic pines were dominant components of Longleaf Pine Flatwoods, Sandhills, and Clayhills. Today there are few virgin tracts remaining of these communities in Florida. Citrus groves, pine plantations, agricultural lands, and residential and commercial developments occupy former longleaf pinelands. In 1936 about 7.6 million acres of forests, dominated by longleaf pines, were present in Florida. By 1987 this acreage had shrunk to 950,000 acres—a loss of 88 percent in 51 years! Only 38 percent of the current acreage of sandhill habitat is in public lands. The largest remaining stands of old-growth longleaf pine in the Southeast are located on the 463,000-acre Eglin Air Force Base that spans Santa Rosa, Okaloosa, and Walton counties in the Panhandle (Map 3).

Other names that have been used to describe the Sandhill community include High Pine, Pine-Turkey Oak Sandridge, Turkey Oak Barrens, Longleaf Pine-Xeric Oak Woods, Sand Ridges, and Sandhill Pine Forest. It has been estimated that Sandhill originally covered about 20 percent of Florida. Often the coverage was continuous, spanning thousands of acres in the Panhandle and northern two-thirds of the peninsula. Sandhills today are fragmented and scattered in parts of the Panhandle, north-central Florida, and down the sandy ridges of the peninsula and adjacent areas. Longleaf pine Sandhills once blanketed most of the southern part of the Lake Wales Ridge of south-central Florida. Slash pine or a mix of slash and longleaf pines now grow on the few Florida Sandhills still left on the Ridge.

Sandhills are one of the most characteristic and recognizable upland communities in Florida. These parklike woodlands are located on high, dry

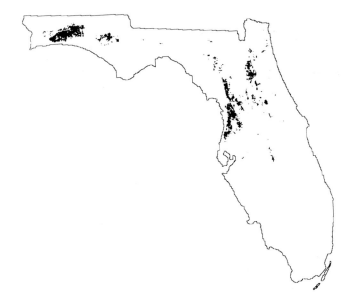

Map 3. Distribution of Sandhill community in Florida. (From Florida Land Cover, Sharon B. Arnold, Landsat Thematic Mapper Satellite, 1985–1989, Florida Game and Fresh Water Fish Commission, Tallahassee.)

ground, often on gently rolling hills of deep, usually yellowish to cream-colored sands (photos 100 and 101). The trees are widely spaced with an open canopy that readily allows sunlight to reach the ground. Because Sandhills are well drained and lack the hardpan characteristic of flat-woods, these drier sites serve as important groundwater recharge areas for replenishing the Florida aquifer. Water runoff and evaporation are minimal. The marine-deposited sands are relatively sterile but support a surprisingly extensive and varied flora.

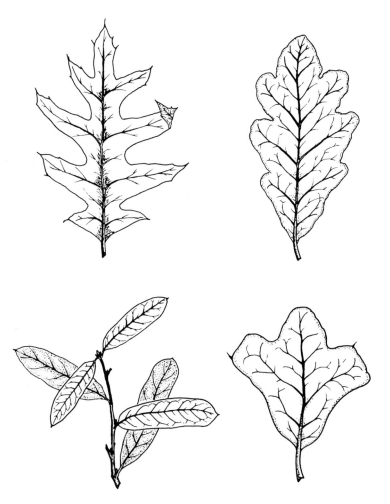

3. *Upper Left:* Turkey oak leaf (*Quercus laevis*). *Upper Right:* Sand post oak leaf (*Quercus margaretta*). *Lower Left:* Bluejack oak leaf (*Quercus incana*). *Lower Right:* Blackjack oak leaf (*Quercus marilandica*).

4. Persimmon leaf (*Diospyros virginiana*).

Longleaf pine, the signature species, forms the main overstory, interspersed with scattered turkey oak (*Quercus laevis,* photo 102; Figure 3). Because of the relationship between these two trees, Sandhills are often called Longleaf Pine-Turkey Oak Associations. In areas where the pines have been harvested, turkey oak may become the most common tree, forming oak woodlands. On many sites, sand post oak (*Q. margaretta,* Figure 3) and bluejack oak (*Q. incana,* Figure 3) are intermixed with the turkey oak because these species can tolerate dry conditions and low intensity fires. Blackjack oak (*Q. marilandica,* Figure 3) is not common in Florida and is limited to the more clayey soils of the upper Panhandle. Unlike the short-lived sand pine (*Pinus clausa*) that is characteristic of Sand Pine Scrub, longleaf pines may live 300 years or more. Fires every 2 to 5 years are needed to maintain Sandhills. Without fires Sandhills eventually succeed to hardwood hammocks.

A diversity of low-growing woody trees and scrubs forms the understory of most Sandhills. Little is known about the understory in virgin Sandhills. Today the understory may include endemic oaks, persimmon (*Diospyros virginiana,* Figure 4), deerberry (*Vaccinium stamineum,* photo 136), saw palmetto, and other woody or semiwoody shrubs and vines.

The ground cover is notably herbaceous. Several species of grasses, many perennials, and wildflowers dominate the ground cover. Perennial grasses include wiregrasses (*Aristida* spp.) and lopsided Indiangrass (*Sorghastrum secundum,* photo 165). Wiregrass (*Aristida beyrichiana,* photo 101) is nearly universally present in Florida Sandhills.

Common herbaceous and woody wildflowers forming the ground cover include the following: narrow-leaf pawpaw (*Asimina angustifolia*, photo 104), sandhill milkweed (*Asclepias humistrata*, photo 106), velvet-leaf milkweed (*A. tomentosa*, photo 107), butterfly weed (*A. tuberosa*, photo 108), greeneyes (*Berlandiera pumila*, photo 111), greeneyes or Florida dandelion (*B. subacaulis*, photo 112), goldenaster (*Chrysopsis scabrella*, photo 115), pink-scale gay feather or blazing star (*Liatris elegans*, photo 117), blazing star (*L. pauciflora*, 118), roserush (*Lygodesmia aphylla*, photo 119), silk-grass (*Pityopsis graminifolia*, photo 123), pineland ginseng or squarehead (*Tetragonotheca helianthoides*, photo 125), silver croton (*Croton argyranthemus*, photo 138), wild buckwheat or dog-tongue (*Eriogonum tomentosum*, photo 168), and New Jersey tea (*Ceanothus americanus*, photo 170).

Many species of wildflowers are common to Sandhills, Scrubs, and Pine Flatwoods. These include yellow buttons (*Balduina angustifolia*, photo 110), prickly-pear cactus (*Opuntia humifusa*, photo 129), clammey weed (*Polanisia tenuifolia*, photo 130), gopher apple (*Licania michauxii*, photo 133), and alicia (*Chapmannia floridana*, photo 145). In contrast, gallberry (photo 14) and fetterbush or shiny lyonia (photo 48), so common in flatwoods, are notably lacking in Sandhills.

Sandhills include several endemic plants on the state and federal lists of endangered species, although fewer than occur in the Florida Scrub. Clasping warea (*Warea amplexifolia*, photo 127) and Carter's mustard (*W. carteri*, photo 128) of central peninsular Florida and toothed basil or toothed savory (*Calamintha dentata*, photo 160) of the Panhandle are Sandhill species on the federal endangered list.

The Clayhill or Upland Pine Forest community occurs on the dry hills of extreme northern Florida. Other names are Longleaf Pine Upland Forest, Loblolly-Shortleaf Upland Forest, Longleaf Pine Savannah, and High Pine. Some ecologists do not recognize Clayhills as being distinct from Sandhills and generally group them under the name of High Pine.

Clayhills are found in the upper half of the Panhandle spanning the counties from Escambia to Madison. Well-developed Clayhills can be seen in the region called the Tallahassee Red Hills (Map 1).

Upland Pine Forests, like Sandhills, give one the impression of rolling parklike woodlands with an open, airy overstory of widely spaced stately pines. Longleaf pines and wiregrasses dominated the forests in the past. In many areas today the longleaf has been harvested and replaced by shortleaf pine (*Pinus echinata*) and loblolly pine. Saw palmetto may also be present. Bracken fern (*Pteridium aquilinum*) can be as variably abundant in Clayhills as in the Sandhills. As in Sandhills, a dense ground cover of grasses and wildflowers is present in Clayhills. For the most part, the same species of wildflowers found in Sandhills and mesic Pine Flatwoods occur in Clayhills.

Unlike Sandhills, soils of Clayhills consist of considerable amounts of loamy clays, mixed with sand. The clay retains moisture and increases the fertility of the soils in contrast to the drier, deeper, sterile sands of Sandhills. Often Clayhill soils are drier than those of Pine Flatwoods. Fire is crucial in maintaining the integrity and diversity of both Clayhills and Sandhills. Without periodic fires, hardwoods encroach on both habitats. Like most other pinelands of Florida, the Upland Pine Forest has been degraded by logging operations and by conversion to agricultural lands for plantations.

Scrubs

Scrub is a xeric or dry community that occurs on well-drained, sandy soils that lack appreciable organic materials. The surface sands of some scrubs are loose and extremely white; these sands are often called "sugar sands." Sands of other scrubs are yellowish, more compact, and similar to those of Sandhills. In Florida's interior, the deep white sands may indicate a more ancient scrub, though this has been debated. Nonetheless, Scrub occurs on water-deposited sand or beach ridges and wind-deposited dunes created along past shorelines of marine origin.

The Scrub community exists in several types. Scrub may be located inland or coastally. Scrub vegetation may be a Sand Pine Scrub (photo 175), an Oak Scrub (photo 176), or a Rosemary Scrub (photo 177). In the Panhandle, Woody Goldenrod Scrub is recognized; however, the distribution is coastal and limited. The woody or bush goldenrod (*Chrysoma pauciflosculosa*, photo 381) of this scrub is short-lived. The goldenrod is the first woody plant to displace grasses on the inner dune ridges of the Panhandle coast.

Sand Pine Scrub in Florida is characterized by an overstory dominated by sand pines (photo 175). The overstory may be open or form a closed canopy. Compared with other pine species, sand pine is relatively short-lived (50 to 90 years). In both coastal and inland scrubs, it is not unusual to find mature stands of sand pines that lean. Along with the overstory of sand pines there is an understory that consists of one or more species of oaks, particularly scrub or sand live oak (*Quercus geminata*, photo 178), Chapman's oak (Figure 2), and myrtle oak (Figure 2). Other woody plants found may include saw palmetto, Florida rosemary (*Ceratiola ericoides*, photo 177), garberia (*Garberia heterophylla,* photo 185), rusty lyonia (photo 193), tallowwood or hog plum (*Ximenia americana,* photo 205), wild olive (*Osmanthus megacarpus,* photo 207), scrub hickory (*Carya floridana,* photo 179), and silk bay (*Persea humilis*) with blackish branches and evergreen leaves whose lower surfaces are silky to the touch. Not all of these plants will occur in a given scrub. The evergreen, thick leaves of many of these woody plants are probably adaptations to moisture retention due to living in an arid, harsh environment. Sand pines are relatively shallow-rooted, and mature trees are susceptible to being blown over when former windbreaks are removed; trees diseased from root rot are also commonly blown down.

The herbaceous layer of the various scrubs in Florida is sparsely vegetated with low-growing woody plants and herbaceous wildflowers. Wildflowers that form this layer may include Britton's beargrass (*Nolina brittoniana,* photo 181), Curtiss' milkweed (*Asclepias curtissii,* photo 184), Florida bonamia or scrub morning-glory (*Bonamia grandiflora,* photo 192), scrub balm or Lloyd's mint (*Dicerandra frutescens,* photo 204), woody wireweed (*Polygonella myriophylla,* photo 209), sandhill wireweed (*P. robusta,* photo 210), and the widespread gopher apple (photo 133). Nonflowering lichens, such as British soldier moss (*Cladonia leporina,* photo 180), the sand spikemoss (*Selaginella arenicola,* photo 180), and various species of lichens are common. Open patches of bare sand are also common in our scrubs.

Oak Scrub and Rosemary Scrub are similar to Sand Pine Scrub except that the pine overstory may be lacking or very sparse. Oaks usually dominate Oak Scrub, whereas Florida rosemary dominates Rosemary Scrub. Extensive Oak Scrub today occupies the east-coastal ridges, the south end of the Lake Wales Ridge, and parts of Hardee, Manatee, and Hillsborough counties (Map 4).

Sand Pine Scrub is fire-maintained as are Sandhills and Pine Flatwoods, but burning of the scrub should be at longer periods (20 or more years). The sparse ground cover makes scrubs more difficult to ignite than Sandhills and Pine Flatwoods. Sand pines, unlike longleaf pines, retain their lower dead branches thereby allowing a fire to climb up into the crowns of the pines. The dead branches ensure a hot, fast-burning fire that rejuvenates the scrub by releasing minerals into the sandy soils. Sand pines located in the peninsula may release their seeds from the closed cones due to the heat of a fire, but apparently for some peninsular sand pines, fire is not necessary for the cones to release their seeds. Sand pines of the Panhandle do not require fire for seed release. Because of the infrequency of fire, oaks

Map 4. Distribution of Oak Scrub community in Florida. (From Florida Land Cover, Sharon B. Arnold, Landsat Thematic Mapper Satellite, 1985–1989, Florida Game and Fresh Water Fish Commission, Tallahassee.)

and other hardwoods may become so dense and thicketlike that the scrub is difficult to walk through.

Most of the peninsular scrub is inland, occurs in isolated patches, and occupies the sand ridges of the Central Highlands that also support Sandhills. More than 82 percent of these xeric uplands of the highlands have disappeared. Today, the "Big Scrub" in the Ocala National Forest, Marion County, is the largest existing tract of inland Sand Pine Scrub (Map 5).

Along the Atlantic and the Gulf coasts of the peninsula are scrubs that occupy old dunes. Similarily in the Panhandle there are scrubs that are narrowly restricted along the Gulf coast and on barrier islands, beginning just west of the Ochlockonee River in Franklin County, Florida, to Baldwin County, Alabama.

Coastal scrubs are not the same as inland scrubs even though the vegetation of both may have the same or similar species. Coastal scrub is maintained by fire and salt spray from the ocean, whereas inland scrubs are fire-maintained. Sand pines and Florida rosemary are common dominants of inland scrub; saw palmetto and yaupon holly (*Ilex vomitoria*, photo 380) often characterize the coastal scrub.

Map 5. Distribution of Sand Pine Scrub community in Florida. (From Florida Land Cover, Sharon B. Arnold, Landsat Thematic Mapper Satellite, 1985–1989, Florida Game and Fresh Water Fish Commission, Tallahassee.)

It has been estimated that 40 to 60 percent of the plant species found today in scrubs of Florida are endemic. Many of these are endangered or threatened and among the rarest of plants in the continental United States. Twenty-one endangered or threatened species listed by the U.S. Fish and Wildlife Service occur on the sandy spine of Lake Wales Ridge, which traverses the center of the peninsula (Map 1). Examples of these species include the Florida gay feather or scrub blazing star (*Liatris ohlingerae*, photo 187), scrub balm or Lloyd's mint (photo 204), pygmy fringe tree (*Chionanthus pygmaeus*, photo 206), and scrub plum (*Prunus geniculata*, photo 211). Because of the uniqueness of the Lake Wales Ridge ecosystem, selected areas of the ridge have recently been designated collectively as the Lake Wales Ridge National Wildlife Refuge. This is the only national wildlife refuge set aside to protect plants.

Florida scrubs are among the oldest communities, dating back about 20 million years. Some ecologists believe that the community is indeed the oldest. Florida scrub is less extensive today than in the past because the climate has become wetter and because the habitat has been needlessly destroyed. Many people view a Sand Pine Scrub or an Oak Scrub as a wasteland, aesthetically unpleasing, and useful only for housing developments, shopping centers, golf courses, and citrus groves. The fact that Oak Scrub is endemic and Sand Pine Scrub is nearly endemic in Florida has not been a factor in their preservation by developers. Florida's scrub community is disappearing at an alarming rate—almost 90 percent of the original scrub of central Florida is already gone.

Temperate Hardwood Forests

Florida's hardwood forests are fragmented; that is, large continuous acreage of these forests is not present in Florida today. Florida's hardwood forests are often called hammocks, and these occur statewide.

Hammocks vary in size, soil types, slope gradient, soil moisture, plant composition, and geographical location. Based on measures of soil moisture content, hammocks may be xeric (dry), mesic (moist-wet), or hydric (very wet). Hammocks confined to slopes are often bordered by other communities such as a Sandhill or a Floodplain Forest.

The Temperate Hardwood Forest is commonly called "woods." The major components of the forests are deciduous trees, either saplings or mature trees. Florida's Temperate Hardwood Forests are best developed in the north-central peninsula and the upper section of the Panhandle. Most Temperate Hardwood Hammocks range from low slope to mid slope.

The Temperate Hardwood Forests in Florida belong to the deciduous forest formation so characteristic of the eastern section of the United States. Our temperate hardwoods have been here for a very long time, perhaps as long as 25 million years, and may well be the oldest major community found in Florida. There is evidence of mesic hardwoods in the northern sector of Florida from the beginning of the state's terrestrial history. This vegetation type was probably originally restricted to riverine habitats and to margins around lakes and sinkholes where the forests can still be found. Florida's Temperate Hardwood Forests are probably southern extensions of the Appalachian-Piedmont system.

Florida's Temperate Hardwood Forests today are unique and diverse with considerable species richness, especially in the large number of tree species present. In fact, the largest number of species of trees per unit area found in the temperate forests of the eastern United States occurs in certain northern forests of Florida. There is a decrease in tree species diversity for hammocks of the peninsula; however, there is an increased diversity of evergreen trees in hammocks located along the peninsula's central ridges.

Florida's Temperate Hardwood Forests grow on soils that are rich and alluvial in origin and contain varying amounts of nutrients, sands, and clays. Peats do not accumulate.

As in Pine Flatwoods and other major forest types, Temperate Hardwood Forests are vertically stratified, having an overstory, an understory, and a ground layer of low-growing herbaceous plants. The overstory and understory strata are less defined for hammocks of the peninsula compared with those of the Panhandle. The species of plants comprising the "strata" vary, but the overstory and understory are generally quite diverse. No single species of plant is characteristic of and dominant in all Temperate Hardwood Forests in Florida. There are, however, several species with restricted distributions.

Attempts to describe and classify our hardwood forests have resulted in a large, often confusing array of names. Examples of these include Mesic Hammock, Climax Hardwoods, Upland Hardwoods, Upland Mixed Forest, Temperate Broad-leaved Evergreen Forest, Slope Forest, Ravine Forest, Beech-Magnolia Climax, Oak-Magnolia Climax, Pine-Oak-Hickory Forest, Pine-Oak Forest, Southern Mixed Hardwood Forest, Clay Hills Hammocks, and Piedmont Forest. For this section, I follow the classifications Upland Hardwood Forest and Upland Mixed Forest, as delineated by the Florida Natural Inventory Areas' 1990 "Guide to the Natural Communities of Florida." Both types of forests have very similar plant composition. Slope Forest, Bluff, and Floodplain communities of that guide are presented as separate subsets of the Upland Hardwood Forest.

Upland Hardwood Forests

The Upland Hardwood Forest is most common in the northern half of the Panhandle (photo 212). This closed-canopy forest type occurs on rolling hills but may also be associated with Floodplain Forests and Bluffs. Outcrops of limestones are present, and soils are rich with varying amounts of sand and clays. These mesic, rich woods consist of mostly deciduous trees, although pines (*Pinus* spp.) and southern red cedar (*Juniperus silicicola*) may be found. A substantial leaf litter is usually present, adding to the moisture of the soils. Light penetration through the closed canopy may be minimal. Unlike many other Florida communities, fire is rare and not important in the maintenance of these forests, but when fire does occur it can be destructive.

The overstory vegetation of the Upland Hardwood Forest may consist of southern magnolia (*Magnolia grandiflora*), American beech (*Fagus grandifolia*, photo 213; Figure 5), spruce pine (*Pinus glabra*, photo 214), sweetgum (*Liquidambar styraciflua*, Figure 5), basswood (*Tilia ameri-*

cana, Figure 5), mockernut hickory (*Carya alba,* Figure 6), pignut hickory (*C. glabra,* Figure 6), white oak (*Quercus alba,* Figure 7), Shumard oak (*Q. shumardii,* Figure 7), and tulip poplar (*Liriodendron tulipifera*), which has tulip-shaped leaves. Smaller woody trees and bushes comprising the understory include Florida flame azalea (*Rhododendron austrinum,* photo 218), redbud (*Cercis canadensis,* photo 219), red buckeye (*Aesculus pavia,* photo 220), silverbell (*Halesia diptera,* photo 227), the well-known flowering dogwood (*Cornus florida*), and saplings of overstory trees that may or may not become a part of the overstory. The endemic Torreya or gopherwood (*Torreya taxifolia,* photo 231) and Florida yew (*Taxus floridana*) are present in a few Upland Hardwood Forests in Jackson, Gadsden, and Liberty counties. Both species are on the verge of extinction.

Although trees and shrubs figure prominently in our Upland Hardwood Forests, there exists a bountiful flora of herbaceous wildflowers within the

5. *Upper:* American beech leaf (*Fagus grandifolia*). *Lower Left:* Sweetgum leaf (*Liquidambar styraciflua*). *Lower Right:* Basswood leaf (*Tilia americana*).

6. *Left:* Mockernut hickory leaf (*Carya alba*). *Right:* Pignut hickory leaf (*Carya glabra*).

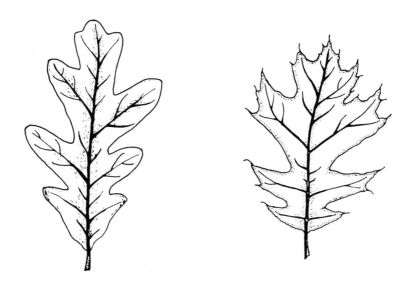

7. *Left:* White oak leaf (*Quercus alba*). *Right:* Shumard oak leaf (*Quercus shumardii*).

bounds of these woods. Examples include hairy angelica (*Angelica ven-enosa*, photo 215), black snakeroot (*Sanicula canadensis*, photo 216), Michaux's or Carolina lily (*Lilium michauxii*, photo 221), wakerobin (*Trillium decipiens*, photo 222), Indian pink (*Spigelia marilandica*, photo 223), crested coralroot (*Hexalectris spicata*, photo 224), and violets such as *Viola sororia* (photo 228). Many of these wildflowers also occur in the Upland Mixed Forests.

Slope Forests

The Slope Forest of Florida is a unique type of Upland Hardwood Forest that deserves special attention. It is a closed-canopy, mesic forest of upland hardwoods located on steeps, slopes, ravines, and bluffs (photo 229). Because of these locations this forest is also known as Ravine Forest, Bluff Forest, and Steepheads. Some may call it a Beech-Magnolia Forest or a calcareous hammock. The forest is shaded, cool, and moist. A thick leaf litter often accumulates from the large number of deciduous trees present. Higher elevations tend to be drier than the lower sites.

The Slope Forests of the Marianna Lowlands or Marianna Redlands (Jackson County) are famous and have been well studied (Map 1). The northern spring wildflowers, ferns, and mosses that grow in this and surrounding regions have attracted professional botanists as well as amateurs for many years. In these forests one can observe wildflowers in Floodplain Forests, in calcareous woods, on limestone outcroppings (photo 230), alongside Bluffs, in sinks, and down steepheads (i.e., steep slopes at the heads of ravines where erosion occurs). One of the few steepheads found beyond the borders of the Panhandle occurs at Gold Head Branch State Park in Clay County.

Species richness, disjunct distributions, and endemism of plants are high in our Slope Forests, which have the greatest diversity of plants in the state. These forests may resemble our ancestral forests; they contain relicts whose relationship extends to forests of the Piedmont and Southern Appalachian mountains.

The Slope Forests in the Marianna Lowlands and Apalachicola Bluffs and Ravines are well known for having northern-forest species of wildflowers as though latitudinal zones were nonexistent. Excellent examples of disjunct relict species in the Marianna area are the leafcup *Polymnia laevigata* (photo 234) and false rue-anemone (*Enemion biternatum*, photo 246). Present also are several rare and unique plants at the extreme southern limits of their known distributions in Florida; these plants probably predate the last glaciation. Northern wildflowers that barely enter the state include the green-flowered yeatesia (*Yeatesia viridiflora,* photo 232), may-apple (*Podophyllum peltatum,* photo 238), wakerobin (*Trillium maculatum,* photo 240), little sweet Betsy (*T. underwoodii,* photo 241), moonseed (*Menispermum canadense,* photo 242), bloodroot (*Sanguinaria canadensis,* photo 243), wild columbine (*Aquilegia canadensis,* photo 244), and lousewort or wood betony (*Pedicularis canadensis,* photo 247). You would not expect to see either the mayapple or the columbine anywhere in Florida. The endangered Torreya tree (photo 231) and few-flowered croomia (*Croomia pauciflora,* photo 248) occur only in certain Slope Forests. Florida Caverns State Park on the Chipola River and Torreya State Park on the Apalachicola River are among the most interesting, exciting, and pleasant places to visit in all Florida, and they are readily accessible to the public.

Bluffs

Cliff, bank, and slope are synonyms for the Bluff community. Bluffs are often exposed, unstable slopes along waterways (e.g., streams, rivers, and Floodplain Forest) where erosion is a constant factor (photo 250). These Bluffs support sparse vegetation, if present at all, consisting of weedy wildflowers like ragweed (*Ambrosia* spp.), dog fennel (*Eupatorium* spp.), goldenrods (*Solidago* spp.), and various grasses. Bluffs with calcareous and moist soils often have a lush growth of ferns, mosses, and nonweedy wildflowers (photo 251).

The Apalachicola River Bluffs and Ravines, located in Liberty and Gadsden counties, are probably the best known Bluffs in Florida (photo 250, Map 1). Some of the trees may be 200 years old and may be virgin. There are numerous endemic and disjunct species. Because the vegetation of this community is closely associated with the Slope Florest, I have included the Bluff section herein, knowing that Bluffs can be found in Upland Mixed Forests and other habitats. Many of the wildflowers growing on the Apalachicola River Bluffs and Ravines are the same species of the Slope Forest. These include the forget-me-not (*Myosotis macrosperma,* photo 254), Allegheny spurge (*Pachysandra procumbens,* photo 255), twining tragia (*Tragia cordata,* photo 257), lance-leaved wakerobin (*Trillium lancifolium,* photo 258), yellow passion-flower (*Passiflora lutea,* photo 259), spikegrass (*Chasmanthium latifolium,* photo 260), twoflower medic (*Melica mutica,* photo 261), blue phlox (*Phlox divaricata,* photo 262), rue anemone (*Thalictrum thalictroides,* photo 263), parsley haw (*Crataegus marshallii,* photo 264), and oakleaf hydrangea (*Hydrangea quercifolia,* photo 265).

Floodplain Forests

This bottomland hardwood forest is usually associated with alluvial rivers (photo 266). Common trees found in Florida's Floodplain Forests include sweetgum (Figure 5), planer tree (*Planera aquatica,* Figure 8), red maple (*Acer rubrum,* Figure 8), water oak (*Quercus nigra,* Figure 8), and swamp chestnut oak (*Q. michauxii,* Figure 9).

Floodplain Forests are subjected to shallow inundations. The rich soils range from coarse sands to clay with organic matter received during periods of flooding. During the dry season standing water is absent and soils

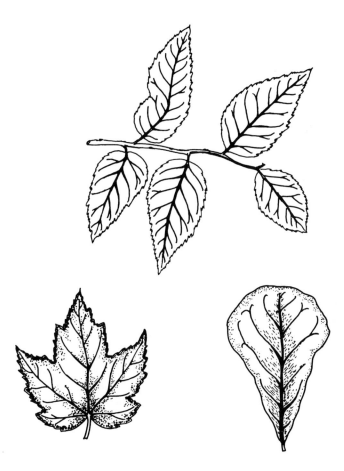

8. *Upper:* Planer tree leaf (*Planera aquatica*). *Lower Left:* Red maple leaf (*Acer rubrum*). *Lower Right:* Water oak leaf (*Quercus nigra*).

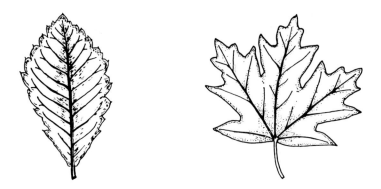

9. *Left:* Swamp chestnut oak (*Quercus michauxii*). *Right:* Sugar maple leaf (*Acer saccharum*).

become well aerated. Diversity of herbaceous species is greater when the area is not inundated. During periods of low moisture a lush herbaceous growth may occur. Examples of wildflowers found in Floodplain Forests include possum haw or winterberry (*Ilex decidua*, photo 267), spring-cress (*Cardamine bulbosa*, photo 269), swamp buttercup (*Ranunculus hispidus* var. *nitidus*, photo 273), Virginia willow (*Itea virginica*, photo 274), mazus (*Mazus pumilis*, photo 275), and monkeyflower (*Mimulus alatus*, photo 276).

Upland Mixed Forests

The physical aspects of the environment and the vegetation composition of the Upland Mixed Forest (also commonly called Southern Mixed Hardwood Forest) are similar to those of the Upland Hardwood Forest (photo 277). Both are closed-canopy forests often located on rolling hills with limestone at or near the ground surface. Canopy species diversity is large. A notable difference between the two forest types is the near absence in the Upland Mixed Forest of American beech (photo 213; Figure 5), white oak (Figure 7), and other more northern species that typically occur in the Upland Hardwood Forests. Slash and loblolly pines and woody evergreen plants often predominate. Furthermore, Upland Mixed Forests are more commonly distributed in the north and central peninsula of Florida than in the Panhandle, where the Upland Hardwood Forests prevail. It is not uncommon for Sandhills, Pine Flatwoods, Bluffs, and/or a Floodplain Forest to border an Upland Hardwood Forest.

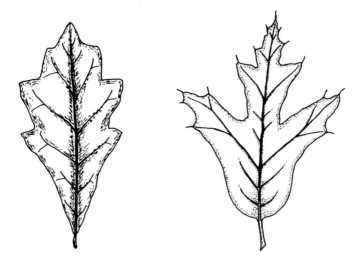

10. *Left:* Bluff oak (*Quercus austrina*). *Right:* Southern red oak (*Quercus falcata*).

Many hardwoods are shared between the Upland Hardwood Forest and Upland Mixed Forest including southern magnolia, flowering dogwood, persimmon (Figure 4), sweetgum (Figure 5), sugar maple (*Acer saccharum,* Figure 9), bluff oak (*Quercus austrina,* Figure 10), southern red oak (*Q. falcata,* Figure 10), chinquapin (*Castanea pumila,* Figure 11), redbud (photo 219), winged sumac (*Rhus copallinum,* photo 280), American holly (*Ilex opaca* var. *opaca,* photo 282), devil's-walkingstick (*Aralia spinosa,* photo 283), cross-vine (*Bignonia capreolata,* photo 285), Virginia live oak (photo 278), laurel cherry (*Prunus caroliniana,* photo 303), and horse sugar or sweetleaf (*Symplocos tinctoria,* photo 308). Understory species include strawberry bush (*Euonymus americanus,* photo 287), sweet pinxter azalea (*Rhododendron canescens,* photo 290), sparkleberry (*Vacci-*

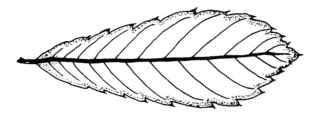

11. Chinquapin (*Castanea pumila*).

nium arboreum, photo 291), wax myrtle (*Myrica cerifera,* photo 298), and wafer ash or common hoptree (*Ptelea trifoliata,* photo 306).

Most wildflowers that are found growing in the Upland Mixed Forest are also found in other ecological communities, especially Sandhills and Pine Flatwoods. However, characteristic species include rattlesnake master (*Polianthes virginica,* photo 279), eastern poison oak (*Toxicodendron pubescens,* photo 281), coralbean (*Erythrina herbacea,* photo 292), milkpea (*Galactia regularis,* photo 293), yellow jessamine or Carolina jasmine (*Gelsemium sempervirens,* photo 296), squawroot (*Conopholis americana,* photo 301), jumpseed (*Polygonum virginianum,* photo 302), partridge berry (*Mitchella repens,* photo 305), wild sarsaparilla (*Smilax pumila,* photo 307), rose verbena (*Glandularia canadensis,* photo 309), and Walter's violet (*Viola walteri,* photo 310).

Coastal Uplands

Beaches, dunes, ridges, swales, strands, coastal grasslands, coastal scrubs, hammocks, shell mounds, barrier islands, mangrove swamps, salt flats, and salt marshes are all communities of Florida's coasts. Of the contiguous 48 states, Florida has the longest coastline—1,200 miles exclusive of the Keys. Except for the Big Bend of the Gulf Coast and Mangrove Forests at the southern and southwestern tip of the peninsula, the coastline of Florida is sandy and marked by numerous barrier islands. Florida has more acreage (200,000 acres) of barrier island uplands than any of the contiguous 48 states. More than 60 percent of this coastal upland acreage has been developed. The coasts of the Panhandle and northeast Florida, with the most pristine beaches and dunes of white "sugar sands," have not been developed as extensively as have other coastlines in Florida.

Coastal communities are harsh places for both the plants and animals that make their homes there. These environments, especially those nearest the Atlantic Ocean and the Gulf of Mexico, are ever changing not only through the physical forces of nature but also through the actions of the inhabitants. Plants growing in these maritime areas are subjected to hurricanes, winter storms, shifting sands, erosive waves, sand abrasion, intense sunlight, nutrient poor soils, desiccation, salt spray deposition, and destructive activities of humans and other animals. Just walking or driving on the dunes damages the plants growing there more than one might realize. Not only are the plants trampled and broken, but also erosion of the dune may occur. Salt sprays kill the growing tips of woody plants such as the seagrape (*Coccoloba uvifera*, photo 368) and Florida privet (*Forestiera segregata*, photo 396). These plants often display a "pruned" appearance from effects of the salt spray. Because of the infrequency of onshore winds along Florida's southwest coast, spray-pruned plants are not prevalent there.

Many plants living in coastal areas have reduced foliage, are brittle, and are fleshy (succulent). Succulent types in our coastal environments include sea purslane (*Sesuvium portulacastrum*, photo 314), samphire (*Blutaparon vermiculare*, photo 317), beach elder (*Iva imbricata*, photo 322), saltwort (*Batis maritima*, photo 324), sea rocket (*Cakile lanceolata*, photo 326), annual glasswort (*Salicornia bigelovii*, photo 328), perennial glasswort (*Salicornia perennis*, photo 329), Christmasberry (*Lycium carolinianum*, photo 344), inkberry (*Scaevola plumieri*, photo 362), and false foxglove (*Agalinis maritima*, photo 371). These species represent a variety of plant families. Many of these salt-loving plants (halophytes) have wide ranges. Other halophytes include the seabeach atriplex or seabeach orach (*Atriplex pentandra*, photo 327), southern sea blite (*Suaeda linearis*, photo 331), saltgrass (*Distichlis spicata*, photo 342), and Virginia dropseed (*Sporobolus virginicus*, photo 343).

Coastal communities tend to occur in distinct zones as a response to soil types, wind-driven sand movements, and erosion, and through tolerance to windblown salt spray deposition. Three main coastal zones in Florida can be distinguished: (1) pioneer, (2) transition, and (3) stable. The coastal plant habitats within each zone occur more or less in linear strips that parallel the coast. Different opinions among specialists exist regarding names for these zones. I follow the terminology of Johnson and Barbour (1990) from their chapter in the book *Ecosystems of Florida*, and the 1993 summary entitled "An Assessment of Florida's Remaining Coastal Upland Natural Communities: Final Summary Report" by Johnson and Muller of Florida Natural Areas Inventory.

One must realize that the plants themselves do not always fit nicely in one particular zone. Species such as the beach tea (*Croton punctatus*, photo 336) and the federally listed endangered sea oats (*Uniola paniculata*, photos 313, 378) occur in more than one zone and are distributed nearly throughout all coastal areas of Florida. Other species like the endangered beach peanut (*Okenia hypogaea*, photo 341) of the southeast coast and woody or bush goldenrod (*Chrysoma pauciflosculosa*, photo 381) of the Panhandle have restricted distributions in Florida.

Pioneer Zone

Beach Dunes

The Beach Dune area embraces both the upper beaches and foredunes and lies nearest the coast (photos 311 and 312). No vascular plants grow along beaches below the high tide mark because the area changes daily.

Beach Dune is the most uniform and the most stressed of the coastal areas. It is easy to recognize because many of the plants that grow here are familiar, widespread beach species. Beach Dune shares the fewest number of species with the more inland coastal areas. The area may be sparsely or densely vegetated. Grasses, vines, and mostly herbaceous plants grow here.

Plants that colonize the wave-deposited beaches and windblown foredunes are among the hardiest of coastal species because these areas are exceptionally harsh and contain little organic matter. Both beaches and foredunes are ever changing and experience the brunt of storm surges and salt sprays. Plant species of the Beach Dune areas are typically dispersed by oceanic currents and therefore continuously recolonize the land. Many of these plant species are pantropical in distribution; that is, they also occur across the tropical zone.

Perennial species are more abundant than are annuals. The plants growing on the beaches and foredunes accumulate and retain windblown sands. Foredunes are usually built by grasses such as bitter panicum (*Panicum amarum*, photo 377) and sea oats, which have extensive root systems (photo 313). Such species are called beach and dune formers and stabilizers. Sea oats are widely distributed plants of Florida's coasts. The seeds have a low tolerance for salt water, and mature plants do not do well if watered continuously with salt water. The thick leaves, however, allow the plants to tolerate the salt spray.

Other common Beach Dune species include the wide-ranging sea purslane (photo 314), water pennywort or beach pennywort (*Hydrocotyle bonariensis,* photo 318), beach sunflower (photo 320), beach elder (photo 322), sea rocket (photo 326), saltwort or Russian thistle (*Salsola kali,* photo 330), beach morning-glory (*Ipomoea imperati,* photo 332), railroad-vine (*I. pes-caprae,* photo 333), seaside or woody spurge (*Chamaesyce mesembrianthemifolia,* photo 335), seaside bean (*Canavalia rosea,* photo 337), Virginia dropseed (photo 343), sand or ground cherry (*Physalis walteri,* photo 345), and coastal vervain or beach verbena (*Glandularia maritima,* photo 347).

Transition Zone

The transition zone or backdunes lies between the pioneer zone and the stable zone and is intermediate in environmental exposures caused by coastal stresses (photo 348). The zone protects the more inland sites from severe storms. Soils of the transition zone are deep sands with a high organic content.

Many plant species growing in the transition zone also occur in the pioneer or stable zones. Vegetation may be patchy and species composition varies from one geographic locale to another. Two fairly widespread plant communities found in Florida's transition zone are Coastal Strand and Coastal Grassland.

Coastal Strands

Vegetation growing on and amid sand dunes as a continuous, narrow strip along high energy shorelines of both coasts constitutes the coastal strand. About 50 percent (13,000 acres) of this community exists today. Coastal developments have been the main factors for this reduction. The Coastal Strand is sometimes called the woody community because many woody or partially woody plants grow here. Widespread and common vines like greenbrier (*Smilax auriculata,* photo 93), Virginia creeper (*Parthenocissus quinquefolia,* photo 97), southern fox grape or muscadine (*Vitis rotundifolia,* photo 98), and summer grape (*V. aestivalis,* photo 406) grow in the Coastal Strand. These vines can also be found in the pioneer and stable zones of certain geographical areas as well as in areas located beyond the coastal borders.

Saw palmetto and yaupon holly (photo, 380) are common, characteristic plants of the Coastal Strand and Coastal Scrub. Nearly continuous stretches of saw palmetto occur along the northeast Atlantic Coast to about St. Lucie County, where its dominance diminishes. Here and farther south along the east Florida coast saw palmetto gives way to seagrape, twinberry or nakedwood (*Myrcianthes fragrans,* photo 365), and tough bumelia or buckthorn (*Sideroxylon tenax,* photo 370). Still farther south, blackbead (*Pithecellobium keyense,* photo 359) becomes abundant.

It is not uncommon to find plants in the Coastal Strand that are stunted or dwarfed forms of ordinary forest trees like red bay (photo 393) and cabbage palm. Low-growing dense thickets containing saw palmetto, coralbean (photo 292), Spanish dagger or Spanish bayonet (*Yucca aloifolia,* photo 349), prickly-pear cactus (*Opuntia stricta,* photo 352), necklace pod (*Sophora tomentosa,* photo 360), twinberry (photo 365), seagrapes (photo

368), tough bumelia (photo 370), yaupon holly (photo 380), and Florida privet (photo 396) occur behind the foredunes along much of the east coast. Many of these woody species are spray-pruned and resemble a sheared hedge. Herbs or semiwoody plants in the Coastal Strand include beach sunflower (photo 320), coastal vervain or beach verbena (photo 347), narrow-leaved hoary pea (*Tephrosia angustissima*, photo 361), and inkberry (photo 362).

The Coastal Strand on the southwest Florida coast tends to occur as shrubby islands in Coastal Grasslands or as open stands of low-growing shrubs. These include bay cedar (*Suriana maritima*, photo 346), gray nicker or nickerbean (*Caesalpinia bonduc*, photo 357), coin-vine (*Dalbergia ecastophyllum*, photo 358), myrsine (*Myrsine floridana*, photo 422), snowberry (*Chiococca alba*, photo 426), marlberry (*Ardisia escallonioides*, photo 444), and joewood (*Jacquinia keyensis*, photo 457). All the above plants except joewood can be found in the Atlantic Coastal Strand.

The Coastal Strand, like that found along the Atlantic and southwest coasts, does not exist in the Panhandle or in the Keys. In the Panhandle Woody Goldenrod Scrub constitutes the strand area, and Coastal Rock Barrens constitutes the area in the Keys.

Coastal Grasslands

Grasslands occur in all coastal regions, except in the Keys. Grasslands are especially developed along Cape Canaveral and the Panhandle, where they form an important component of the transition zone (photo 373). Coastal Grasslands consist primarily of herbaceous plants and lie just inland of the Beach Dune. Characteristic grasses include bushy bluestem or beardgrass (*Andropogon glomeratus*, photo 375), hairgrass (*Muhlenbergia capillaris*, photo 376), bitter panicum (photo 377), and sea oats (photo 378). Hairgrass may dominate grassy flats behind the foredunes in all coastal areas. In the Panhandle the grasslands have been invaded by the woody goldenrod. In many Coastal Grasslands of northeast Florida and northward, nongrass plants like the viny greenbrier (photo 93), tread softly (photo 137), water or beach pennywort (photo 318), railroad-vine (photo 333), beach tea (photo 336), inkberry (photo 362), sand bean (*Strophostyles helvula*, photo 374), and camphorweed (*Heterotheca subaxillaris*, photo 467) may be common.

Often associated with Coastal Grasslands are interdunal grassy swales (photo 312). Swales lie between the dune ridges and can be seen in all Coastal Uplands except those in the Keys. These are low-lying, periodically flooded areas with fresh to brackish water. Herbaceous vegetation in the swales includes grasses and herbs such as the marsh pink (*Sabatia stellaris,* photo 340).

Much of the transition zone has disappeared or continues to be altered. Elevated areas adjacent to the coast are prime sites for resort or residential development. Before development took place, the vegetation and land comprising the transition zone was continuous along the shorelines. Today the zone consists of patchy stretches of vegetation. In South Florida especially, a large part of the transition zone is invaded by aggressive exotics like Brazilian pepper and Australian pine.

Stable Zone

The stable zone is the most inland and consists of dunes that are old, stabilized, and well protected from the salt spray and storms. The zone experiences the least coastal stresses. Soils contain a lot of organic material. The plant communities resemble those inland, away from the coast. The stable zone contains the Coastal Scrub and Temperate Maritime Forest (Temperate Maritime Hammock or simply Forest of some writers).

Coastal Scrubs

The Scrub community occurs in both the transition and stable zones (photo 379). A number of species that occur in the Coastal Strand also occur in Florida's Coastal Scrubs.

Four general types of Coastal Scrub in Florida can be identified: Woody Goldenrod Scrub, Rosemary Scrub, Sand Pine Scrub, and Oak Scrub. All four types occur in the Panhandle. Oak Scrub is the most common type, but it does not occur along the southwest coast or in the Keys. Most people who mention Coastal Scrub usually are referring to Oak Scrub. Scrub vegetation and Upland Hardwood Forests are probably the oldest plant communities in south Florida. Scrub live oak (photo 178) and myrtle oak are major elements in nearly all Florida scrubs, including Coastal Scrub. Other important components include saw palmetto, southern red cedar, Chapman's oak (Figure 2), scrub hickory (photo 179), Florida rosemary, Feay's palafox (photo 188), tallowwood (photo 205), wild or scrub olive (photo 207), wax myrtle (photo 298), tough bumelia (photo 370), wild sage or wild lantana (*Lantana involucrata,* photo 372), and Feay's prairie-clover (*Dalea feayi,* photo 383). All the above species, except the lantana, commonly occur in scrubs that are more inland.

Although Coastal Scrub is similar to inland scrubs (e.g., Sand Pine Scrub, Rosemary Scrub) it is not exactly the same thing. First, sand pine and rosemary are not codominants in the coastal sites as they are for inland scrubs. Second, Sand Pine Scrub is fire maintained, whereas Coastal Scrubs are maintained by fire and salt spray.

Temperate Coastal Hammocks

Temperate Coastal or Maritime Hammocks can be found in all of Florida's coastal areas except the Keys, where Rockland Tropical Hammocks prevail. Many of the same plants occur in the two communities (photo 385). Temperate Coastal Hammocks are very limited in the Panhandle.

Large trees and a rich understory of smaller woody plants and vines form the coastal hammocks. Many of the woody species are salt-tolerant evergreens. The species of trees that form the canopy layer vary geographically, but often cabbage palm, Virginia live oak (photo 278), and red bay (photo 393) are characteristic. In the Panhandle and the northeast region of Florida, southern magnolia and southern red cedar are prominent. In the extreme western Panhandle, scrub or sand live oak (photo 178) and southern red cedar replace the Virginia live oak and cabbage palm. In the more southern locations of the southeast and southwest sections of Florida, red bay and live oak are replaced by poisonwood (*Metopium toxiferum*, photo 433), gumbo-limbo (*Bursera simarouba*, photo 438), lancewood (*Nectandra coriacea*, photo 440), strangler fig (*Ficus aurea*, photo 442), white stopper (*Eugenia axillaris*, photo 445), and other tropical species.

Both temperate and tropical species intermingle to form the understory. Examples include beautyberry (photo 96), twinberry or nakedwood (photo 365), yaupon holly (photo 380), pavonia (*Pavonia spinifex*, photo 395), rouge plant (*Rivina humilis*, photo 397), snowberry (photo 426), marlberry (photo 444), hackberry or sugarberry (*Celtis laevigata*, Figure 12), and especially in the southwest coastal area, agaves and cacti. Yaupon holly is a characteristic plant of the Panhandle and northeast section of Florida. The same species of vines that occur in the Coastal Strand and other sites can be found in the Temperate Maritime Hammocks. Terrestrial and epiphytic ferns and various species of bromeliads and orchids are commonly found in these hammocks. Breaks in the canopy permit the development of a sparse herbaceous layer.

The stable zone is a prime area for erecting commercial and residential developments. Many Temperate Maritime Hammocks have been destroyed and more continue to disappear.

12. Hackberry or sugarberry (*Celtis laevigata*).

Shell Mounds

Shell mounds or middens are special vegetated places that have attracted the attention of many people. These mounds were made by early Indians who inhabited Florida before the arrival of the Spanish. Shell mounds were more prevalent in the past than they are today because of their needless destruction. These ancient landmarks were located primarily along the coasts and along inland rivers such as the St. Johns. Shell mounds located along the coasts are largely composed of oyster shells, whereas those along the St. Johns River and other inland waterways are primarily of shells of freshwater molluscs. Perhaps the most famous and one of the largest Florida shell mounds today is Turtle Mound at north Canaveral National Seashore in Volusia County (photo 407). This mound has been in existence since at least the 1500s.

Vegetation on shell mounds may be a closed canopy of tropical and temperate hardwoods or a shrubby community. Though similar to hammocks, shell mounds differ from those communities in that the mounds are man-made. Plants often found on shell mounds include cabbage palm, hackberry (Figure 12), Virginia live oak (photo 278), coralbean (photo 292), prickly-pear cactus (photo 352), twinberry (photo 365), red bay (photo 393), pavonia (photo 395), wild plumbago (*Plumbago scandens,* photo 398), wild coffee (*Psychotria nervosa,* photo 401), snowberry (photo 426), and marlberry (photo 444).

Rockland Pinelands (Subtropical Pine Forests)

Extreme South Florida, including the Keys, is known for its tropiclike climate of high humidity, high temperatures, and a long growing period. Here, the environment differs from that elsewhere in the state. Mean sea level is below 20 feet for most sites in this part of Florida.

Stretching from Miami, to Homestead, to Everglades National Park, and on the Lower Florida Keys, the pine forests are intimately associated with outcroppings of limestones that are hard on the surface, but soft below where not exposed to the air. This is the land of Rockland Pinelands (Pine Rocklands or Subtropical Pine Forests). These forests also formerly occurred on north Key Largo. One of the first writers to mention pine forests growing on limestone in South Florida was Bernard Romans, writing in 1775.

Though never covering the large area of Sandhills or Pine Flatwoods in Florida, the Rockland Pineland habitat is nonetheless unique and distinct from these and other pinelands (photo 408). Rockland Pinelands consist of slash pine (*Pinus elliottii* var. *densa*), the only pine variety that consistently grows on limestone. The terrain is flat and well drained because of the porosity of the limestone. A hardpan similar to that in most Pine Flatwoods is not present in the Rockland Pinelands. How any vegetation, let alone a pine forest, can grow on the limestone with little or no soil is amazing.

Rockland Pinelands occur today or formerly occurred on three geologic limestone formations located in three geographical regions of South Florida. The three limestone formations are the youngest in North America. The Miami Rock Ridge, an extension of the Atlantic Coastal Ridge and composed of Miami limestone, extends from Miami, to Homestead, and to the Long Pine Key area in Everglades National Park (Map 1). Key Largo limestone supports the Upper Keys (i.e., from Soldier Key to Big Pine Key). The pine stands formerly on north Key Largo were known to occur only on Key Largo limestone. These stands were not destroyed by human development, but possibly by sea level rise. The Lower Keys (i.e., from Big Pine

Key to Key West) are on outcrops of Miami limestone. Large patches of pines are found on Big Pine Key and Cudjoe Key. Tamiami limestone is the third major outcropping and it underlies the southeastern one-third of Big Cypress Swamp. Stands of pinelands in Big Cypress Swamp are not well developed but are widely scattered and include many cypress heads.

Soils in the Rockland Pinelands vary from organic deposits of a few inches in depth, with some accumulation of sands and marl, to practically bare limestone. Deep, acid, sandy soils that are present elsewhere in the state are absent here. In the pinelands on Long Pine Key, the weakened limestone surface in places may collapse, forming sharp-edged solution holes that can make walking difficult (photo 409). A person may injure a leg by stepping into a hidden hole with razor-sharp limestone edges.

Vegetation of the Rockland Pinelands represents a mixture of tropical and temperate species. Tropicals outnumber the temperate species and are the same as or related species to those found in the West Indies and Bahamas. The degree of endemism among the plants of the Rockland Pinelands is among the highest in Florida.

As with other pine associations in Florida, the understory consists of low-growing woody species. Only in places protected from fire is there a subcanopy of tree-sized plants such as beautyberry (photo 96), Virginia live oak (photo 278), silver thatch palm (*Coccothrinax argentata,* photo 412), and wild tamarind (*Lysiloma latisiliquum,* photo 439). Species in the shrub layer that occur beyond the tropical limits include common peninsular species such as winged sumac (photo 280) and wax myrtle (photo 298). Individual small, fire-pruned live oaks are common in the shrub area on Long Pine Key.

The shrub layer is nearly universal and mainly kept low by recurring fires. Most of the plants in the shrub layer, however, are tropicals including locust-berry (*Byrsonima lucida,* photo 420), Spanish leather (*Tetrazygia bicolor,* photo 421), varnish leaf (*Dodonaea viscosa,* photo 427), Mexican alvaradoa (*Alvaradoa amorphoides,* photo 429), and marlberry (photo 444). Mexican alvaradoa is extremely limited in distribution to a few places on western Long Pine Key and around Castellow Hammock in the pinelands. The diversity of shrubby members of Rubiaceae including indigo-berry (*Randia aculeata,* photo 403), snowberry (photo 426), velvet-seed (*Guettarda scabra*), with rough leaves and globose red berrylike fruit, and Indian mulberry (*Morinda royoc*), with six whitish petals and yellowish, fleshy fruits, is noteworthy.

Open areas on the ground not covered with shrubs support a diverse cover of herbs in the Rockland Pinelands. Many herbaceous plants are perennials and most wildflowers bloom and fruit for more than six months of the year. Wildflowers that form the ground layer include Rockland ruellia (*Ruellia succulenta,* photo 410), Blodgett's cynanchum (*Cynanchum blodgettii,* photo 413), pineland clustervine (*Jacquemontia curtissii,* photo 415), Rockland spurge (*Chamaesyce conferta,* photo 416), Bahama senna (*Senna mexicana* var. *chapmanii,* photo 419), pine-pink (*Bletia purpurea,* photo 423), and Boykin's polygala (*Polygala boykinii,* photo 425). Growing alongside these tropical plants are temperate species with wide distributions in Florida: poison ivy (photo 8), white-tops or star rush (photo 43), butterfly weed (photo 108), coralbean (photo 292), pineland heliotrope (*Heliotropium polyphyllum,* photo 414), and yellow thistle (*Cirsium horridulum*).

Farther south in the Lower Keys the herbaceous vegetation becomes impoverished. Many temperate species found in the Upper Keys fail to reach the Lower Keys, including Key West.

As in Pine Flatwoods and Sandhills, periodic fires are necessary to maintain the Rockland Pinelands. Normally the fires are surface blazes that readily burn and consume the understory plants and what litter exists. The open canopy of the pine trees does not permit crown fires to form. Fires not only stimulate blooming in many plants but also prevent the pine forest from developing into a Rockland Hardwood Hammock. Tropical storms and hurricanes can be destructive to the habitat. Trees are felled, and these storms may enhance the spread of exotic species.

Strict conservation efforts must be employed to protect and maintain the existing acreage (about 31,000 acres) of the Rockland Pinelands of South Florida. More than 95 percent of this community has already been destroyed by development for houses and for farming. Problems with drift smoke are complicating management of small pine preserves in settled areas.

Rockland Hardwood Hammocks

Closely allied to the Rockland Pinelands are Rockland Hardwood Hammocks, often called Tropical Hardwood Hammocks. These closed, broad-leaved forests are located on many of the same rockland areas as the pinelands: Miami Rock Ridge, the Florida Keys, and the southeastern end of Big Cypress Swamp. Most tropical hammocks occur today on Key Largo and Elliott Key of the Upper Keys and on Big Pine Key, No Name Key, the Torch Keys, Ramrod Key, Summerland Key, Cudjoe Key, and

Sugarloaf Key in the Lower Keys. North Key Largo Hammock is the largest Caribbean Basin tropical hardwood forest in the continental United States. Beyond the Florida Keys, most remaining parcels of Tropical Hardwood Hammocks occur on Sanibel and Captiva islands (Lee County) and on shell mounds in the Ten Thousand Islands.

Rockland Hardwood Hammocks are vegetated islands, surrounded by Rockland Pinelands, marshes, or cypress forests (photo 431). Hammocks in the Big Cypress Swamp are usually associated with marshes and cypress forests instead of Rockland Pinelands. Tropical Hardwood Hammocks generally lie on outcroppings of limestone rock. The hammocks vary in size and plant species composition. Today there are about 15,000 acres remaining of tropical hammocks.

The number of Rockland Hardwood Hammocks has been reduced by commercial and residential development, road construction, power line erection, and other construction. Hammocks have fared better than the pinelands; relatively few have been totally eliminated. Probably most of the "out-of-context" hammocks that remain amid city park lawns or isolated in farm fields are doomed.

Hammocks are not prone to flooding and burning. Calcareous substrates are characteristic of South Florida hammocks. The organic soils are better developed than those of Rockland Pinelands, but still, soils in the hammocks are sparse, consisting mainly of decayed vegetation with some sands and crumbled limestones. Trees are notably shallow-rooted. Strong winds such as occur during a hurricane can severely damage a hammock by uprooting or breaking off large trees. Hurricane Donna caused such destruction at Mahogany Hammock in September 1960, as did Hurricane Andrew in March 1994 along Gumbo-Limbo Trail in Everglades National Park. Humidity is often high and a spicy odor may be detected in the interiors of dense hammocks. The interiors of many hammocks are unexpectedly open and can be walked through; however, hammock margins are often dense and form a tangled, junglelike growth.

An amazing thing about Rockland Hardwood Hammocks is their great diversity of species of broad-leaved trees, shrubs, and vines. More than 150 woody, native species of trees and shrubs have been listed from hammocks of South Florida. These plants blend together, forming a dense, nearly evergreen forest. Most of the trees and shrubs are more commonly found in the West Indies than in South Florida. The flora of South Florida's Rockland Hardwood Hammocks is similar in structure to many of the West Indian coastal stands and similar floristically to stands in the northern Bahamas.

The trees that form the dense canopy may reach 50 feet or more in height. Common canopy tree species include willow bustic (*Sideroxylon salicifolium,* photo 428), royal palm (*Roystonea elata,* photo 432), poison-wood (photo 433), gumbo-limbo (photo 438), wild tamarind (photo 439), lancewood (photo 440), West Indian mahogany (*Swietenia mahagoni,* photo 441), the infamous strangler fig (*Ficus aurea,* photo 442) that "strangles" its host (commonly cabbage palm), the shortleaf fig or wild banyan tree (*Ficus citrifolia,* photo 443), satinleaf (*Chrysophyllum olivi-forme,* photo 454), and paradise tree (*Simarouba glauca,* photo 455). To-day royal palms are not widespread and occur only in a few restricted hammocks including those at Collier-Seminole State Park, Fakahatchee Strand State Preserve, and Royal Palm Hammock at the eastern end of Long Pine Key.

Understory plants of small trees and shrubs include a large variety of species such as twinberry (photo 365), wild coffee (photo 401), myrsine (photo 422), marlberry (photo 444), white stopper (photo 445), coffee colubrina or snake-bark (*Colubrina arborescens,* photo 450), coffee colubrina or Cuban colubrina (*C. cubensis,* photo 451), inkwood (*Exothea paniculata,* photo 453), and satinleaf (photo 454). The latter species can become a canopy tree. White stopper is found in nearly every Rockland Hardwood Hammock. The related Spanish stopper (*Eugenia foetida*) may be found and can be recognized by its rounded leaves and somewhat rank smell. The two coffee colubrinas are limited to Long Pine Key in the Everglades, but occur in the Keys. A number of these tropical trees and shrubs extend northward along both the east and west coasts of Florida.

Most of the above-named species occur in the Rockland Pinelands, but usually as shrubs or low-growing trees because of the frequent fires in the pinelands. The Florida trema (*Trema micranthum,* photo 458) may become common in hammocks after a hurricane or other disturbance. Along with these characteristic plants are woody vines with temperate and tropical affinities: poison ivy (photo 8), Virginia creeper (photo 97), southern fox grape (photo 98), and hairy tournefort (*Tournefortia hirsutissima,* photo 435).

The Rockland Hardwood Hammocks of South Florida have a very sparse grass-herb ground cover. The dense canopy of trees prevents adequate sunlight from reaching the ground. Grasses such as the basket-grass or woodsgrass (*Oplismenus hirtellus*), *Dichanthelium dichotomum, Lasiacis divaricata,* and a number of ground orchids (e.g., various ladies'-tresses, *Spiranthes* spp) may be found on the ground. None of these species is limited to the southern tropical areas.

There are ferns present in these hammocks as well as various species of epiphytic orchids (e.g., clam shell orchid *Anacheilium cochleatum,* photo 447) and terrestrial ones (e.g., wild coco *Eulophia alta,* photo 448). South Florida has the largest number of epiphytic ferns, bromeliads, and orchids found in the continental United States. Common bromeliads in the hammocks include the two wild pines, *Tillandsia balbisiana* (photo 436) and *Tillandsia fasciculata* (photo 437).

Rockland Pinelands and associated Rockland Hardwood Hammocks are among the most periled communities in Florida. Both are limited in distribution, are under constant development pressure, and are being invaded by aggressive exotic plants.

Ruderal Sites

Lawns, roadsides, pastures, vacant lots, abandoned agricultural lands, old fields, parks, fence rows, and railroad rights-of-way are all Ruderal Sites, also commonly called Disturbed Sites (photo 460). The total area of Florida uplands classified as "ruderal" is about 14.5 million acres (42 percent of the uplands), and that acreage continues to grow as the natural communities are destroyed or modified to suit the needs or desires of man. Any natural community presented in this book can become a ruderal one. The occurrence of one or more wildflower species in a disturbed site may indicate what type of natural community was present before the site was disturbed.

Not only do weedy, aggressive, and noxious wildflowers make their homes in Ruderal Sites, but many species are also components of the natural communities. To the homeowner and gardener perhaps most ruderal species are simply "weeds." These plants, though they can be a nuisance and are not desired, often have flowers that are delicate and quite beautiful when viewed under magnification. Their showy appearance is limited because of their small size.

Weedy species usually have wide-ranging distributions, occur in more than one disturbed site, and are not native to Florida or to the United States. Many species have entered the state using their own means of dispersal and without the help of man. Exotic species, on the other hand, are often introduced, intentionally or accidentally, and usually these plants cause problems to the native vegetation and are costly to get rid of. Brazilian pepperbush and water hyacinth are classic examples of exotic introductions in Florida that have escaped and spread into the natural communities as invasive pests.

Florida, with its warm climate and long growing season, has become home to many of these costly pests. The adaptability of many weedy forms, such as partridge-pea (*Chamaecrista fasciculata*, photo 477) and lion's-ear (*Leonotis nepetifolia*, photo 488), explains why the same plants observed in Florida can be found growing in the Midwest and the northeastern United States. Regardless of our likes or dislikes, weedy and exotic species form a large and important component of Florida's wildflowers.

An entire book could be filled with our wildflowers classified as ruderal types. Because of the large numbers of natural upland communities and of wildflowers represented therein, I have chosen to present a limited number of wildflowers that are commonly observed in disturbed areas. Representatives of spring, summer, autumn, and winter wildflowers are shown in the photos.

PART II *Species Descriptions*

Pine Flatwoods

1. Longleaf Pine Flatwoods, Brevard County, Florida. October 26, 1996. Note the dense understory of saw palmetto (*Serenoa repens*).

Above: 2. Young longleaf pine (*Pinus palustris*) showing the characteristic white bud. July 26, 1996.

Right: 3. Burned Slash Pine Flatwoods, Tosohatchee State Reserve, Orange County, Florida. May 3, 1996.

4. Oak Hammock with a parklike appearance formed by Virginia live oak (*Quercus virginiana*). This hammock is surrounded by Sand Pine Scrub and Pine Flatwoods. University of Central Florida, Orange County, Florida. March 1995.

5. Cabbage Palm Flatwoods, Tosohatchee State Reserve, Orange County, Florida. May 23, 1997.

6. Scrubby Slash Pine Flatwoods with a grassy coastal swale, Cape Canaveral Air Station, Brevard County, Florida. July 3, 1996. Note the few pines and dense growth of saw palmetto (*Serenoa repens*).

7. Dry Prairie, Kissimmee Prairie, Okeechobee County, Florida. June 13, 1997.

8. Poison Ivy

Anacardiaceae (cashew or sumac family)
Toxicodendron radicans (Linnaeus) Kuntze

Description: Deciduous perennial. Low herb
or woody vine that climbs by aerial roots.
Leaves alternate, petioled. Leaflets 3, thin,
widest near the base, toothed. Flowers small,
greenish white. Petals 5. Drupe whitish.

Flowering time: February–May.

Habitat: Pine flatwoods, upland hardwoods,
upland mixed forests, coastal and tropical
hammocks, and ruderal.

Range: Throughout.

Comment: Plant turns orangish red to brown
in the fall. Sap of plant may cause a severe
rash in some people. Allergic reactions to
smoke from burning plants may even occur.
Indians used the ivy to treat ringworm. Birds
eat the berries, which are rich in vitamin C.

Synonym: *Rhus radicans* Linnaeus

9. Dog Banana
or Reticulate Pawpaw

Annonaceae (custard apple family)
Asimina reticulata Shuttleworth ex Chapman

Description: Woody, deciduous shrub up to
4.5 ft tall. Leaves alternate, leathery, elliptic
to oblong. Sepals 3, deciduous. Flowers in
upper leaf axils, nodding, creamy white. Petals 6; inner 3 with purplish bases. Ripe berry
oblong, yellowish green, edible.

Flowering time: January–July.

Habitat: Pine flatwoods, sandhills, coastal
scrub, and ruderal.

Range: North Florida: Counties east of Dixie,
Gilchrist, Union, and Baker, except Putnam
and St. Johns. Central Florida: Throughout.
South Florida: Throughout, except Monroe
and the Keys.

Comment: Endemic to Florida. Flowers appear before or with leaf emergence on growth
of the previous year. Seminole Indians made a
tea from the flowers for kidney disorders.

Synonym: *Pityothamnus reticulatus*
(Shuttleworth ex Chapman) Small

10. White Squirrel-banana or Beautiful Pawpaw

Annonaceae (custard apple family)
Deeringothamnus pulchellus Small

Description:: Small, woody shrub to 1 ft tall. Foliage and flowers fragrant. Leaves alternate, leathery, persistent on the plant, mostly glabrous at maturity. Blades reticulate, apex round. Flowers white or pinkish, singly in leaf axils. Ripe berry to 2 inches long, yellowish, edible.

Flowering time: April–May.

Habitat: Pine flatwoods.

Range: Central Florida: Orange. South Florida: Charlotte and Lee.

Comment: Federally endangered and endemic to Florida.

Synonym: *Asimina pulchella* (Small) Rehder & Dayton

11. Yellow Squirrel-banana or Rugel's Pawpaw

Annonaceae (custard apple family)
Deeringothamnus rugelii (B. L. Robinson) Small

Description: Low shrub to 8 inches tall. Leaves alternate, leathery, oblong to elliptic. Flowers yellowish, fragrant, nodding in the leaf axils. Petals 6–15, linear, fleshy. Stamens no more than 25. Ripe berry cylindric, yellow green, to 2.5 inches long.

Flowering time: April.

Habitat: Wet pine flatwoods.

Range: Central Florida: Volusia.

Comment: Federally endangered and endemic to Florida. Species named for Ferdinand Rugel (1806–1878), who traveled in the southern states in the early 1840s and discovered several new species while in Florida. Most of Rugel's discoveries were named by R. J. Shuttleworth, an Englishman living in Switzerland. Reports of this pawpaw occurring in Seminole County are incorrect.

Synonym: *Asimina rugelii* B. L. Robinson

12. Button Snakeroot
or Rattlesnake Master

Apiaceae or Umbelliferae (carrot or parsley family)
Eryngium yuccifolium Michaux

Description: Perennial with a stout, glabrous stem 3 ft tall or more. Stems branched above. Leaves alternate, narrow, stiff, lowermost to 3 ft long. Margins prickly, veins parallel. Flowers tiny, numerous, in compact, ovoid, hard heads that terminate the branches. Petals 5, greenish or whitish. Fruit a schizocarp.

Flowering time: May–September.

Habitat: Pine flatwoods, sandhills, floodplains, marshes, and coastal flatwoods.

Range: Panhandle: Throughout, except Gulf. North Florida: Throughout, except Gilchrist, Lafayette, Suwannee, Madison, Hamilton, and Marion. Central Florida: Throughout, except Indian River. South Florida: Throughout, except Glades, Hendry, Monroe, Dade, and the Keys.

Comment: The Timucuan and Creek Indians used the roots for neuralgia and the leaves for dysentery. Chewing the root increases saliva flow. A related species, *Eryngium aromaticum*, is a low-growing plant with spreading stems. It occurs in dry pinelands. The small, compact heads have a bluish or lead color. Leaves are stiff, deeply clefted and spine-tipped.

Synonym: *Eryngium synchaetum* (A. Gray ex J. M. Coulter & Rose) J. M. Coulter & Rose

13. Large Gallberry
or Sweet Gallberry

Aquifoliaceae (holly family)
Ilex coriacea (Pursh) Chapman

Description: Perennial, evergreen, woody shrub to 4 ft tall or more. May form dense colonies. Leaves alternate, petioled, blades widest at the middle. Margins smooth or with small teeth. Male and female flowers on separate plants. Flowers white, clustered in the leaf axils. Petals 5–9, united at the base. Mature drupe, globose, black, shiny.

Flowering time: April.

Habitat: Wet pine flatwoods and other wet areas.

Range: Panhandle: Throughout, except Holmes. North Florida: Throughout, except Bradford and Flagler. Central Florida: Hernando, Lake, Orange, Seminole, Volusia, and Polk.

14. Inkberry or Gallberry

Aquifoliaceae (holly family)
Ilex glabra (Linnaeus) A. Gray

Description: Perennial, evergreen, woody shrub to 6 ft tall or more. May form colonies. Leaves alternate, broaden upward. Margins near apices usually toothed. Male and female flowers on separate plants. Flowers white. Male flowers in axillary clusters; female flowers usually solitary. Petals usually 6, united at the base. Mature fruit drupe globose, black.

Flowering time: March–June.

Habitat: Wet to mesic pine flatwoods, thickets, sinks, prairies, and coastal swales.

Range: Throughout, except the Keys.

Comment: Common names come from the plant's black and bitter fruits.

15. Fragrant Milkweed or Large-flower Milkweed

Asclepiadaceae (milkweed family)
Asclepias connivens Baldwin

Description: Perennial, erect herb to 2 ft tall. Sap milky. Leaves opposite, sessile, fleshy. Flower clusters (umbels) in the upper part of the plant. Calyx 5-lobed. Corolla lobes 5, greenish white, reflexed. Hoods large, curved, white. Seedpods erect, long, narrow, opening to release the hair-tufted seeds.

Flowering time: May–August.

Habitat: Moist pine flatwoods.

Range: Panhandle: Wakulla, Leon, Liberty, Franklin, Calhoun, Gulf, Bay, Walton, Okaloosa, and Santa Rosa. North Florida: Alachua, Bradford, Baker, Clay, Nassau, Duval, and St. Johns. Central Florida: Manatee, Hillsborough, Pasco, Highlands, Polk, Lake, Orange, and Brevard. South Florida: Charlotte.

Comment: Some taxonomists place milkweeds in the dogbane family (Apocynaceae).

Synonym: *Anantherix connivens* (Baldwin) Feay

16. Michaux's Milkweed

Asclepiadaceae (milkweed family)
Asclepias michauxii Decaisne

Description: Herb to 16 inches tall with a weak-branched stem. Sap milky. Leaves mostly opposite, linear. The many leaves are glabrous or have hairy veins. Flowers in a terminal, solitary cluster (umbel). Calyx 5-lobed. Corolla lobes 5, pinkish white, reflexed; lobe tips dark rose. Seedpods erect, glabrous, opening to release the hair-tufted seeds.

Flowering time: April–August.

Habitat: Pine flatwoods, sandhills, and wet areas.

Range: Panhandle: Throughout, except Jefferson, Leon, Wakulla, and Holmes. North Florida: Counties east of Hamilton, Suwannee, Gilchrist, Union, and north of Marion and Flagler.

Comment: This plant honors the Frenchman André Michaux (1746–1802), who was the official botanist of King Louis XVI. Michaux spent 11 years botanizing in the United States, Canada, and the Bahamas. He visited Florida in the spring of 1788, at the time of the Second Spanish period.

17. Pedicellate Milkweed or Savannah Milkweed

Asclepiadaceae (milkweed family)
Asclepias pedicellata Walter

Description: Perennial herb. Stems slender, hairy, to 2 ft tall (usually less). Sap milky. Leaves opposite, sessile. Lower leaves reduced, upper ones narrow. Flowers erect, cylindric, greenish yellow. Flowers terminal or in the upper leaf axils. Seedpods erect, opening to release the hair-tufted seeds.

Flowering time: April–October.

Habitat: Pine flatwoods, scrubs, and ruderal.

Range: Panhandle: Throughout, except Gadsden, Jackson, Calhoun, Holmes, Washington, Santa Rosa, and Escambia. North Florida: Dixie, Levy, Columbia, Baker, Union, Bradford, Alachua, Marion, Putnam, Clay, Duval, and Nassau. Central Florida: Throughout, except Pasco, Hardee, Seminole, and Indian River. South Florida: Charlotte, Lee, Collier, Dade, Palm Beach, Martin, and Glades.

Comment: A related species, *Asclepias longifolia*, is found in wet pine flatwoods and meadows throughout the state. Stems slender, leafy, to about 28 inches tall. Leaves are very narrow and have ciliated margins. Corolla greenish white with purple tips.

Synonym: *Podostigma pedicellata* (Walter) Vail

18. Leopard's-bane

Asteraceae or Compositae (daisy or sunflower family)
Arnica acaulis (Walter) Britton et al.

Description: Perennial herb with an erect, hairy stem to 2.5 ft tall. Basal leaves ovate with parallel veins; upper leaf surface pubescent. Lower stem leaves opposite, sessile, toothed or entire. Heads of yellow disk and yellow ray florets. Ray florets toothed at apex. Fruit an achene.

Flowering time: April–May.

Habitat: Pine flatwoods and roadsides.

Range: Panhandle: Jackson and Liberty.

Comment: Only species of genus in the South.

19. Wormwood

Asteraceae or Compositae (daisy or sunflower family)
Artemisia campestris Linnaeus subsp. *caudata* (Michaux) H. M. Hall & Clements

Description: Weedy, shrublike herb to 3 ft tall or more. Stems woody at the base, glabrous, roundish. Leaves alternate, grasslike, clustered at the base and reduced above. Inflorescence elongated, forming large clusters (panicles). Bases of floral branches with many narrow leaves. Flowers small, greenish yellow, tubular. Fruit an achene.

Flowering time: September.

Habitat: Pine flatwoods, sandhills, and ruderal.

Range: Central Florida: Lake, Orange, Polk, and Osceola.

Synonym: *Artemisia caudata* Michaux

20. Snakeroot Aster or Coyote-thistle Aster

Asteraceae or Compositae (daisy or sunflower family)
Aster eryngiifolius Torrey & A. Gray

Description: Perennial with a rigid, sparsely haired stem to 2.5 ft tall. Basal leaves grass-like. Upper leaves alternate, sessile, reduced. One or more heads terminate the flowering stalk. Heads large, hard, prickly. Ray florets white or pinkish. Disk florets reddish yellow. Fruit an achene.

Flowering time: May–August.

Habitat: Pine flatwoods and wet areas.

Range: Panhandle: Counties west of Jefferson to Okaloosa.

21. White-topped Aster

Asteraceae or Compositae (daisy or sunflower family)
Aster reticulatus Pursh

Description: Perennial to 3 ft tall. Often forming dense colonies. Stems and leaves glandular, pubescent. Leaves alternate, ellip-tic, veiny. Margins entire or nearly so. Ray florets white, drooping. Disk florets yellowish to reddish. Bracts whitish with green midribs. Fruit an achene.

Flowering time: February–November.

Habitat: Wet pine flatwoods and other wet areas.

Range: Panhandle: Throughout, except Jefferson, Washington, Okaloosa, Santa Rosa, and Escambia. North Florida: Throughout, except Lafayette, Citrus, Levy, and Dixie. Central Florida: Throughout. South Florida: Glades and Lee.

Synonym: *Doellingeria reticulata* (Pursh) Greene

22. Walter's Aster

Asteraceae or Compositae (daisy or sunflower family)
Aster walteri Alexander

Description: Perennial with rough, erect or decumbent stems to 2 ft tall. Basal leaves small. Stem leaves alternate, sessile, small, triangular. Heads few, terminating on branchlets. Heads of pale purple ray florets and reddish yellow disk florets. Fruit an achene.

Flowering time: November–January.

Habitat: Pine flatwoods, sandhills, and ruderal.

Range: North Florida: Marion, Levy, Taylor, Alachua, Union, Bradford, Putnam, St. Johns, Duval, and Nassau. Central Florida: Lake, Orange, Seminole, Osceola, and Manatee.

Comment: Named for the Englishman Thomas Walter (ca. 1740–1789), who resided near Charleston, South Carolina, in the late 1700s. Walter wrote *Flora Caroliniana*.

Synonym: *Aster squarrosus* Walter

23. Balduina

Asteraceae or Compositae (daisy or sunflower family)
Balduina uniflora Nuttall

Description: Perennial with a pubescent, ribbed stem to 3 ft tall. Stems unbranched, terminated with a single flower. Basal leaves to 4 inches long. Stem leaves alternate, linear, reduced upward. Heads showy, yellow. Ray florets toothed. Disk buttonlike, yellow, honeycombed when dried. Fruit an achene.

Flowering time: July–November.

Habitat: Pine flatwoods, sandhills, scrubs, and moist areas.

Range: Panhandle: Throughout, except Jefferson and Holmes. North Florida: Hamilton, Columbia, Suwannee, Alachua, Baker, Bradford, Clay, Nassau, Duval, St. Johns, and Flagler.

Comment: Genus honors Dr. William Baldwin (1777–1819), navy surgeon and native of Pennsylvania, who visited Florida in the spring of 1817.

Synonym: *Endorima uniflora* (Nuttall) Barnhart

24. Hairy Trilisa

Asteraceae or Compositae (daisy or sunflower family)
Carphephorus paniculatus (J. F. Gmelin) Herbert

Description: Perennial to 3 ft tall or more. Stems hairy, sticky. Basal leaves in a rosette. Stem leaves alternate, sessile, numerous, reduced above. Flowers purple, mostly in a terminal, elongated cluster. Fruit an achene.

Flowering time: August–December.

Habitat: Pine flatwoods and mesic areas.

Range: Panhandle: Throughout, except Escambia, Walton, Holmes, and Bay. North Florida: Throughout, except Jefferson, and Lafayette. Central Florida: Throughout, except Manatee and De Soto. South Florida: Throughout, except Lee, Glades, Hendry, Broward, Dade, the Keys, and Monroe.

Comment: A taller relative in pine flatwoods is the vanilla plant or deer-tongue (*Carphephorus odoratissima*), which smells like the flavoring. The vanilla plant has a glabrous stem and clasping leaves. *Carphephorus carnosus* of moist pine flatwoods is usually less than 3 ft tall. Most leaves are basal, narrow, and entire. The terminal purple flowers have hairy, spine-tipped bracts.

Synonym: *Trilisa paniculata* (J. F. Gmelin) Cassini

25. Goldenaster

Asteraceae or Compositae (daisy or sunflower family)
Chrysopsis subulata Small

Description: Perennial to 3 ft tall. Stems with loose-tangled hairs. Basal leaves spatulate. Stem leaves alternate, spatulate to linear. Flower heads yellow, drooping, surrounded with curved-tipped bracts. Fruit an achene.

Flowering time: February–December; mostly late June–August.

Habitat: Pine flatwoods, scrubs, and ruderal.

Range: North Florida: Marion, Alachua, Flagler, and St. Johns. Central Florida: Throughout, except Sarasota, De Soto, and St. Lucie. South Florida: Collier.

Comment: Endemic to Florida and one of our earliest goldenasters to flower.

26. Leavenworth's Tickseed

Asteraceae or Compositae (daisy or sunflower family)
Coreopsis leavenworthii Torrey & A. Gray

Description: Perennial to 5 ft tall. Stems slender, glabrous, branched above. Leaves opposite, narrow, lobed or unlobed. Ray florets yellow, toothed. Disk florets dark. Fruit an achene.

Flowering time: January–December.

Habitat: Pine flatwoods, roadside ditches, and other ruderal areas.

Range: Panhandle: Throughout, except Leon, Liberty, Calhoun, Gulf, Holmes, Okaloosa, and Escambia. North Florida: Throughout, except Madison, Hamilton, Nassau, and Clay. Central Florida: Throughout. South Florida: Throughout.

Comment: Endemic to Florida. Named for Dr. Melines Conkling Leavenworth (1796–1862), a Yale graduate and army surgeon who was stationed in 1838 at Fort King, northeast of Tampa, during the Second Seminole War. Hot infusion made from this tickseed was used externally for heat prostration by Seminole Indians. *Coreopsis* means bedbug, apparently referring to the shape of the seeds.

Synonym: *Coreopsis lewtonii* Small

27. Swamp Coreopsis

Asteraceae or Compositae (daisy or sunflower family)
Coreopsis nudata Nuttall

Description: Stem slender, glabrous, branched above, to 4 ft tall. Leaves alternate, few, thick, rushlike. Lower leaves long-tapered. Heads showy, ray florets pink purple, disk pale yellow. Fruit an achene.

Flowering time: March–June.

Habitat: Wet pine flatwoods, roadside ditches, and wet areas.

Range: Panhandle: Throughout, except Leon and Holmes. North Florida: Alachua, Union, Bradford, Baker, Duval, and Nassau.

Comment: Resembles the cosmos.

28. Florida Elephant's-foot

Asteraceae or Compositae (daisy or sunflower family)
Elephantopus elatus Bertoloni

Description: Perennial to 2 ft tall or more. Stems stout, hairy, branched above. Basal rosette of elliptic to lanceolate leaves; lower leaf surfaces hairy. Stem leaves alternate, sessile, elliptic, reduced above. Flowers small, tubular, pale purple, subtended by 3 leaflike, hairy bracts. Fruit an achene.

Flowering time: June–November.

Habitat: Pine flatwoods, sandhills, upland mixed forests, and ruderal.

Range: Panhandle: Throughout, except Bay and Santa Rosa. North Florida: Throughout. Central Florida: Throughout. South Florida: Throughout, except Hendry, Monroe, and the Keys.

29. False Hoarhound

Asteraceae or Compositae (daisy or sunflower family)
Eupatorium rotundifolium Linnaeus

Description: Perennial herb to 3 ft tall or more. Stems solid, hairy. Leaves opposite, roundish, sessile or nearly so. Blades toothed, gland-dotted, reduced above. Flowering branches opposite. Flowers white, florets tubular. Outer bracts with golden dots. Fruit an achene.

Flowering time: May–November.

Habitat: Moist to wet pine flatwoods and ruderal.

Range: Panhandle: Throughout, except Walton. North Florida: Throughout, except Lafayette. Central Florida: Throughout. South Florida: Throughout, except Glades, Hendry, Palm Beach, Broward, Dade, the Keys, and Monroe.

Comment: Leaves of this species and others of the genus were used by Timucuan and Creek Indians to induce vomiting. The related semaphore eupatorium (*Eupatorium mikanioides*) can be found in wet pine flatwoods and salt marshes. The inflorescence of white terminal flowers and long petioles of the somewhat diamond-shaped, toothed leaves distinguish this species.

Synonyms: *Eupatorium pubescens* Muhlenberg; *Eupatorium verbenaefolium* Michaux

30. Sneezeweed

Asteraceae or Compositae (daisy or sunflower family)
Helenium autumnale Linnaeus

Description: Clump-forming, perennial to 6 ft tall. Stems branched, glabrous. Stem leaves alternate, elliptic to lanceolate. Margins toothed or entire. Leaf bases extending down on the stem. Heads showy, long-stalked, yellow. Ray florets toothed. Disk buttonlike. Fruit an achene.

Flowering time: June–October.

Habitat: Pine flatwoods, bluffs, and floodplains.

Range: Panhandle: Wakulla, Franklin, Liberty, Gadsden, Washington, and Jackson. North Florida: Taylor. Central Florida: Orange and Lake.

Comment: American Indians used the plant for colds and intestinal worms. A lactone, helenalin, is an antitumor agent in members of the genus. Powdered leaves induce sneezing.

Synonyms: *Helenium latifolium* Miller; *Helenium parviflorum* Nuttall

31. Silk-grass

Asteraceae or Compositae (daisy or sunflower family)
Pityopsis oligantha (Chapman ex Torrey & A. Gray) Small

Description: Perennial herb to 1 ft tall or more. Stems slender, usually single. Stems and flower stalks glandular. Leaves alternate, grasslike, silvery. Basal leaves exceeding the few stem leaves. Margins entire. Flowering heads 2–4, showy, on naked stalks. Disk and ray florets yellow. Rays 10 in number. Bracts of the heads overlapping. Fruit an achene.

Flowering time: April–May.

Habitat: Pine flatwoods, cypress pond margins, and other moist areas.

Range: Panhandle: Counties west of Jefferson, except Okaloosa.

Synonyms: *Chrysopsis oligantha* Chapman ex Torrey & A. Gray; *Heterotheca oligantha* (Chapman ex Torrey & A. Gray) Harms

32. Blackroot

Asteraceae or Compositae (daisy or sunflower family)
Pterocaulon pycnostachyum (Michaux) Elliott

Description: Perennial herb with thick, black roots. Stems winged, hairy, to 2.5 ft tall. Leaves alternate, lanceolate, sessile. Blades white below, greenish and purplish above. Flowers tubular, small, in a terminal, woolly spike. Fruit an achene.

Flowering time: March–November.

Habitat: Pine flatwoods, sandhills, and ruderal.

Range: Throughout, except Dixie, Madison, Jefferson, Gadsden, Jackson, and Holmes.

Comment: A decoction of the root has been used to treat colds and menstrual cramps; a tea was taken for backache.

Synonym: *Pterocaulon undulatum* C. Mohr

33. Mohr's Susan

Asteraceae or Compositae (daisy or sunflower family)
Rudbeckia mohrii A. Gray

Description: Slender, branched herb to 4 ft tall. Stems glabrous. Leaves alternate, few, glabrous, reduced above. Blades narrow, margins entire. Heads showy, terminating at a long stalk. Ray florets yellow, drooping. Disk conic or flat, florets dark. Fruit an achene.

Flowering time: July–October.

Habitat: Wet pine flatwoods and cypress swamps.

Range: Panhandle: Jefferson, Wakulla, Franklin, Liberty, Calhoun, Gulf, Bay, and Washington. North Florida: Taylor.

Comment: Plant honors the German-born Dr. Charles Theodore Mohr (1824–1901), a druggist who lived in Mobile, Alabama. From the 1850s to the 1880s, Dr. Mohr collected and wrote on a number of plant species ranging from mosses to grasses. Genus commemorates Professor Olof Rudbeck (1630–1702) and son, the predecessors of Linnaeus at Uppsala, Sweden.

34. St. John's Susan

Asteraceae or Compositae (daisy or sunflower family)
Rudbeckia nitida Nuttall

Description: Perennial to 4 ft tall or more. Stems slender, glabrous, few-branched above. Leaves alternate, sessile, unlobed. Lower leaf surface rough. Flowers showy, long-stalked, terminal. Ray florets yellow, drooping. Disk cylindric to conic, florets reddish brown. Fruit an achene.

Flowering time: July.

Habitat: Pine flatwoods and ruderal.

Range: Panhandle: Gulf and Bay. North Florida: Marion, Baker, Clay, and St. Johns.

Comment: Endangered in Florida.

Synonym: *Rudbeckia glabra* de Candolle

35. Rosinweed

Asteraceae or Compositae (daisy or sunflower family)
Silphium asteriscus Linnaeus

Description: Coarse, perennial herb with a rough stem, to 3 ft tall or more. Leaves alternate and opposite, rough to the touch. Lower leaf surface veiny. Lower leaves not lobed. Leaf margins toothed. Heads yellow, showy, solitary, few-flowered. Rays toothed. Involucre bracts large. Fruit an achene.

Flowering time: April–September.

Habitat: Pine flatwoods, upland mixed forests, and ruderal.

Range: Panhandle: Throughout, except Santa Rosa, Holmes, Washington, and Gulf. North Florida: Taylor, Dixie, and Levy. Central Florida: Pasco, Pinellas, Hillsborough, and Manatee. South Florida: Lee.

Comment: A related species is *Silphium compositum,* which is found in sandhills and dry, upland mixed forests. The stem is glabrous and nearly leafless. The basal leaves are often large and lobed.

Synonyms: *Silphium simpsonii* Greene, *Silphium dentatum* Elliott; *Silphium gracile* A. Gray

36. Chapman's Crownbeard

Asteraceae or Compositae (daisy or sunflower family)
Verbesina chapmanii J. R. Coleman

Description: Herb with a rough stem to 2 ft tall. Leaves mostly opposite, reduced above. Blades rough, entire or toothed, elliptic, broadest near the middle. Heads 1–5 per stem, bracts with stiff hairs. Ray florets lacking. Disk florets tubular, yellow orange. Fruit an achene.

Flowering time: July–August.

Habitat: Pine flatwoods and wet areas.

Range: Panhandle: Franklin, Liberty, Gulf, Bay, Washington, and Walton.

Comment: Endemic to and threatened in Florida.

37. Carolina Rock-rose

Cistaceae (rock-rose family)
Helianthemum carolinianum (Walter) Michaux

Description: Hairy perennial, to 1 ft tall. Basal leaves may be absent at flowering time. Stem leaves alternate, short-petioled, hairy. Lower leaves spatulate, reduced above. Flowers showy, 1 inch across, terminal. Sepals 5, unequal. Petals 5, yellow. Stamens numerous, orange. Fruit a small capsule.

Flowering time: February–April.

Habitat: Pine flatwoods, sandhills, dry woods, and old fields.

Range: Panhandle: Counties west of Jefferson, except Washington, Gulf, Bay, and Escambia. North Florida: Taylor, Gilchrist, Suwannee, Hamilton, Columbia, Baker, Levy, Marion, Alachua, Putnam, Clay, Duval, and St. Johns. Central Florida: Citrus south along the coast to Manatee; Polk, Lake, Orange, Seminole, and Volusia.

Comment: Flowers last for 1 day; petals easily fall off. *Helianthemum corymbosum*, a related species in sandy areas, has flowers about 0.5 inch across and in terminal clusters.

Synonym: *Crocanthemum carolinianum* (Walter) Spach

38. Sweet Pepperbush or Summersweet

Clethraceae (white alder family)
Clethra alnifolia Linnaeus

Description: Deciduous, woody shrub to 7 ft tall or more. Leaves alternate, petioled. Blades widest near the middle, narrow at the base, pale below. Veins prominent, margins toothed near apex. Flowers in terminal or axillary, elongated clusters (racemes). Sepals 5, hairy. Petals 5, white. Stamens 10, filaments glabrous. Capsule globose, pubescent.

Flowering time: June–September.

Habitat: Wet pine flatwoods and other wet areas.

Range: Panhandle: Throughout. North Florida: Madison, Taylor, Gilchrist, Hamilton, Columbia, Baker, Nassau, and Duval. Central Florida: Lake.

Comment: Shrub spreads by underground stems and can be used as a yard plant. Flowers fragrant and attract bees and butterfies. Only member of the family in Florida.

39. Sandweed

Clusiaceae or Guttiferae (St. John's-wort family)
Hypericum exile W. P. Adams

Description: Woody subshrub with a glabrous stem, less than 3 ft tall. Leaves opposite, clustered, needlelike, glabrous. Margins entire. Glands of the leaves usually drying black. Inflorescence terminal. Sepals 5, needlelike, some longer than the petals. Petals 5, orange yellow. Stamens many. Fruit a capsule.

Flowering time: April–May.

Habitat: Pine flatwoods.

Range: Panhandle: Santa Rosa, Washington, Bay, Gulf, Franklin, Liberty, and Wakulla.

Comment: Endemic to Florida. Plant formerly placed in the family Hyperiaceae. A related species, *Hypericum chapmanii,* is also endemic to the Panhandle. This woody shrub may exceed 3 ft tall. Bark of the trunk is soft and spongy. Leaves needlelike, 0.5 inch long or more, sessile. Sepals 5, needlelike, one-fourth inch long or more. Petals 5, yellow.

40. Bedstraw St. John's-wort

Clusiaceae or Guttiferae (St. John's-wort family)
Hypericum galioides Lamarck

Description: Perennial shrub to 3 ft tall or more. Stem glabrous, brownish, woody below. Leaves opposite, narrow, often broader at the tip. Margins turned down. Clusters of small leaves in axils of larger leaves. Flowers in leaf axils and terminal. Sepals 5, nearly equal. Petals 5, orange yellow. Stamens many. Fruit a pointed capsule.

Flowering time: May–July.

Habitat: Wet pine flatwoods, floodplains, and swamps.

Range: Panhandle: Throughout, except Escambia. North Florida: Throughout, except Gilchrist, Marion, Putnam, Bradford, Putnam, Clay, Duval, and Nassau. Central Florida: Hillsborough. South Florida: Absent.

Comment: Plant formerly placed in the family Hyperiaceae.

Synonym: *Hypericum ambiguum* Elliott

41. St. Andrew's-cross

Clusiaceae or Guttiferae (St. John's-wort family)
Hypericum hypericoides (Linnaeus) Crantz

Description: Evergreen, perennial herb or small shrub to 3 ft tall or more. Stem branched, reddish brown, base usually woody. Leaves opposite, linear or elliptic, sessile. Flowers terminal, in axils of leaves. Sepals 4, unequal in size. Petals 4, yellow. Stamens many. Fruit an ovoid capsule.

Flowering time: January–December.

Habitat: Pine flatwoods, floodplains, calcareous hammocks, upland mixed forests, and ruderal.

Range: Throughout Florida, except Glades, Hendry, and the Keys.

Comment: Plant formerly placed in the family Hyperiaceae.

Synonyms: *Ascyrum hypericoides* Linnaeus; *Ascyrum linifolium* Spach

42. St. Peter's-wort

Clusiaceae or Guttiferae (St. John's-wort family)
Hypericum tetrapetalum Lamarck

Description: Evergreen, perennial herb or shrub to 3 ft tall. Stem glabrous, woody at the base. Leaves opposite, sessile, clasping. Blades heart-shaped. Margins entire. Sepals 4, unequal in size. Petals 4, yellow. Fruit an ellipsoid capsule.

Flowering time: January–December.

Habitat: Pine flatwoods, sandhills, and ruderal.

Range: Panhandle: Throughout, except Escambia, Santa Rosa, Holmes, Jackson, Washington, Gadsden, and Leon. North Florida: Throughout, except Union. Central Florida: Throughout. South Florida: Throughout, except Monroe and the Keys.

Comment: Plant formerly placed in the family Hyperiaceae. *Hypericum myrtifolium* often occurs in mesic pine flatwoods. The species has leaflike sepals, 5 yellow petals, and evergreen leaves that clasp the stem. Another pine flatwoods relative is Edison's ascyrum (*Hypericum edisonianum*), limited to Highlands, De Soto, and Glades counties. Stem mostly unbranched, except near the top where branches form a spreading, flat-topped appearance. Petals yellow, of equal size.

Synonym: *Ascyrum tetrapetalum* (Lamarck) Vail ex Small

43. White-tops or Star Rush

Cyperaceae (sedge family)
Rhynchospora colorata (Linnaeus) H. Pfeiffer

Description: Erect herbs from perennial, elongated rhizomes. Stem slender, nearly 2 ft tall. Leaves alternate, narrow, flat or folded. Petal-like bracts 7 or fewer, radiating from the center, base white. Fruit an achene.

Flowering time: February–November.

Habitat: Mesic pine flatwoods, wet prairies, and other wet areas.

Range: Throughout Florida, except Santa Rosa, Walton, Holmes, Washington, Calhoun, and Leon.

Comment: A similar species, *Rhynchospora latifolia*, is stouter, taller, and has 7 or more bracts with larger white areas.

Synonym: *Dichromena colorata* (Linnaeus) Hitchcock

44. Dew-threads

Droseraceae (sundew family)
Drosera tracyi (Diels) Macfarlane

Description: Herb with elongated, bladeless leaves to 16 inches long. Leaves threadlike with many sticky glands for catching insects. Flower stalk long, hairy, glandular. Petals 5, rose purple or white. Sepals 5. Stamens 5. Fruit a capsule, seeds minute.

Flowering time: April–May.

Habitat: Wet pine flatwoods and other wet areas.

Range: Panhandle: Throughout, except Washington.

Comment: Professor S. M. Tracy (1847–1920), native of Vermont and longtime resident of Mississippi, traveled extensively in Florida in the early 19th century. Two much smaller, low-growing sundews in wet pine flatwoods and other wet sites are *Drosera brevifolia* and *Drosera capillaris*. The former has white flowers, the latter pink flowers.

45. Tarflower

Ericaceae (heath family)
Bejaria racemosa Ventenat

Description: Woody, evergreen shrub to 7 ft tall or more. Twigs pubescent. Leaves alternate, entire, ovate to elliptic. Lower leaf surfaces whitish green to pinkish. Flowers white to pinkish, in an elongated-branched inflorescence (raceme). Fragrant and sticky. Calyx lobes 6 or 7. Petals 6 or 7. Stamens 12 to 14. Fruit a globose, sticky capsule.

Flowering time: April–September.

Habitat: Pine flatwoods and scrubs.

Range: North Florida: Throughout, except Madison, Hamilton, Suwannee, and Lafayette. Central Florida: Throughout, except Indian River and De Soto. South Florida: Throughout, except Glades, Monroe, and the Keys.

Comment: The sticky flowers catch flies and other insects, hence the plant's common name. The commonly used name, *Befaria,* is incorrect.

46. Dwarf Huckleberry

Ericaceae (heath family)
Gaylussacia dumosa (Andrews) Torrey & A. Gray

Description: Woody shrub with a slender stem to 2 ft tall. Leaves alternate, short-petioled. Lower leaf surface veiny with amber dots. Blades entire, widest at the middle, apex sharp-pointed. Margins glandular. Flowers in terminal clusters (racemes). Corolla bell-shaped, 5-parted, white to pinkish. Berry black, globose, edible.

Flowering time: March–May.

Habitat: Pine flatwoods, sandhills, scrubs, acid swamps, and dry bluffs.

Range: Panhandle: Throughout, except Holmes and Bay. North Florida: Throughout, except Madison, Dixie, and Union. Central Florida: Throughout, except De Soto. South Florida: Throughout, except Hendry, Broward, Dade, Monroe, and the Keys.

Comment: A taller relative that is common in pine flatwoods is the dangleberry (*Gaylussacia frondosa* var. *tomentosa*). Flowers are small, bell-shaped, greenish, and clustered. Leaves deciduous, pale, and pubescent below.

Synonym: *Lasiococcus dumosus* (Andrews) Small

47. Wicky or Hairy Wicky

Ericaceae (heath family)
Kalmia hirsuta Walter

Description: Evergreen shrub to 2 ft tall. Twigs hairy. Leaves alternate, sessile. Blades hairy, elliptic to lanceolate. Flowers in leaf axils. Sepals 5, hairy. Petals 5, pink with red near the stamen pockets. Stamens 10, seated in reddish pockets of the corolla. Fruit a globose, glandular capsule.

Flowering time: May–September.

Habitat: Pine flatwoods, sandhills, scrubs, and coastal swales.

Range: Panhandle: Throughout, except Washington. North Florida: Throughout, except Suwannee. Central Florida: Lake.

Comment: Flowers similar to the mountain laurel, *Kalmia latifolia,* found mainly in the Panhandle. The wicky is a smaller plant and has smaller leaves. Genus honors Peter Kalm (1715–1779) of Sweden, who in the mid-1700s botanized in Philadelphia, Delaware, New Jersey, and as far north as Quebec. Kalm's mentor was Carolus Linnaeus (1707–1778), who gave us the binomial name (genus, species) used today.

Synonym: *Kalmiella hirsuta* (Walter) Small

48. Fetterbush or Shiny Lyonia

Ericaceae (heath family)
Lyonia lucida (Lamarck) K. Koch

Description: Woody, evergreen shrub to 6 ft tall or more, branches smooth. Leaves alternate, leathery, shiny above. Blades elliptic or ovate. Margins entire. Submarginal vein parallels the leaf margin (magnification needed). Flowers clustered in leaf axils, urn-shaped, red, pink, or white. Calyx and corolla 5-lobed. Stamens 5. Capsule smooth, ovoid to urn-shaped, with thickened sutures.

Flowering time: November–June.

Habitat: Pine flatwoods, scrubs, upland mixed forests, and wet areas.

Range: Panhandle: Throughout. North Florida: Throughout, except Suwannee. Central Florida: Throughout, except De Soto. South Florida: Throughout, except Charlotte, Hendry, Monroe, and the Keys.

Comment: Plants growing in wet areas may reach 12 ft tall. Shiny lyonia is used as a landscape plant and can be purchased at many native plant nurseries. The related staggerbush (*Lyonia fruticosa*), with urn-shaped white flowers, is common in pine flatwoods. This evergreen shrub usually does not exceed 6 ft tall. Leaves usually with flat margins, reduced near the end of the branches. Some leaves are rusty in color.

Synonym: *Desmothamnus lucidus* (Lamarck) Small

49. Shiny Blueberry

Ericaceae (heath family)
Vaccinium myrsinites Lamarck

Description: Branched, evergreen shrub to 2 ft tall (usually less). Leaves alternate, ovate to elliptic, glossy green above and with stalked, reddish glands below (magnification needed). Flowers in clusters. Corolla urn-shaped, whitish pink or white. Berry, globose, blue black when ripe, edible.

Flowering time: November–June.

Habitat: Pine flatwoods, sandhills, upland mixed forests, and scrubs.

Range: Panhandle: Throughout, except Escambia, Bay, Gulf, Washington, and Liberty. North Florida: Throughout. Central Florida: Throughout. South Florida: Throughout, except Monroe and the Keys.

Comment: A similar species, Darrow's blueberry, *Vaccinium darrowii*, has dull, glaucous leaves and lacks the stalked glands on the lower surface. A taller relative is the highbush blueberry (*Vaccinium corymbosum*), also found in pine flatwoods. This variable species has white, urn-shaped flowers that are often suffused with pink. Leaves are mostly glabrous beneath. Berry is edible and dull blue.

Synonym: *Cyanococcus myrsinites* (Lamarck) Small

50. Hatpins, Shoe Buttons, or Bantam-buttons

Eriocaulaceae (pipewort family)
Syngonanthus flavidulus (Michaux) Ruhland

Description: Perennial with a slender, pubescent, flowering stem to 1 ft tall. Leaves grasslike, in a dense rosette. Bases of leaves hairy. Flowers small, whitish yellow, in a hemispheric head terminating each stem. Bracts below the head straw-colored. Fruit a small capsule.

Flowering time: January–September.

Habitat: Mesic pine flatwoods, marshes, coastal swales, and pond margins.

Range: Panhandle: Throughout, except Holmes, Jackson, and Gadsden. North Florida: Throughout, except Taylor. Central Florida: Throughout, except De Soto. South Florida: Throughout, except Hardy, Broward, Monroe, and the Keys.

Comment: A related species in mesic pine flatwoods is the bog button (*Lachnocaulon anceps*). The hairy, flowering stem is usually less than 12 inches tall and terminated by a grayish head of tiny flowers.

51. Three-seeded Mercury

Euphorbiaceae (spurge family)
Acalypha gracilens A. Gray

Description: Annual weedy herb with a branched, pubescent stem to 2 1/2 ft tall. Leaves alternate with two lateral veins extending from the base. Blades elliptic, hairy. Axil spike with female flowers near its base; male flowers in an interrupted spike above. Petals absent. Leaflike bracts with triangular teeth. Fruit a schizocarp.

Flowering time: June–November.

Habitat: Pine flatwoods, sandhills, hammocks, beaches, and ruderal.

Range: Panhandle: Throughout, except Santa Rosa and Gulf. North Florida: Throughout, except Madison, Lafayette, Union, and St. Johns. Central Florida: Throughout, except Osceola and St. Lucie. South Florida: Charlotte, Glades, Martin, and Collier.

52. White Wild Indigo

Fabaceae or Leguminosae (bean or pea family)
Baptisia alba (Linnaeus) Ventenat

Description: Perennial herb to 3 ft tall or more. Stem solitary, smooth, branched above. Leaves alternate, compound. Leaflets 3, elliptic to ovate. Flowers pea-shaped, white, in a terminal or axillary inflorescence. Legume black, inflated.

Flowering time: March–May.

Habitat: Pine flatwoods, upland mixed forests, and riverbanks.

Range: Panhandle: Throughout, except Santa Rosa, Okaloosa, and Bay. North Florida: Madison, Hamilton, Suwannee, Columbia, Baker, Lafayette, Taylor, Dixie, Alachua, Marion, and Levy. Central Florida: Citrus and Lake.

Comment: Plant turns black when dried.

Synonyms: *Baptisia lactea* sensu (Clewell 1985) non (Rafinesque) Thieret; *Baptisia leucantha* sensu Small 1933, non Torrey & A. Gray

53. Scare-weed

Fabaceae or Leguminosae (bean or pea family)
Baptisia simplicifolia Croom

Description: Perennial, branched herb to 3 ft tall. Leaves alternate, unifoliate, sessile. Blades ovate, notched at the apex, shiny above, pale below. Flowers in terminal clusters (racemes), pea-shaped, yellow or greenish yellow. Fruit a black, woody legume.

Flowering time: June–September.

Habitat: Pine flatwoods and sandhills.

Range: Panhandle: Gadsden, Leon, Liberty, Franklin, and Wakulla.

Comment: Endemic to and threatened in Florida. Plant turns black when dried. Hardy Bryan Croom (1797–1837) discovered the species near Quincy, Florida.

54. Sensitive Briar

Fabaceae or Leguminosae (bean or pea family)
Mimosa quadrivalvis Linnaeus var. *angustata* (Torrey & A. Gray) Barneby

Description: Perennial herb with prostrate, prickly stems. Leaves alternate, compound. Leaflets small, closing when touched. Flowers many, sessile, arranged in a pink, globose head. Legume prickly.

Flowering time: January–December.

Habitat: Pine flatwoods, sandhills, upland mixed forests, and mesic areas.

Range: Panhandle: Throughout, except Holmes, Bay, Gulf, Wakulla, and Jefferson. North Florida: Throughout, except Union, Bradford, and Flagler. Central Florida: Throughout, except Hardee, De Soto, Manatee, and Sarasota. South Florida: Martin, Palm Beach, and Dade.

Synonym: *Schrankia microphylla* (Dryander ex Smith) J. F. Macbride

55. Zornia
or Marsilea Sandweed

Fabaceae or Leguminosae (bean or pea family)
Zornia bracteata J. F. Gmelin

Description: Annual or perennial. Prostrate or low erect herb with a branched, wiry stem. Forms mats. Leaves alternate, petioled, compound. Leaflets mostly 4, narrow. Flowers few, in a long-stalked axillary spike. Flowers pea-shaped, orange yellow. Legume bristly, divided into constrictions (a loment).

Flowering time: July–September.

Habitat: Pine flatwoods, sandhills, and ruderal.

Range: Panhandle: Throughout, except Santa Rosa, Jackson, Calhoun, Bay, Gadsden, Leon, and Jefferson. North Florida: Madison, Hamilton, Columbia, Suwannee, Gilchrist, Marion, Alachua, Putnam, and Duval. Central Florida: Throughout, except Osceola, Indian River, St. Lucie, Okeechobee, Hardee, De Soto, and Manatee. South Florida: Dade.

56. Bartram's Sabatia

Gentianaceae (gentian family)
Sabatia bartramii Wilbur

Description: Perennial with branched, smooth stems to 3 ft tall. Basal leaves spatulate, in a rosette. Stem leaves opposite, sessile, linear. Upper leaves narrower than the stem. Sepal lobes narrow, 8–12. Petals 8–12, pink, center yellow bordered by red. Stamens 5. Fruit a capsule.

Flowering time: June–August.

Habitat: Wet pine flatwoods, bogs, cypress swamps, margins of ponds, and ruderal.

Range: Panhandle: Throughout, except Walton, Jackson, Gadsden, and Jefferson. North Florida: Taylor, Dixie, Levy, Marion, Alachua, Bradford, Baker, Nassau, Duval, Clay, St. Johns, and Flagler. Central Florida: Throughout, except Lake, Seminole, Highlands, and St. Lucie. South Florida: Throughout, except Glades, Hendry, and the Keys.

Comment: Another pink multipetaled species is *Sabatia dodecandra*, which has upper leaves wider than the stem. *Sabatia grandiflora* is another related species that can be found in mesic pine flatwoods and other sites. This species has linear, sessile leaves and rose flowers of 5 large petals. Stem branched, glabrous, to 3 ft tall or more.

57. Narrow-leaved Sabatia

Gentianaceae (gentian family)
Sabatia brevifolia Rafinesque

Description: Annual herb with a smooth, branched stem to 20 inches tall or more. Stem leaves opposite, glabrous, narrow, sessile. Inflorescence with alternate branches. Flowers white with a yellow center. Calyx lobes 5, lobes bristlelike. Petals 5. Fruit a small capsule.

Flowering time: June–December.

Habitat: Pine flatwoods and moist areas.

Range: Panhandle: Throughout, except Escambia and Holmes. North Florida: Throughout, except Lafayette, Suwannee, Gilchrist, and Levy. Central Florida: Throughout, except Sumter. South Florida: Throughout, except Monroe, Dade, and the Keys.

Synonym: *Sabatia elliottii* Steudel

58. Yellow-star Grass

Hypoxidaceae (yellow-star grass family)
Hypoxis juncea Smith

Description: Perennial with a thin, hairy stem to 9 inches tall. Leaves basal, few, threadlike, V-shaped in cross section Flowers solitary or few, star-shaped. Outer 3 tepals greenish beneath and inner 3 yellow. Stamens 6. Fruit a narrow capsule with black seeds.

Flowering time: January–December.

Habitat: Moist to wet pine flatwoods.

Range: Panhandle: Santa Rosa, Okaloosa, Walton, Bay, Liberty, Franklin, Gadsden, Leon, and Jefferson. North Florida: Throughout, except Gilchrist and Madison. Central Florida: Throughout. South Florida: Martin, Palm Beach, Collier, Lee, Charlotte, and Glades.

Comment: Some authors place this plant in the amaryllis family (Amaryllidaceae). A similar species, *Hypoxis curtissii*, has much wider leaves.

59. Bartram's Ixia

Iridaceae (iris family)
Calydorea caelestina (W. Bartram) Goldblatt & Henrich

Description: Perennial herb to 1 ft tall, arising from a brownish bulb. Basal leaves usually 2, narrow. Flower stem erect, unbranched, with 1 or 2 small leaves. Flowers about 2 inches across. Tepals nearly identical. Stamens 3, erect. Fruit an erect capsule with brown seeds.

Flowering time: April–June.

Habitat: Pine flatwoods and wet prairies.

Range: Northeast Florida: Baker, Bradford, Union, Duval, Clay, Putnam, and St. Johns.

Comment: Endemic to and endangered in Florida. Plant responds positively to burning the habitat. Plant's name denotes its discoverer, William Bartram (1739–1823) of Pennsylvania, who came to Florida in 1765 with his father, John. In 1766 William established a short-lived plantation on the St. Johns River. From April 1773 until 1778, William traveled extensively in Florida and throughout the Southeast. William's observations are recorded in his famous book, *Travels,* where the ixia is illustrated. A related species of wet pine flatwoods, hammocks, and marshes is the endemic celestial lily (*Nemastylis floridana*). The 6 violet blue tepals are narrower and more pointed than those of Bartram's ixia. Leaves few, linear, bases stalked.

Synonyms: *Salpingostylis caelestina* (W. Bartram) Small; *Sphenostigma caelestinum* (W. Bartram) R. C. Foster

60. White Birds-in-a-nest

Lamiaceae or Labiatae (mint family)
Macbridea alba Chapman

Description: Perennial herb to 15 inches tall. Stem angled, simple or few-branched. Tight-bracted clusters bearing the flowers terminate the stem. Leaves opposite, sessile, spatulate, glandular. Flowers white, 2-lipped. Stamens 4. Fruits of 4 nutlets.

Flowering time: June–July.

Habitat: Pine flatwoods, savannas, and wet areas.

Range: Panhandle: Bay, Calhoun, Gulf, Franklin, and Liberty.

Comment: Endemic to and endangered in Florida. Genus commemorates Dr. James McBride, a skilled physician and student of natural history, who died at the early age of 33.

61. Godfrey's Obedient Plant

Lamiaceae or Labiatae (mint family)
Physostegia godfreyi Cantino

Description: Erect herb. Stem 2 ft tall or more, branched above. Leaves opposite, narrow, reduced above. Flowers paired, small, pale purple. Corolla 2-lipped. Lower lip 3-lobed with dark purple lines. Fruits of 4 nutlets.

Flowering time: June–July.

Habitat: Pine flatwoods and moist areas.

Range: Panhandle: Walton, Bay, Gulf, Calhoun, Liberty, Franklin, and Wakulla.

Comment: Endemic to Florida. Plant name honors Robert K. Godfrey, who made major contributions to our knowledge of Florida and Georgia plants.

62. Yellow Butterwort

Lentibulariaceae (bladderwort family)
Pinguicula lutea Walter

Description: Perennial herb to 1 ft tall or more. Basal leaves yellow green, in rosettes. Upper leaf surfaces viscid. A single yellow flower terminates the leafless flowering stalk. Calyx 5-lobed. Corolla 5-lobed, 2-lipped with a cylindric spur. Fertile stamens 2. Fruit a capsule.

Flowering time: November–May.

Habitat: Wet pine flatwoods, ruderal, and other wet areas.

Range: Panhandle: Throughout, except Escambia, Holmes, and Washington. North Florida: Throughout, except Madison, Taylor, Suwannee, Lafayette, Union, and Dixie. Central Florida: Throughout, except Sarasota and De Soto. South Florida: Charlotte, Lee, Collier, Glades, and Martin.

Comment: Insects are trapped and digested on the viscid leaves. Threatened in Florida. A similar threatened species with purplish flowers with purple veins is the blue butterwort (*Pinguicula caerulea*).

63. Small Butterwort

Lentibulariaceae (bladderwort family)
Pinguicula pumila Michaux

Description: Perennial, succulent herb to 12 inches tall. Basal leaves in rosettes. Upper leaf surfaces viscid. A single flower terminates the leafless flowering stalk. Calyx 5-lobed. Corolla 5-lobed, pale blue, pink, violet, or whitish. Base of flower bears a spur. Stamens 2. Fruit a capsule.

Flowering time: December–May.

Habitat: Wet pine flatwoods.

Range: Panhandle: Throughout, except Escambia, Santa Rosa, Okaloosa, Holmes, Jackson, and Washington. North Florida: Throughout, except Madison and Lafayette. Central Florida: Throughout, except Sarasota, De Soto, Okeechobee, Indian River, and St. Lucie. South Florida: Throughout, except Glades and Hendry.

Comment: Insects are trapped and digested on the viscid leaves. Threatened in Florida.

64. Yellow Colic-root

Liliaceae (lily family)
Aletris lutea Small

Description: Slender herb to 3 ft tall or more. The pointed, yellow green leaves form a basal rosette. Flowering stalk arises from the rosette's center. Stem leaves reduced. Inflorescence terminal, spikelike. Flowers yellow, outer surfaces bumpy. Tepals 6, fused. Stamens 6. Fruit a 3-parted capsule.

Flowering time: February–July.

Habitat: Moist pine flatwoods and wet ruderal sites.

Range: Panhandle: Throughout, except Jefferson and Gadsden. North Florida: Throughout, except Madison, Taylor, Suwannee, Lafayette, Gilchrist, Dixie, and Levy. Central Florida: Throughout, except Indian River and Sarasota. South Florida: Throughout, except Glades, Broward, and the Keys.

Comment: Some authors place this plant in the Melanthiaceae or Nartheciaceae. A similar but much shorter species with yellow flowers is *Aletris aurea,* found in the Panhandle.

65. White Colic-root

Liliaceae (lily family)
Aletris obovata Nash

Description: Perennial, glabrous herb to 3 ft tall or more. Leaves mainly in a basal rosette. Flowering stalk arises from the rosette's center. Stem leaves reduced. Inflorescence terminal, spikelike. Flowers small, ovoid, white with a bumpy outer surface. Tepals 6. Stamens 6, anthers reddish. Fruit a 3-parted capsule.

Flowering time: April–June.

Habitat: Moist pine flatwoods and savannas.

Range: Panhandle: Leon, Wakulla, Liberty, and Franklin. North Florida: Throughout. Central Florida: Citrus.

Comment: Some authors place this plant in the Melanthiaceae or Nartheciaceae. A similar species with white, tubular flowers is *Aletris bracteata,* found in Dade, Monroe, and the Keys.

66. Pine Lily, Catesby's Lily, or Southern Red Lily

Liliaceae (lily family)
Lilium catesbaei Walter

Description: Erect herb with a leafy stalk to 2 ft or more. Basal leaves lacking. Leaves alternate, sessile, reduced above. Flowers erect, solitary. Tepals reddish orange with yellow bases and dots of purplish brown. Capsule cylindrical, with brown seeds.

Flowering time: July–October.

Habitat: Wet pine flatwoods, savannas, and other wet areas.

Range: Panhandle: Throughout, except Holmes, Leon, and Jefferson. North Florida: Throughout, except Madison, Suwannee, Lafayette, Dixie, and Levy. Central Florida: Throughout, except Sumter and Indian River. South Florida: Throughout, except Glades, Hendry, Dade, Broward, Monroe, and the Keys.

Comment: Named for the English naturalist Mark Catesby (1679–1749), who came to Charleston, South Carolina, in 1722. Although Catesby wrote a famous work (2 volumes, 1730–1747), *Natural History of the Carolina, Florida, and the Bahama Islands,* it is doubtful that Catesby visited any part of present-day Florida. Species threatened in Florida.

67. Crow-poison or Osceola's Plume

Liliaceae (lily family)
Zigadenus densus (Desrousseaux) Fernald

Description: Perennial herb to 3 ft tall or more. Main leaves basal, grasslike. Leaves 1–3, enclosed by a purplish sheath. Stem leaves reduced. Flowering stalk glabrous. Flowers numerous, congested into a terminal, elongated cluster. Tepals 6, white or pinkish. Stamens 6. Fruit a capsule.

Flowering time: March–May.

Habitat: Wet pine flatwoods, savannas, and roadside ditches.

Range: Panhandle: Throughout, except Holmes and Jefferson. North Florida: Throughout, except Madison, Taylor, Lafayette, Suwannee, Dixie, Gilchrist, and Levy. Central Florida: Throughout, except Citrus, Hernando, Sumter, Brevard, Indian River, Sarasota, and De Soto. South Florida: Glades, Collier, and Lee.

Comment: Some authors place this plant in the Melanthiaceae or Nartheciaceae. Humans and cattle have been poisoned from the plant. Osceola (?1800–1838) was a prominent Seminole Indian chief whose rebellion resulted in the Second Seminole War in Florida.

Synonym: *Tracyanthus angustifolius* (Michaux) Small

68. Creeping Camus or Camass

Liliaceae (lily family)
Zigadenus glaberrimus Michaux

Description: Glabrous, perennial, clumped herb to 4 ft tall. Basal leaves linear. Stems leafy, reduced above. Flowers yellow white, tepals 6. Two greenish glands occur at the base of each inner flower segment. Stamens 6. Fruit a capsule.

Flowering time: July–September.

Habitat: Pine flatwoods and wet sites.

Range: Panhandle: Walton to (including) Escambia; Calhoun, Gulf, Liberty, Franklin, Wakulla, Leon, and Gadsden.

Comment: Some authors place this plant in the Melanthiaceae or Tofieldiaceae. Plant poisonous.

69. Tall Meadow Beauty

Melastomataceae (meadow beauty family)
Rhexia alifanus Walter

Description: Perennial herb with a smooth stem to 3 ft tall. Leaves opposite, sessile, 3-veined, glabrous. Flowers showy, terminal. Sepals 4. Petals 4, rose lavender, glandular beneath. Base of urn-shaped flowers with glandular hairs. Stamens 8, anthers curved, over ⅛ inch long. Capsule glandular, urn-shaped.

Flowering time: May–August.

Habitat: Moist pine flatwoods, sandhills, and wet areas.

Range: Panhandle: Throughout. North Florida: Madison, Columbia, Baker, Bradford, Alachua, Putnam, Clay, Nassau, Duval, St. Johns, and Flagler. Central Florida: Volusia and Orange.

Comment: The dried, urn-shaped capsules of the larger species of *Rhexia* can be found in the winter and used in dried flower arrangements.

70. Yellow Meadow Beauty

Melastomataceae (meadow beauty family)
Rhexia lutea Walter

Description: Perennial herb with a branched, 4-angled, hairy stem to 2 ft tall. Leaves opposite, sessile, 3-veined. Margins ciliate. Sepals 4. Petals 4, yellow. Stamens 8, anthers less than ⅛ inch long. Capsule urn-shaped, mostly glabrous.

Flowering time: May–July.

Habitat: Wet pine flatwoods and bogs.

Range: Panhandle: Throughout, except Jefferson, Gadsden, and Washington. North Florida: Counties east of Columbia, Gilchrist, Marion, and Lake; north of Seminole and Brevard.

Comment: Only *Rhexia* in North America with yellow flowers.

71. Pale Meadow Beauty

Melastomataceae (meadow beauty family)
Rhexia mariana Linnaeus

Description: Branched, perennial, herb to 2 ft tall or more. Leaves opposite, 3-veined. Margins toothed. Flowers showy; pink, rosy pink, or white. Urn-shaped flower base with glandular hairs. Sepals 4. Petals 4. Stamens 8, anthers curved, over ⅛ inch long. Capsule glandular, urn-shaped.

Flowering time: March–November.

Habitat: Wet pine flatwoods, prairies, and ruderal.

Range: Panhandle: Throughout. North Florida: Throughout. Central Florida: Throughout. South Florida: Charlotte, Lee, Collier, Glades, Hendry, Martin, and Palm Beach.

Comment: The petals of this and other members of *Rhexia* fall off easily, especially in the afternoon.

Synonym: *Rhexia lanceolata* Walter

72. Common Meadow Beauty

Melastomataceae (meadow beauty family)
Rhexia virginica Linnaeus

Description: Perennial herb to 3 ft tall. Stems hairy, 4-angled, usually branched above. Leaves opposite, 3-veined, nearly sessile. Margins ciliate. Sepals 4. Petals 4, lavender. Stamens 8, anthers curved, over ⅛ inch long. Capsule urn-shaped.

Flowering time: July–October.

Habitat: Wet pine flatwoods, cypress pond margins, riverbanks, and ruderal.

Range: Panhandle: Throughout, except Holmes. North Florida: Madison, Hamilton, Columbia, Baker, Bradford, Putnam, Nassau, Duval, St. Johns, and Flagler.

Comment: Young leaves can be used as a salad for a sweet, acid taste. Tubers have a nutty taste. Two wet pine flatwoods species with short, straight anthers, purple flowers, mostly unbranched stems, and ovate leaves are *Rhexia nuttallii* and *Rhexia petiolata*. The former has many glandular hairs on the urn-shaped capsules and lacks hairs on both leaf surfaces, whereas the latter lacks hairs on the capsules and only the lower leaf surface is hairy.

73. Downy Myrtle

Myrtaceae (myrtle family)
Rhodomyrtus tomentosa (Aiton) Hasskarl

Description: Woody, evergreen shrub to 6 ft tall or more. Stems covered with soft hairs. Leaves opposite, grayish woolly below. Margins entire. Flowers showy, in leaf axils. Calyx 5-lobed. Petals 5, rosy pink. Stamens many. Berries purple.

Flowering time: May.

Habitat: Pine flatwoods and scrubby flatwoods.

Range: Central Florida: Pasco, Hillsborough, Manatee, De Soto, Highlands, and St. Lucie. South Florida: Martin, Palm Beach, Charlotte, Lee, and Collier.

Comment: Native to Asia and Australia. An invasive escapee from cultivation. Fruit used for making pies and jellies.

74. Bearded Grass-pink
Orchidaceae (orchid family)
Calopogon barbatus (Walter) Ames

Description: Terrestrial orchid with a slender stalk to 1 ft tall. Basal leaves 1 or 2, grasslike, less than $^1/_5$ inch wide. Inflorescence of 4 or 5 terminal flowers. Flowers purple or pale pink. Petals widest below the middle. Lip uppermost with tuft of hairs extending to apex. Fruit a capsule.

Flowering time: February–June.

Habitat: Wet pine flatwoods, prairies, and other wet areas.

Range: Panhandle: Escambia, Bay, Gulf, Liberty, Franklin, Wakulla, Gadsden, and Jefferson. North Florida: Taylor, Levy, Marion, Alachua, Union, Baker, Flagler, Putnam, Clay, St. Johns, Duval, and Nassau. Central Florida: Throughout, except Sumter, Seminole, Manatee, Sarasota, Hardee, De Soto, Okeechobee, and Indian River. South Florida: Charlotte, Lee, Martin, and Palm Beach.

Comment: Threatened in Florida.

Synonym: *Limodorum parviflorum* Nash

75. Multi-flowered Grass-pink
Orchidaceae (orchid family)
Calopogon multiflorus Lindley

Description: Terrestrial orchid with a slender stalk to 16 inches tall. Basal leaves 1 or 2, grasslike, less than $^1/_5$ inch wide. Inflorescence terminal with 3 to 15 flowers. Flowers deep rose or magenta. Petals widest above the middle. Lip uppermost with hairs not extending to the apex. Fruit a capsule.

Flowering time: March–May.

Habitat: Pine flatwoods and prairies.

Range: Panhandle: Franklin, Liberty, Walton, and Okaloosa. North Florida: Dixie, Levy, Alachua, Putnam, Clay, Nassau, Duval, and St. Johns. Central Florida: Pasco, Pinellas, Hillsborough, Manatee, Sarasota, Hardee, Highlands, Osceola, Orange, Seminole, Brevard, Indian River, and St. Lucie. South Florida: Martin, Palm Beach, Dade, Collier, and Lee.

Comment: Threatened in Florida. Flowering increases after the habitat is burned.

Synonym: *Limodorum multiflorum* (Lindley) C. Mohr

76. Pale Grass-pink

Orchidaceae (orchid family)
Calopogon pallidus Chapman

Description: Terrestrial orchid to 28 inches tall (usually less). Leaves basal, grasslike, usually absent at flowering time. Flowers rose pink or white. Petals broadly lance-falcate. Lateral sepals reflexed. Lip uppermost with tuft of hairs. Fruit a capsule.

Flowering time: April–May.

Habitat: Pine flatwoods and wet areas.

Range: Panhandle: Jefferson, Wakulla, Liberty, Franklin, Gulf, Bay, Okaloosa, Santa Rosa, and Escambia. North Florida: Levy, Marion, Alachua, Union, Clay, Nassau, Duval, and St. Johns. Central Florida: Sarasota, Pinellas, Hillsborough, Pasco, Polk, Highlands, Orange, Volusia, and St. Lucie. South Florida: Martin, Palm Beach, Dade, Collier, and Lee.

Comment: Threatened in Florida.

Synonym: *Limodorum pallidum* (Chapman) C. Mohr

77. Rose-orchid or Rosebud Orchid

Orchidaceae (orchid family)
Cleistes divaricata (Linnaeus) Ames

Description: Terrestrial orchid with a glabrous stem to 32 inches tall. Leaf solitary, located above the middle of the flowering stalk. Flowers showy, terminal, usually solitary, magenta pink to white. Petals form a tube. Lip veined. Sepals narrow, erect, dark maroon brown. Fruit a capsule.

Flowering time: April–May.

Habitat: Wet pine flatwoods and sandhills.

Range: Panhandle: Jefferson west to Escambia, except Holmes, Washington, Jackson, and Gadsden. North Florida: Hamilton, Columbia, Baker, Union, Bradford, Alachua, Marion, Putnam, Clay, Duval, Nassau, and St. Johns. Central Florida: Lake.

Comment: Threatened in Florida.

78. Yellow-fringed Orchid

Orchidaceae (orchid family)
Platanthera ciliaris (Linnaeus) Lindley

Description: Terrestrial orchid with a glabrous, stout stalk to 3 ft tall. Larger leaves the lowest. Leaves alternate, lanceolate. Inflorescence terminal, flower clusters bright yellow or deep orange. Lip deeply fringed. Spur slender, longer than the flower pedicel. Fruit a capsule.

Flowering time: July–August.

Habitat: Wet pine flatwoods, bluffs, and marshes.

Range: Panhandle: Jefferson to (including) Escambia, except Holmes and Franklin. North Florida: Throughout, except Taylor, Lafayette, Gilchrist, Levy, Marion, and Baker. Central Florida: Volusia, Brevard, Orange, Lake, Hernando, Pasco, Hillsborough, Manatee, Polk, De Soto, and Highlands.

Comment: Threatened in Florida.

Synonyms: *Blephariglotis ciliaris* (Linnaeus) Rydberg; *Habenaria ciliaris* (Linnaeus) R. Brown

79. Orange Rein-orchid or Yellow Fringeless Orchid

Orchidaceae (orchid family)
Platanthera integra (Nuttall) A. Gray ex Beck

Description: Terrestrial orchid with a glabrous stalk to 2 ft tall. Upper stem leaves reduced. Blades oblong to lanceolate. Inflorescence a terminal cluster of small yellow orange flowers. Lip shallow-toothed, but not fringed. Spur about $1/5$ inch long. Fruit a capsule.

Flowering time: August–October.

Habitat: Wet pine flatwoods and marshes.

Range: Panhandle: Throughout, except Holmes, Gadsden, Leon, and Jefferson. North Florida: Clay, Duval, and Nassau. Central Florida: Orange, Osceola, Polk, and Highlands.

Comment: Threatened in Florida.

Synonyms: *Gymnadeniopsis integra* (Nuttall) Rydberg; *Habenaria integra* (Nuttall) Sprengel

80. Snowy Orchid or Bog-torch

Orchidaceae (orchid family)
Platanthera nivea (Nuttall) Luer

Description: Terrestrial orchid with a glabrous stalk to 3 ft. Larger leaves near the base keeled. Blades narrow. Inflorescence a terminal, elongated cluster of snowy white flowers. Lip uppermost, not fringed, linear. Spur slender, curved up. Fruit a capsule.

Flowering time: May–July.

Habitat: Wet pine flatwoods and other wet sites.

Range: Panhandle: Throughout, except Jefferson, Gadsden, and Okaloosa. North Florida: Taylor, Levy, and counties east of Columbia and north of Marion. Central Florida: Pasco, Pinellas, Hillsborough, Polk, Lake, Orange, Osceola, Indian River, St. Lucie, Brevard, and Volusia. South Florida: Charlotte, Lee, Collier, Dade, Palm Beach, and Martin.

Comment: Threatened in Florida.

Synonyms: *Gymnadeniopsis nivea* (Nuttall) Rydberg; *Habenaria nivea* (Nuttall) Sprengel

81. Rose Pogonia or Snake-mouth Pogonia

Orchidaceae (orchid family)
Pogonia ophioglossoides (Linnaeus) Ker-Gawler

Description: Terrestrial orchid to 20 inches tall. Stalk glabrous. Single leaf near middle of stalk; present at time of flowering. Leaflike bract just below the flower. Flowers 1–3 (usually 1), terminal, tubular, rose pink. Lower petal with yellow or brown hairs, fringed at the tip. Fruit a capsule.

Flowering time: April–July.

Habitat: Wet pine flatwoods and other wet areas.

Range: Panhandle: Throughout, except Gadsden and Jackson. North Florida: Throughout, except Madison, Taylor, Dixie, Suwannee, Union, and Bradford. Central Florida: Citrus, Lake, Seminole, Volusia, Brevard, St. Lucie, Orange, Osceola, Polk, Highlands, Pasco, Pinellas, and Hillsborough. South Florida: Martin and Palm Beach.

Comment: Wide-ranging from Newfoundland to Minnesota to Florida. Threatened in Florida.

82. Grass-leaved Ladies'-tresses

Orchidaceae (orchid family)
Spiranthes praecox (Walter) S. Watson

Description: Slender, nearly glabrous, terrestrial herb to 36 inches tall (usually less). Leaves narrow, mostly basal and may be lacking at flowering time. Flowers in a dense to loose spiral, 1-sided spike. Flowers white with green veins. Lip thin, roundish, wavy-edged. Fruit a capsule.

Flowering time: April–May.

Habitat: Wet pine flatwoods, sandhills, marshes, and swamps.

Range: Panhandle: Throughout, except Jefferson, Holmes, Washington, and Calhoun. North Florida: Throughout, except Lafayette, Gilchrist, and Marion. Central Florida: Throughout, except De Soto, Okeechobee, and Indian River. South Florida: Collier, Martin, Palm Beach, Broward, and Dade.

Comment: Threatened in Florida.

Synonym: *Ibidium praecox* (Walter) House

83. Bottlebrush Threeawn

Poaceae or Gramineae (grass family)
Aristida spiciformes Elliott

Description: Erect, perennial grass to 3 ft tall. Leaf blades erect, flat at the base, becoming inturned toward apex. Flowering head spike-like, 4–6 inches long, bristly. Bristles (awns) to ½ inch long. Head resembles a bottlebrush when opened. Fruit a grain.

Flowering time: July–November.

Habitat: Pine flatwoods, sandhills, sand pine scrub, savannas, brackish marshes, and coastal swales.

Range: Panhandle: Throughout, except Leon, Gadsden, Jackson, Washington, and Holmes. North Florida: Throughout, except Suwannee and Lafayette. Central Florida: Throughout. South Florida: Throughout, except Hendry, Monroe, Dade, and the Keys.

84. White Bachelor's Button

Polygalaceae (milkwort family)
Polygala balduinii Nuttall

Description: Annual or biennial herb to 28 inches tall. Basal leaves not persistent. Stem leaves alternate, reduced above. Inflorescence usually dense, terminal, somewhat flat-topped. Lateral sepals large, petallike. Flowers white or greenish white. Fruit a capsule.

Flowering time: March–July, November.

Habitat: Wet pine flatwoods, marshes, and coastal swales.

Range: Panhandle: Escambia, Walton, Bay, Gulf, Liberty, Franklin, and Wakulla. North Florida: Throughout, except Madison, Baker, Suwannee, Union, Bradford, Clay, Putnam, and Marion. Central Florida: Throughout, except Sumter, Manatee, Hardee, and De Soto. South Florida: Throughout.

Comment: Common name reflects an old belief that cows would increase their milk production if they ate certain species of milkworts.

Synonym: *Pilostaxis balduinii* (Nuttall) Small

85. Drumheads

Polygalaceae (milkwort family)
Polygala cruciata Linnaeus

Description: Annual with a 3-angled, glabrous stem to 1 ft tall. Leaves in whorls of 3 or 4 usually. Lower leaves spatulate, upper leaves smaller and narrow. Heads cylindrical, terminal, densely flowered. Lateral sepals large, petallike. Flowers rose purple or greenish. Fruit a capsule.

Flowering time: May–October.

Habitat: Wet pine flatwoods and wet lowlands.

Range: Panhandle: Throughout. North Florida: Throughout, except Madison, Hamilton, Columbia, Suwannee, Lafayette, Taylor, and Gilchrist. Central Florida: Throughout, except Sarasota, Hardee, and De Soto. South Florida: Collier, Martin, Palm Beach, and Broward.

Synonym: *Polygala ramosior* (Nash ex B. L. Robinson) Small

86. Procession Flower or Few-flowered Milkwort

Polygalaceae (milkwort family)
Polygala incarnata Linnaeus

Description: Glabrous herb to 28 inches tall (usually less). Stem slender, glabrous, grooved. Leaves near base opposite or whorled. Stem leaves alternate, narrow. Inflorescence a terminal, cylindric cluster. Lateral sepals large, petallike. Flowers rose purple (rarely white). Petals 3, lower petal fringed. Fruit a capsule.

Flowering time: April–September.

Habitat: Pine flatwoods, sandhills, cypress swamp margins, and dry woods.

Range: Panhandle: Throughout. North Florida: Throughout, except Madison, Lafayette, Gilchrist, and Putnam. Central Florida: Throughout, except Seminole, Sumter, Manatee, De Soto, Indian River, and St. Lucie. South Florida: Throughout, except Charlotte, Glades, Hendry, and Monroe (except the Keys).

Synonym: *Galypoda incarnata* (Linnaeus) Nieuwland

87. Wild Bachelor's Button

Polygalaceae (milkwort family)
Polygala nana (Michaux) de Candolle

Description: Clumped herb with several glabrous stems to 6 inches tall. Leaves mostly in a basal rosette. Stem leaves alternate, few. Lateral sepals large, petallike. Flowers greenish yellow, in thimble-shaped, solitary clusters terminating the stems. Fruit a capsule.

Flowering time: March–October.

Habitat: Moist pine flatwoods, coastal swales, and other moist areas.

Range: Panhandle: Throughout, except Washington and Gulf. North Florida: Throughout. Central Florida: Throughout, except Indian River. South Florida: Charlotte, Glades, Martin, Palm Beach, Lee, and Collier.

Comment: Plant turns blue green when dried. The orange milkwort or candyweed, *Polygala lutea*, has orange flowers; the roots smell like wintergreen.

Synonym: *Pilostaxis nana* (Michaux) Rafinesque ex Small

88. Yellow Bachelor's Button or Big Yellow Milkwort

Polygalaceae (milkwort family)
Polygala rugelii Shuttleworth ex Chapman

Description: Stem glabrous to 32 inches tall (usually less). Leaves alternate, smooth. Lower leaves the larger, widest at or near the base. Lateral sepals large, petallike. Flowers lemon yellow. Inflorescence a compact, thimble-shaped cluster with a pointed apex. Lower flowers loose. Fruit a capsule.

Flowering time: January–December.

Habitat: Moist pine flatwoods and moist ruderal sites.

Range: North Florida: Lafayette, Columbia, Suwannee, Hamilton, Dixie, Levy, Gilchrist, Alachua, Marion, Putnam, and Flagler. Central Florida: Throughout. South Florida: Throughout, except Glades, Broward, Monroe, and the Keys.

Comment: Endemic to Florida. A related species of moist pine flatwoods is *Polygala setacea*. This very slender plant has small, narrow-pointed heads of tiny, greenish white flowers.

Synonym: *Pilostaxis rugelii* (Shuttleworth ex Chapman) Small

89. Pine-hyacinth

Ranunculaceae (buttercup or crowfoot family)
Clematis baldwinii Torrey & A. Gray

Description: Terrestrial herb with a stem to 2 ft tall. Leaves opposite, linear to lanceolate. Leaves may be divided into narrow segments. Flowers purplish, usually solitary, bell-shaped with a thin, crisped margin. Calyx 4-lobed. Petals lacking. Plumose achene.

Flowering time: November–August.

Habitat: Pine flatwoods.

Range: North Florida: Levy, Suwannee, Columbia, Hamilton, Marion, and Flagler. Central Florida: Throughout, except De Soto and St. Lucie. South Florida: Throughout, except Martin and the Keys.

Comment: Endemic to the Florida Peninsula. Plant used by Seminole Indians to treat sunstroke.

Synonym: *Viorna baldwinii* (Torrey & A. Gray) Small

90. White-top Pitcher-plant

Sarraceniaceae (pitcher-plant family)
Sarracenia leucophylla Rafinesque

Description: Perennial herb to 3 ft tall. Leaves tubular and forming a hood with undulate margins. Lower part of leaves green, upper part white with red reticulations. Flowers solitary. Sepals 5, dark red. Petals 5, broad, dark red. Style umbrellalike. Stamens numerous. Fruit a capsule, seeds many.

Flowering time: March–July.

Habitat: Wet pine flatwoods and other wet areas.

Range: Panhandle: Liberty, Franklin, Bay, Gulf, Calhoun, Holmes, Walton, Okaloosa, Santa Rosa, and Escambia.

Comment: Endangered in Florida. Insectivore.

91. Hooded Pitcher-plant

Sarraceniaceae (pitcher-plant family)
Sarracenia minor Walter

Description: Herbaceous perennial, mostly under 20 inches. Leaves erect, hollow, with a hood arching over each tubular leaf. White or translucent blotches occur on the upper part of the leaves. Flowers terminal, nodding, pale yellow. Sepals and petals 5. Style umbrellalike. Stamens numerous. Fruit a capsule, seeds many.

Flowering time: Usually March–May; October.

Habitat: Wet pine flatwoods and other wet areas.

Range: Panhandle: Gadsden, Liberty, Franklin, Leon, Wakulla, and Jefferson. North Florida: Throughout, except Lafayette. Central Florida: Throughout, except Citrus, Hernando, Pinellas, Manatee, Sarasota, Hardee, St. Lucie, Indian River, and Brevard.

Comment: This is the most common and widespread of our pitcher-plants. Insectivore. Threatened in Florida.

92. Parrot Pitcher-plant

Sarraceniaceae (pitcher-plant family)
Sarracenia psittacina Michaux

Description: Tubular leaves with curved hoods. Leaves lie nearly flat on the ground. Base tapered, marked with white patches. Flowers erect, nodding, solitary. Sepals 5. Petals 5, reddish. Style umbrellalike. Stamens numerous. Fruit a capsule, seeds many.

Flowering time: April–July.

Habitat: Wet pine flatwoods and other wet areas.

Range: Panhandle: Throughout, except Jefferson. North Florida: Baker and Nassau.

Comment: The curved hood suggests a parrot's bill. Threatened in Florida. The purple pitcher-plant (*Sarracenia purpurea*) and trumpets (*Sarracenia flava*) can be found in wet pine flatwoods in the Panhandle. The former has maroon flowers and urn-shaped basal leaves with exposed orifices. Trumpets have tall, trumpet-shaped leaves that are hooded at the top; flowers yellow. Both species are threatened.

93. Greenbrier or Catbrier

Smilacaceae (greenbrier family)
Smilax auriculata Walter

Description: Vine with stout, woody, green stems usually lacking spines. Plant often forms tangled thickets. Leaves alternate, evergreen, and leathery. Margins entire. Leaf shape variable, often with a pointed apex and lobed base. Flowers fragrant, greenish, in axillary clusters. Berry round, black.

Flowering time: April–July.

Habitat: Pine flatwoods, upland mixed forests, and scrubs.

Range: Panhandle: Throughout, except Jefferson and Washington. North Florida: Throughout, except Hamilton, Gilchrist, and Union. Central Florida: Throughout. South Florida: Collier, Martin, Palm Beach, and Broward.

Comment: The wild sarsaparilla (*Smilax glauca*) differs from the above in having spines and thin, wide leaves that are grayish white below.

94. Hairy Melochia

Sterculiaceae (chocolate family)
Melochia spicata (Linnaeus) Fryxell

Description: Annual to 3 ft tall or more. Stems hairy, lying flat or ascending. Leaves alternate, hairy, sessile or nearly so. Margins toothed. Flowers sessile, in leaf axils or terminal. Calyx 5-lobed. Petals 5, pink purplish. Fruit a 5-valved capsule.

Flowering time: April.

Habitat: Pine flatwoods and ruderal.

Range: North Florida: Lafayette. Central Florida: Pinellas, Sarasota, De Soto, and Highlands. South Florida: Charlotte, Lee, Collier, Dade, Glades, and Hendry.

Synonyms: *Melochia villosa* (Miller) Fawcett & Rendle; *Melochia hirsuta* Cavanilles

95. Piriqueta

Turneraceae (turnera family)
Piriqueta caroliniana (Walter) Urban

Description: Perennial herb to 20 inches tall. Stems hairy or nearly glabrous. May form colonies. Leaves alternate, mostly toothed, pubescent. Flowers terminal, yellow to yellow orange. Calyx 5-lobed. Petals 5, thin, veiny, easily detached. Stamens 5. Fruit a 3-parted capsule.

Flowering time: February–November.

Habitat: Pine flatwoods, sandhills, hammocks, and ruderal.

Range: Panhandle: Escambia, Santa Rosa, Jackson, Gadsden, Calhoun, Bay, Leon, Wakulla, and Jefferson. North Florida: Throughout, except Union. Central Florida: Throughout, except Indian River and Hardee. South Florida: Throughout.

96. Beautyberry, Beautybush, or French Mulberry

Verbenaceae (vervain or verbena family)
Callicarpa americana (Linnaeus)

Description: Woody shrub to 6 ft tall or more. Leaves opposite, petioled. Blades ovate to elliptic, hairy below. Flowers small, in axillary clusters. Calyx 5-lobed. Corolla 5-lobed, pinkish. Stamens 4. Fruit globose, fleshy, purplish.

Flowering time: April–October.

Habitat: Pine flatwoods, hammocks, and roadsides.

Range: Panhandle: Throughout. North Florida: Throughout, except Hamilton. Central Florida: Throughout. South Florida: Throughout.

Comment: Widely used for ornamental plantings. Ripened fruit is used for making jellies, and mockingbirds enjoy the berries. Formerly used in the South for dropsy. This plant has traditionally been placed in Verbenaceae, but recent evidence indicates that it might best be placed with the mints (Lamiaceae).

97. Virginia Creeper or Woodbine

Vitaceae (grape family)
Parthenocissus quinquefolia (Linnaeus) Planchon

Description: Climbing, woody vine with tendrils opposite the leaves. Leaves alternate, petioled, compound. Leaflets usually 5 emerging from the same point. Leaflets variable, green or red. Flowers small. Calyx flat, without lobes. Petals 5. Stamens 5. Berry globose, black or dark blue.

Flowering time: May–July.

Habitat: Pine flatwoods, hammocks, coastal sites, and wet woods.

Range: Panhandle: Throughout, except Santa Rosa, Holmes, Washington, Bay, and Calhoun. North Florida: Throughout, except Madison, Taylor, and Bradford. Central Florida: Throughout, except Hardee and Highlands. South Florida: Throughout, except Charlotte.

Comment: Vine wide-ranging in many habitats. Timucuan and Creek Indians used the roots of this plant to treat gonorrhea.

98. Southern Fox Grape, Scuppernong, or Muscadine

Vitaceae (grape family)
Vitis rotundifolia Michaux

Description: Climbing, woody vine with unbranched tendrils opposite the leaves. Young branches angled with few hairs. Leaves alternate, simple, petioled. Margins with large teeth. Flowers small, greenish, in axillary clusters. Berry edible, black purple.

Flowering time: March–April.

Habitat: Pine flatwoods, dry hammocks, and coastal sites.

Range: Panhandle: Throughout, except Santa Rosa, Washington, and Bay. North Florida: Throughout. Central Florida: Throughout. South Florida: Throughout, except Monroe.

Comment: Jellies, jams, and wine can be made from the grapes. Timucuans and Creek Indians used the fruit for a blue dye.

Synonym: *Muscadinia munsoniana* (J. H. Simpson ex Munson) Small

99. Yellow-eyed Grass

Xyridaceae (yellow-eyed grass family)
Xyris caroliniana Walter

Description: Herb with a rigid, twisted, leafless stalk to 28 inches tall. Leaves basal, shorter than the flowering stalk. Leaves narrow; bases brownish. Flowers in an ovoid, conelike head. Sepals 3 (2 keel-shaped, 1 membranous). Petals 3, white. Fertile stamens 3, alternating with 3 brushlike staminoides. Fruit a capsule.

Flowering time: June–September.

Habitat: Mesic pine flatwoods.

Range: Panhandle: Throughout. North Florida: Throughout, except Madison, Taylor, Levy, Gilchrist, Suwannee, and St. Johns. Central Florida: Throughout. South Florida: Throughout, except Hendry.

Comment: Most species of yellow-eyed grasses should be identified using technical keys. This is our only white one. American Indians used a root tea made from this species for diarrhea.

Synonyms: *Xyris flexuosa* Muhlenberg ex Elliott; *Xyris pallescens* (C. Mohr) Small

Sandhills and Clayhills

100. Sandhill at Salt Springs Island, Ocala National Forest, Marion County, Florida. November 2, 1996.

Left: 101. Sandhill at Riverside Island, Ocala National Forest, Marion County, Florida. November 2, 1996. Note the lush growth of wiregrass (*Aristida beyrichiana*).

Below: 102. Young turkey oak (*Quercus laevis*), a characteristic tree of Sandhills. The leaf may remind one of a wild turkey's foot. April 13, 1996.

103. Twinflower or Blue Twinflower

Acanthaceae (acanthus family)
Dyschoriste oblongifolia (Michaux) Kuntze

Description: Herb to 8 inches tall or more. Stems and leaves pubescent. Leaves opposite, sessile, narrow. Margins entire. Flowers in leaf axils. Calyx pubescent, 5-lobed, lobes bristlelike. Corolla 5-lobed, blue or purplish with dark streaks. Stamens 4. Fruit a small capsule.

Flowering time: March–November.

Habitat: Sandhills, pine flatwoods, and upland mixed forests.

Range: Panhandle: Throughout, except Wakulla and counties west of Jackson, Liberty, and Gulf. North Florida: Throughout, except Flagler. Central Florida: Throughout, except Indian River, Okeechobee, and St. Lucie. South Florida: Charlotte, Lee, Collier, Martin, and Palm Beach.

104. Narrow-leaf Pawpaw

Annonaceae (custard apple family)
Asimina angustifolia Rafinesque

Description: Perennial shrub to 4 ft tall. Leaves alternate, narrow at the base. Blades narrow, leathery. Flowers in leaf axils, white. Sepals 3. Petals 6. Inner petals with corrugated bases. Fruit an ellipsoid berry.

Flowering time: April–July; November.

Habitat: Sandhills, pine flatwoods, scrubs, secondary woods, and ruderal.

Range: Panhandle: Throughout, except Gulf, Okaloosa, Santa Rosa, and Escambia. North Florida: Counties west of Duval, Clay, and Marion; Putnam. Central Florida: Hernando, Pasco, Hillsborough, and Lake.

Comment: New leaves appear before flowers. A similar pawpaw of sandhills of central and north Florida is *Asimina incana*. Leaves are ovate to elliptic, and the flowers have outer white petals and inner cream-colored ones with a yellow corrugated zone. The dwarf pawpaw (*Asimina pygmaea*) of sandhills and dry pinelands grows to about 20 inches tall. The flowers are pink maroon, axillary, and drooping. Leaves are elliptic to oblong.

Synonym: *Asimina longifolia* Kral

105. Bluestar or Blue Dogbane

Apocynaceae (dogbane family)
Amsonia ciliata Walter

Description: Perennial to 3 ft tall. Sap milky. Leaves alternate, many, grasslike. Flowers pale blue or whitish, star-shaped. Calyx 5-lobed. Corolla 5-lobed, glabrous outside, hairy within. Seedpods long, erect, usually paired.

Flowering time: April–November.

Habitat: Sandhills, scrubs, and pine flatwoods.

Range: Peninsula: Throughout, except Holmes, Bay, Gulf, and Jefferson. North Florida: Taylor, Hamilton, Suwannee, Clay, Putnam, Alachua, Marion, and Levy. Central Florida: Citrus, Hernando, Pasco, Hillsborough, Polk, Highlands, Sumter, Lake, and Orange.

106. Sandhill Milkweed

Asclepiadaceae (milkweed family)
Asclepias humistrata Walter

Description: Glabrous perennial with prostrate or ascending stems to 3 ft long (usually less). Leaves opposite, sessile, broad. Blades dull green with pink veins. Sap milky. Flowers in terminal clusters, mostly pink to lavender. Calyx 5-lobed. Corolla 5-lobed, lobes reflexed. Seedpods erect, narrow, opening to release hair-tufted seeds.

Flowering time: March–April.

Habitat: Sandhills, scrubs, pine flatwoods, and dry ruderal sites.

Range: Panhandle: Throughout, except Jefferson, Holmes, and Washington. North Florida: Throughout, except Union. Central Florida: Throughout, except Brevard, Indian River, St. Lucie, Okeechobee, Hardee, De Soto, and Sarasota.

Comment: Some taxonomists place the milkweeds (Asclepiadaceae) in the dogbane family (Apocynaceae).

107. Velvet-leaf Milkweed

Asclepiadaceae (milkweed family)
Asclepias tomentosa Elliott

Description: Herb with milky sap. Stems hairy, to 2 ft tall (usually less). Leaves opposite, petioled, hairy. Flowers in terminal or axillary clusters. Calyx 5-lobed. Corolla 5-lobed, greenish. Seedpods erect, opening to release hair-tufted seeds.

Flowering time: May–August.

Habitat: Sandhills, dunes, scrubs, and dry ruderal sites.

Range: Panhandle: Leon, Wakulla, Liberty, and Franklin. North Florida: Levy, Taylor, Lafayette, Columbia, Marion, Putnam, Flagler, Clay, Duval, and Nassau. Central Florida: Throughout, except Seminole, Manatee, Sarasota, Hardee, Okeechobee, St. Lucie, and Indian River. South Florida: Collier.

Comment: A slender milkweed often seen in sandhills, scrubs, and other dry areas is *Asclepias verticillata*. The small flowers are greenish white, and the opposite or whorled leaves are very narrow. Another milkweed with narrow, opposite leaves that may be found in sandy pinelands is *Asclepias cinerea*. The flowers are lavender to nearly white.

108. Butterfly Weed or Pleurisy-root

Asclepiadaceae (milkweed family)
Asclepias tuberosa Linnaeus

Description: Pubescent, perennial herb to 2 ft tall or more. Stems rough, erect or sprawling. Milky sap lacking. Leaves mostly alternate, sessile or nearly so. Flowers orangish to reddish, in terminal or axillary clusters. Calyx 5-lobed. Corolla 5-lobed, reflexed. Seedpod tapered at both ends, opening to release hair-tufted seeds.

Flowering time: February–October.

Habitat: Sandhills, pine flatwoods, secondary woods, pastures, and sandy ruderal sites.

Range: Panhandle: Throughout, except Escambia, Holmes, and Washington. North Florida: Throughout. Central Florida: Throughout, except Hardee and Indian River. South Florida: Throughout, except Broward, Hendry, Glades, Hardee, Monroe, and the Keys.

Comment: Widely used in ornamental plantings. Named the pleurisy-root because Indians chewed the roots to treat pleurisy and other ailments. Roots are poisonous.

Synonyms: *Asclepias decumbens* Linnaeus; *Asclepias rolfsii* Britton ex Vail

109. White-topped Aster

Asteraceae or Compositae (daisy or sunflower family)
Aster tortifolius Michaux

Description: Perennial herb to 3 ft tall. Stems branched above, hairy. Leaves alternate, sessile, pubescent. Upper leaves spatulate. Ray florets few, narrow, creamy white. Disk florets yellowish. Phyllaries hairy, white with green tips. Fruit an achene.

Flowering time: April; July–December.

Habitat: Sandhills, pine flatwoods, upland mixed forests, oak scrub, and secondary woods.

Range: Panhandle: Throughout, except Gulf and Santa Rosa. North Florida: Throughout, except Madison, Lafayette, and Union. Central Florida: Throughout, except Sumter and Indian River. South Florida: Glades, Lee, Collier, Broward, Dade, and Martin.

Comment: A relative that can be found in sandhills and dry pine flatwoods is *Aster concolor.* Stems silky, leafy, to 28 inches tall. Leaves elliptic or narrow, sessile, silky. Heads of violet purple ray florets and yellow disk florets.

Synonyms: *Sericocarpus acutisquamosus* (Nash) Small; *Sericocarpus bifoliatus* Porter

110. Yellow Buttons

Asteraceae or Compositae (daisy or sunflower family)
Balduina angustifolia (Pursh) B. L. Robinson

Description: Annual. Stems to 3 ft tall, widely branched. Leaves alternate, entire, narrow. Heads showy, 1–2 inches across. Ray florets yellow, sterile. Disk florets yellow, fertile. Mature heads become honeycombed. Fruit an achene.

Flowering time: January–December.

Habitat: Sandhills, scrubs, dunes, and pine flatwoods.

Range: Panhandle: Throughout, except Jefferson, Leon, Jackson, and Holmes. North Florida: Throughout, except Union, Duval, St. Johns, and Flagler. Central Florida: Throughout, except Hardee and Okeechobee. South Florida: Throughout, except Charlotte, Glades, Hendry, Monroe, and the Keys.

Synonym: *Actinospermum angustifolium* (Pursh) Torrey & A. Gray

111. Greeneyes

Asteraceae or Compositae (daisy or sunflower family)
Berlandiera pumila (Michaux) Nuttall

Description: Perennial herb from large roots. Stems to 3 ft tall or more, hairy. Leaves alternate, petioled, downy and paler below. Margins toothed or scalloped. Heads showy. Ray florets yellow, sterile. Unopened disk florets greenish reddish. Fruit an achene.

Flowering time: March–July.

Habitat: Sandhills and open dry woods.

Range: Panhandle: Throughout, except Jefferson. North Florida: Throughout, except Taylor, Dixie, and Union. Central Florida: Volusia and Brevard.

Synonym: *Berlandiera humilis* Small

112. Greeneyes or Florida Dandelion

Asteraceae or Compositae (daisy or sunflower family)
Berlandiera subacaulis (Nuttall) Nuttall

Description: Perennial herb with large roots. Stems hairy, to 20 inches tall (usually less). Leaves mostly basal, lobed. A head terminates a long stalk. Ray florets yellow, fertile. Disk florets greenish becoming yellowish when open. Fruit an achene.

Flowering time: January–November.

Habitat: Sandhills, pine flatwoods, upland mixed forests, and ruderal.

Range: Panhandle: Jefferson and Leon. North Florida: Throughout, except Madison, Gilchrist, Union, Bradford, Nassau, Duval, St. Johns, and Flagler. Central Florida: Throughout, except Hardee, Okeechobee, Indian River, and St. Lucie. South Florida: Lee and Dade.

Comment: Endemic to Florida. Genus of plant honors Jean Louis Berlandier (1805–1851), a Swiss, who collected plants in Texas and Mexico.

113. Paint Brush

Asteraceae or Compositae (daisy or sunflower family)
Carphephorus corymbosus (Nuttall) Torrey & A. Gray

Description: Perennial herb with hairy, leafy stems to 3 ft tall or more. Basal leaves present at flowering time. Stem leaves alternate, sessile. Inflorescence a terminal cluster of bright pink, tubular florets. Ray florets lacking. Fruit an achene.

Flowering time: September–December.

Habitat: Sandhills, pine flatwoods, scrubby flatwoods, upland mixed forests, and ruderal.

Range: Panhandle: Bay and Liberty. North Florida: Throughout. Central Florida: Throughout. South Florida: Throughout, except Glades, Hendry, Dade, and the Keys.

114. Goldenaster

Asteraceae or Compositae (daisy or sunflower family)
Chrysopsis linearifolia Semple

Description: Biennial herb with glabrous inflorescence, stem, and upper leaves. Plant to 3 ft tall or more. Basal rosette leaves white cottony, mostly absent at flowering time. Stem leaves alternate, linear; lower leaves becoming dried. Ray and disk florets yellow. Fruit an achene.

Flowering time: September–November.

Habitat: Sandhills, scrubs, and other dry sites.

Range: Panhandle: Walton to Franklin; Gadsden. North Florida: Marion. Central Florida: Volusia, Brevard, Orange, Osceola, Polk, Hernando, Hillsborough, and Manatee. South Florida: Lee, Collier, and Dade.

Comment: Endemic to Florida.

115. Goldenaster

Asteraceae or Compositae (daisy or sunflower family)
Chrysopsis scabrella Torrey & A. Gray

Description: Biennial herb. Stems rough, glandular, to 3 ft tall or more. Basal leaves white cottony, toothed, spatulate. Stem leaves alternate, sessile. Blades entire, rough, sticky to the touch. Inflorescence branched, flower heads yellow and sticky. Fruit an achene.

Flowering time: July–November.

Habitat: Sandhills, sandy riverbanks, and sandy disturbed sites.

Range: North Florida: Taylor, Dixie, Levy, Marion, Alachua, Columbia, Clay, Putnam, and Flagler. Central Florida: Throughout, except Pinellas, Manatee, Hardee, De Soto, and Indian River. South Florida: Throughout, except Hendry, Dade, and Monroe.

Comment: Plant slightly fragrant.

Synonym: *Heterotheca scabrella* (Torrey & A. Gray) R. W. Long

116. Dog Fennel

Asteraceae or Compositae (daisy or sunflower family)
Eupatorium compositifolium Walter

Description: Perennial, viscid herb with woody, branched stems to 3 ft tall or more. Stem leaves linear; lower ones opposite, upper ones alternate. Heads of numerous, tubular, white florets. Ray florets absent. Flowers fragrant. Fruit an achene.

Flowering time: July–November.

Habitat: Sandhills, pine flatwoods, old fields, secondary woods, and ruderal.

Range: Panhandle: Throughout, except Washington and Jefferson. North Florida: Throughout, except Union. Central Florida: Throughout, except Pasco, Sarasota, Hendry, De Soto, Okeechobee, Indian River, and St. Lucie. South Florida: Palm Beach and Dade.

Comment: Similar to *Eupatorium capillifolium,* which has narrower and finer leaf segments.

117. Pink-scale Gay Feather or Blazing Star

Asteraceae or Compositae (daisy or sunflower family)
Liatris elegans (Walter) Michaux

Description: Perennial herb from a globose rootstock. Stems to 4 ft, finely haired. Lowest stem leaves linear, gland-dotted. Upper stem leaves alternate, reduced. Heads pink to purple or white, arranged in a terminal cluster. Ray florets absent. Inner phyllaries petaloid, pink. Fruit an achene.

Flowering time: September–October.

Habitat: Sandhills and mesic longleaf pinelands.

Range: Panhandle: Throughout, except Wakulla, Gulf, and Bay. North Florida: Madison, Taylor, Holmes, Suwannee, Columbia, Alachua, Marion, Nassau, Duval, St. Johns, and Clay.

Comment: Our only blazing star with a feathery pappus (magnification needed).

Synonym: *Laciniaria elegans* (Walter) Kuntze

118. Blazing Star or Gay Feather

Asteraceae or Compositae (daisy or sunflower family)
Liatris pauciflora Pursh

Description: Perennial with a glabrous stem to 3 ft tall. Lower leaves linear. Flower heads stalked, purple, arranged on one side of a curved main stalk. Ray florets lacking. Fruit an achene.

Flowering time: September–October.

Habitat: Sandhills, scrubs, and pine flatwoods.

Range: Panhandle: Santa Rosa. North Florida: Throughout, except Lafayette, Gilchrist, Union, Baker, Nassau, and Flagler. Central Florida: Citrus, Hernando, Pasco, Hillsborough, Polk, Lake, and Orange.

Comment: A related species of pinelands and ruderal sites is *Liatris tenuifolia*. Stems are glabrous, to 3 ft tall or more. Basal rosette consists of long and narrow leaves. Stem leaves rapidly reduced in size upward. Flower heads not one-sided, stalked, usually of 5 purple florets. Involucre bracts blunt- or sharp-tipped, margins translucent. Another blazing star found in sandhills and pine flatwoods is *Liatris gracilis*. Stems hairy, to 3 ft tall or more. Basal rosette lacking. Lower leaves petioled, spatulate. Upper leaves linear, sessile, reduced. Flower heads not one-sided, stalked, usually of 5 light purple florets. Involucre bracts blunt-tipped, margins ciliate.

Synonym: *Laciniaria pauciflora* (Pursh) Kuntze

119. Roserush or Rushweed

Asteraceae or Compositae (daisy or sunflower family)
Lygodesmia aphylla (Nuttall) de Candolle

Description: Perennial herb. Stem rushlike, to 3 ft tall. Sap milky. Basal leaves few, narrow, long. Stem leaves scalelike or absent. Corolla pink or pale rose; sometimes white. Ray florets toothed at the tips. Disk florets lacking. Fruit an achene.

Flowering time: March–November.

Habitat: Sandhills, dry pinelands, dry prairies, and sandy soils.

Range: Panhandle: Throughout, except Gulf, Franklin, and Leon. North Florida: Throughout, except Madison, Jefferson, Baker, Bradford, St. Johns, and Dixie. Central Florida: Throughout. South Florida: Throughout, except Hendry, Monroe, Dade, and the Keys.

120. Coastal-plain Palafox

Asteraceae or Compositae (daisy or sunflower family)
Palafoxia integrifolia (Nuttall) Torrey & A. Gray

Description: Partially woody herb to 3 ft tall or more. Stems hairy, branching. Leaves alternate, narrow, reduced above. Flowers in a flat-topped terminal inflorescence. Flowers tubular, white or pink, anthers purplish. Ray florets lacking. Fruit an achene.

Flowering time: September–November.

Habitat: Sandhills, sand pine scrub, and coastal hammocks.

Range: Panhandle: Liberty, Franklin, and Leon. North Florida: Throughout, except Hamilton, Lafayette, Baker, and Union. Central Florida: Throughout, except Okeechobee. South Florida: Collier, Martin, Palm Beach, and Dade.

Comment: The name honors José Palafox, a Spanish general who fought against the armies of Napoleon Bonaparte.

121. Phoebanthus

Asteraceae or Compositae (daisy or sunflower family)
Phoebanthus grandiflorus (Torrey & A. Gray) S. F. Blake

Description: Perennial herb. Stem mostly unbranched, to 3 ft tall or more. Leaves mainly alternate, entire, narrow. Stem and leaves rough. Heads showy, sunflowerlike. Disk and ray florets yellow. A single flower usually terminates the stem. Fruit an achene.

Flowering time: May–October.

Habitat: Sandhills, pine flatwoods, and oak scrub.

Range: North Florida: Hamilton, Columbia, Baker, Suwannee, Levy, Alachua, Marion, Putnam, and Clay. Central Florida: Throughout, except Hardee and St. Lucie. South Florida: Martin, Palm Beach, and Broward.

Comment: Endemic to peninsular Florida.

122. Phoebanthus

Asteraceae or Compositae (daisy or sunflower family)
Phoebanthus tenuifolius (Torrey & A. Gray) S. F. Blake

Description: Perennial herb to 3 ft tall or more. Stem rough, mostly unbranched. Leaves alternate or opposite, very narrow, entire, rough. Heads showy, sunflowerlike. Disk and ray florets yellow. Single flower usually terminates the stem. Fruit an achene.

Flowering time: May–July.

Habitat: Sandhills and pine flatwoods.

Range: Panhandle: Calhoun, Liberty, Gadsden, Leon, Gulf, and Franklin.

Comment: Similar to *Phoebanthus grandiflorus*, except for the narrower leaves and geographical location. Endemic to Florida.

123. Silk-grass, Goldenaster, or Pityopsis

Asteraceae or Compositae (daisy or sunflower family)
Pityopsis graminifolia (Michaux) Nuttall

Description: Perennial, grasslike herb with silvery, silky stems to 3 ft tall or more (usually less). Leaves alternate, mostly basal, grasslike, silvery, veins parallel. Heads of yellow disk and ray florets. Fruit an achene.

Flowering time: January–December.

Habitat: Sandhills, scrubs, pine flatwoods, bogs, upland mixed forests, and ruderal.

Range: Present in the Keys and all counties, except the mainland part of Monroe.

Comment: Plant often occurs in colonies.

Synonyms: *Chrysopsis graminifolia* (Michaux) Elliott; *Heterotheca graminifolia* (Michaux) Shinners

124. Sandhill Coneflower or Soft-haired Coneflower

Asteraceae or Compositae (daisy or sunflower family)
Rudbeckia mollis Elliott

Description: Annual herb to 3 ft tall, branched above. Stems and leaves grayish green with soft hairs. Stem leaves alternate, sessile. Leaf margins toothed. Flowers showy, ray florets yellow. Disk flattened, brown or purplish. Fruit an achene.

Flowering time: June–July.

Habitat: Sandhills, open woods, and roadsides.

Range: Panhandle: Bay, Holmes, and Walton. North Florida: Throughout, except Union, Bradford, and Flagler.

Comment: Resembles black-eyed Susan, *Rudbeckia hirta*, but is distinguished by having soft hairs and a flat central disk.

125. Pineland Ginseng or Squarehead

Asteraceae or Compositae (daisy or sunflower family)
Tetragonotheca helianthoides Linnaeus

Description: Perennial herb with a branched stem to 3 ft tall or more. Leaves opposite, sessile. Heads solitary, showy, terminal, yellow. Ray and disk florets fertile. Ray florets toothed at the tips, narrowing at the base. Four large green bracts below the flower form a square. Fruit an achene.

Flowering time: April–June.

Habitat: Sandhills and upland mixed forests.

Range: Panhandle: Throughout, except Washington, Bay, Gulf, and Franklin. North Florida: Marion, Alachua, Lafayette, Madison, and Columbia. Central Florida: Citrus and Lake.

126. Fall Gromwell

Boraginaceae (borage family)
Onosmodium virginianum (Linnaeus) de Candolle

Description: Perennial herb with rough stems to 32 inches tall. Leaves alternate, entire, strongly veined. Flowers in a leafy, curved inflorescence that opens gradually at maturity. Calyx deeply 5-lobed. Corolla 5-lobed, lobes narrow, pubescent, yellow to orange. Fruit a schizocarp.

Flowering time: March–May.

Habitat: Sandhills, pine flatwoods, and upland mixed forests.

Range: Panhandle: Throughout, except Holmes and Gulf. North Florida: Throughout, except Hamilton, Union, Bradford, Nassau, and Flagler. Central Florida: Citrus, Hernando, Pasco, Hillsborough, Polk, Highlands, Lake, Orange, Seminole, and Volusia.

127. Clasping Warea

Brassicaceae or Cruciferae (mustard family)
Warea amplexifolia (Nuttall) Nuttall

Description: Annual to 2 ft tall or more. Stem
slender, finely haired, branched above. Leaves
alternate, smooth, clasping the stem. Flowers
whitish turning rose purple. Sepals 4, narrow,
reflexed. Petals 4, widened at apex from a
filamentlike base. Stamens 6. Seedpod (silique) stalked, elongated, curved, to 3 inches
long.

Flowering time: September.

Habitat: Sandhills and dry pinelands.

Range: Central Florida: Lake, Orange, Polk,
and Osceola.

Comment: Federally endangered and endemic
to Florida. Genus honors Nathaniel P. Ware
(1780–1854), who made extensive collections
of Florida plants along the east coast in the
fall of 1821. Thomas Nuttall (1786–1859)
published an account of Ware's plants.

128. Carter's Warea
or Carter's Mustard

Brassicaceae or Cruciferae (mustard family)
Warea carteri Small

Description: Annual herb with glabrous, slender stems to 3 ft tall. Leaves alternate, narrow
or wedge-shaped. Flowers in clusters. Sepals
4, narrow. Petals 4, white or tinged with
purple. Stamens 6. Seedpod (silique) stalked,
elongated, curved, to 2.5 inches long.

Flowering time: September–December.

Habitat: Sandhills and sand pine scrub.

Range: Central Florida: Brevard, Polk, and
Highlands. South Florida: Glades.

Comment: Federally endangered and endemic
to Florida.

129. Prickly-pear Cactus

Cactaceae (cactus family)
Opuntia humifusa (Rafinesque) Rafinesque

Description: Perennial with fleshy stems of flattened pads. Spines gray to whitish, 1 or 2 per cluster. Spines may be absent. Flowers showy, solitary. Sepals greenish yellow, intergrading with petals. Petals many, bright yellow. Stamens many. Berry pear-shaped, purplish.

Flowering time: March–August.

Habitat: Sandhills, pine flatwoods, coastal scrub, and dry ruderal areas.

Range: Panhandle: Counties west of Jefferson, except Calhoun, Washington, and Holmes. North Florida: Throughout, except Madison, Taylor, Union, and Bradford. Central Florida: Throughout, except Hardee, De Soto, and Indian River. South Florida: Throughout, except Glades and Hendry.

Comment: Ripened fruit can be eaten raw or made into jellies and marmalade.

Synonyms: *Opuntia compressa* J. F. Macbride; *Opuntia cumulicola* Small

130. Clammy Weed or Pineland Catchfly

Capparaceae (caper family)
Polanisia tenuifolia Torrey & A. Gray

Description: Annual herb to 3 ft tall with alternate-branched stems. Plant glandular, sticky. Leaves alternate, leaflets 1–3, thread-like. Sepals 4, reflexed. Petals 4, unequal in size. Stamens 9–12. Seedpod to 2.5 inches long, slender, glandular.

Flowering time: May–September.

Habitat: Sandhills, scrubs, dry pine flatwoods, and ruderal.

Range: Panhandle: Jackson and Liberty. North Florida: Levy, Columbia, Marion, Putnam, and Clay. Central Florida: Citrus, Lake, Orange, Polk, Osceola, Brevard, Indian River, St. Lucie, and Highlands. South Florida: Martin, Palm Beach, Dade, Collier, Lee, and Charlotte.

Comment: Some authors combine Capparaceae with Brassicaceae.

Synonym: *Aldenella tenuifolia* (Torrey & A. Gray) Greene

131. Pine-barrens Sandwort

Caryophyllaceae (pink family)
Minuartia caroliniana (Walter) Mattfeld

Description: Perennial herb with prostrate stems forming a basal cushion. Leaves opposite, small, narrow. Flowers small, usually numerous, stalked. Sepals 5. Petals 5, white, broadened at the apex. Stamens 10. Fruit a small capsule.

Flowering time: April–May.

Habitat: Sandhills and pond margins.

Range: Panhandle: Okaloosa, Walton, Holmes, Washington, Bay, Jackson, and Calhoun.

Comment: The wire plant (*Stipulicida setacea*) is a related species found in sandhills, scrubs, and other dry sites. The species grows to about 8 inches tall. Stems wiry, forking and branched with each slender branch terminating in a cluster of a few white flowers. Stem leaves opposite, minute. Basal leaves usually not present. Petals 3, stamens 3.

Synonyms: *Arenaria caroliniana* Walter; *Sabulina caroliniana* (Walter) Small

132. Sand Squares

Caryophyllaceae (pink family)
Paronychia rugelii (Chapman) Shuttleworth ex Chapman

Description: Annual or biennial with erect, branched stems to 20 inches tall. Leaves opposite, narrow. Flowers tiny, white to pinkish, in dense square clusters. Petals lacking. Fruit a utricle.

Flowering time: July–September.

Habitat: Sandhills, pine flatwoods, scrubs, and disturbed sites.

Range: Panhandle: Leon and Wakulla. North Florida: Counties west of Columbia to Jefferson. Counties west of Union, Bradford, Putnam, and Volusia. Central Florida: Pinellas, Pasco, Hernando, Citrus, Sumter, Lake, and Highlands.

Synonym: *Gastronychia herniarioides* (Michaux) Small

133. Gopher Apple

Chrysobalanaceae (chrysobalanus family)
Licania michauxii Prance

Description: Shrub to 1 ft tall or more. Leaves alternate, leathery, veiny, oblong. Upper surface glabrous. Flower clusters terminal and in the upper axils of the leaves. Flowers creamy white, pubescent. Calyx 5-lobed. Petals 5. Stamens 15. Fruit ovoid, edible but nearly tasteless.

Flowering time: March–August.

Habitat: Sandhills, pine flatwoods, and scrubs.

Range: Panhandle: Throughout west of Jefferson. North Florida: Throughout, except Madison, Hamilton, and Union. Central Florida: Throughout, except De Soto. South Florida: Throughout, except Glades, Hendry, and Monroe. Occurs in the Keys.

Comment: Plant spreads by underground stems.

Synonym: *Chrysobalanus oblongifolius* Michaux

134. Little St. Andrew's-cross

Clusiaceae or Guttiferae (St. John's-wort family)
Hypericum suffruticosum W. P. Adams & N. Robson

Description: Dwarf shrub with an angled stem to 6 inches tall. Leaves opposite, oblong or elliptic. Flowers usually solitary, yellow. Outer sepals 2, ovate. Inner sepals absent. Petals 4. Fruit a capsule.

Flowering time: May–August.

Habitat: Sandhills and pine flatwoods.

Range: Panhandle: Throughout, except Washington, Leon, Wakulla, and Jefferson. North Florida: Counties east of Hamilton, Lafayette, Gilchrist and north of Marion, Putnam, and Flagler.

Synonym: *Ascyrum pumilum* Michaux

135. Roseling
Commelinaceae (spiderwort family)
Cuthbertia ornata Small

Description: Perennial herb to 2 ft tall. Stems slender. Leaves alternate, with narrow leaves. Flowering scapes overtopping the leaves. Flowers pink, fragile, terminal. Petals 3. Stamens 5, pink, the filaments with delicate, beadlike hairs. Fruit a small capsule.

Flowering time: February to October.

Habitat: Sandhills, scrubs, and dry ruderal areas.

Range: North Florida: Alachua and Marion. Central Florida: Throughout, except Indian River, Okeechobee, and De Soto. South Florida: Lee, Collier, Palm Beach, Martin, and Glades.

Comment: Endemic to Florida. Another roseling of sandy soils is *Cuthbertia rosea*. It is a taller plant, the flower bracts are shorter, and leaves wider than in *Cuthbertia ornata*.

136. Deerberry
Ericaceae (heath or blueberry family)
Vaccinium stamineum Linnaeus

Description: Deciduous, woody shrub to 5 ft tall or more. Leaves alternate, thin, oval or broadened upward, often white beneath. Flowers in leafy clusters. Calyx 5-lobed. Corolla 5-lobed, white. Stamens extend beyond petals. Ripe berry, globose, dark blue.

Flowering time: February–May.

Habitat: Sandhills, pine flatwoods, scrubs, and upland mixed forests.

Range: Panhandle: Throughout. North Florida: Throughout. Central Florida: Throughout, except De Soto, Okeechobee, and Indian River. South Florida: Martin and Palm Beach.

Synonym: *Polycodium depressum* Small

137. Tread Softly

Euphorbiaceae (spurge family)
Cnidoscolus stimulosus (Michaux) Englemann & A. Gray

Description: Perennial herb with a milky sap, stiff stinging hairs, and stems to 3 ft tall (usually less). Leaves alternate, variously lobed, toothed, palmately veined. Male flowers uppermost, female flowers lowermost. Calyx of male and female flowers white, petallike. Petals lacking. Female flower with 3-lobed ovary. Stamens 10. Fruit a capsule.

Flowering time: January–December.

Habitat: Sandhills, scrubs, pine flatwoods, ruderal, and coastal areas.

Range: Panhandle: Throughout, except Holmes, Gulf, and Jefferson. North Florida: Throughout, except Taylor and Union. Central Florida: Throughout except Osceola, Okeechobee, and Hardee. South Florida: Throughout, except Hendry, Glades, Charlotte, and Monroe.

Comment: Some people have severe reactions to stinging hairs.

Synonym: *Bivonea stimulosa* (Michaux) Rafinesque

138. Silver Croton

Euphorbiaceae (spurge family)
Croton argyranthemus Michaux

Description: Perennial herb. Stem brownish, to 2 ft tall. Leaves alternate, petioled. Margins entire. Lower leaf surfaces silvery. Flowers small, terminal, white. Male and female flowers separate, but on the same plant. Male flowers with petals. Fruit a capsule.

Flowering time: April–August.

Habitat: Sandhills, scrubs, and upland mixed forests.

Range: Panhandle: Throughout, except Gulf, Wakulla, and Jefferson. North Florida: Throughout, except Dixie, Union, St. Johns, and Flagler. Central Florida: Throughout, except Pasco, Brevard, Indian River, St. Lucie, Okeechobee, Highlands, Hardee, De Soto, Manatee, and Sarasota.

Comment: Plant has been named the "healing croton" because the milky sap has been used to treat cuts and scratches. *Croton michauxii* (formerly *Crotonopsis linearis*) occurs in many Florida sandhills. Scrublike, widely branched, to about 2 ft tall. Densely covered with star-shaped hair (magnification needed) with reddish spotting. Leaves opposite, linear. Inflorescence a terminal spike. Lower flowers female, upper ones male. Flowers 5-parted. Pistils 3. Stamens 5. Fruit 1-seeded; seeds black.

139. Queen's Delight or Queen's Root

Euphorbiaceae (spurge family)
Stillingia sylvatica Linnaeus

Description: Perennial herb with milky sap. Stems smooth, to 3 ft tall (usually less). Leaves alternate, margins finely toothed, narrow or wide. Flowers in a terminal, greenish yellow or reddish spikelike inflorescence. Petals lacking. Male flowers uppermost; female flowers below. At the spike's base are 3-lobed, smooth capsules.

Flowering time: February–October.

Habitat: Sandhills, flatwoods, scrubs, sinks, and upland mixed forests.

Range: Panhandle: Throughout, except Escambia, Okaloosa, Washington, and Leon. North Florida: Dixie, Taylor, Suwannee, Alachua, Putnam, Clay, Duval, Nassau, and St. Johns. Central Florida: Throughout, except Sumter, Manatee, Sarasota, Hardee, and De Soto. South Florida: Throughout, except Glades and the Keys.

Comment: Queen's delight was used to treat constipation and to induce vomiting. The plant is a component of S.S.S. Tonic sold today.

Synonym: *Stillingia angustifolia* (Muller Argoviensis) Engelmann ex S. Watson

140. Joint-vetch

Fabaceae or Leguminosae (bean or pea family)
Aeschynomene viscidula Michaux

Description: Prostrate, sticky, perennial herb. Stems slender to 3 ft tall. Leaves alternate, hairy, leaflets 3–5. Flowers few, pea-shaped, pale yellow with a yellow center bordered by red. Legume jointed (loment), hairy.

Flowering time: July–September.

Habitat: Sandhills, scrubs, pine flatwoods, margins of salt marshes, and ruderal.

Range: Panhandle: Escambia, Santa Rosa, Okaloosa, Walton, Bay, Gulf, Franklin, Wakulla, and Leon. North Florida: Taylor, Dixie, Levy, Marion, Alachua, Bradford, Columbia, Putnam, Clay, and Duval. Central Florida: Citrus, Hernando, Pasco, Pinellas, Hillsborough, Polk, Highlands, Osceola, Sumter, Lake, Orange, and Volusia. South Florida: Dade.

Comment: Native to tropical America.

Synonym: *Secula viscidula* (Michaux) Small

141. Hairy Milk Vetch

Fabaceae or Leguminosae (bean or pea family)
Astragalus villosus Michaux

Description: Hairy, perennial herb. Stems prostrate to 8 inches long. Leaves compound, leaflets 9–17. Flowers pea-shaped, yellow, in terminal clusters. Calyx 5-lobed. Legume hairy, curved.

Flowering time: March–April.

Habitat: Sandhills, scrubs, pine flatwoods, and disturbed sites.

Range: Panhandle: Throughout, except Holmes, Jackson, Calhoun, Bay, Gulf, and Wakulla. North Florida: Madison, Hamilton, Columbia, Baker, Clay, Suwannee, Lafayette, Taylor, Dixie, Gilchrist, Alachua, and Marion. Central Florida: Citrus, Hernando, Lake, and Orange.

Synonym: *Phaca intonse* (E. Sheldon) Rydberg ex Small

142. Pineland Wild Indigo

Fabaceae or Leguminosae (bean or pea family)
Baptisia lanceolata (Walter) Elliott

Description: Bushy perennial with hairy stems to 3 ft tall. Leaves alternate, compound. Leaflets 3, widest at the middle, 2–3 inches long. Flowers pea-shaped, about 1 inch long, yellow, in leaf axils. Calyx 5-lobed, hairy. Stamens 10. Legume woody, to ¾ inch long.

Flowering time: March–May.

Habitat: Sandhills, pine flatwoods, scrubs, and upland mixed forests.

Range: Panhandle: Throughout, except Holmes and Jefferson. North Florida: Nassau, Baker, Union, Bradford, Clay, Putnam, St. Johns, and Flagler. Central Florida: Volusia, Orange, Hernando, Citrus, Hillsborough, and Polk.

Comment: *Baptisia lecontii* is a related woody shrub found in sandhills and scrubs. Flowers yellow, pea-shaped, about [1/2] inch long. Leaflets 3, grayish green, 1 inch long or less. Legume small, oval.

Synonym: *Baptisia elliptica* Small

143. Cat-bells or Gopher-weed

Fabaceae or Leguminosae (bean or pea family)
Baptisia perfoliata (Linnaeus) R. Brown

Description: Perennial shrub to 3 ft tall. Stems glabrous, arching. Leaves alternate, dull green, 1-foliate, ovate. Stem penetrates each leaf. Flowers solitary, pea-shaped, yellow. Legume small.

Flowering time: June–July.

Habitat: Sandhills and disturbed sites.

Range: Central Florida: Orange and Osceola.

144. Butterfly-pea

Fabaceae or Leguminosae (bean or pea family)
Centrosema virginianum (Linnaeus) Bentham

Description: Herbaceous, trailing and climbing vine. Leaves alternate, leaflets 3, narrow to elliptic. Veins on lower surfaces of leaflets raised. Flowers showy, upturned. Corolla bluish or pinkish blotched with white. Upper petal spurred. Legume flat, linear with a long tip.

Flowering time: February–October.

Habitat: Sandhills, upland mixed forests, pine flatwoods, ruderal, and coastal strand.

Range: Panhandle: Throughout, except Washington and Wakulla. North Florida: Throughout, except Taylor, St. Johns, and Flagler. Central Florida: Throughout, except Osceola, Okeechobee, Hardee, and De Soto. South Florida: Throughout, except Glades and Monroe.

Comment: A similar endemic species found in dry areas is *Centrosema arenicola*. Veins on the lower surfaces of the 3 leaflets are not raised.

Synonym: *Bradburya virginiana* (Linnaeus) Kuntze

145. Alicia

Fabaceae or Leguminosae (bean or pea family)
Chapmannia floridana Torrey & A. Gray

Description: Erect, sticky, pubescent herb to 3 ft tall. Leaves alternate, 3–7 leaflets. Inflorescence terminal. Flowers pea-shaped, yellow, upper petal large and ovoid. Flowers usually closed by noon. Legume (loment), hairy, divided into segments.

Flowering time: April–October.

Habitat: Sandhills, scrubs, pine flatwoods, and sandy woods.

Range: North Florida: Clay, Putnam, and Marion. Central Florida: Sumter, Lake, Orange, Seminole, Hillsborough, Polk, Osceola, Manatee, Sarasota, Hardee, De Soto, and Highlands.

Comment: Endemic to the peninsula. Name honors Dr. Alvan Wentworth Chapman (1809–1899), who wrote *Flora of the Southern United States,* the standard manual for southern plants for many years. Chapman, a medical doctor and a native of Southampton, Massachusetts, came to Florida around 1835. He lived in Quincy, in Marianna, and at the time of his death in Apalachicola. Chapman's grave is at Apalachicola.

146. Butterfly-pea

Fabaceae (bean and pea family)
Clitoria mariana Linnaeus

Description: Perennial twining or trailing herbaceous vine. Leaves alternate, petioled, leaflets 3. Leaflets entire, mostly glabrous, broadest near the base. Flowers pea-shaped, blue or lilac with purplish streaks. Spur lacking. Calyx tube cylindric. Legume flattened, narrow, to 2 [1/2] inches long.

Flowering time: April–September.

Habitat: Sandhills, flatwoods, scrubs, and upland mixed forests.

Range: Panhandle: Throughout, except Washington, Calhoun, and Gulf. North Florida: Throughout, except Madison, Hamilton, Union, Bradford, Gilchrist, and Flagler. Central Florida: Citrus, Hernando, Pinellas, Hillsborough, Manatee, Sarasota, Highlands, Polk, Lake, Orange, Seminole, Volusia, Brevard, and Indian River. South Florida: Palm Beach.

Synonym: *Martiusia mariana* (Linnaeus) Small

147. Summer-farewell

Fabaceae or Leguminosae (bean or pea family)
Dalea pinnata (J. F. Gmelin) Barneby var. *pinnata*

Description: Perennial herb with branched, glabrous stems to 2 ft tall. Leaves alternate, glabrous. Leaflets 3–11, linear. Flowers white, small, in terminal, headlike spikes. Legume hairy, 1–2 seeded.

Flowering time: September–November.

Habitat: Sandhills and sand pine scrub.

Range: Panhandle: Okaloosa, Holmes, Jackson, Washington, Bay, Franklin, Leon, and Jefferson. North Florida: Throughout, except Hamilton, Lafayette, Baker, Union, Bradford, Nassau, and Flagler. Central Florida: Throughout, except Brevard, Indian River, St. Lucie, Okeechobee, De Soto, Manatee, and Sarasota. South Florida: Martin.

Synonyms: *Kuhnistera pinnata* (J. F. Gmelin) Kuntze; *Petalostemon pinnatum* (J. F. Gmelin) S. F. Blake

148. Wild Indigo or Carolina Indigo

Fabaceae or Leguminosae (bean or pea family)
Indigofera caroliniana Miller

Description: Slender-branched shrub to 6 ft tall. Woody below, herbaceous above. Leaves compound. Leaflets 9–15; tiny spine terminates each leaflet. Flowers small, pea-shaped, yellow brownish to pinkish. Calyx 5-lobed, hairy. Legume drooping, usually 2-seeded.

Flowering time: May–August.

Habitat: Sandhills, scrubs, pine flatwoods, secondary woods, and ruderal.

Range: Panhandle: Throughout, except Santa Rosa, Holmes, Washington, Bay, Gulf, Calhoun, and Jefferson. North Florida: Throughout, except Hamilton, Suwannee, Lafayette, Gilchrist, Baker, Nassau, Duval, Bradford, and St. Johns. Central Florida: Throughout, except Pasco, Sumter, Manatee, Hardee, De Soto, Okeechobee, Indian River, and St. Lucie. South Florida: Lee, Collier, Palm Beach, Dade, and Broward.

149. Hairy Bush-clover

Fabaceae or Leguminosae (bean or pea family)
Lespedeza hirta (Linnaeus) Hornemann

Description: Perennial to 4 ft tall. Stems hairy, leafy. Leaflets 3, roundish. Flowers small, in dense clusters located in the leaf axils. Flowers pea-shaped, yellowish white with a purplish spot. Calyx 5-lobed, hairy. Jointed legume (loment) hairy.

Flowering time: May; September–October.

Habitat: Sandhills, scrubs, pine flatwoods, upland mixed forests, and secondary woods.

Range: Panhandle: Throughout, except Calhoun, Bay, and Gulf. North Florida: Throughout, except Lafayette, Baker, Union, Bradford, and Flagler. Central Florida: Throughout, except Sumter, Brevard, Indian River, Okeechobee, Highlands, Hardee, Manatee, and Sarasota.

150. Sky-blue Lupine

Fabaceae or Leguminosae (bean or pea family)
Lupinus diffusus Nuttall

Description: Perennial, hairy herb to 3 ft tall. Leaves alternate, unifoliate, midvein prominent. Flowers in a terminal, spikelike inflorescence. Calyx 2-lipped. Flowers pea-shaped, blue. Upper petal bears a white spot. Legume hairy, about 1 inch long.

Flowering time: February–May.

Habitat: Sandhills, sand pine scrub, pine flatwoods, oak scrub, and coastal strand.

Range: Panhandle: Escambia, Santa Rosa, Okaloosa, Walton, Bay, and Jackson. North Florida: Levy, Suwannee, Columbia, Marion, Alachua, Putnam, Flagler, St. Johns, Clay, and Duval. Central Florida: Throughout, except Okeechobee. South Florida: Martin, Palm Beach, Broward, Lee, and Charlotte.

Synonym: *Lupinus cumulicola* Small

151. Sundial Lupine

Fabaceae or Leguminosae (bean or pea family)
Lupinus perennis Linnaeus

Description: Perennial herb to 2 ft tall. Stems slender, erect or spreading, glabrous or hairy. Leaves alternate, compound. Leaflets 7–11, arising from the same point. Flowers in a terminal, spikelike inflorescence. Calyx 2-lipped. Flowers pea-shaped, bluish purple (rarely pink or white). Legume hairy.

Flowering time: March–April.

Habitat: Sandhills.

Range: Panhandle: Throughout, except Holmes, Gulf, and Jefferson. North Florida: Madison, Hamilton, Columbia, Suwannee, Lafayette, Clay, Duval, and Nassau.

Comment: Seeds are poisonous. American Indians drank a leaf tea for nausea and internal hemorrhage. The plant has been used in fodder to fatten horses and boost their energy levels.

Synonym: *Lupinus nuttallii* S. Watson

152. Lady Lupine

Fabaceae or Leguminosae (bean or pea family)
Lupinus villosus Willdenow

Description: Perennial herb usually less than 3 ft tall. Stems and leaves with long hairs. Leaves alternate, long-stalked, elliptic. Flowers pea-shaped, in a terminal, spikelike inflorescence. Calyx 2-lipped. Petals deep pink to purple with a reddish purple center. Legume with long, white hairs.

Flowering time: March–May.

Habitat: Sandhills, scrubs, and upland mixed forests.

Range: Panhandle: Throughout, except Holmes, Washington, Gulf, and Jefferson. North Florida: Throughout, except Baker, Union, Bradford, Putnam, St. Johns, Flagler, and Marion. Central Florida: Citrus and Polk.

153. Gulf Coast Lupine

Fabaceae or Leguminosae (bean or pea family)
Lupinus westianus Small var. *westianus*

Description: Stout perennial with shaggy hairs. Stem woody, branches herbaceous. Herb or small shrub to 3.5 ft tall. Flowers pea-shaped, crowded, in a terminal spikelike inflorescence. Flowers purplish blue with a spot of deep purple. Legume with shaggy hairs.

Flowering time: April–May.

Habitat: Sandhills, scrubs, and coastal dunes.

Range: Panhandle: Franklin, Gulf, Bay, Washington, Walton, Okaloosa, Santa Rosa, and Escambia.

Comment: Threatened and endemic to Florida.

154. Fine-leaf Orbexilum

Fabaceae or Leguminosae (bean or pea family)
Orbexilum lupinellus (Michaux) Isely

Description: Perennial herb with stems to 2 ft tall. Plant obscurely pubescent. Leaves alternate, compound, petioles long and filiform. Leaflets 5–7, filiform. Inflorescence (raceme) axillary, long-stalked, loosely flowered. Calyx 5-lobed, dotted with glands. Flowers small, pea-shaped, purple or violet with dark veins. Legume crescent-shaped, wrinkled.

Flowering time: May–July.

Habitat: Sandhills.

Range: Panhandle: Escambia, Okaloosa, Walton, Leon, and Wakulla. North Florida: Taylor, Madison, Hamilton, Suwannee, Levy, Alachua, Marion, Putnam, Clay, and Duval. Central Florida: Hernando, Lake, Orange, Volusia, Hillsborough, and Polk.

Synonyms: *Psoralea lupinellus* Michaux; *Rhytidomene lupinellus* (Michaux) Rydberg

155. Buckroot

Fabaceae or Leguminosae (bean or pea family)
Pediomelum canescens (Michaux) Rydberg

Description: Perennial, woody-branched shrub to 3 ft tall. Stems with grayish hairs. Leaves alternate, leaflets 1 or 3. Calyx 5-lobed, hairy. Flowers pea-shaped, blue or violet. Stamens 10. Legume ovoid.

Flowering time: May–July.

Habitat: Sandhills, pine flatwoods, open woods, and bogs.

Range: Panhandle: Throughout, except Holmes, Jackson, Gulf, Liberty, and Jefferson. North Florida: Throughout, except Union, Gilchrist, and Flagler. Central Florida: Throughout, except Brevard, Indian River, St. Lucie, Okeechobee, Hardee, De Soto, Manatee, and Sarasota.

Synonym: *Psoralea canescens* Michaux

156. Michaux's Rhynchosia

Fabaceae or Leguminosae (bean or pea family)
Rhynchosia michauxii Vail

Description: Herb prostrate, trailing or twining. Stems with gray hairs. Leaves alternate, leaflet 1. Blades ovoid, hairy, longer than wide. Margins entire. Calyx lobes 5, hairy. Flowers pea-shaped, yellow, clustered in the leaf axils. Fruit a legume.

Flowering time: July–August.

Habitat: Sandhills, secondary woods, and ruderal.

Range: Panhandle: Okaloosa and Jackson. North Florida: Taylor, Dixie, Levy, Marion, Alachua, Putnam, and Clay. Central Florida: Throughout, except Osceola, Brevard, Indian River, St. Lucie, Okeechobee, Highlands, Hardee, and De Soto. South Florida: Martin.

Comment: Another prostrate species found in sandhills is *Rhynchosia cinerea*. It has 3 leathery leaflets; the terminal one is the largest. Flowers pea-shaped, yellow, clustered in the leaf axils.

157. Dollar-weed

Fabaceae or Leguminosae (bean or pea family)
Rhynchosia reniformis de Candolle

Description: Perennial herb to 10 inches tall. Stems hairy, angled. Leaves alternate, petioled, 1–3 (usually 1). Blade roundish, veiny. Calyx 5-lobed, hairy. Flowers pea-shaped, yellow, often clustered. Legume hairy, glandular, about [1/2] inch long.

Flowering time: April–September.

Habitat: Sandhills, scrubs, and dry pinelands.

Range: Panhandle: Throughout, except Holmes, Bay, Gulf, and Wakulla. North Florida: Throughout, except Taylor and Flagler. Central Florida: Throughout, except Brevard, Indian River, St. Lucie, Okeechobee, Osceola, De Soto, Manatee, Sarasota, and Pinellas.

Synonyms: *Rhynchosia simplicifolia* (Walter) Wood; *Rhynchosia intermedia* (Torrey & A. Gray) Small

158. Goat's Rue or Devil's Shoestring

Fabaceae or Leguminosae (bean or pea family)
Tephrosia virginiana (Linnaeus) Persoon

Description: Perennial to 2.5 ft tall. Stems woody at the base, herbaceous and grayish green above. Leaves alternate, compound, petioled. Leaflets many. Calyx 5-lobed, hairy. Flowers pea-shaped, white yellow tinged with pink or rose. Legume hairy, linear, flattened.

Flowering time: April–July; October.

Habitat: Sandhills and upland mixed forests.

Range: Panhandle: Escambia, Okaloosa, Walton, Gadsden, Liberty, Leon, and Jefferson. North Florida: Duval, Clay, and Putnam. Central Florida: Citrus, Hernando, Polk, Lake, and Orange.

Comment: Plant is poisonous. *Tephrosia chrysophylla,* common in sandhills, has wedge-shaped leaflets that are shiny above and hairy below. The entire plant appears to be pressed into the sand.

Synonym: *Cracca virginiana* Linnaeus

159. Sandspur or Sandbur

Krameriaceae (rattany family)
Krameria lanceolata Torrey

Description: Perennial with prostrate stems
and erect branches. Leaves alternate, narrow,
silky gray. Corolla irregular. Sepals 4 or 5,
petallike, red purplish within. Petals 5, 2
thick and scalelike. Stamens 4, united to the
petals. Fruit a woody bur.

Flowering time: May–June.

Habitat: Sandhills.

Range: Panhandle: Okaloosa, Walton, and
Liberty. North Florida: Hamilton, Columbia,
Baker, Levy, Alachua, Putnam, and Clay. Cen-
tral Florida: Citrus, Hernando, Pasco,
Hillsborough, Polk, Highlands, Lake, and Or-
ange.

Comment: The only *Krameria* species in the
Southeast. Most species occur in the southwestern U.S deserts. Plant parasitic on persimmon, turkey oak, longleaf pine, and various herbs.

Synonym: *Krameria spathulata* Small ex
Britton

160. Toothed Basil
or Toothed Savory

Lamiaceae or Labiatae (mint family)
Calamintha dentata Chapman

Description: Aromatic shrub to 2 ft tall.
Leaves opposite, sessile. Surfaces covered
with dots and hairs. Margins of lower leaves
have toothed apices. Flowers 2-lipped, pinkish with purplish spots. Lower lip lobed. Fruit
of 4 nutlets.

Flowering time: March–October.

Habitat: Sandhills and dry bluffs.

Range: Panhandle: Walton, Washington, Bay,
Jackson, Gadsden, Liberty, and Wakulla.

Synonym: *Clinopodium dentatum* (Chapman)
Kuntze

161. Pennyroyal

Lamiaceae or Labiatae (mint family)
Piloblephis rigida (W. Bartram ex Bentham)
Rafinesque

Description: Aromatic herb to 1 ft tall. Stems woody, branched, leafy. Leaves numerous, needlelike, entire. Flowers many, in compact, silky terminal heads. Corolla purplish, 2-lipped. Lower lip with dark dots. Stamens 4. Fruit of 4 nutlets.

Flowering time: January–June.

Habitat: Sandhills, pine flatwoods, oak scrub, dry prairies, and ruderal.

Range: North Florida: Suwannee, Alachua, Marion, Putnam, and St. Johns. Central Florida: Throughout. South Florida: Throughout, except the Keys.

Synonym: *Satureja rigida* W. Bartram ex Bentham

162. Horsemint

Lamiaceae or Labiatae (mint family)
Pycnanthemum floridanum E. Grant & Epling

Description: Erect, aromatic perennial. Stems branched, 4-angled, to 4 ft tall. Leaves opposite, petioled. Upper leaves ashy gray. Flowers many, sessile, in dense terminal clusters. Corolla lavender or white, 2-lipped. Calyx 5-lobed. Stamens 4. Fruit of 4 nutlets.

Flowering time: July–August.

Habitat: Sandhills and secondary pinelands.

Range: Panhandle: Jackson and Leon. North Florida: Madison, Levy, Marion, Alachua, Putnam, Clay, Duval, St. Johns, and Flagler. Central Florida: Volusia, Seminole, and Hernando.

163. Skullcap

Lamiaceae or Labiatae (mint family)
Scutellaria multiglandulosa (Kearney) Small
ex R. M. Harper

Description: Perennial herb. Stems angled,
hairy, to 15 inches tall. Leaves opposite, glandular. Margins turned down. Flowers pale
blue or white, 2-lipped. Stamens 4. Fruit of 4
nutlets.

Flowering time: March–April.

Habitat: Sandhills and scrubs.

Range: Panhandle: Leon and Escambia.
North Florida: Throughout, except Union,
Nassau, Duval, St. Johns, and Flagler. Central
Florida: Citrus, Hernando, Sumter, and Lake.

Comment: *Scutellaria arenicola,* also found in
sandhills and dry areas, has pale blue flowers.
Upper stem leaves below the inflorescence
toothed. Leaf margins not turned down.

164. Feather-shank

Liliaceae (lily family)
Schoenocaulon dubium (Michaux) Small

Description: Herb with a leafless flowering
stem to 3 ft tall or more. Basal leaves grasslike, smooth, to 20 inches long. Flowers opposite, in clusters of 2 or 3, short-petioled, arranged in a terminal wandlike spike (raceme).
Flowers small, globular, greenish. Stamens 6,
filaments purplish. Fruit a capsule.

Flowering time: April–August.

Habitat: Sandhills.

Range: North Florida: Levy, Gilchrist,
Alachua, Marion, and Putnam. Central Flor-
ida: Throughout, except Pinellas,
Hillsborough, Manatee, Sarasota, Hardee, De
Soto, Okeechobee, Indian River, and St.
Lucie. South Florida: Glades, Martin, and
Broward.

Comment: Only species in this genus in Florida. This species is placed in Melanthiaceae
or Tofieldiaceae by some authors.

165. Lopsided Indiangrass

Poaceae or Gramineae (grass family)
Sorghastrum secundum (Elliott) Nash

Description: Perennial grass with
stems (culms) to 6 ft tall or more.
Stem base pubescent. Leaves elongated, flat becoming inturned at the
tips. Leaf surfaces rough. Inflorescence terminal, densely flowered on
one side of branches, drooping.
Flower heads (spikelets) paired,
brownish to golden brown. Long,
twisted, hairy awns occur on the
spikelets. Fruit a grain.

Flowering time: August–December.

Habitat: Sandhills, pine flatwoods,
scrubs, and secondary pinelands.

Range: Panhandle: Throughout, ex-
cept Jefferson, Calhoun, and Gulf.
North Florida: Throughout, except
Lafayette, Union, and Bradford. Cen-
tral Florida: Throughout, except
Sumter. South Florida: Throughout,
except Broward, Monroe, and
Hendry.

166. Downy Phlox

Polemoniaceae (phlox family)
Phlox pilosa Linnaeus

Description: Perennial to 2 ft tall.
Stems mostly unbranched. Leaves opposite, sessile, linear to lanceolate,
base hairy. Flowers tubular, stalked.
Calyx 5-lobed. Corolla 5-lobed, tube
usually hairy, pink to dark lavender.
Stamens 5, not extending beyond the
corolla tube opening. Fruit a capsule.

Flowering time: April–July.

Habitat: Sandhills, dry bluffs, open
secondary woods, and thickets.

Range: Panhandle: Throughout, ex-
cept Bay and Wakulla. North Florida:
Throughout, except Levy, Lafayette,
Union, Bradford, Nassau, Clay, and
Flagler. Central Florida: Citrus,
Hernando, Pinellas, Hillsborough,
Lake, Polk, and Seminole.

Comment: A related species found in
sandhills and pine flatwoods is *Phlox
nivalis*. This is a prostrate, evergreen,
semi-woody plant. Corolla 5-lobed,
pink to rose. Leaves many, narrow,
often in clusters.

167. Scrub Buckwheat

Polygonaceae (buckwheat or knotweed family)
Eriogonum longifolium Nuttall var. *gnaphalifolium* Gandoger

Description: Perennial or annual herb with silvery, hairy stems to 3 ft tall or more. Basal leaves long, narrow, silvery below, green above. Stem leaves alternate, narrow. Flowers silvery, silky-pubescent, often nodding. Sepals 6, greenish white, linear. Petals lacking. Fruit an achene.

Flowering time: May–September.

Habitat: Sandhills and scrubs.

Range: North Florida: Marion and Putnam. Central Florida: Sumter, Lake, Orange, Polk, Osceola, and Highlands.

Comment: This threatened variety is endemic to Florida.

Synonym: *Eriogonum floridanum* Small

168. Wild Buckwheat or Dog-tongue

Polygonaceae (buckwheat or knotweed family)
Eriogonum tomentosum Michaux

Description: Herbaceous evergreen perennial to 3 ft tall or more. Stems branched, pubescent. Basal leaves long. Stem leaves sessile, in whorls of 3–5, hairy, whitish or tan below. Flowers clustered in the upper branches. Sepals 6, white or pinkish. Petals lacking. Stamens 9. Fruit an achene.

Flowering time: March–December.

Habitat: Sandhills and dry pinelands.

Range: Panhandle: Throughout, except Jefferson. North Florida: Throughout, except Madison, Hamilton, Taylor, Lafayette, Union, Nassau, St. Johns, and Flagler. Central Florida: Throughout, except Volusia, Seminole, Brevard, Indian River, St. Lucie, Okeechobee, Hardee, De Soto, Sarasota, Manatee, and Pinellas.

169. Leather Flower

Ranunculaceae (buttercup or crowfoot family)
Clematis reticulata Walter

Description: Sprawling or climbing vine, hairy to nearly glabrous. Leaflets 3–9, leathery, coarsely veined. Flowers fragrant, solitary, terminal. Sepals 4, urn-shaped, bluish or reddish. Petals absent. Stamens many, hairy. Achene with persistent hairy style.

Flowering time: May–June.

Habitat: Sandhills and upland mixed forests.

Range: Panhandle: Okaloosa, Walton, Holmes, Washington, Jackson, Gadsden, Leon, Franklin, and Jefferson. North Florida: Throughout, except Union, Bradford, and Flagler. Central Florida: Throughout, except Pinellas, Manatee, Sarasota, Hardee, De Soto, Okeechobee, St. Lucie, Indian River, and Osceola.

Synonym: *Viorna reticulata* (Walter) Small

170. New Jersey Tea or Redroot

Rhamnaceae (buckthorn family)
Ceanothus americanus Linnaeus

Description: Deciduous shrub to 3 ft tall. Leaves alternate, pubescent, strongly 3-veined below. Margins toothed. Flowers many, in terminal or axillary clusters. Sepals 5. Petals 5, white or gray white. Stamens 5. Fruit 3-lobed, somewhat fleshy.

Flowering time: April–July.

Habitat: Sandhills, pine flatwoods, upland mixed forests, and thickets.

Range: Panhandle: Throughout, except Bay, Gulf, Calhoun, and Franklin. North Florida: Madison, Hamilton, Suwannee, Gilchrist, Columbia, Baker, Alachua, Marion, Putnam, and Duval. Central Florida: Citrus, Hernando, Pasco, Hillsborough, Polk, Highlands, Sumter, Lake, and Orange.

Comment: Dried leaves from the plant were used to make tea in colonial times. Root tea was used for dysentery, asthma, sore throat, and respiratory ailments. Alkaloids in the roots may lower blood pressure. Redroot (*Ceanothus microphyllus*) is a showy and characteristic plant of sandhills. Stem is often yellowish. Leaves small, evergreen, entire, oblong or roundish. Flower heads globose, white, flowers small.

171. Sand Blackberry

Rosaceae (rose family)
Rubus cuneifolius Pursh

Description: Perennial to 3 ft tall or more. Stems erect or arching, prickly. Leaves alternate, compound. Leaflets 3 or 5. Green above, white or grayish below. Margins toothed. Sepals 5, green, hairy. Petals 5, white or pink. Stamens numerous. Fruit a cluster of globular drupelets, edible, black when ripe.

Flowering time: February–June.

Habitat: Sandhills, pine flatwoods, upland mixed forests, sandy thickets, and ruderal.

Range: Panhandle: Throughout, except Santa Rosa, Holmes, Washington, and Bay. North Florida: Throughout, except Dixie and Union. Central Florida: Throughout, except Osceola, Polk, Indian River, and Sarasota. South Florida: Palm Beach and Broward. The highbush blackberry (*Rubus argutus*) is common in thickets and woods of north Florida. Leaflets are green or lighter colored on the lower surface.

Synonym: *Rubus inferior* L. H. Bailey

172. Slender Beard Tongue

Scrophulariaceae (figwort family)
Penstemon australis Small

Description: Perennial with hairy, glandular stems to 2 ft tall. Stem leaves opposite, glabrous to pubescent. Lower leaves the largest, spatulate. Flowers at the end of a slender stalk. Corolla 2-lipped, pinkish to violet with reddish purple lines. Lower lip 3-lobed. Fertile stamens 4. Infertile stamen hairy. Fruit a capsule.

Flowering time: March–May.

Habitat: Sandhills, flatwoods, and secondary woods.

Range: Panhandle: Throughout, except Bay and Franklin. North Florida: Madison, Taylor, Lafayette, Suwannee, Columbia, Alachua, Levy, Marion, and Putnam. Central Florida: Citrus, Hernando, Lake, and Polk.

Comment: The hairy, infertile stamen is the "beard tongue."

173. Beard Tongue

Scrophulariaceae (figwort family)
Penstemon multiflorus Chapman ex Bentham

Description: Perennial to 3 ft tall or more.
Stems glabrous, reddish. Branches opposite.
Basal leaves in rosettes. Stem leaves opposite,
sessile, margins entire to glabrous. Flowers
bell-shaped, nodding. Corolla 5-lobed, white,
2-lipped. Lower lip 3-lobed. Fertile stamens 4.
Infertile stamen hairy. Fruit a capsule.

Flowering time: April–September.

Habitat: Sandhills, pine flatwoods, and ruderal.

Range: Panhandle: Throughout, except
Okaloosa, Walton, Holmes, and Jefferson.
North Florida: Throughout, except Flagler.
Central Florida: Throughout, except Semi-
nole, Pinellas, Hardee, De Soto, Okeechobee,
Indian River, and St. Lucie. South Florida:
Martin, Glades, Collier, and Dade.

174. Stylodon

Verbenaceae (vervain or verbena family)
Stylodon carneus (Medikus) Molderke

Description: Perennial to 3 ft tall or more.
Stems pubescent, 4-angled. Leaves opposite,
sessile. Blades elliptic or oblong, hairy, surfaces rough. Margins toothed. Flowers small,
on wandlike spikes. Spikes terminal or axillary. Calyx 5-lobed with glandular hairs. Corolla 5-lobed, pink or pinkish lavender. Stamens 4. Fruit a schizocarp.

Flowering time: April–August; October.

Habitat: Sandhills, pine flatwoods, upland
mixed forests, marshes, and ruderal.

Range: Panhandle: Throughout, except Gulf.
North Florida: Taylor, Dixie, Lafayette, Su-
wannee, Columbia, Hamilton, Alachua,
Marion, Putnam, Clay, Duval, and St. Johns.
Central Florida: Volusia, Seminole, Orange,
Lake, Polk, Hernando, and Pasco. South Flor-
ida: Martin.

Synonyms: *Stylodon caroliniensis* (Walter)
Small; *Verbena carnea* Medikus

Scrubs

175. Sand Pine Scrub, Ocala National Forest, Marion County, Florida. August 20, 1996. Sand pines (*Pinus clausa*) have short, usually paired needles, small cones, and numerous branches often growing low along the trunk. The myrtle oak (*Quercus myrtifolia*) seen at the edge is a common plant of Florida scrubs.

176. Oak Scrub, Allen David Broussard Catfish Creek Preserve, Polk County, Florida. April 13, 1996. This scrub is allied with the Central Highlands of the Peninsula. Note the scrub live oak (*Quercus geminata*) and saw palmetto (*Serenoa repens*).

177. Rosemary Scrub at Lake Cane and Marsha Park, Orange County, Florida. September 5, 1990. Florida rosemary (*Ceratiola ericoides*) is an evergreen that is characteristic of Florida scrubs.

Above: 178. Sand live or scrub live oak (*Quercus geminata*), a characteristic tree of both coastal and inland scrubs as well as other dry habitats. The dark green, glossy, down-turned leaves are characteristic of this species. Photograph was taken at Santa Rosa Island, Santa Rosa County, Florida. July 18, 1996.

Right: 179. Scrub hickory (*Carya floridana*) occurs in inland and coastal scrubs. This endemic species can be identified by its 5 or 7 leaflets with rusty pubescence below, and by the dry habitat where it is found. Note the spikelike inflorescence of male flowers (catkin). Photograph was taken at Allan David Broussard Catfish Creek State Preserve. April 13, 1996.

180. Sand spikemoss (*Selaginella arenicola*), a small, non-flowering plant that is common in Florida's scrubs. British soldier moss (*Cladonia leporina*), a lichen identified by the red tops, can also be seen. Photograph was taken near Montverde, Lake County, Florida. August 24, 1996.

181. Britton's Beargrass or Scrub Beargrass

Agavaceae (century plant family)
Nolina brittoniana Nash

Description: Stem stiff, woody to 6 ft tall or more. Basal leaves long, straplike. Stem leaves alternate, few, glabrous, narrow. Flowers on erect branches. Perianth white, 6-parted. Stamens 6, each attached to a petal. Capsules with 3 thin wings.

Flowering time: March–June.

Habitat: Sand pine scrub and dry pinelands.

Range: North Florida: Marion. Central Florida: Lake, Hernando, Orange, Polk, Osceola, and Highlands.

Comment: Federally endangered and endemic to Florida.

182. Flag Pawpaw

Annonaceae (custard apple family)
Asimina obovata (Willdenow) Nash

Description: Woody, perennial shrub to 9 ft tall or more. Leaves alternate, broadened upward. Lower leaves petioled. Flowers nodding, terminal. Sepals 3. Petals 6, white or greenish white. Inner 3 petals with maroon, corrugated bases. Stamens many. Berry ellipsoid, usually clustered.

Flowering time: March–May.

Habitat: Sand pine scrub, coastal dunes, dry sand ridges, and pine flatwoods.

Range: North Florida: Suwannee, Hamilton, Columbia, Baker, Levy, Marion Alachua, Clay, Putnam, Duval, and Flagler. Central Florida: Throughout, except Pinellas, Sarasota, Hardee, De Soto, and Okeechobee. South Florida: Glades and Dade.

Comment: Flowers emerge after leaves appear. Endemic to Florida.

Synonym: *Pityothamnus obovatus* (Willdenow) Small

183. Four-petal Pawpaw

Annonaceae (custard apple family)
Asimina tetramera Small

Description: Woody, aromatic shrub to 9 ft tall or more. Bark reddish brown becoming gray. Leaves alternate, yellow green to deep green. Blades broadened upward. Flowers in upper leaf axils. Sepals 4. Petals 6. Outer 3 are pink-tipped and dark maroon at the base; inner 3 petals maroon. Stamens many. Berry greenish yellow, oblong, often clustered.

Flowering time: May.

Habitat: Sand pine scrub on old dunes inland from the coast.

Range: South Florida: Martin and Palm Beach.

Comment: Federally endangered and endemic to Florida. Plants may be found with 3 or 5 sepals or 3 petals.

Synonym: *Pityothamnus tetramerus* (Small) Small

184. Curtiss' Milkweed

Asclepiadaceae (milkweed family)
Asclepias curtissii A. Gray

Description: Perennial herb with slender, pubescent stems to 2 ft tall or more. Sap milky. Leaves opposite, petioled, nearly glabrous. Flowers clusters at the upper part of the plant. Corolla lobes 5, greenish white, reflexed. Purplish lines occur on the small flowers. Seedpods solitary, narrow, opening to release the hair-tufted seeds.

Flowering time: July–September.

Habitat: Scrubs and sandhills.

Range: North Florida: Clay and Marion. Central Florida: Hernando, Pasco, Pinellas, Hillsborough, Polk, Highlands, Lake, Orange, Osceola, Volusia, Brevard, Indian River, and St. Lucie. South Florida: Martin, Palm Beach, Broward, Collier, and Lee.

Comment: Endangered and endemic to Florida. Prefers leached white sand scrub. Name honors Allen Hiram Curtiss (1845–1907), a Virginian who came to Florida in 1875. Curtiss settled in Jacksonville and collected nearly 1,500 species in seven years. During 1880–1881 he traveled about the Keys. After 1900, Curtiss botanized in other southern states and the West Indies.

Synonym: *Oxypteryx curtissii* (A. Gray) Small

185. Garberia

Asteraceae or Compositae (daisy or sunflower family)
Garberia heterophylla (W. Bartram) Merrill & F. Harper

Description: Woody, perennial evergreen shrub to 7 ft tall. Leaves alternate, grayish green. Blades paddle-shaped, entire. Flowers tubular, rose purple, in clusters. Floral bracts narrow. Ray florets absent. Fruit an achene.

Flowering time: March; October–December.

Habitat: Sand pine scrub and oak scrub.

Range: North Florida: Marion, Putnam, and Clay. Central Florida: Throughout, except Pasco, Sarasota, De Soto, Okeechobee, and St. Lucie. South Florida: Martin.

Comment: Threatened and endemic to Florida. Name honors Dr. Abram P. Garber (1838–1881) of Pennsylvania, who came to Florida for his tuberculosis in 1876. Garber worked mostly in northeast Florida, but did get to Miami.

Synonym: *Garberia fruticosa* (Nuttall) A. Gray

186. Chapman's Blazing Star

Asteraceae or Compositae (daisy or sunflower family)
Liatris chapmanii Torrey & A. Gray

Description: Perennial herb with leafy, hairy, stiff stems to 2 ft tall or more. Leaves alternate. Lower leaves linear, the largest. Flowers in a dense spike of many pink purplish florets. Ray florets lacking. Seeds purple. Fruit an achene.

Flowering time: August–October.

Habitat: Scrubs, sandhills, and dunes.

Range: Panhandle: Throughout, except Holmes. North Florida: Suwannee, Columbia, and Putnam. Central Florida: Volusia, Seminole, Brevard, Orange, Polk, Hernando, Hillsborough, Pinellas, Manatee, Sarasota, Highlands, Okeechobee, Indian River, and St. Lucie. South Florida: Martin, Palm Beach, Broward, Dade, Collier, and Lee.

Synonym: *Laciniaria chapmanii* (Torrey & A. Gray) Kuntze

187. Florida Gayfeather or Scrub Blazing Star

Asteraceae or Compositae (daisy or sunflower family)
Liatris ohlingerae (S. F. Blake) B. L. Robinson

Description: Perennial herb with pubescent stems to 3 ft tall or more. Leaves alternate, narrow, glabrous. Flowers rose purple in heads terminating the branches. Ray florets lacking. Fruit an achene.

Flowering time: July–October.

Habitat: Sand pine scrub or white sand scrub.

Range: Central Florida: Polk and Highlands.

Comment: Federally endangered and endemic to central Florida.

Synonym: *Ammopursus ohlingerae* (S. F. Blake) Small

188. Feay's Palafox

Asteraceae or Compositae (daisy or sunflower family)
Palafoxia feayi A. Gray

Description: Perennial herb or shrub to 9 ft tall (usually less). Base woody, herbaceous branches above. Lower leaves opposite, upper ones alternate. Leaves evergreen, reduced above, rough to the touch. Heads few, long-stalked, in a terminal spreading inflorescence. Flowers tubular, white or pinkish, anthers dark. Fruit an achene.

Flowering time: March–November.

Habitat: Scrubs, dry pine flatwoods, and ruderal.

Range: North Florida: Marion. Central Florida: Throughout, except Hernando, Pasco, Sumter, Seminole, and Okeechobee. South Florida: Throughout, except Charlotte, Lee, Hendry, Monroe, and the Keys.

Comment: Endemic to Florida.

189. Sand Pine Whitlow-wort

Caryophyllaceae (pink family)
Paronychia chartacea
Fernald subsp. *chartacea*

Description: Stems prostrate, mat-forming, branching to 8 inches long. Leaves opposite, small, margins turned down. Sepals 5, whitish. Petals absent. Fruit a small capsule.

Flowering time: April–July; October.

Habitat: Sand pine scrub.

Range: Central Florida: Lake, Orange, Polk, De Soto, and Highlands.

Comment: Endemic to Florida and federally endangered.

190. Woody Pinweed

Cistaceae (rock-rose family)
Lechea deckertii Small

Description: Perennial herb with basal rosettes. Stems branched at the woody base. Branches leafy, sparingly pubescent. Leaves opposite, numerous. Flowers minute. Sepals 5, outer 2 linear, inner 3 ovate (the largest). Petals 3, reddish. Fruit a small capsule.

Flowering time: August–September.

Habitat: Scrubs and sandhills.

Range: Panhandle: Wakulla and Franklin. North Florida: Levy, Marion, Putnam, and Clay. Central Florida: Lake, Orange, Pinellas, Polk, Osceola, and Highlands. South Florida: Charlotte, Collier, Martin, and south to the Keys.

Synonym: *Lechea myriophylla* Small

191. Matted Sandweed

Clusiaceae or Guttiferae (St. John's-wort family)
Hypericum reductum (Svenson) W. P. Adams

Description: Small, shrublike herb with woody stems to 20 inches tall. Stems red bronze, erect and decumbent. Leaves opposite, sessile, needlelike. Margins glandular. Sepals 5, narrow, leaflike. Petals 5, yellow. Stamens many. Fruit a small capsule.

Flowering time: April–September.

Habitat: Scrubs, sandhills, coastal dunes, pine flatwoods, and pond margins.

Range: Panhandle: Franklin, Washington, Bay, Walton to and including Escambia. North Florida: Marion, Alachua, Suwannee, Columbia, Hamilton, Putnam, Flagler, St. Johns, Clay, and Duval. Central Florida: Throughout, except De Soto. South Florida: Charlotte, Glades, Lee, Hendry, Collier, and Martin.

Comment: Scrub hypericum (*Hypericum cumulicola*), an endemic and federally endangered species, occurs in white sand and sand pine scrub of Highlands and Polk counties. Petals 5, yellow. Stamens grouped in fours.

192. Florida Bonamia or Scrub Morning-glory

Convolvulaceae (morning-glory family)
Bonamia grandiflora (A. Gray) Hallier f.

Description: Perennial, prostrate vine. Leaves alternate, sessile. Blades widest near the base. Flowers solitary, showy, in leaf axils. Sepals pubescent, pointed. The blue to blue purple, funnel-shaped corollas have a white throat. Styles 2. Fruit a capsule.

Flowering time: May–November.

Habitat: Sand pine scrub.

Range: North Florida: Marion. Central Florida: Lake, Orange, Hillsborough, Polk, Manatee, Sarasota, and Highlands.

Comment: Federally endangered and endemic to Florida. *Stylisma patens* is a common morning-glory in scrubs and sandhills. The plant has trailing stems, white flowers that are about 1 inch across, and mostly narrow leaves.

193. Rusty Lyonia or Staggerbush

Ericaceae (heath family)
Lyonia ferruginea (Walter) Nuttall

Description: Evergreen shrub or small tree to 15 ft tall or more. Upper stems and lower leaf surfaces with a rusty pubescence, especially in young leaves. Leaves alternate, leathery. Margins entire, turned down. Flowers in axillary clusters of the upper branches. Corolla urn-shaped, white or pinkish. Stamens 10. Capsules with thickened sutures.

Flowering time: January–April.

Habitat: Sand pine scrub and dry flatwoods.

Range: Panhandle: Throughout, except Escambia, Santa Rosa, Holmes, Washington, and Jackson. North Florida: Throughout, except Madison, Lafayette and Gilchrist. Central Florida: Throughout, except Manatee, Sarasota, Hardee, De Soto, and Indian River. South Florida: Glades and Palm Beach.

Comment: Flowers appear on wood of the previous season. Species is gathered for use in ornamental plant industry. Silk leaves are attached to cut-off trunks to make "artificial potted plants" for offices and similar places.

Synonym: *Xolisma ferruginea* (Walter) A. Heller

194. Pine-sap or False Beechdrops

Ericaceae (heath family)
Monotropa hypopithys Linnaeus

Description: Erect, herbaceous, succulent perennial lacking chlorophyll; probably saprophytic or parasitic. Stems pink, fleshy, hairy, to 4 inches tall. Leaves alternate, yellowish, thin. Sepals 2. Corolla 4- or 5-lobed. Stamens 10. Ovary pink, hairy. Ring of hairs below stigma. Fruit a 5-parted capsule.

Flowering time: November.

Habitat: Oak scrub, sand pine scrub, and mixed temperate forests.

Range: Panhandle: Okaloosa and Walton. North Florida: Marion. Central Florida: Lake.

Comment: Plant turns black when dried.

195. Indian Pipe

Ericaceae (heath family)
Monotropa uniflora Linnaeus

Description: Erect, smooth, succulent perennial to 10 inches tall. Stems solitary or in clusters. Leaves alternate, sessile, white, scalelike. Herb white to rosy pink, nodding. Petals usually 5, inside hairy, outside smooth. Fruit a 5-parted capsule.

Flowering time: November.

Habitat: Scrubs and mixed temperate hardwood forests.

Range: Panhandle: Escambia, Okaloosa, Walton, Washington, Jackson, Liberty, Leon, and Wakulla. North Florida: Suwannee, Columbia, Gilchrist, Marion, Alachua, Putnam, Clay, Duval, and St. Johns. Central Florida: Citrus, Hernando, Hillsborough, Manatee, Sarasota, Highlands, Polk, Osceola, Orange, Lake, Volusia, Brevard, and St. Lucie. South Florida: Martin and Palm Beach.

Comment: Species is a mycoparasite, parasitizing mycorrhizal fungi of roots of plants. Plant turns black when dried. Physicians once used a tea from the plant as a sedative for nervous irritability. American Indians and early settlers treated sore eyes with the plant's juice. Water extracts are antibacterial.

Synonym: *Monotropa brittonii* Small

196. Pigeon-wing

Fabaceae or Leguminosae (bean or pea family)
Clitoria fragrans Small

Description: Perennial herb with 1 or more stems to 1 ft tall or more. Stem slender, slightly zigzag, purplish-tinged. Leaves alternate, compound. Leaflets 3, narrow. Flowers showy, pea-shaped, fragrant. Petals 5. Large petal pale purple with purplish lines. Throat white. Legume to about 3 inches long, spine-tipped.

Flowering time: June–July.

Habitat: White sand scrub.

Range: Central Florida: Lake, Orange, Polk, and Highlands.

Comment: Federally endangered and endemic to central Florida. Small, apetalous flowers that self-fertilize appear later in the season.

Synonym: *Martiusia fragrans* (Small) Small

197. Avon Park Rattlebox

Fabaceae or Leguminosae (bean or pea family)
Crotalaria avonensis DeLaney & Wunderlin

Description: Erect, bluish green perennial with yellowish hairs. Flowering stems mostly 1–3 ft tall. Leaves alternate, unifoliate, petiole reddish brown or green. Flowers pea-shaped, yellow with brownish red lines. Calyx 5-lobed, brownish red, hairy. Legume inflated, tan, grayish or maroon.

Flowering time: mid-March–September.

Habitat: White sand scrub.

Range: Central Florida: Polk and Highlands.

Comment: Federally endangered and endemic to central Florida.

198. Elliott's Milk Pea

Fabaceae or Leguminosae (bean or pea family)
Galactia elliottii Nuttall

Description: Evergreen twining, erect or trailing vine with hairs. Lower part of stem woody. Leaves alternate, compound. Leaflets 7–9. Flowers white, pea-shaped, showy. Legume linear, compressed, hairy.

Flowering time: April–October.

Habitat: Sand pine scrub, dry pine flatwoods, and sandhills.

Range: North Florida: Suwannee, Taylor, Columbia, Baker, Alachua, Nassau, Duval, St. Johns, Flagler, Clay, Putnam, Marion, and Levy. Central Florida: Throughout. South Florida: Throughout, except Charlotte, Hendry, Broward, Dade, and Monroe (except the Keys).

Comment: This is our only white-flowered milk pea. Contrary to the name, these plants do not have a milky sap. Name honors Stephen Elliott (1771–1830).

199. Scrub Lupine or McFarlin's Lupine

Fabaceae or Leguminosae (bean or pea family)
Lupinus westianus Small var. *aridorum* (McFarlin ex Beckner) Ilsey

Description: Hairy herb with erect or reclining stems to 16 inches tall or more. Leaves unifoliate, silky-haired, petioled. Blades elliptic or ovate. Flowers terminal, in elongated spikes. Calyx 5-lobed, hairy. Corolla pea-shaped, purplish with a deep reddish purple center. Legume covered profusely with silky white hairs.

Flowering time: March–April.

Habitat: White sand scrub.

Range: Central Florida: Orange and Polk.

Comment: Endangered and endemic to Florida.

Synonym: *Lupinus aridorum* McFarlin ex Beckner

200. Ashe's Savory or Ashe's Calamintha

Lamiaceae or Labiatae (mint family)
Calamintha ashei (Weatherby) Shinners

Description: Aromatic, woody-branched shrub to 2 ft tall. Leaves opposite, clustered, grayish green. Blades narrow, margins turned down. Flowers pale lavender with dark dots. Calyx 2-lipped. Corolla 2-lipped, tube straight, outside hairy. Stamens 4. Fruit of 4 nutlets.

Flowering time: April–June.

Habitat: Sand pine scrub and sandhills.

Range: North Florida: Marion. Central Florida: Volusia, Lake, Polk, and Highlands. South Florida: Glades.

Comment: Threatened in Florida.

Synonym: *Clinopodium ashei* (Weatherby) Small

201. Red Basil

Lamiaceae or Labiatae (mint family)
Calamintha coccinea (Nuttall ex Hooker)
Bentham

Description: Woody, loosely branched shrub to 3 ft tall or more. Leaves opposite, evergreen, leathery, about ½ inch long. Blades slightly broader upward. Flowers red, solitary or clustered, in the upper leaf axils. Calyx 2-lipped, reddish-tipped. Corolla 2-lipped, upper lobes the shorter. Stamens 4. Fruit of 4 nutlets.

Flowering time: April–November.

Habitat: Sand pine scrub.

Range: Panhandle: Escambia, Santa Rosa, Walton, Holmes, Washington, Bay, Gulf, Franklin, and Wakulla. Central Florida: Citrus, Hernando, Pasco, Hillsborough, Seminole, Orange, Osceola, and Indian River.

Synonym: *Clinopodium coccineum* (Nuttall ex Hooker) Kuntze

202. Conradina

Lamiaceae or Labiatae (mint family)
Conradina canescens A. Gray

Description: Aromatic, woody, bushy-branched shrub to 20 inches tall. Leaves opposite, grayish, clustered. Blades narrow, lower surface with flattened hairs. Flowers bent upward, in leaf axils. Calyx 2-lipped, hairy. Corolla 2-lipped, purplish with dark spots, with pubescent tube. Stamens 4. Fruit of 4 nutlets.

Flowering time: March–November.

Habitat: Sand pine scrub and sandhills.

Range: Panhandle: Escambia, Santa Rosa, Walton, Bay, Gulf, and Franklin. Central Florida: Hernando, Polk, and Highlands.

Synonyms: *Conradina brevifolia* Shinners; *Conradina puberula* Small

203. Long-spurred Balm or Robin's Mint

Lamiaceae or Labiatae (mint family)
Dicerandra cornutissima Huck

Description: Shrubby, aromatic perennial. Stems woody, glabrous, to 20 inches tall. Leaves opposite, narrow. Margins entire. Foliage and flowers glandular. Calyx 2-lipped, tubular. Corolla 2-lipped, rose pink with purplish lines and spots. Tube bent. Stamens 4, extending beyond the corolla. Fruit of 4 nutlets.

Flowering time: September.

Habitat: Sand pine scrub.

Range: North Florida: Marion. Central Florida: Sumter.

Comment: Federally endangered and endemic to Florida. The common name is for Robin Huck, who described the mint.

204. Scrub Balm or Lloyd's Mint

Lamiaceae or Labiatae (mint family)
Dicerandra frutescens Shinners

Description: Aromatic, woody, bushy-branched shrub to 20 inches tall. Leaves opposite, numerous, narrow. Foliage and flowers glandular. Flowers paired, in the leaf axils of upper stems. Calyx 2-lipped, whitish. Corolla 2-lipped, tubular, white with rose purple dots. Stamens 4, anthers lavender, spurred. Fruit of 4 nutlets.

Flowering time: September–October.

Habitat: Oak scrub.

Range: Central Florida: Polk and Highlands.

Comment: Federally endangered and endemic to Florida. The common name is for Lloyd Shinners, who described the mint.
Christman's mint (*Dicerandra christmanii*), located in Highlands County, has cream-colored flowers with purple spots. Anthers are brilliant yellow. Leaves have a eucalyptus-oil scent.

205. Tallowwood or Hog Plum

Olacaceae (ximenia or olax family)
Ximenia americana Linnaeus

Description: Woody shrub or small tree to 20
ft tall or more. Stems bear dark branches and
sharp spines. Foliage yellowish green. Leaves
alternate, leathery, entire. Flowers small, yellow white, hairy within. Sepals and petals 4.
Stamens 8. Fruit yellow, fleshy, edible.

Flowering time: September–October.

Habitat: Scrubs, hammocks, pinelands, and
ruderal.

Range: North Florida: Levy, Marion,
Alachua, Putnam, Clay, Duval, and Flagler.
Central Florida: Throughout, except Volusia,
Sumter, Pasco, De Soto, and Okeechobee.
South Florida: Throughout, except Charlotte
and Glades.

Comment: Name honors a Spanish monk,
Francisco Ximenes, who published on plants
and animals of Mexico in 1615.

206. Pygmy Fringe Tree

Oleaceae (olive family)
Chionanthus pygmaeus Small

Description: Shrub or small tree to 6 ft tall.
Leaves opposite, leathery. Blades elliptic, margins entire. Flowers axillary, drooping. Calyx
4-lobed. Corolla white or greenish white, the
lobes 4, about H inch long. Stamens 2. Drupe
purplish.

Flowering time: February–April; November.

Habitat: Sand pine scrub.

Range: Central Florida: Lake, Osceola, Polk,
Highlands, Hillsborough, and Manatee.

Comment: Federally endangered and endemic
to Florida.

207. Wild Olive or Scrub Olive

Oleaceae (olive family)
Osmanthus megacarpus (Small) Small ex
Little

Description: Woody shrub or small tree 9 ft
tall or more. Leaves opposite, petioled, shiny.
Blades leathery, margins entire. Flowers in axillary clusters, fragrant. Calyx 4-lobed. Corolla white, 4-lobed. Stamens 2. Ripe drupe
dark purple.

Flowering time: January–May.

Habitat: Sand pine scrub.

Range: North Florida: Marion, Alachua, and
Columbia. Central Florida: Throughout, ex-
cept Pasco, Indian River, St. Lucie,
Okeechobee, and Hardee.

Comment: A similar species with smaller fruit
is *Osmanthus americana*, found in moist
woods and hammocks.

Synonym: *Amarolea megacarpa* (Small) Small

208. Wild Coco or Giant Orchid

Orchidaceae (orchid family)
Pteroglossaspis ecristata (Fernald) Rolfe

Description: Terrestrial orchid to 3 ft tall or
more. Flower stalk arises at one side of a leaf
cluster. Leaves basal, grasslike, long. Flowers
clustered at the end of a long stalk. A long,
pointed bract supports each flower. Sepals
and 2 lateral petals greenish. Lip brown. Fruit
a capsule.

Flowering time: April–August.

Habitat: Sand pine scrub and sandhills.

Range: Panhandle: Wakulla. North Florida:
Throughout, except Madison, Hamilton,
Lafayette, Suwannee, Gilchrist, Union,
Nassau, St. Johns, and Flagler. Central Flor-
ida: Throughout, except Sarasota, Pasco,
Sumter, Indian River, St. Lucie, and
Okeechobee. South Florida: Martin, Collier,
and Dade.

Comment: Threatened in Florida.

Synonym: *Eulophia ecristata* (Fernald) Ames

209. Woody Wireweed or Sandlace

Polygonaceae (buckwheat or knotweed family)
Polygonella myriophylla (Small) Horton

Description: Woody shrub with prostrate branches. Plant forms dark green mats. Leaves alternate, many, dark green. Ocreae nonciliate. Flowers white, many, in short clusters. Petals lacking. Fruit an achene.

Flowering time: April–November.

Habitat: Sand pine scrub.

Range: Central Florida: Orange, Osceola, Polk, and Highlands.

Comment: Federally endangered and endemic to Florida. A related, erect species found in scrubs is *Polygonella polygama*. This shrubby plant, 1–2 ft tall, has somewhat paddle-shaped leaves. The small, white or pink flowers are in elongated clusters. Petals absent.

Synonym: *Dentoceras myriophylla* Small

210. Sandhill Wireweed

Polygonaceae (buckwheat or knotweed family)
Polygonella robusta (Small) G. L. Nesom & V. M. Bates

Description: Woody, brittle shrub with smooth stems to 3 ft tall. Leaves alternate, clustered, linear. Ocreae nonciliate. Flowers in many spikelike clusters. Sepals 5, white or pinkish, inner ones fringed. Petals absent. Stamens 8. Fruit an achene.

Flowering time: March–November.

Habitat: Sand pine scrub, sandhills, and riverbanks.

Range: Panhandle: Bay, Franklin, and Wakulla. North Florida: Madison, Taylor, Lafayette, Suwannee, Gilchrist, Alachua, Levy, and Marion. Central Florida: Throughout, except Volusia, Seminole, Pasco, Sarasota, De Soto, and Okeechobee. South Florida: Glades, Martin, and Palm Beach.

Comment: Endemic to Florida. A related species, *Polygonella gracilis*, is a tall, slender jointweed that commonly flowers in the fall. The smooth stem is dull green, bearing alternate leaves. Sepals 5, white, tiny. Petals lacking.

Synonyms: *Polygonella fimbriata* (Elliott) Horton var. *robusta* (Small); *Thysanella robusta* Small

211. Scrub Plum

Rosaceae (rose family)
Prunus geniculata R. M. Harper

Description: Woody, densely branched shrub to 3 H ft tall. Branches spiny, appear zigzag. Leaves alternate, petioled, widest at the middle. Margins minutely toothed. Flowers small, solitary, sessile. Calyx rose red. Petals 5, white. Stamens many. Plums about I inch long.

Flowering time: February–March.

Habitat: Sand pine scrub.

Range: Central Florida: Lake, Orange, Polk, and Highlands.

Comment: Federally endangered and endemic to Florida. Two unrelated species of Florida scrubs with spiny, zigzag stems are scrub ziziphus (*Ziziphus celata*) and tough bumelia (*Sideroxylon tenax,* photo 370). The federally endangered ziziphus is restricted to Highlands and Polk counties, whereas the bumelia occurs throughout the peninsula. Both species may occur in the same site. Both have paddle-shaped, alternate leaves and small, 5-parted white flowers. Lower leaf surface of the bumelia often has brownish pubescence and the fruit is black. The ziziphus lacks the brown hairs and the fruit is green.

Temperate Hardwood Forests

Upland Hardwood Forests

212. Upland Hardwood Forest, Torreya State Park, Liberty County, Florida. March 12, 1997.

Left: 213. American beech (*Fagus grandifolia*) at Falling Waters Recreation Area, Washington County, Florida. July 19, 1996. Note the smooth, gray bark of this characteristic tree of the Upland Hardwood Forest.

Below: 214. A young spruce pine (*Pinus glabra*) at San Felasco Hammock State Preserve, Alachua County, Florida. May 19, 1997.

215. Hairy Angelica

Apiaceae or Umbelliferae (carrot or parsley family)
Angelica venenosa (Greenway) Fernald

Description: Perennial to 3 ft tall. Stems hairy near the top. Leaves divided, upper petioles expanded. Leaflets thickish, widest at the middle. Margins finely toothed. Flowers tiny, in flat-topped clusters (umbels) lacking bracts below. Petals, sepals, and stamens each 5. Fruit a schizocarp.

Flowering time: July.

Habitat: Upland hardwood forests.

Range: Panhandle: Jackson, Gadsden, and Leon.

Comment: Leaves were smoked to discourage the use of tobacco.

Synonym: *Angelica villosa* (Walter) Britton et al.

216. Black Snakeroot

Apiaceae or Umbelliferae (carrot or parsley family)
Sanicula canadensis Linnaeus

Description: Perennial herb with glabrous, branched stems to 2[1/2] ft tall (usually less). Leaves long-petioled, compound. Leaves thin, lower ones segmented. Segments toothed, widest at or above the middle. Upper leaves reduced. Flowers small, in globose heads. Petals 5, white to greenish. Styles no longer than the bristles of the ovary or fruit (magnification needed). Fruit a schizocarp.

Flowering time: February–July.

Habitat: Calcareous upland hardwood forests, river swamps, bluffs, and secondary woods.

Range: Panhandle: Throughout, except Calhoun, Gulf, Bay, Washington, and Holmes. North Florida: Throughout, except Hamilton, Lafayette, Gilchrist, Baker, Union, Bradford, and Putnam. Central Florida: Throughout, except Pinellas, Osceola, Brevard, Indian River, St. Lucie, Okeechobee, Highlands, Hardee, De Soto, Manatee, and Sarasota.

Comment: American Indians used the powdered root for the heart and to stimulate menses. Leaves contain allantoin and were used for bruises and inflammations.

Synonym: *Sanicula floridana* E. P. Bicknell

217. Southern Black Haw, Blue Haw, or Rusty Haw

Caprifoliaceae (honeysuckle family)
Viburnum rufidulum Rafinesque

Description: Deciduous shrub or small tree. Bark blocky. Leaves opposite, unlobed. Blades elliptic, finely toothed, shiny green above, reddish brown below hairs especially on the veins. Flowers white, clustered in the leaf axils. Sepals 5, small. Corolla 5-lobed. Stamens 5. Drupe oblong, blue or purplish.

Flowering time: March–April.

Habitat: Calcareous upland hardwood forests, bluffs, and secondary woods.

Range: Panhandle: Counties west of Jefferson, except Holmes, Bay, Gulf, and Franklin. North Florida: Levy, Marion, Alachua, Putnam, Clay, Suwannee, Columbia, and Hamilton. Central Florida: Citrus and Hernando.

Comment: Some taxonomists place the viburnums in the family Adoxaceae.

218. Florida Flame Azalea or Orange Azalea

Ericaceae (heath family)
Rhododendron austrinum (Small) Rehder

Description: Deciduous shrub to 9 ft tall or more, branches loose. Leaves alternate, pubescent, broadest at or above the middle. Margins minutely toothed. Flowers fragrant, clustered, showy. Blooms before or as leaves appear. Calyx 5-lobed. Corolla tubular, 5-lobed, yellow orange to orange. Stamens and pistil extend beyond the corolla. Fruit a cylindrical capsule.

Flowering time: March–April.

Habitat: Upland hardwood forests, bluffs, slopes of moist ravines, and floodplains. Prefers acid soils.

Range: Panhandle: Throughout, except Jefferson, Wakulla, Gulf, and Bay. North Florida: Baker.

Comment: Endangered in Florida. Often used in yards as an ornamental.

Synonym: *Azalea austrina* Small

219. Redbud or Judas Tree

Fabaceae or Leguminosae (bean or pea family)
Cercis canadensis Linnaeus

Description: Deciduous, wide-spreading tree to 25 ft tall or more. Bark smooth. Leaves alternate, petioled. Blades thin, dull green, broadly heart-shaped. Margins entire. Flowers clustered, usually appear on previous year's wood before or as leaves emerge. Calyx reddish. Corolla pea-shaped, pinkish to purple. Legume flat, thin-walled.

Flowering time: January–March.

Habitat: Upland hardwood forests, bluffs, and secondary woods.

Range: Panhandle: Escambia, Santa Rosa, Washington, Holmes, Jackson, Liberty, Franklin, Gadsden, Leon, and Jefferson. North Florida: Madison, Hamilton, Columbia, Suwannee, Dixie, Gilchrist, Levy, Alachua, Marion, Clay, and Duval. Central Florida: Citrus, Hernando, Sumter, Lake, and Polk.

Comment: Often planted as an ornamental in yards and along streets. Legend says that Judas Iscariot, betrayer of Christ, hanged himself on a relative of the redbud.

220. Red Buckeye

Hippocastanaceae (horsechestnut or buckeye family)
Aesculus pavia Linnaeus

Description: Deciduous shrub or small tree to 30 ft tall (usually less). Bark smooth. Leaves opposite, long-petioled, compound. Leaflets usually 5, emerging from a common point. Blades smooth, tapered at the base, conspicuously veined. Margins finely toothed. Flowers red to yellow red in a terminal, showy inflorescence. Calyx 5-lobed. Petals 4. Fruit a round, brownish capsule.

Flowering time: January–April.

Habitat: Calcareous upland hardwood forests, bluffs, slope forests, margins of swamps, and sandhills.

Range: Panhandle: Escambia, Santa Rosa, Washington, Jackson, Liberty, Franklin, Gadsden, Leon, and Jefferson. North Florida: Madison, Hamilton, Columbia, Suwannee, Dixie, Gilchrist, Levy, Marion, Alachua, Clay, and Duval. Central Florida: Citrus, Hernando, Sumter, Lake, Polk, Orange, and Seminole.

Comment: Some botanists place the horsechestnuts in the Sapindaceae. Plant is poisonous.

221. Michaux's Lily or Carolina Lily

Liliaceae (lily family)
Lilium michauxii Poiret

Description: Glabrous perennial to 4 ft tall. Leaves sessile, whorled, blades 3–7. Blades widest at or above the middle. Margins smooth. Flowers showy, nodding, red orange, tips of tepals usually bent back. Inner bases of tepals yellow, purple-spotted. Anthers long, reddish. Fruit an erect capsule; seeds brownish.

Flowering time: July.

Habitat: Upland hardwood forests.

Range: Panhandle: Jackson, Gadsden, and Liberty.

Comment: This beautiful lily is worthy of cultivation. Blooming of this species is promoted by fire.

222. Wakerobin

Liliaceae (lily family)
Trillium decipiens J. D. Freeman

Description: Erect, perennial herb with a slender stem to 1 ft tall. Leaves 3, sessile, veiny. Blades mottled light to dark green, widest at the middle. Margins entire. Flower single, just above the 3 leaves. Sepals 3, green. Petals 3, usually greenish or greenish yellow with purple. Petals mostly less than 3 times as long as wide. Fruit a berry.

Flowering time: February–March.

Habitat: Calcareous upland hardwood forests, slope forests, and bluffs.

Range: Panhandle: Jackson and Walton.

Comment: Many botanists place this plant in the Trilliaceae. This plant is an exceptionally tall wakerobin.

223. Indian Pink

Loganiaceae (logania family)
Spigelia marilandica (Linnaeus) Linnaeus

Description: Erect perennial to 35 inches tall.
Stems 4-angled, smooth. Leaves opposite,
sessile, glabrous, 4–7 pairs on the stem. Flowers showy. Calyx and corolla 5-lobed. Corolla
erect, tubular, red outside, yellow within.
Fruit a capsule, broader than long.

Flowering time: April–July.

Habitat: Calcareous upland hardwood forests
and bluffs.

Range: Panhandle: Santa Rosa, Jackson,
Gadsden, Liberty, Leon, Jefferson, and
Wakulla.

Comment: American Indians and physicians
used the plant as a tea to expel intestinal
parasites, especially in children. An alkaloid
in the Indian pink may cause convulsions, increased heart rate, and death.

224. Crested Coralroot
or Cock's-comb

Orchidaceae (orchid family)
Hexalectris spicata (Walter) Barnhart

Description: Terrestrial, leafless orchid lacking green color. Stems scaly, to 20 inches tall.
Flowers 2-lipped, in a loose terminal spike.
Corolla yellowish, spurless. Lip purplish,
streaked.

Flowering time: June–August.

Habitat: Upland hardwood forests, upland
mixed forests, and calcareous hammocks.

Range: Panhandle: Jackson, Calhoun, Liberty,
Gadsden, and Leon. North Florida: Suwan-
nee, Columbia, Alachua, Taylor, Levy, Duval,
and St. Johns. Central Florida: Sarasota,
Pasco, Hernando, Citrus, Sumter, Lake,
Brevard, and St. Lucie. South Florida: Lee.

Comment: Endangered in Florida. Species is a
mycoparasite.

225. Shadow Witch

Orchidaceae (orchid family)
Ponthieva racemosa (Walter) C. Mohr

Description: Perennial, terrestrial orchid to 2 ft tall. Flowering stalks hairy, reddish brown to greenish. Leaves mostly basal in a rosette; stem leaves scalelike. Flowers white to green, wide-spreading in a terminal spikelike inflorescence. Petals nearly triangular. Lip uppermost, white with green stripes.

Flowering time: November–December.

Habitat: Upland hardwood forests, river swamps, and springs.

Range: Panhandle: Bay, Jackson, Liberty, Gadsden, Leon, Wakulla, and Jefferson. North Florida: Taylor, Hamilton, Columbia, Duval, Alachua, Putnam, Marion, and Levy. Central Florida: Citrus, Hernando, Sumter, Lake, Volusia, Seminole, Orange, Brevard, Osceola, Polk, Highlands, and De Soto. South Florida: Lee, Collier, Monroe (except the Keys), and Dade.

Comment: Threatened in Florida.

226. Texas Anemone

Ranunculaceae (buttercup or crowfoot family)
Anemone berlandieri Pritzel

Description: Perennial herb. Stems up to 1 ft tall, arising from a brown bulb. Lower leaves arise from the bulb, but disappear later in the season. Leaves long-petioled, terminating in 3 leaflets, each lobed. Upper midstem leaves sessile, each has 3 linear segments. A single flower terminates the flowering stalk. Tepals have 7–14 lobes, white pinkish. Fruiting head conical.

Flowering time: April.

Habitat: Calcareous upland hardwood forests.

Range: Coastal counties: Citrus to Jefferson.

Comment: Rare in Florida.

Synonym: *Anemone caroliniana* sensu Small 1933, non Walter

227. Silverbells, Two-winged Silverbells, or Snowdrop Tree

Styraceae (storax family)
Halesia diptera Ellis

Description: Deciduous large shrub or small tree to 20 ft tall or more. Leaves alternate, petioled. Margins toothed, apices pointed. Flowers showy, bell-shaped, drooping, in clusters of 3–5. Calyx pubescent, 4-lobed. Petals 4, white, separate or nearly so. Stamens 8. Fruits with 2 wings.

Flowering time: March–April.

Habitat: Upland hardwood forests, slope forests, bluffs, and floodplains.

Range: Panhandle: Throughout, except Escambia, Okaloosa, Bay, Gulf, and Wakulla. North Florida: Suwannee.

Comment: Similar to the Carolina silverbell (*Halesia carolina*), which has 4-winged fruits, fused petals, and narrower leaves.

228. Violet

Violaceae (violet family)
Viola sororia Willdenow

Description: Low-growing, pubescent perennial. Leaves long-petioled. Blades green, hairy, margins toothed. Flowers solitary, long-stalked, 2-lipped. Sepals 5. Petals 5, violet purple or lilac. Lower petals spurred at the base. Fruit a capsule.

Flowering time: March.

Habitat: Upland hardwood forests and bluffs.

Range: Panhandle: Throughout, except Holmes, Bay, and Gulf. North Florida: Taylor, Dixie, Levy, Suwannee, Columbia, Alachua, Marion, Putnam, and Duval. Central Florida: Throughout, except Indian River, St. Lucie, and Okeechobee.

Slope Forests

229. Slope Forest, Chattahoochee, Gadsden County, Florida. March 12, 1997. The large tree is an American beech (*Fagus grandifolia*).

Left: 230. Limestone outcropping at Florida Caverns State Park, Jackson County, Florida. March 11, 1997.

Below: 231. Torreya or gopherwood (*Torreya taxifolia*) at Chattahoochee Nature Park, Gadsden County, Florida. March 12, 1997. This species is endemic to Gadsden, Liberty, and Jackson counties, Florida, and adjacent Decatur County, Georgia. Considered endangered everywhere.

232. Green-flowered Yeatesia

Acanthaceae (acanthus family)
Yeatesia viridiflora (Nees von Esenbeck) Small

Description: Erect perennial to 2 ft tall. Leaves opposite, petioled. Blades thin, upper surfaces sparsely pubescent. Margins entire. Flowers white to pinkish, sessile, in compact bracted spikes. Calyx 5-lobed. Corolla 2-lipped, lower lip 3-lobed. Stamens 2. Fruit a glabrous capsule.

Flowering time: May–July.

Habitat: Slope forests, bluffs, and calcareous woods.

Range: Panhandle: Jackson, Gadsden, Liberty, Leon, and Jefferson.

Synonym: *Dicliptera halei* Riddell

233. Atamasco-lily or Rain-lily

Amaryllidaceae (amaryllis family)
Zephyranthes atamasca (Linnaeus) Herbert

Description: Perennial. A single flower usually terminates the flowering stalk that reaches 1 ft tall or more. Leaves grasslike, sharp-edged, arising near the plant's base. Flowers with 6 tepals, white or pinkish. Stamens 6, shorter than the style. Fruit a capsule; seeds black.

Flowering time: January–December.

Habitat: Slope forests, bluffs, moist pine flatwoods, river swamps, meadows, and ruderal.

Range: Panhandle, Throughout, except Santa Rosa, Okaloosa, Washington, Bay, Calhoun, Gulf, and Franklin. North Florida: Throughout. Central Florida: Throughout, except Seminole, Brevard, Indian River, St. Lucie, Okeechobee, Hardee, De Soto, and Sarasota.

Comment: Threatened in Florida. Bulbs were used by Seminole Indians to treat toothache. Horses, cattle, and chickens have been poisoned by eating this lily. The bulb is the most toxic part of the plant.

Synonym: *Atamosco atamasca* (Linnaeus) Greene

234. Leafcup

Asteraceae or Compositae (daisy or sunflower family)
Polymnia laevigata Beadle

Description: Widely branched perennial. Stems glabrous, to 3 ft tall or more. Leaves opposite, glabrous. Blades broad, oval or deltoid, pinnately lobed. Flower heads small, not showy. Ray florets whitish. Disk florets yellowish. Fruit an achene.

Flowering time: May–July; October–November.

Habitat: Slope forests and calcareous hammocks.

Range: Panhandle: Jackson.

235. Bear's-foot or Yellow Leafcup

Asteraceae or Compositae (daisy or sunflower family)
Polymnia uvedalia (Linnaeus) Linnaeus

Description: Perennial herb with hollow stems 3 ft tall or more. Stems ribbed, mostly glabrous, mottled with purple. Leaves opposite, broad, palmately veined, 3- to 5-lobed. Petioles leafy. Leaf surfaces rough. Flowers axillary and terminal. Heads showy, yellow. Rays toothed at the apices. Fruit an achene.

Flowering time: June–December.

Habitat: Slope forests, bluffs, coastal hammocks, and upland mixed forests.

Range: Panhandle: Throughout, except Holmes, Washington, Calhoun, Gulf, and Jefferson. North Florida: Columbia, Levy, Alachua, Marion, Putnam, and Duval. Central Florida: Citrus, Sumter, Lake, Volusia, Orange, Brevard, Osceola, Polk, and Pinellas.

Synonym: *Smallanthus uvedalia* (Linnaeus) MacKenzie

236. Green Dragon

Araceae (arum family)
Arisaema dracontium (Linnaeus) Schott

Description: Erect perennial to 3 ft tall. Leaves solitary, petioled, compound. Leaflets unequal, 5–17. Flowers numerous, whitish, on a long-tapered spadix. Spadix surrounded by a leafy bract, the spathe. Spathe thin, long-tapered. Female flowers at the base of the spadix; male flowers midway. Sepals and petals lacking. Ripe fruit a cluster of red berries.

Flowering time: March–May.

Habitat: Slope forests, floodplains, bluffs, and moist hammocks.

Range: Panhandle: Walton, Washington, Jackson, Calhoun, Liberty, Franklin, Gadsden, and Leon. North Florida: Madison, Suwannee, Columbia, Taylor, Dixie, Levy, Marion, Alachua, Clay, Duval, St. Johns, and Flagler. Central Florida: Citrus, Hernando, Pasco, Sumter, Lake, Orange, Seminole, Volusia, and Brevard.

Comment: Calcium oxalate crystals in the plant cause intense burning if eaten fresh. Dried and aged roots can be eaten and were used by American Indians for female disorders.

Synonym: *Muricauda dracontium* (Linnaeus) Small

237. Jack-in-the-pulpit or Indian Turnip

Araceae (arum family)
Arisaema triphyllum (Linnaeus) Torrey

Description: Erect perennial to 2 ft tall. Stem leaf single, compound, leaflets 3. Flowers small in a spadix ("Jack" or "Parson"): female flowers at the base, male flowers near the middle. Spadix surrounded by a large, bract, the spathe ("pulpit"). Spathe hooded, may be striped with purple. Sepals and petals lacking. Ripe fruit a cluster of red berries.

Flowering time: January–June.

Habitat: Slope forests, floodplains, bluffs, and hammocks.

Range: Panhandle: Escambia, Oklaloosa, Holmes, Jackson, Calhoun, Liberty, Gadsden, and Leon. North Florida: Levy, Marion, Alachua, Suwannee, Columbia, Putnam, and Duval. Central Florida: Throughout, except Pasco, Sarasota, Indian River, and St. Lucie. South Florida: Collier.

Comment: Plant contains calcium oxalate crystals that irritate mucous membranes. American Indians boiled and ate the rootlike bulb or made flour from it, hence the name "Indian turnip." Other uses include treatments for sores, boils, and respiratory ailments.

Synonym: *Arisaema acuminatum* Small

238. Mayapple or Mandrake

Berberidaceae (barberry family)
Podophyllum peltatum Linnaeus

Description: Perennial, glabrous herb. Stems to 20 inches tall. Leaves 1 or 2, blades flat, deeply lobed. Leaf petiole attached to center of blade. Flowers solitary, white, nodding. Fragrant. Sepals 6, dropping early. Petals 6–9. Fruit round, edible, yellowish to purplish when ripe.

Flowering time: March–April.

Habitat: Slope forests, bluffs, and calcareous hammocks.

Range: Panhandle: Jackson.

Comment: Florida is the southernmost point in the range of the species. Plant contains antitumor alkaloids. Etoposide, a semisynthetic derivative of the mayapple, is FDA-approved for testicular and small-cell lung cancers. Indians used root extracts to treat worms, syphilis, tumors, and skin disorders. Seeds, roots, and leaves are poisonous eaten in large amounts.

239. Sweet-scrub, Spicebush, or Carolina Allspice

Calycanthaceae (strawberry-shrub or sweet-shrub family)
Calycanthus floridus Linnaeus

Description: Shrub to 3 ft tall or more. Aromatic. Leaves opposite, widest near the middle, veiny above, apices narrower. Margins entire. Flowers showy, reddish to purplish brown. Sepals and petals similar, strap-shaped. Stamens many. Fruit fleshy, many-seeded.

Flowering time: April–May.

Habitat: Slope forests, bluffs, and floodplain forests.

Range: Panhandle: Escambia, Santa Rosa, Okaloosa, Walton, Jackson, Liberty, Wakulla, Gadsden, and Leon. North Florida: Suwannee.

Comment: Crushed leaves have a sweet odor. Plant can be used as a landscape plant for both sunny and shady areas. Seeds are poisonous. Endangered in Florida.

240. Wakerobin

Liliaceae (lily family)
Trillium maculatum Rafinesque

Description: Glabrous perennial to 1 ft tall. Leaves 3, sessile, broad. Blades mottled light and dark green with veins in a network. Flower single, just above the leaves. Sepals 3, green. Petals 3, maroon, narrowly spatulate, 4 or more times as long as wide. Stamens 6. Fruit a berry.

Flowering time: February–March.

Habitat: Slope forests and calcareous hammocks.

Range: Panhandle: Jackson and Jefferson. North Florida: Suwannee, Columbia, and Alachua.

Comment: Many botanists place this plant in the Trilliaceae.

Synonym: *Trillium ludovicianum* sensu Small 1933, non Harbison

241. Little Sweet Betsy

Liliaceae (lily family)
Trillium underwoodii Small

Description: Perennial to 8 inches tall. Leaves 3, sessile. Blades narrow, mottled light and dark green with veins in a network. Flower single, just above the leaves. Sepals 3, green. Petals 3, usually purple, elliptic, usually 4 times as long as wide. Stamens 6. Fruit a berry.

Flowering time: January–March.

Habitat: Slope forests and bluffs.

Range: Panhandle: Bay, Jackson, Liberty, Gadsden, Leon, and Jefferson. North Florida: Madison, Hamilton, Columbia, and Suwannee.

Comment: Many botanists place this plant in the Trilliaceae. Earliest of our 4 species of trilliums to flower. Usually shorter in height than *Trillium dicipiens*.

242. Moonseed

Menispermaceae (moonseed family)
Menispermum canadense Linnaeus

Description: Slender, twining vine. Leaves alternate, simple. Blades 3–7 lobed, glabrous above, margins smooth. Petiole long, attached just inside the lower surface of the leaf. Inflorescence terminal or axillary. Male and female flowers separate. Flowers clustered, small, greenish white or yellowish. Stamens 12–24. Fruit bluish black, fleshy, in hanging clusters.

Flowering time: June–August.

Habitat: Slope forests.

Range: Panhandle: Jackson, Gadsden, Liberty and Jefferson. North Florida: Alachua.

Comment: Physicians historically used a tincture from the roots as a laxative, and for arthritis, syphilis, and indigestion. Children eating the seeds and fruits have died. Some people evidently confuse this plant with wild grapes.

243. Bloodroot

Papaveraceae (poppy family)
Sanguinaria canadensis Linnaeus

Description: Erect succulent, glabrous perennial to 1 ft tall. Roots thick with a red orange bitter juice. Leaves solitary, long-petioled. Blades thin, pale green, veiny. Margins deeply lobed or toothed. Flowers white, solitary at the end of a leafless stalk. Sepals 2, dropping after flowering. Petals usually 8, unequal. Stamens 24.

Flowering time: February–March.

Habitat: Slope forests, bluffs, and calcareous hammocks.

Range: Panhandle: Walton, Washington, Liberty, Jackson, Gadsden, Leon, and Jefferson. North Florida: Hamilton.

Comment: American Indians used the red juice as an insect repellent, for warts, for war paint, and for dyeing clothes and baskets yellow-orange. A mordant was not needed. The alkaloid sanguinarine has shown to have antiseptic, anesthetic, and anticancer properties. Sanguinarine is commercially used as a plaque-inhibiting agent in toothpaste, mouthwashes, and rinses. The toxic plant should not be ingested.

244. Wild Columbine or Red Columbine

Ranunculaceae (buttercup or crowfoot family)
Aquilegia canadensis Linnaeus

Description: Perennial herb with leafy stems. Leaves alternate, compound, divided in threes. Leaflets with short, fingerlike lobes. Flowers tubular, nodding, red and yellow, terminal. Sepals 5, yellow. Petals 5, each with a backward-directed, hollow spur. Fruit a ring-like capsule. Seeds black, shiny.

Flowering time: March–April.

Habitat: Slope forests and calcareous woods.

Range: Panhandle: Jackson, Washington, and Liberty.

Comment: Endangered in Florida. Can be grown as an ornamental at least as far south as Orlando. This plant is potentially poisonous, but the American Indians chewed the root for diarrhea and stomach ailments. The tiny black seeds were rubbed into the hair to control lice.

Synonym: *Aquilegia australis* Small

245. Virgin's Bower or Woodbine

Ranunculaceae (buttercup or crowfoot family)
Clematis catesbyana Pursh

Description: Climbing herbaceous vine. Stems angled, pubescent. Leaves opposite, compound, petioled. Leaflets usually 3, thin, toothed. Young leaflets grayish white below. Flowers clustered in leaf axils. Sepals 4, petal-like, white. Petals lacking. Stamens numerous. Seed with a feathery attachment.

Flowering time: July–August.

Habitat: Slope forests, calcareous woods, and river swamps.

Range: Panhandle: Jackson, Washington, Gadsden, Liberty, Franklin, and Leon. North Florida: Dixie, Levy, Marion, Alachua, and Duval. Central Florida: Citrus, Hernando, Pasco, Lake, and Volusia.

Synonym: *Clematis micrantha* Small

246. False Rue-anemone

Ranunculaceae (buttercup or crowfoot
family)
Enemion biternatum Rafinesque

Description: Delicate perennial to 8 inches
tall. Leaves petioled, basal. Leaves compound, leaflets usually 3 with fingerlike lobes.
Leaves below flowers usually simple, sessile.
Flowers stalked, terminal or in leaf axils. Sepals 5, white, petallike. Petals lacking. Stamens many. Pistils 3–6.

Flowering time: January–April.

Habitat: Slope forests, bluffs, and calcareous
woods.

Range: Panhandle: Jackson and Washington.

Synonym: *Isopyrum biternatum* (Rafinesque)
Torrey & A. Gray

247. Lousewort or Wood Betony

Scrophulariaceae (figwort family)
Pedicularis canadensis Linnaeus

Description: Stout, hairy perennial to 16
inches tall. May form colonies. Lower leaves
in a basal cluster. Stem leaves alternate.
Blades deeply lobed, ferny. Flowers sessile, in
dense terminal heads. Sepals united, unequal.
Corolla 2-lipped, yellow to reddish brown.
Upper lip hoodlike, lower lip 3-lobed. Stamens 4. Fruit an asymmetrical, flattened capsule.

Flowering time: March–April.

Habitat: Slope forests, bluffs, and upland
mixed forests.

Range: Panhandle: Walton, Jackson,
Gadsden, and Leon. North Florida: Columbia
and Clay.

Comment: Lice were thought to live in the
hairs of this plant, hence the name "lousewort." Parasitic on trees and herbaceous
plants. A variety of uses by American Indians
include treating diarrhea, heart conditions,
coughs, and anemia. The roots were thought
to be an aphrodisiac.

248. Few-flowered Croomia

Stemonaceae or Croomiaceae (croomia family)
Croomia pauciflora (Nuttall) Torrey

Description: Glabrous herb with simple stems to 16 inches tall. Forms colonies. Leaves alternate, thin, petioled, near the top of the stem. Blades with prominent paralleled veins. Flowers small, nodding, arising from leaf axils. Sepals 4-lobed, green. Petals 4-lobed, greenish with purple. Stamens 4; filaments maroon, anthers yellow. Fruit a capsule.

Flowering time: March–April.

Habitat: Slope forests, bluffs, and ravines.

Range: Panhandle: Gadsden and Liberty.

Comment: Often found with the torreya (*Torreya taxifolia*). Endangered in Florida. Plant honors Hardy Bryan Croom (1797–1837), a native of Lenoir County, North Carolina. He moved to Quincy, Florida, in 1830. Croom discovered the torreya. He and his family were killed in a steamship wreck in 1837.

249. Wood-nettle

Urticaceae (nettle family)
Laportea canadensis (Linnaeus) Weddell

Description: Perennial herb with stinging hairs. Stems to 3 ft tall or more. Leaves alternate, petioled. Blades widest at the middle, margins toothed. Male and female flowers separate. Sepals 5-lobed, greenish or greenish white. Petals lacking. Fruit an achene, crescent-shaped, often with persistent recurved stigma.

Flowering time: April.

Habitat: Slope forests, floodplains, and calcareous hammocks.

Range: Panhandle: Jackson and Liberty.

Synonym: *Urticastrum divaricatum* (Linnaeus) Kuntze

Bluffs

Above: 250. Apalachicola River Bluffs, Liberty County, Florida. December 16, 1991. Photo by David Leonard.

Left: 251. A Bluff site with moist, calcareous soils, Liberty County, Florida. March 23, 1994. Note the ferns and blue phlox (*Phlox divaricata*).

252. Small's Sunflower

Asteraceae or Compositae (daisy or sunflower family)
Helianthus resinosus Small

Description: Perennial to 6 ft tall or more. Stems rough. Leaves opposite below, alternate above. In smaller plants all leaves are opposite. Blades ovate, rough, paler below, gland-dotted. Heads few, yellow, on long stalks, rough. Bracts and florets glandular. Fruit an achene.

Flowering time: July–September.

Habitat: Bluffs and dry woods.

Range: Panhandle: Leon, Liberty, Gadsden, Jackson, and Walton.

253. Wild Comfrey

Boraginaceae (borage family)
Cynoglossum virginianum Linnaeus

Description: Hairy perennial to 2½ ft tall. Leaves mostly basal, large, long-petioled. Upper stem leaves alternate, reduced, sessile. Inflorescence long-stalked. Calyx 5-lobed. Corolla 5-lobed, white or bluish. Stamens 5. Fruits with stiff spines.

Flowering time: March–April.

Habitat: Bluffs and floodplain forests.

Range: Panhandle: Liberty.

Comment: Rare in Florida. Cherokee Indians made a root tea from the plant for bad memory, itching of the genitals, cancer, and milky urine. Leaves were smoked like tobacco.

254. Forget-me-not

Boraginaceae (borage family)
Myosotis macrosperma Engelmann

Description: Annual or biennial to 2.5 ft tall.
Stems branched. Leaves alternate, simple,
widest at the middle. Flowers in a terminal,
spirallike coil. Calyx 5-lobed, lobes unequal.
Corolla 5-lobed, white. Fruit a schizocarp.

Flowering time: March–April.

Habitat: Bluffs and floodplains.

Range: Panhandle: Jackson, Liberty,
Gadsden, Leon, and Jefferson.

255. Allegheny Spurge

Buxaceae (box family)
Pachysandra procumbens Michaux

Description: Perennial with reclining stems to
8 inches long. Lower leaves scalelike; upper
leaves large, clustered toward the upper end.
Leaves alternate, evergreen, pubescent. Blades
mottled dark and light green. Margins
toothed. Inflorescence a spike. Male flowers
in the upper part of the spike, female flowers
below. Tepals 4, greenish purplish. Stamens 4,
filaments white.

Flowering time: February–April.

Habitat: Calcareous bluffs and upland calcareous woods.

Range: Panhandle: Jackson.

Comment: Endangered in Florida.

256. Wood Spurge

Euphorbiaceae (spurge family)
Euphorbia commutata Engelmann ex A. Gray

Description: Herb to 16 inches tall. Upper stem leaves alternate, sessile. Lower stem leaves petioled, elliptic, entire. Bracteal leaves broader than long, entire. Cyathia yellow. Involucre glands with hornlike processes. Petaloid appendages absent. Fruit a 3-parted, smooth capsule.

Flowering time: February–April.

Habitat: Bluffs, calcareous hammocks, and streambanks.

Range: Panhandle: Jackson and Gadsden. North Florida: Levy and Marion.

Synonym: *Galarhoeus austrinus* (Small) Small

257. Twining Tragia

Euphorbiaceae (spurge family)
Tragia cordata Michaux

Description: Herb with twining stems. Leaves long-petioled. Blades coarsely toothed, widest at the base. Male and female flowers separate, in elongated stalks. Female sepals wider than those of the male. Petals lacking. Stamens 3–5. Fruit a 3-parted, pubescent capsule.

Flowering time: September.

Habitat: Calcareous bluffs.

Range: Gadsden, Jackson, and Liberty.

Synonym: *Tragia macrocarpa* Willdenow

258. Lance-leaved Wakerobin

Liliaceae (lily family)
Trillium lancifolium Rafinesque

Description: Erect, slender perennial to 10 inches tall. Leaves 3, sessile, narrowly lanceolate, mottled. Veins form a network. Single flower just above the leaves. Sepals 3, green. Petals 3, narrow, greenish or with some purple. Stamens 6, strongly incurved. Fruit a berry.

Flowering time: February–March.

Habitat: Bluffs.

Range: Panhandle: Jackson and Gadsden.

Comment: Endangered in Florida. Many botanists place this plant in the Trilliaceae.

259. Yellow Passion-flower

Passifloraceae (passion-flower family)
Passiflora lutea Linnaeus

Description: Perennial vine, climbing or trailing with tendrils. Leaves alternate, petioled. Blades shallowly and bluntly 3-lobed, 3-veined, margins entire. Flowers 1–3 in leaf axils. Flowers yellow green, about 1 inch across. Calyx 5-lobed, green. Petals 5, yellowish green. Corona of many green segments. Stamens 5, united as a tube. Mature berry black.

Flowering time: June–July.

Habitat: Bluffs and ruderal.

Range: Panhandle: Throughout, except Okaloosa, Holmes, Bay, Gulf, Wakulla, and Jefferson. North Florida: Dixie, Lafayette, Suwannee, Columbia, Alachua, Marion, Clay, and Duval. Central Florida: Hernando, Lake, and Brevard.

Comment: A related species, the maypop (*Passiflora incarnata*), occurs in ruderal sites. It differs from the above by having large, lavender flowers.

260. Spikegrass

Poaceae or Gramineae (grass family)
Chasmanthium latifolium (Michaux) Yates

Description: Perennial, colonial grass. Leaves toothed. Stems (culms) glabrous, leafy, to 3 ft tall or more. Blades lanceolate, mostly glabrous. Inflorescence loose. Flower heads flattened, long-stalked, drooping, green. Fruit a grain or caryopsis.

Flowering time: June–October.

Habitat: Bluffs and floodplains.

Range: Panhandle: Escambia, Santa Rosa, Washington, Jackson, Calhoun, Liberty, Franklin, Gadsden, and Leon. North Florida: Suwannee, Clay, Duval, and St. Johns.

Synonym: *Uniola latifolia* Michaux

261. Twoflower Medic

Poaceae or Gramineae (grass family)
Melica mutica Walter

Description: Perennial grass to 32 inches tall. Stem mostly glabrous, bearing leaves to 6 inches long. Blades sparsely haired. Inflorescence to 8 inches long. Fertile florets 2. Fruit a grain or caryopsis.

Flowering time: March–April.

Habitat: Bluffs, slope forests, and floodplains.

Range: Panhandle: Escambia, Jackson, Liberty, Gadsden, Bay, Gulf, Franklin, Leon, and Jefferson. North Florida: Levy, Taylor, Marion, Putnam, St. Johns, and Flagler. Central Florida: Hernando and Citrus.

262. Blue Phlox

Polemoniaceae (phlox family)
Phlox divaricata Linnaeus

Description: Perennial herb to 1 ft tall. Leaves opposite, usually 4 pairs on the flowering stem. Blades elliptic to lanceolate, pubescent. Inflorescence open, loose. Calyx 5-lobed, lobes linear. Corolla 5-lobed, pale lavender. Stamens 5, below opening of corolla tube. Fruit a 3-valved capsule.

Flowering time: February–April.

Habitat: Bluffs, slope forests, and calcareous hammocks.

Range: Panhandle: Jackson, Gadsden, and Liberty.

263. Rue Anemone or Windflower

Ranunculaceae (buttercup or crowfoot family)
Thalictrum thalictroides (Linnaeus) A. J. Eames & B. Boivin

Description: Glabrous, perennial herb to 10 inches tall. Leaves basal or stemmed. Leaf petioles wiry. Leaves at the top of the stem with several stalked leaflets. Leaflet tips rounded. Flower stalks threadlike. Tepals 5–10, delicate, white or pinkish. Stamens many. Fruit an achene lacking the stalk of the pistil.

Flowering time: March–April.

Habitat: Limestone bluffs.

Range: Panhandle: Gadsden and Leon.

Comment: Endangered in Florida. A root tea was used by American Indians for diarrhea and vomiting.

Synonym: *Anemonella thalictroides* (Linnaeus) Spach

264. Parsley Haw

Rosaceae (rose family)
Crataegus marshallii Eggleston

Description: Small, deciduous tree to 25 ft tall. Branches scaly, thorny. Leaves alternate, petioled, frilly, triangular, 5–7 lobed. Blades hairy, margins gland-toothed. Flowers in showy clusters. Sepals 5, gland-toothed. Petals 5, white to pinkish. Stamens many, anthers red. Fruit red, globose, fleshy, with a hard core.

Flowering time: March–April.

Habitat: Bluffs and floodplains.

Range: Panhandle: Throughout, except Franklin, Gulf, and Bay. North Florida: Hamilton, Columbia, Suwannee, Gilchrist, Alachua, Levy, and Marion. Central Florida: Hernando, Pasco, Hillsborough, and Polk.

Comment: A related species of north-central Florida and the Panhandle is *Crataegus uniflora.* Its leaves are narrow at the base. Leaf margins at the base lack teeth. Flowers white, solitary.

265. Oakleaf Hydrangea or Graybeard

Saxifragaceae (saxifrage family)
Hydrangea quercifolia W. Bartram

Description: Deciduous, multibranched shrub to 6 ft tall or more. Bark peeling, orangish. Leaves opposite, yellowish green, usually 3–7 lobed. Margins toothed. Flowers in a large, terminal cluster. Tepals 4, creamy white.

Flowering time: May–July.

Habitat: Calcareous bluffs, ravines, and streambanks.

Range: Panhandle: Escambia, Santa Rosa, Walton, Washington, Bay, Jackson, Calhoun, Liberty, Gadsden, Leon, and Wakulla. North Florida: Marion.

Comment: Used in landscaping. Horses and cows have been poisoned by eating this plant.

Floodplain Forests

266. Floodplain Forest with standing water, Torreya State Park, Liberty County, Florida. Photo by Richard Owen. March 30, 1991. The water will dissipate during drier conditions.

267. Possum Haw or Winterberry

Aquifoliaceae (holly family)
Ilex decidua Walter

Description: Deciduous large shrub or small tree to 25 ft tall or more. Leaves alternate, dark green, paler below, and may be crowded at the ends of branches. Blades widest at or above the middle. Teeth of leaf margins gland-tipped (magnification needed). Male and female flowers on separate plants, in sessile clusters in leaf axils. Fruit a reddish drupe.

Flowering time: March–April.

Habitat: Floodplains, upland hardwood forests, and thickets.

Range: Panhandle: Throughout, except Gulf and Bay. North Florida: Madison, Hamilton, Columbia, Union, Alachua, Gilchrist, Suwannee, Taylor, Dixie, and Levy. Central Florida: Citrus, Pasco, Pinellas, Hillsborough, Manatee, Hardee, and De Soto.

Comment: Threatened in Florida.

Synonym: *Ilex curtissii* (Fernald) Small

268. Cut-leaved Coneflower or Golden Glow

Asteraceae or Compositae (daisy or sunflower family)
Rudbeckia laciniata Linnaeus

Description: Perennial herb to 8 ft tall, forms colonies. Stems glabrous or hairy, ribbed or angled. Leaves alternate, sessile or nearly so. Lower leaf blades toothed, deeply dissected. Flowers showy, long-stalked. Ray florets yellow, disk florets greenish yellow. Achenes brown, 4-angled.

Flowering time: July–September.

Habitat: Floodplains and ruderal.

Range: Panhandle: Walton, Liberty, Gadsden, and Leon. North Florida: Levy.

Synonym: *Rudbeckia heterophylla* Torrey & A. Gray

269. Spring-cress

Brassicaceae or Cruciferae (mustard family)
Cardamine bulbosa (Schreber ex
Muhlenberg) Britton et al.

Description: Perennial to 24 inches tall.
Leaves alternate. Basal leaves petioled,
rounded. Margins entire to shallowly
toothed. Stem leaves sessile, reduced above.
Flowers white, inflorescence terminal. Sepals
4, greenish with white margins. Petals 4. Fruit
a narrow, stalked capsule (silique).

Flowering time: February–April.

Habitat: Floodplains and bluffs.

Range: Panhandle: Jackson, Gadsden, and
Liberty. North Florida: Levy, Alachua,
Putnam, and Duval. Central Florida: Semi-
nole, Orange, Hillsborough, Polk, and
Osceola.

Comment: Young plants can be used in salads
and impart a taste of horseradish.

270. Pink-root

Loganiaceae (logania family)
Spigelia loganioides (Torrey & A. Gray ex
Endlicher & Fenzl) Alph. de Candolle

Description: Delicate herb to 12 inches tall.
Leaves opposite, sessile. Margins entire.
Flowers terminal or in the leaf axils. Calyx
tubular, lobes 5, linear. Corolla funnel-
shaped, lobes 5, white. Fruit a capsule.

Flowering time: April–July.

Habitat: Floodplains, wet woods, and
swamps.

Range: Levy, Marion, and Sumter.

Comment: Endemic to and endangered in
Florida.

Synonym: *Coelostylis loganioides* Torrey and
A. Gray ex Endlicher & Fenzl

271. Halberd-leaved Marshmallow

Malvaceae (mallow family)
Hibiscus laevis Allioni

Description: Glabrous, shrubby perennial to 8 ft tall. Leaves alternate, petioled. Blades lobed at the base, margins toothed. Flower solitary, showy, supported by a whorl of bracts. Sepals 5, triangular. Petals 5, pink with purplish throat. Fruit a glabrous capsule; seeds pubescent.

Flowering time: June–October.

Habitat: Floodplains and riverbanks.

Range: Panhandle: Escambia, Washington, Jackson, Gadsden, Calhoun, Gulf, Liberty, Franklin, and Leon.

Synonym: *Hibiscus militaris* Cavanilles

272. Leatherleaf or Leather Flower

Ranunculaceae (buttercup or crowfoot family)
Clematis crispa Linnaeus

Description: Climbing or trailing perennial vine, nearly glabrous. Stems angled. Leaves opposite, compound, leaflets 3–11. Flowers solitary, nodding, rose to violet. Sepals 4, petallike, tips usually reflexed. Margins of sepals thin, crisp, wavy. Petals lacking. Stamens numerous. Fruit an achene with persisting plumose style.

Flowering time: March–October.

Habitat: Floodplains.

Range: Panhandle: Throughout. North Florida: Throughout, except Madison, Union, Clay, Flagler, and Marion. Central Florida: Hernando, Hillsborough, Manatee, Polk, De Soto, Osceola, Orange, Seminole, Volusia, and Brevard.

Synonyms: *Viorna crispa* (Linnaeus) Small; *Viorna obliqua* Small

273. Swamp Buttercup

Ranunculaceae (buttercup or crowfoot family)
Ranunculus hispidus var. *nitidus* (Chapman) T. Duncan

Description: Sprawling or erect pubescent perennial. Leaves alternate, simple or 3-lobed. Flowering stems slender, pubescent. Flowers yellow, appearing waxy. Petals 5. Sepals usually 5, reflexed. Fruit an achene with a corky rim.

Flowering time: February–May.

Habitat: Floodplains and wet hammocks.

Range: Panhandle: Jackson, Gadsden, Leon, and Wakulla. North Florida: Levy, Duval, and Nassau. Central Florida: Citrus and Lake.

Synonym: *Ranunculus carolinianus* de Candolle

274. Virginia Willow

Saxifragaceae (saxifrage family)
Itea virginica Linnaeus

Description: Slender-branched, deciduous shrub to 6 ft tall (usually less). Leaves alternate, petioled. Blades elliptic or widest at the middle. Tips pointed. Margins finely toothed. Flowers white, small, numerous, in a terminal, drooping inflorescence. Calyx deeply 5-lobed. Petals 5-lobed, longer than the stamens. Stamens 5. Fruit a hairy, 2-parted capsule.

Flowering time: February–June.

Habitat: Floodplains, swamps, along streambanks, and calcareous hammocks.

Range: Panhandle: Throughout. North Florida: Throughout, except Union. Central Florida: Throughout, except Sarasota, De Soto, and Indian River. South Florida: Glades, Martin, Palm Beach, Broward, Collier, and Lee.

Comment: Can be used as an ornamental plant in both dry and wet sites. Some authors divide Saxifragaceae into several families and place this plant in Iteaceae.

275. Mazus

Scrophulariaceae (figwort family)
Mazus pumilis (Burnman f.) Steenis

Description: Mostly prostrate, pubescent herb from a basal rosette. Leaves opposite, spatulate. Blades distally toothed, purplish below. Petioles winged. Flowers solitary, blue or pale lavender, terminal. Calyx 5-lobed, lobes narrow. Corolla 2-lipped, ½ inch long or less. Lower lip 3-lobed, lobes broad. Stamens 4. Fruit a capsule.

Flowering time: January; March–October.

Habitat: Floodplains and ruderal.

Range: Panhandle: Escambia, Walton, Jackson, Calhoun, Liberty, and Leon. North Florida: Alachua and Duval. Central Florida: Orange, Seminole, Pinellas, and Hillsborough. South Florida: Broward and Dade.

Comment: Introduced from Southeast Asia.

Synonym: *Mazus japonicus* (Thunberg) Kuntze

276. Monkeyflower

Scrophulariaceae (figwort family)
Mimulus alatus Aiton

Description: Perennial herb to 3 ft tall or more. Stems winged, 4-angled, glabrous. Leaves opposite, petioled. Blades tapered at the base, margins toothed. Flowers solitary, from leaf axils. Calyx 5-lobed. Corolla 2-lipped, bluish to white with yellow spot. Lower lip 3-lobed, the largest. Fruit a capsule.

Flowering time: July–October.

Habitat: Floodplains, marshes, and calcareous seepages.

Range: Panhandle: Gadsden, Liberty, Jackson, Holmes, Walton, and Santa Rosa.

Upland Mixed Forests

277. Upland Mixed Hardwood Forest at San Felasco Hammock State Preserve, Alachua County, Florida. May 19, 1997.

278. Virginia live oak (*Quercus virginiana*) near Montverde, Lake County, Florida. August 1996.

279. Rattlesnake Master

Agavaceae (century plant family)
Polianthes virginica (Linnaeus) Shinners

Description: Succulent perennial with slender stalks to 6 ft tall. Leaves basal, narrow, 1 ft long, may be blotched with purple. Flowers tubular, greenish yellow, in a spikelike inflorescence. Stamens 6. Fruit a 3-parted capsule, with black seeds.

Flowering time: July.

Habitat: Upland mixed forests, dry rocky woods, sandhills, and secondary woods.

Range: Panhandle: Escambia, Okaloosa, Washington, Jackson, Gadsden, Liberty, Leon, and Wakulla. North Florida: Dixie, Columbia, Alachua, and Putnam. Central Florida: Hernando.

Synonyms: *Agave virginica* Linnaeus; *Manfreda virginica* (Linnaeus) Rose

280. Winged Sumac or Shining Sumac

Anacardiaceae (cashew or sumac family)
Rhus copallinum Linnaeus

Description: Deciduous shrub or small tree to 22 ft tall or more. Bark thin, reddish brown. Stems densely pubescent. Leaves alternate, compound, nearly glabrous above and pubescent below. Leaflets 9–23, sessile, entire or nearly so, leaf stem (rachis) winged. Flower clusters terminal. Sepals small, greenish. Petals greenish white. Fruit a dull red, pubescent drupe.

Flowering time: June–September.

Habitat: Upland mixed forests, sandhills, pine flatwoods, floodplains, and ruderal.

Range: Throughout Florida, except Broward, De Soto, Gulf, and Bay.

Comment: Timucuan and Creek Indians used the roots of this plant to treat dysentery. The ripe berries were a source for a dark tan dye, and children chewed the berries to treat bedwetting and mouth sores.

281. Eastern Poison Oak

Anacardiaceae (cashew or sumac family)
Toxicodendron pubescens Miller

Description: Shrub to 3 ft tall or more (usually less). Stems mostly erect. Leaves alternate, compound. Leaflets 3, thickish, tips blunt. Margins entire, toothed, or lobed. Flowers in loosely branched clusters in the leaf axils. Sepals 5. Petals 5, greenish yellow. Drupe greenish to pale yellowish white, pubescent.

Flowering time: March–May.

Habitat: Upland mixed forests, sandhills, secondary woods, and scrubs.

Range: Panhandle: Jefferson, Leon, Wakulla, Gadsden, Liberty, Jackson, Walton, Okaloosa, and Escambia. North Florida: Madison, Lafayette, Suwannee, Levy, Dixie, Gilchrist, Alachua, Marion, Putnam, and Clay.

Comment: Sap of plant can cause allergic skin reactions.

Synonyms: *Rhus toxicodendron* Linnaeus; *Toxicodendron toxicarium* Gillis

282. American Holly

Aquifoliaceae (holly family)
Ilex opaca Aiton var. *opaca*

Description: Small, evergreen shrub or tree to 50 ft tall. Bark grayish, often warty. Leaves alternate, dark green, leathery. Margins usually with sharp spines. Male and female flowers on separate plants. Petals 4, white. Stamens 4. Drupe globose, red or orange.

Flowering time: March–April.

Habitat: Upland mixed forests and bluffs.

Range: Panhandle: Throughout, except Holmes. North Florida: Throughout. Central Florida: Citrus, Hernando, Pinellas, Hillsborough, Polk, Manatee, De Soto, Highlands, Sumter, Lake, Orange, Seminole, and Volusia. South Florida: Charlotte.

Comment: Fruits provide food for birds in the winter. Branches and leaves are used for holiday decorations. Species commercially exploited in Florida. An endemic variety (var. *cumicola*) of this holly, commonly known as the scrub holly, occurs in drier habitats.

283. Devil's-walkingstick

Araliaceae (ginseng family)
Aralia spinosa Linnaeus

Description: Deciduous shrub or small tree to 30 ft tall. Trunk and branches with many stout spines. Leaves alternate, large, spiny, twice-compound. Leaflets ovate or elliptic, opposite, toothed. Flowers small, greenish white, in a large, branched terminal cluster to 2 ft long. Petals 5. Stamens 5. Berry purplish black.

Flowering time: June–July.

Habitat: Upland mixed forests and secondary woods.

Range: Panhandle: Leon, Gadsden, Liberty, Franklin, Jackson, Washington, Walton, and Okaloosa. North Florida: Suwannee, Columbia, Dixie, Levy, Gilchrist, Alachua, Marion, Putnam, Clay, Duval, Nassau, St. Johns, and Flagler. Central Florida: Citrus, Hernando, Pasco, Hillsborough, Sumter, Lake, Polk, Osceola, Volusia, Brevard, and St. Lucie.

Comment: Some authors merge this family with Apiaceae (Umbelliferae). A tincture of berries was used for toothaches and rheumatic pain by early settlers. Consuming large amounts of the berries can be fatal.

284. Green-crowned Milkweed or Antelope-horn

Asclepiadaceae (milkweed family)
Asclepias viridis Walter

Description: Perennial herb with a stout stem to 2 ft tall. Stem usually unbranched, glabrous. Sap milky. Leaves alternate, short-petioled, ovate to oblong. Flowers many, stalked, greenish purple. Sepals 5-lobed. Corolla 5-lobed, lobes erect. Seedpods broad and ovoid, opening to release hair-tufted seeds.

Flowering time: April.

Habitat: Upland mixed forests and calcareous ravines.

Range: Panhandle: Gadsden and Liberty. North Florida: Levy. Central Florida: Citrus, Hernando, Sumter, and Lake. South Florida: Dade and the Keys.

Comment: Some authors include milkweeds in Apocynaceae.

Synonym: *Asclepiodora viridis* (Walter) A. Gray

285. Cross-vine

Bignoniaceae (bignonia or trumpet vine family)
Bignonia capreolata Linnaeus

Description: Woody, evergreen, perennial vine. Usually climbs high using tendrils. Leaves opposite, evergreen, 2 leaflets. Flowers in leaf axils, tubular, fragrant. Calyx 5-lobed, lobes small. Corolla 5-lobed, reddish orange and yellow. Fruit a beanlike capsule.

Flowering time: March–April.

Habitat: Upland mixed forests, thickets, floodplains, and hammocks.

Range: Panhandle: Throughout, except Holmes, Washington, and Gulf. North Florida: Hamilton, Suwannee, Lafayette, Dixie, Levy, Marion, Alachua, Union, Bradford, Clay, Duval, and Nassau. Central Florida: Citrus, Hernando, Polk, Seminole, and Volusia.

Comment: Stem in cross section shows a cross, hence the common name. The trumpet vine or trumpet-creeper (*Campsis radicans*) is found in habitats similar to the above. It can be distinguished by the tubular red to orange flowers and compound leaves with 7 or more serrated leaflets.

Synonym: *Anisostichus capreolata* (Linnaeus) Bureau

286. Possum Haw

Caprifoliaceae (honeysuckle family)
Viburnum nudum Linnaeus

Description: Deciduous, perennial shrub or small tree to 18 ft tall or more. Leaves opposite, petioled, simple. Lower leaf surface gland-dotted. Margins usually entire. Flowers in a stalked, flat-topped cluster. Petals 5-lobed, creamy white. Sepals 5. Fruit reddish turning dark blue.

Flowering time: March–April.

Habitat: Wet, upland mixed forests, pine flatwoods, swamps, and bogs.

Range: Panhandle: Throughout, except Gulf. North Florida: Throughout, except Levy north to Jefferson, Madison, Gilchrist, Suwannee, and Flagler. Central Florida: Lake, Orange, Hernando, Pasco, Hillsborough, Manatee, Polk, Hardee, De Soto, Highlands, and Volusia.

Comment: Much evidence indicates that viburnums should be in the family Adoxaceae. A bark tea made by American Indians was used as a diuretic and a tonic, and for diabetes.

Synonym: *Viburnum cassinoides* Linnaeus

287. Strawberry Bush or Hearts-a-bustin'

Celastraceae (bitter sweet or staff-tree family)
Euonymus americanus Linnaeus

Description: Straggling, perennial shrub to 6 ft tall. Leaves opposite, thin, widest at or below the middle. Blades sessile or nearly so, minutely toothed. Flowers in leaf axils. Sepals 5. Petals 5, green or green purplish. Stamens 5. Warty, red capsule, splitting when mature to reveal orange red seeds.

Flowering time: January–April.

Habitat: Mesic upland mixed forests, hammocks, floodplains, and bluffs.

Range: Panhandle: Jefferson west to (including) Escambia, except Walton, Washington, Bay, and Gulf. North Florida: Hamilton, Suwannee, Columbia, Duval, Alachua, Clay, Putnam, Flagler, Marion, and Levy. Central Florida: Citrus, Hernando, Pasco, Hillsborough, Polk, Hardee, Highlands, Sumter, Lake, Orange, Seminole, and Volusia.

Comment: Physicians once used the bark as a tonic, expectorant, and laxative. Eating the fruits may cause unconsciousness and vomiting.

288. Dog-hobble

Ericaceae (heath family)
Leucothoe axillaris (Lamarck) D. Don

Description: Woody, evergreen, perennial to 3 ft tall or more. Leaves alternate, leathery, paler below, widest at or near the middle. Petiole short. Margins entire or finely toothed. Flower clusters compact, in leaf axils. Flowers urn-shaped, 5-lobed, white. Fruit a brown, round capsule.

Flowering time: February–April.

Habitat: Low, mixed forests and streambanks.

Range: Panhandle: Counties west of Jefferson, except Franklin, Gulf, and Washington. North Florida: Hamilton, Gilchrist, Baker, Nassau, Duval, Clay, Marion, and Putnam.

Comment: Plant is used as an ornamental. A closely related species is the fetterbush (*Leucothoe racemosa*). It has flowers in elongated, axillary racemes and the membranous leaves are deciduous.

289. Climbing Heather or Climbing Pieris

Ericaceae (heath family)
Pieris phyllyreifolia (Hooker) de Candolle

Description: Nonparasitic, evergreen shrub with weak or vinelike branches. Plant ascends trees by creeping under the bark. Leaves alternate, leathery. Margins weakly toothed near apex, entire. Flower clusters elongated in leaf axils. Calyx 5-lobed, lobes triangular. Flowers urn-shaped with 5 white corolla lobes. Fruit a capsule.

Flowering time: October–March.

Habitat: Upland mixed forests, sandhills, cypress ponds, moist pinelands, and white cedar swamps.

Range: Panhandle: Throughout, except Escambia, Holmes, Gadsden, and Jefferson. North Florida: Taylor, Madison, Hamilton, Columbia, Lafayette, Alachua, and Marion. Central Florida: Lake.

Comment: Plant climbs on pond cypress, titi trees, Atlantic white cedars, cabbage palms, and pines.

Synonym: *Ampelothamnus phyllyreifolius* (Hooker) Small

290. Sweet Pinxter Azalea or Wild Azalea

Ericaceae (heath family)
Rhododendron canescens (Michaux) Sweet

Description: Thinly branched, deciduous shrub to 15 ft tall. Leaves alternate, hairy, narrow at the base. Margins with short hairs. Flowers sticky, in terminal clusters. Corolla trumpet-shaped, pale pink to dark rose. Stamens and pistil extend beyond the corolla. Fruit a cylindrical to elongate-ovate brown capsule.

Flowering time: February–May.

Habitat: Upland mixed forests, pine flatwoods, bay swamps, sinks, and bluffs.

Range: Panhandle: Throughout, except Holmes and Gulf. North Florida: Hamilton, Columbia, Baker, Union, Bradford, Alachua, Marion, Clay, Duval, St. Johns, and Nassau.

Comment: Flowers open before or with appearance of first leaves. Commercially exploited and protected in Florida. The swamp honeysuckle (*Rhododendron viscosum*) of wetter areas has showy white flowers that are glandular. This species blooms mainly in the summer.

Synonym: *Azalea canescens* Michaux

291. Sparkleberry, Farkleberry, or Tree Huckleberry

Ericaceae (heath family)
Vaccinium arboreum Marshall

Description: Woody, deciduous shrub or small tree to 27 ft tall (usually less). Bark reddish brown. Leaves alternate, widest at or above the middle. Margins usually entire. Flowers urn-shaped, small, white, long-stalked. Berry shiny, black.

Flowering time: April and May.

Habitat: Upland mixed forest, sandhills, coastal hammocks, dunes, and oak scrub.

Range: Panhandle: Throughout. North Florida: Throughout. Central Florida: Throughout except Seminole, Orange, Osceola, Highlands, Indian River, and St. Lucie. South Florida: Charlotte and Lee.

Comment: Fruit can be used for making jam and jelly. Birds and other wildlife eat the fruit. Leaves, roots, and bark were used to treat diarrhea and dysentery.

Synonym: *Batodendron arboreum* (Marshall) Nuttall

292. Coralbean or Cherokee Bean

Fabaceae or Leguminosae (bean or pea family)
Erythrina herbacea Linnaeus

Description: Deciduous, perennial shrub to 3 ft tall or more. Branches viny, prickly. Leaves alternate. Leaflets 3, triangular. Flowers showy in terminal, spikelike racemes. Corolla tubular, 5-lobed, red. Upper lobe narrow, folded. Legume elongated. Seeds hard, red, poisonous.

Flowering time: December–June.

Habitat: Upland mixed forests, thickets, tropical hammocks, coastal dunes, sandhills, and pine flatwoods.

Range: Panhandle: Santa Rosa, Okaloosa, Walton, Jackson, Gulf, Franklin, Liberty, Gadsden, and Leon. North Florida: Throughout, except Madison, Lafayette, Baker, and Bradford. Central Florida: Throughout, except De Soto and Okeechobee. South Florida: Throughout, except Glades, Hendry, and Broward.

Comment: Used in ornamental plantings. Plants in South Florida may become small trees. Flowers appear before or during leaf development.

Synonym: *Erythrina arborea* (Chapman) Small

293. Milk-pea

Fabaceae or Leguminosae (bean or pea family)
Galactia regularis (Linnaeus) Britton et al.

Description: Perennial with prostrate, trailing stems. Not a vigorous twining vine. Leaves alternate. Leaflets 3, leathery, glabrous above. Calyx hairy, 4-lobed. Flowers pea-shaped, reddish purple. Legume hairy.

Flowering time: April–October.

Habitat: Upland mixed forests, sandhills, scrubs, and pine flatwoods.

Range: Panhandle: Throughout, except Holmes, Jackson, and Jefferson. North Florida: Throughout. Central Florida: Throughout. South Florida: Throughout, except Charlotte and Monroe (except Keys).

Synonyms: *Galactia fasciculata* Vail; *Galactia prostrata* Small

294. Yellow Star Anise

Illiciaceae (anise or star anise family)
Illicium parviflorum Michaux ex Ventenat

Description: Aromatic, evergreen shrub to 7 ft tall. Leaves alternate, petioled, margins entire. Flowers nodding. Tepals 6–12, yellow. Stamens 6 or 7. Fruit star-shaped.

Flowering time: March–July.

Habitat: Wet upland mixed forests and swamps.

Range: North Florida: Marion. Central Florida: Polk, Lake, Orange, Seminole, and Volusia.

Comment: The aromatic odor from crushing the leaves comes from ethereal oil in the plant's tissues. Endangered in Florida. A related shrub found in the Panhandle is the star anise (*Illicium floridanum*), which has many reddish purple tepals. This shrub is also aromatic and has a similar star-shaped fruit.

295. Rough Skullcap

Lamiaceae or Labiatae (mint family)
Scutellaria integrifolia Linnaeus

Description: Perennial herb to 2 ft tall. Stems 4-angled. Leaves opposite, toothed. Leaves below flowers narrow and entire. Flowers 2-lipped, blue to violet. Upper corolla lobes fused appearing hooked. Lower lip of 3 fused lobes, center white. Calyx 5-lobed, hairy. Stamens 4. Fruit of 4 nutlets.

Flowering time: March–November.

Habitat: Upland mixed forests, pine flatwoods, sandhills, marshes, cypress swamps, and ruderal.

Range: Panhandle: Throughout, except Bay. North Florida: Throughout, except Suwannee, Lafayette, Gilchrist, and Levy. Central Florida: Throughout, except Citrus, Lake, Pinellas, De Soto, and Indian River. South Florida: Lee and Charlotte.

Synonym: *Scutellaria integrifolia* Linnaeus var. *hispida* Bentham

296. Yellow Jessamine or Carolina Jasmine

Loganiaceae (logania family)
Gelsemium sempervirens (Linnaeus) Aiton f.

Description: Evergreen, perennial, climbing or trailing vine. Stems woody, slender, reddish brown. Leaves opposite, petioled. Blades smooth, elliptic to lanceolate. Flowers tubular, yellow, fragrant. Calyx and corolla 5-lobed. Capsule compressed; seeds many.

Flowering time: December–April.

Habitat: Upland mixed forests, pine flatwoods, bluffs, floodplains, and ruderal.

Range: Panhandle: Throughout, except Washington and Gulf. North Florida: Throughout. Central Florida: Throughout, except Indian River, St. Lucie, and Okeechobee. South Florida: Martin.

Comment: Plant poisonous. Used as an ornamental and does well on trellises. A similar species in the Panhandle is *Gelsemium rankinii*, which lacks the fragrant odor and occurs in wetter areas.

297. Poppy Mallow or Wine-cup

Malvaceae (mallow family)
Callirhoe papaver (Cavanilles) A. Gray

Description: Perennial herb to 1 ft tall. Branches ascending or spreading. Basal leaves in a rosette. Stem leaves alternate with long petioles. Leaf segments 3–5. Flowers solitary on long stalks. Calyx 5-lobed; 3 bracts below. Petals 5, rosy red to deep crimson with a white blotch at the base. Stamens many, filaments united forming a tube.

Flowering time: March–May.

Habitat: Upland mixed forests and roadsides.

Range: Panhandle: Jackson, Gadsden, and Leon. North Florida: Alachua.

Comment: This is a plant of the western U.S. grasslands. Endangered in Florida. The Teton Dakota Indians burned the dried roots of the poppy, believing that it relieved pain. They also inhaled the smoke for colds.

298. Wax Myrtle or Southern Bayberry

Myricaceae (wax myrtle or bayberry family)
Myrica cerifera Linnaeus

Description: Aromatic, evergreen shrub or small tree to 25 ft tall or more. Often with several trunks. Leaves alternate, pubescent below, glandular, narrow at the base. Margins entire or toothed near apices. Male and female flowers on separate plants. Flowers small, in the leaf axils. Fruits globose, grayish, coated with wax.

Flowering time: February–June.

Habitat: Upland mixed forests, pine flatwoods, coastal scrub, coastal strand, Indian middens, and swamps.

Range: Panhandle: Throughout, except Santa Rosa, Holmes, and Gulf. North Florida: Throughout. Central Florida: Throughout. South Florida: Throughout.

Comment: A widespread plant in Florida. The berries were used in colonial times and are still used today for making fragrant candles. Some people are allergic to the wax. Stomachaches, colds, and ulcers were treated with teas made from the plant. The plant is often used in landscaping.

299. Spring Coralroot

Orchidaceae (orchid family)
Corallorhiza wisteriana Conrad

Description: Perennial, mycoparasitic, terrestrial orchid. Stem glabrous, reddish purple, to 14 inches tall. Stem leaves absent or reduced to scales. Flowers green to yellow, tinged with purplish brown. Sepals 3, nearly equal and spreading. Petals 3, lip unlobed, white with purplish spots. Fruit a capsule.

Flowering time: January–February.

Habitat: Upland mixed forests.

Range: Panhandle: Wakulla, Leon, Liberty, Gadsden, Jackson, and Santa Rosa. North Florida: Madison, Hamilton, Suwannee, Columbia, Taylor, Dixie, Levy, Gilchrist, Alachua, Clay, Nassau, and Duval. Central Florida: Citrus, Hernando, Pinellas, Hillsborough, Sarasota, Polk, Highlands, Lake, Orange, Seminole, Volusia, and Brevard.

Comment: Threatened in Florida.

300. Green-fly Orchid

Orchidaceae (orchid family)
Epidendrum conopseum R. Brown

Description: Perennial, epiphytic orchid to 1 ft tall. Leaves 3 or less, glabrous. Margins entire. Flowering stalk slender. Flowers fragrant, green with purple markings. Lip roundish, green, 3-lobed with 2 appendages at the base. Fruit a capsule.

Flowering time: November–June.

Habitat: Moist, upland mixed forests, sinks, and swamps.

Range: Panhandle: Jefferson to (including) Escambia, except Okaloosa, Holmes, Bay, Washington, and Gulf. North Florida: Throughout, except Madison, Lafayette, Union, and Bradford. Central Florida: Throughout, except Pinellas, Sarasota, De Soto, Okeechobee, Indian River, and St. Lucie.

Comment: Threatened in Florida.

Synonym: *Amphiglottis conopsea* (R. Brown) Small

301. Squawroot or Cancerroot

Orobanchaceae (broomrape family)
Conopholis americana (Linnaeus f.) Wallroth

Description: Perennial, terrestrial parasite that resembles a fir cone. Stalks usually many, clustered, brownish yellow. Leaves scalelike, overlapping. Flowers borne from a fleshy stem. Flowers small, 2-lipped, yellowish with purple. Fruit a capsule.

Flowering time: February–April.

Habitat: Parasitic on oak and other tree roots in upland mixed forests and oak woods.

Range: Panhandle: Okaloosa, Jackson, Gadsden, Leon, Jefferson, Wakulla, and Liberty. North Florida: Columbia, Suwannee, Levy, Gilchrist, Alachua, Putnam, Clay, Flagler, St. Johns, Duval, and Nassau. Central Florida: Citrus, Sumter, Lake, and Polk.

302. Jumpseed

Polygonaceae (buckwheat or knotweed family)
Polygonum virginianum Linnaeus

Description: Perennial herb to 32 inches tall. Leaves alternate, tapered at the base. Flowers in a long, terminal, wandlike inflorescence. Calyx 4-lobed, greenish, purplish, to white. Petals absent. Stamens 5. Fruit an achene.

Flowering time: July–November.

Habitat: Upland mixed forests, thickets, bluffs, and floodplains.

Range: Panhandle: Jackson, Gadsden, and Liberty. North Florida: Suwannee, Duval, Alachua, and Marion. Central Florida: Hernando. South Florida: Palm Beach.

Comment: Some botanists place this species and most of the *Polygonum* in the genus *Persicaria.*

Synonym: *Tovara virginiana* (Linnaeus) Rafinesque

303. Laurel Cherry, Cherry Laurel, or Carolina Cherry

Rosaceae (rose family)
Prunus caroliniana (Miller) Aiton

Description: Aromatic, evergreen shrub or tree to 35 ft tall or more. Leaves alternate, leathery, petioled. Upper leaf surfaces dark green, paler below. Margins entire to sparingly toothed. Flowers in elongated, axillary clusters (racemes). Sepals 5. Petals 5, white. Stamens 10. Drupe black, oval.

Flowering time: February–March.

Habitat: Upland mixed forests, bluffs, calcareous hammocks, scrubs, and Indian middens.

Range: Panhandle: Throughout, except Washington, Bay, Gulf, and Calhoun. North Florida: Columbia, Baker, Levy, Marion, Alachua, Clay, Duval, Nassau, St. Johns, and Flagler. Central Florida: Throughout, except Manatee, Hardee, Highlands, Okeechobee, and Osceola.

Comment: Used in ornamental plantings. Hydrocyanic acid poisoning can occur from eating the leaves and other parts. The almond-flavored hydrocyanic acid can be detected by breaking a leaf or twig. A relative of the above species is the hog plum (*Prunus umbellata*), which occurs in upland mixed forests, hammocks, and dry pine woods of central and north Florida and the Panhandle. This deciduous tree has toothed leaf margins, glands at the base of the leaf, and black drupes.

Synonym: *Laurocerasus caroliniana* (Miller) M. Roemer

304. Black Cherry or Wild Cherry

Rosaceae (rose family)
Prunus serotina Ehrhart

Description: Deciduous tree to 50 ft tall or more. Leaves alternate, finely toothed margins. Flowers in elongated, drooping clusters (racemes). Sepals 5. Petals 5, white. Mature drupe dark purple.

Flowering time: February–March.

Habitat: Upland mixed forests, hammocks, river swamps, and ruderal.

Range: Panhandle: Escambia, Walton, Washington, Jackson, Franklin, Wakulla, Liberty, Leon, and Jefferson. North Florida: Taylor, Dixie, Hamilton, Suwannee, Lafayette, Gilchrist, Baker, Bradford, Alachua, Putnam, Clay, Nassau, Duval, and St. Johns. Central Florida: Throughout, except Indian River, St. Lucie, Okeechobee, Osceola, Highlands, and Hardee.

Comment: The reddish brown wood is prized for furniture. An astringent from the bark was used to make cough medicine. Other than the pulp of the fruit, all parts of the plant are poisonous and contain hydrocyanic acid. The almond-flavored hydrocyanic acid can be detected by breaking a leaf or twig.

305. Partridge Berry or Twinberry

Rubiaceae (madder family)
Mitchella repens Linnaeus

Description: Prostrate, evergreen perennial. Leaves opposite, ovoid, glabrous. Flowers paired with the ovaries partly fused. Calyx lobes minute. Corolla 4-lobed, hairy within, white tinged with pink. Stamens 4. Berry red.

Flowering time: December–July.

Habitat: Moist upland mixed forests.

Range: Panhandle: Throughout, except Washington and Calhoun. North Florida: Throughout, except Dixie, Madison, Taylor, Lafayette, Baker, Union, and Bradford. Central Florida: Throughout, except Brevard, Indian River, Okeechobee, Osceola, Hardee, and Sarasota. South Florida: Martin.

Comment: The name honors Dr. John Mitchell (1690–1768), a physician born in England, who spent nearly 50 years in Virginia. Teas from the fruit or leaves were used for childbirth pain, irregular menses, hemorrhoids, and dysentery. External uses were for swellings, hives, and sore nipples.

306. Wafer Ash or Common Hoptree

Rutaceae (rue or citrus family)
Ptelea trifoliata Linnaeus

Description: Deciduous shrub or small tree to 25 ft tall. Bark usually brownish, strongly scented. Leaves alternate, long-petioled, aromatic. Leaflets usually 3, widest at or near the middle, with pellucid dots. Margins toothed or smooth. Flowers greenish white, in terminal clusters. Sepals 5, hairy. Petals 5. Stamens 5. Fruit flattened, winged.

Flowering time: March–May.

Habitat: Upland mixed forests and bluffs.

Range: Panhandle: Okaloosa, Walton, Jackson, Liberty, Gadsden, Leon, and Jefferson. North Florida: Madison, Columbia, Suwannee, Gilchrist, Dixie, Levy, Alachua, Marion, Putnam, Clay, Duval, and Flagler. Central Florida: Volusia, Orange, Lake, Sumter, Polk, and Pasco.

Comment: Fruit has been used as a substitute for hops in making beer. Crushed leaves have a musky odor.

Synonym: *Ptelea baldwinii* Torrey & A. Gray

307. Wild Sarsaparilla or Sarsaparilla Vine

Smilacaceae (greenbrier family)
Smilax pumila Walter

Description: Low-growing, trailing, spineless woody vine. Leaves alternate, evergreen, greenish above, lighter and pubescent below. Leaf petioles hairy. Blades ovate, somewhat heart-shaped at the base, 3-nerved. Flower clusters yellowish, in leaf axils. Mature berry bright red.

Flowering time: Fall.

Habitat: Upland mixed forests, sandhills, pine flatwoods, and bluffs.

Range: Panhandle: Throughout, except Jefferson, Holmes, and Santa Rosa. North Florida: Throughout, except Madison, Gilchrist, Union, and Nassau. Central Florida: Throughout, except Citrus, Brevard, Indian River, St. Lucie, and Okeechobee.

Comment: Another greenbrier found in rich woods, hammocks, and well-drained sites in central and northern Florida is Jackson-vine or lanceleaf greenbrier (*Smilax smallii*). Leaves narrow, lanceolate. Berry dull red to brownish red, borne in clusters. The bullbrier (*Smilax rotundifolia*), a high-climbing, glabrous vine, has ovate leaves, reddish petioles, thin leaf margins, reddish brown-tipped spines, and glabrous leaves.

308. Horse Sugar or Sweet Leaf

Symplocaceae (sweetleaf family)
Symplocos tinctoria (Linnaeus) L'Heritier de Brutelle

Description: Deciduous shrub or small tree to 35 ft tall. Leaves alternate, leathery, sweet tasting. Blades widest at or near the middle. Margins mostly entire. Flowers fragrant, in axillary rounded clusters on previous year's growth. Calyx 5-lobed. Corolla 5-lobed, yellow. Stamens many. Fruit fleshy, 1-seeded.

Flowering time: March–April.

Habitat: Upland mixed forests, bluffs, floodplains, sandhills, and pine flatwoods.

Range: Panhandle: Throughout, except Gulf. North Florida: Madison, Hamilton, Columbia, Baker, Suwannee, Dixie, Gilchrist, Levy, Alachua, Clay, Nassau, Duval, and St. Johns. Central Florida: Hillsborough.

Comment: Flowers appear before leaves. Leaves and inner bark yield a yellow dye. White-tailed deer, horses, and cattle eat the sweet-tasting leaves.

309. Rose Vervain

Verbenaceae (vervain or verbena family)
Glandularia canadensis (Linnaeus) Nuttall

Description: Perennial herb with pubescent stems. Leaves opposite, lobed or dissected. Blades triangular-ovate. Flowers showy, overlapping, in erect solitary spikes. Calyx 5-lobed, tube glandular. Petals 5-lobed, pink or purple. Stamens 5. Fruit of 4 nutlets.

Flowering time: March.

Habitat: Upland mixed forests and ruderal.

Range: Panhandle: Jackson, Gadsden, Leon, and Jefferson. North Florida: Suwannee, Duval, Flagler, Alachua, and Levy. Central Florida: Citrus and Hernando.

Synonyms: *Glandularia lambertii* (Sims) Small; *Verbena canadensis* (Linnaeus) Britton

310. Walter's Violet

Violaceae (violet family)
Viola walteri House

Description: Pubescent herb with 3 or 4 stems arising from a crown. Leaves ovate, green with purplish veins above, purple below. Margins finely toothed. Flowers 2-lipped, bluish violet with dark streaks. Sepals and petals 5. Stamens 5.

Flowering time: February–April.

Habitat: Upland mixed forests and bluffs.

Range: Panhandle: Jackson, Gadsden, Liberty, Leon, Wakulla, and Jefferson. North Florida: Columbia, Gilchrist, and Alachua. Central Florida: Citrus.

Comment: Another purple violet of mixed forests, pine flatwoods, sandhills, and hardwood forests is *Viola palmata*. Leaves widely ovate, unlobed or lobed, and lack the purplish veins. *Viola septemloba* and *Viola triloba* are synonyms of *palmata* according to some botanists. Two common white-flowered violets found in moist to wet areas are the primrose-leaved violet (*Viola primulifolia*) and long-leaf violet (*Viola lanceolata*). The former has wide leaves with scalloped margins, whereas the latter has narrower leaves with shallow-toothed margins.

Coastal Uplands

Beach Dunes

311. Beach Dune at Melbourne Beach, Brevard County, Florida. September 12, 1992. Note the sea oats (*Uniola paniculata*), bitter panicum (*Panicum amarum*), and in the foreground, railroad-vine (*Ipomoea pes-caprae*).

Above: 312. Dune at St. George Island State Park, Franklin County, Florida, showing ridges, interdunal grassy swales, and in the background a pine forest. July 14, 1996.

Left: 313. Sea oats (*Uniola paniculata*) showing the extensive root system that is involved in dune stabilization. October 19, 1996.

314. Sea Purslane or Sea Pickle

Aizoaceae (carpetweed family)
Sesuvium portulacastrum (Linnaeus)
Linnaeus

Description: Succulent, glabrous perennial
with reddish, prostrate or ascending stems.
Roots at the nodes. Leaves opposite, narrow,
green with some red. Flowers solitary, star-
shaped, in leaf axils. Sepals green on the outside, pink inside. Petals lacking. Stamens
more than 5. Fruit a capsule.

Flowering time: January–December.

Habitat: Beach dunes, salt flats, and brackish
marshes.

Range: Coastal counties except Taylor, Gulf,
and Santa Rosa. Inland county: Seminole.

Comment: The salty leaves may be cooked or
used in salads. Plant has been consumed to
treat scurvy and kidney disorders. Similar
species is *Sesuvium maritimum*, which has 5
stamens and white flowers.

315. Chaff Flower

Amaranthaceae (amaranth or pigweed family)
Alternanthera flavescens Kunth

Description: Weedy herb with branched
stems. Leaves opposite, elliptic to ovate. Inflorescence stalked. Heads spikelike, terminal
or in leaf axils. Flowers papery. Sepals 5,
small, whitish. Petals lacking. Fruit a utricle.

Flowering time: April–October; sporadically
at other times.

Habitat: Beach dunes, coastal hammocks,
and coastal strand.

Range: North Florida: Clay. Central Florida:
Brevard, Indian River, St. Lucie, Manatee,
and Sarasota. South Florida: Throughout, except Glades and Hendry.

Comment: Teas made from this plant have
been used for fevers, dropsy, and bronchitis.

Synonym: *Alternanthera ramosissima*
(Martius) Chodat

316. Beach Alternanthera

Amaranthaceae (amaranth or pigweed family)
Alternanthera maritima (Martius) A. Saint-Hilaire

Description: Prostrate, fleshy herb with glabrous stems that root at the nodes. Leaves opposite, glabrous, widest at the middle. Margins entire. Flowers sessile, papery, in axillary straw-colored spikes. Sepals 5, white. Petals lacking. Stamens 5. Fruit a utricle.

Flowering time: May.

Habitat: Beach dunes, coastal strand, and coastal hammocks.

Range: Central Florida: St. Lucie. South Florida: Martin, Palm Beach, Dade, Monroe, and Collier.

Synonym: *Achyranthes maritima* (Martius) Standley

317. Samphire

Amaranthaceae (amaranth or pigweed family)
Blutaparon vermiculare (Linnaeus) Mears

Description: Perennial herb with fleshy, prostrate, branched stems. Leaves opposite, narrow, thick, sessile. Flowers silvery white, papery, in globose or cylindrical spikes. Sepals 5. Petals lacking. Stamens 5. Fruit a utricle.

Flowering time: November.

Habitat: Beach dunes, coastal strand, and saline soils.

Range: Coastal counties: Volusia south to the Keys. Monroe north to Charlotte; Sarasota north to Pasco; Hernando north to Dixie.

Comment: Leaves and stems may be eaten.

Synonym: *Philoxerus vermicularis* (Linnaeus) Smith

318. Water Pennywort or Beach Pennywort

Apiaceae or Umbelliferae (carrot or parsley family)
Hydrocotyle bonariensis Commerson ex Lamarck

Description: Low-growing, glabrous, succulent herb. Stems slender, rooting at the nodes. Leaf stalk attached to leaf's center. Leaves ovoid, margins scalloped. Flowers tiny, 5-lobed, greenish white; usually in compound umbels. Stamens 5. Fruit a schizocarp forming 2 mericarps.

Flowering time: February–September.

Habitat: Beach dunes, coastal grasslands, coastal flatwoods, ponds, ditches, and canals.

Range: Panhandle: Coastal counties to Jefferson. All east coast counties, except Indian River, Broward, and the Keys. West coastal counties: Dixie, Pasco, Lee, and Collier. Inland counties: Marion, Alachua, Bradford, Putnam, and Clay.

Comment: A similar species that is smaller and more common is the marsh pennywort (*Hydrocotyle umbellata*) of wet grounds. It occurs in both inland and coastal areas. Leaves are similar, but the flowers occur in simple umbels.

319. Sea Oxeye or Sea Daisy

Asteraceae or Compositae (daisy or sunflower family)
Borrichia frutescens (Linnaeus) de Candolle

Description: Perennial, branched, grayish green shrub to 3 ft tall or more. Often forms extensive colonies. Leaves opposite, somewhat fleshy. Blades spatulate, grayish green. Heads usually solitary, long-stalked. Disk and ray florets yellow. Phyllaries firm, spine-tipped. Fruit an achene.

Flowering time: January–December.

Habitat: Beach dunes, salt marshes, and salt flats.

Range: Throughout the Keys and coastal counties, except Gulf, Walton, Okaloosa, and Escambia.

Comment: *Borrichia arborescens,* a similar species, lacks the spine-tipped phyllaries, has larger green leaves, and has a more southern distribution. Genus commemorates the Danish botanist Ole Borrichia (1616–1690).

320. Beach Sunflower or Cucumberleaf Sunflower

Asteraceae or Compositae (daisy or sunflower family)
Helianthus debilis Nuttall

Description: Annual herb with erect or decumbent stems. Stems glabrous or rough; may form colonies. Leaves alternate, base broad, long-stalked, rough. Margins entire or toothed. A single flower terminates a long stalk. Heads of yellow ray florets and reddish purplish disk florets. Fruit an achene.

Flowering time: January–December.

Habitat: Beach dunes, coastal strand, coastal grasslands, and ruderal.

Range: Panhandle: Escambia, Jackson, Bay, Gulf, Franklin, and Wakulla. North Florida: Madison, Columbia, Levy, St. Johns, and Flagler. Central Florida: Pinellas, Hillsborough, Manatee, Sarasota, Lake, Orange, Volusia, Brevard, Indian River, and St. Lucie. South Florida: Martin, Palm Beach, Broward, Dade, Lee, and Charlotte.

Comment: Plant makes an attractive ground cover. A variable species with 3 subspecies in Florida. These are not delineated here. Blanket flower (*Gaillardia pulchella*) is a conspicuous plant of coastal sites and is often used as an ornamental. Heads large, terminal. Ray florets usually reddish purple with yellow tips. Disk reddish purple.

321. Marsh Elder

Asteraceae or Compositae (daisy or sunflower family)
Iva frutescens Linnaeus

Description: Perennial, succulent herb or woody shrub to 12 ft tall. Leaves mostly opposite, linear to elliptic, petioled, narrow at the base. Blades pubescent, toothed, with 3 major veins. Flowers tubular, greenish yellow, in axillary or terminal elongated inflorescence. Mature fruit a dark brown achene.

Flowering time: July–September.

Habitat: Beach dunes, salt marshes, and salt flats.

Range: Coastal counties south through the Keys; Monroe, Lee, Charlotte, Levy, Bay, Walton, and Okaloosa.

322. Beach Elder or Marsh Elder

Asteraceae or Compositae (daisy or sunflower family)
Iva imbricata Walter

Description: Perennial, succulent herb or bushy-branched shrub to 3 ft tall. Foliage scented. Leaves mostly alternate, sessile. Blades narrow, widest near the tip. Flowers solitary, greenish white, in axils of leaves. Mature fruit a yellowish brown achene.

Flowering time: June–October.

Habitat: Beach dunes and coastal grasslands.

Range: Coastal counties, except Nassau, Indian River, Martin, Broward, Charlotte, and Pinellas; coastal counties north of Pasco to Wakulla; Bay.

Comment: A widespread coastal plant that is neither a true elder (*Sambucus*) nor a marsh plant. Propagation is possible by seeds and by cuttings of mature stems.

323. Seaside Goldenrod

Asteraceae or Compositae (daisy or sunflower family)
Solidago sempervirens Linnaeus

Description: Perennial herb, mostly glabrous, to 6 ft tall or more. Basal leaves persisting, long, somewhat fleshy. Upper leaves sessile, reduced. Inflorescence a terminal elongated cluster of yellow tubular florets. Ray florets lacking. Mature fruit a pubescent achene.

Flowering time: January–December.

Habitat: Beach dunes, edges of salt marshes and flats, and wet pinelands.

Range: Panhandle: Coastal counties: From Escambia to Jefferson. North Florida: Levy, Marion, Putnam, Flagler, St. Johns, Duval, and Nassau. Central Florida: Throughout, except Sumter, Seminole, Polk, Okeechobee, St. Lucie, and De Soto. South Florida: Throughout, except Glades and the Keys.

Synonym: *Solidago mexicana* Linnaeus

324. Saltwort or Beachwort

Bataceae (saltwort family)
Batis maritima Linnaeus

Description: Low-growing, pale green succulent herb. Often forming colonies. Leaves opposite, sessile, linear. Male and female flowers separate. Flowers tiny, in conelike spikes located in axils of leaves. Male flowers with 4 petals, 4 stamens. Fruit oblong, drooping.

Flowering time: May–September.

Habitat: Beach dunes, mangrove edges, salt flats, and salt marshes.

Range: Panhandle: Bay, Franklin, and Wakulla. North Florida: Taylor, Levy, Marion, Nassau to Volusia. Central Florida: Brevard, St. Lucie, Pinellas, Hillsborough, and Manatee. South Florida: Charlotte, Lee, Collier, Monroe, Dade, the Keys, and Martin.

Comment: Teas made from the plants have been used for asthma and venereal diseases. Raw leaves were consumed for constipation, gout, and rheumatism. Saltwort can be eaten as a pot herb.

325. Seaside Heliotrope

Boraginaceae (borage family)
Heliotropium curassavicum Linnaeus

Description: Usually a sprawling perennial. Herb glabrous, succulent to 16 inches tall. Stem leafy. Leaves alternate, sessile or nearly so, narrow, and pale green. Flowers small, glabrous, in curved spikes. Calyx 5-lobed. Corolla white or bluish, 5-lobed. Fruit a schizocarp producing 4 mericarps.

Flowering time: January–December.

Habitat: Beach dunes and borders of marshes and salt flats.

Range: Coastal counties: Volusia south to Martin, Broward through the Keys, Monroe north to Charlotte, Manatee to Pasco. Taylor and Franklin. Inland counties: Putnam and Seminole.

Comment: Asthma, gout, coughs, rheumatism, sores, and wounds have been treated with this plant. Alkaloids in this heliotrope have killed cattle and horses and produced liver cancer.

326. Sea Rocket

Brassicaceae or Cruciferae (mustard family)
Cakile lanceolata (Willdenow) O. E. Schulz

Description: Annual herb to 2 ft tall.
Branches decumbent or ascending. Leaves alternate, fleshy, toothed or dissected. Petals 4,
white to pale purple. Stamens 6. Fruit of 2
joints, conical at the apex.

Flowering time: April–August.

Habitat: Beach dunes and coastal strand.

Range: Coastal counties: Duval south
through the Keys, Monroe north to Charlotte, Manatee north to Pasco, Levy, Wakulla
west to (including) Escambia.

Comment: Used as a pot herb and to treat
scurvy. Another sea rocket, common along
Florida's northeast coast, is *Cakile endentula*
subsp. *harperi*. Upper joint of fruit 4-angled
with a prominent rib between angles. Lower
joint on upper surface flat.

Synonyms: *Cakile chapmanii* Millspaugh;
Cakile constricta Rodman

327. Sand Atriplex, Seabeach Orach, or Crested Atriplex

Chenopodiaceae (goosefoot family)
Atriplex pentandra (Jacquin) Standley

Description: Annual or perennial. Stems
branched, green, to 2 ft tall. Leaves alternate,
margins entire or toothed. Male and female
flowers separate on the same plant. Male
flowers with a perianth, lacking bracts. Female flowers lacking a perianth, on the lower
parts of male spikes, associated with fleshy
bracts. Fruit a utricle.

Flowering time: May–September.

Habitat: Beach dunes, salt marshes, and
coastal swales.

Range: Coastal counties: Nassau south
through the Keys, Monroe north to Charlotte. Manatee, Pinellas, and Hillsborough.
Taylor, Franklin, Bay, Okaloosa, and Santa
Rosa.

Synonym: *Atriplex arenaria* Nuttall

328. Annual Glasswort

Chenopodiaceae (goosefoot family)
Salicornia bigelovii Torrey

Description: Annual, succulent herb or shrub. Stems jointed, opposite-branching. Main stem to 2 ft tall. Leaves opposite, scalelike. Flowers small, embedded in the upper jointed leaf axils. Spike becomes bright red. Male sepals inconspicuous. Petals lacking. Fruit a utricle.

Flowering time: June–September.

Habitat: Beach dunes, salt marshes, marl soils, and salt flats.

Range: Coastal counties: Nassau, Duval, Volusia, Brevard, St. Lucie, Dade, the Keys, Lee, Manatee, Pasco, Levy to Jefferson, and Wakulla.

Comment: Salty stems can be eaten.

329. Perennial Glasswort

Chenopodiaceae (goosefoot family)
Salicornia perennis Miller

Description: Perennial, succulent herb. Stems jointed, opposite-branching. Stems may become woody with decumbent branches. Greenish turning brownish red. Leaves opposite, scalelike. Flowers small, embedded in the upper jointed leaf axils. Spike to 1¼ inches long, paired, becoming lead color or light brown. Fruit a utricle.

Flowering time: January–November.

Habitat: Beach dunes, salt marshes, salt flats, and marl soils.

Range: Coastal counties: Nassau south to Martin. Dade, the Keys, Monroe, Collier, and Lee. Manatee north to Gulf. Bay.

Comment: The salty stems can be eaten.

Synonym: *Salicornia virginica* sensu Clewell 1985, non Linnaeus

330. Saltwort or Russian Thistle

Chenopodiaceae (goosefoot family)
Salsola kali Linnaeus

Description: Annual herb with branched stems. Leaves succulent, linear. Leaves alternate, spine-tipped. Flowers in leaf axils. Sepals 5-lobed. Petals lacking. Stamens 5. Fruit a utricle enclosed by the calyx.

Flowering time: June–September.

Habitat: Beach dunes.

Range: Coastal counties: Duval, St. Johns, Volusia to Dade. Wakulla, Franklin, and Bay.

Comment: Introduced from Eurasia.

331. Southern Sea Blite or Sea Blite

Chenopodiaceae (goosefoot family)
Suaeda linearis (Elliott) Moquin-Tandon

Description: Fleshy annual to 3 ft tall. Stems glabrous, much-branched. Plant becoming woody. Leaves alternate, linear, entire, fleshy. Flowers green, in leafy-bracteate spikes. Calyx 5-lobed, green, fleshy, lobes keeled. Petals lacking. Stamens 5. Fruit a utricle enclosed by the calyx.

Flowering time: June–October.

Habitat: Beach dunes, salt marshes, salt flats, and marl soils.

Range: Coastal counties: Nassau south to Flagler. Volusia to Palm Beach. Dade and the Keys. Monroe north to Hernando. Citrus and Levy. Taylor, Wakulla, Franklin, and Gulf.

Comment: Young leaves and stem tips may be cooked as pot herbs.

Synonym: *Dondia linearis* (Elliott) A. Heller

332. Beach Morning-glory

Convolvulaceae (morning-glory family)
Ipomoea imperati (Vahl) Grisebach

Description: Trailing, glabrous, perennial vine rooting at the nodes. Leaves alternate, succulent, petioled. Blades linear to ovate, notched. Flowers solitary, in axils of leaves. Corolla funnel-shaped, white with yellow throat or with yellow apex and purplish lobe. Sepals 5-lobed. Petals 5, fused. Stamens 5. Capsule, with 4 large seeds.

Flowering time: June–November.

Habitat: Beach dunes and coastal grasslands.

Range: Panhandle: Escambia, Okaloosa, Walton, Gulf, and Franklin. North Florida: Levy, Nassau, Duval, St. Johns, and Flagler. Central Florida: Volusia, Brevard, St. Lucie, Hernando, and Pinellas. South Florida: Broward, Dade, and Lee.

Comment: One of the first beach invaders after a storm.

Synonym: *Ipomoea stolonifera* (Cirillo) J. F. Gmelin

333. Railroad-vine

Convolvulaceae (morning-glory family)
Ipomoea pes-caprae (Linnaeus) R. Brown

Description: Branched, trailing, glabrous vine rooting at the nodes. Stems stout. Leaves alternate, kidney-shaped, notched at the apex. Flowers large, usually solitary. Sepals unequal. Corolla funnel-shaped, rose purple, darker in the center. Stamens 5. Capsule, with 4 large seeds.

Flowering time: May–November; sporadically at other times.

Habitat: Beach dunes, coastal grasslands, and ruderal.

Range: Panhandle: Escambia, Santa Rosa, Okaloosa, Walton, Franklin, and Wakulla. North Florida: Taylor, Dixie, Levy, Nassau, Duval, St. Johns, and Flagler. Central Florida: Throughout, except Sumter, Seminole, Osceola, Okeechobee, Highlands, Hardee, and Manatee. South Florida: Throughout.

Comment: Plant has been used to treat fevers, gout, rheumatism, tumors, and jellyfish stings. Flowers last one day. Another more descriptive common name for this important beach vine is "Creeper on the Earth by the Sea." "Pes-caprae" means goat's foot, a reference to the shape of the leaves.

334. Sand-dune Spurge

Euphorbiaceae (spurge family)
Chamaesyce bombensis (Jacquin) Dugand

Description: Herb with glabrous, reclining stems. Sap milky. The flexible stems may form mats. Leaves opposite, mostly oblong, more than twice as long as wide. Margins entire, leaf bases unequal. Flowers in cup-shaped involucres called cyathia. Petallike appendages minute or absent. Capsule 3-lobed, glabrous, somewhat depressed. Seeds not angled (magnification needed).

Flowering time: July–October.

Habitat: Beach dunes and coastal grasslands.

Range: Coastal counties: Nassau south through the Keys. Collier north to Pasco, Hernando, Levy, and Franklin to (including) Escambia.

Synonyms:: *Chamaesyce amannioides* (Kunth) Small; *Chamaesyce ingallsii* Small

335. Seaside Spurge or Woody Spurge

Euphorbiaceae (spurge family)
Chamaesyce mesembrianthemifolia (Jacquin) Dugand

Description: Branched herb often woody at the base. Stems to 3 ft tall, fleshy, ascending or erect. Leaves opposite, fleshy, ovate to elliptic. Margins entire and leaf bases unequal. Flowers in cup-shaped involucres called cyathia. Cyathia about $1/16$ inch long. Petaloid appendages white. Capsule glabrous, 3-lobed.

Flowering time: March–October.

Habitat: Beach dunes and coastal strand.

Range: Coastal counties: Flagler south through the Keys. Monroe north to Pasco.

Comment: Milky sap from the plant has been used to treat puncture wounds. Species name often spelled *mesembryanthemifolia*.

Synonym:: *Chamaesyce buxifolia* (Lamarck) Small

336. Beach Tea or Silver-leaf Croton

Euphorbiaceae (spurge family)
Croton punctatus Jacquin

Description: Perennial herb. Stems diffusely branched, pubescent, tan-colored. Often woody at the base. Usually less than 3 ft tall. Leaves alternate, petioled, silvery. Blades elliptic or ovate. Margins entire or undulate. Lower leaf surface silvery. Male flowers above female flowers (1–3). Flowers small, in short clusters. Stamens 10–12. Capsule 3-lobed.

Flowering time: March–December.

Habitat: Beach dunes, coastal grasslands, and coastal strand.

Range: Coastal counties: Nassau south to Martin. Palm Beach to the Keys. Collier north to Pinellas. Franklin through Escambia. Inland counties: Leon and Lake.

337. Seaside Bean or Bay Bean

Fabaceae or Leguminosae (bean and pea family)
Canavalia rosea (Swartz) de Candolle

Description: Prostrate trailing or twining fleshy vine. Leaves alternate, compound. Leaflets 3, ovoid, thick, entire. Leaflets fold as the day progresses. Flowers in the leaf axils. Calyx 2-lipped. Flowers pea-shaped, pink to rose purple. Stamens 10. Legume 4–6 inches long, flattened.

Flowering time: June–December; sporadically at other times.

Habitat: Beach dunes and coastal strand.

Range: Coastal counties: Volusia south through the Keys. Monroe north to Charlotte. Sarasota to Pasco. Levy and Dixie.

Comment: Excellent vine for dry, salty areas. Flowers used as a flavoring and the young seeds and pods are edible when cooked. Mature seeds may be toxic. Seeds disperse via marine waters.

Synonym: *Canavalia maritima* Thouars

338. Small Rattlebox

Fabaceae or Leguminosae (bean and pea family)
Crotalaria pumila Ortega

Description: Low-growing herb with slender stem, often mat-forming. Leaves alternate, petioled. Leaflets 3, middle leaflet the largest. Leaf margins entire, smooth. Calyx 5-lobed. Flowers pea-shaped, yellow, grouped in small clusters. Legume inflated, smooth.

Flowering time: January–December.

Habitat: Beach dunes and pinelands.

Range: Coastal counties from Brevard south to Monroe. Sarasota and the Keys.

Comment: The unrelated (family Onagraceae) evening primrose (*Oenothera humifusa*) is another low-growing plant of beach dunes. The pale yellow flowers, about 1 inch across, have 4 reflexed sepals and 4 petals. Leaves silky, grayish green.

339. Seaside Gentian

Gentianaceae (gentian family)
Eustoma exaltatum (Linnaeus) Salisbury ex G. Don

Description: Annual glabrous herb to 3 ft tall. Leaves opposite, fleshy, sessile, clasping. Blades gray green, elliptic, reduced above. Flowers on long stalks, showy, erect, cupped. Sepals 5 or 6, shorter than the petals. Corolla 5-lobed, rose purple or lavender (sometimes white), darker in the center. Fruit a sticky capsule.

Flowering time: January–November.

Habitat: Beach dunes, wet marshes, coastal flats, hammocks, and disturbed sites.

Range: Coastal counties: Levy to Sarasota. Charlotte to Collier. Monroe, Dade, the Keys, St. Lucie, Indian River, and Brevard. Inland county: Orange.

340. Marsh Pink

Gentianaceae (gentian family)
Sabatia stellaris Pursh

Description: Annual herb to 2 ft tall (usually less). Stems slender, glabrous, branched. Basal leaves usually absent at flowering. Stem leaves opposite, sessile, narrow. Flowers star-shaped, pink or whitish pink with a yellow eye bordered by red. Calyx 5-lobed, lobes narrow. Petals 5, united. Fruit an ovoid capsule.

Flowering time: January–December.

Habitat: Beach dunes, coastal marshes, coastal flats, bogs, coastal swales, coastal grasslands, wet pine flatwoods, and ruderal.

Range: Coastal counties, except Okaloosa, Pasco, Pinellas, and Flagler. Inland counties: Liberty, Baker, Union, Seminole, Orange, Osceola, Okeechobee, Highlands, and Glades.

341. Beach Peanut or Burrowing Four-o'Clock

Nyctaginaceae (four-o'clock family)
Okenia hypogaea Schlechtendal & Chamisso

Description: Annual. Vine sticky, prostrate, densely pubescent. Leaves opposite, fleshy, sticky. Flowers solitary, in axils of leaves. Sepals united, petallike, reddish purple. Petals lacking. Stamens numerous.

Flowering time: April–November.

Habitat: Beach dunes and coastal hammocks.

Range: Central Florida: St. Lucie. South Florida: Martin, Palm Beach, Broward, Dade, and Monroe.

Comment: Showy flowers are infertile. The peanutlike fruit forms and matures underground from nondescript flowers. Plant endangered in Florida.

342. Saltgrass

Poaceae or Gramineae (grass family)
Distichlis spicata (Linnaeus) Greene

Description: Leafy perennial. Stems (culms) glabrous, to 20 inches tall. The wiry culms arise from underground rhizomes and form dense colonies. Leaves narrow, in two rows, margins inrolled, sharp-tipped. Male and female flowers on separate plants. Inflorescence terminal. Seedheads (spikelets) cylindric, compressed, overlapping. Male spike usually overtopping the foliage and longer than the greenish female spike. Fruit a grain or caryopsis.

Flowering time: September–October.

Habitat: Beach dunes, salt marshes, salt flats, coastal grasslands, edges of mangroves, and disturbed areas.

Range: Coastal counties, except Okaloosa, Walton, Bay, Gulf, Broward, Charlotte, and Sarasota.

Comment: Can be used as a lawn grass in coastal areas. Livestock will graze on the grass. Fruit is high in bran and fiber.

343. Virginia Dropseed

Poaceae or Gramineae (grass family)
Sporobolus virginicus (Linnaeus) Kunth

Description: Perennial grass with wiry, leafy stems (culms) to 1.5 ft tall. Plant roots at the nodes from creeping leafy rhizomes. Leaves arranged in two vertical rows with overlapping sheaths. Leaf blades flat at the base, narrow, and prickly at the tips. Flowers tiny, in a slender terminal spike. Fruit a grain or caryopsis.

Flowering time: June–November

Habitat: Beach dunes, salt marshes, salt flats, and coastal disturbed sites.

Range: Panhandle: Escambia, Santa Rosa, Bay, Gulf, Franklin, and Wakulla. North Florida: Taylor, Levy, Nassau, Duval, St. Johns, and Flagler. Central Florida: Volusia, Brevard, Seminole, St. Lucie, Pasco, Pinellas, Hillsborough, Manatee, and Sarasota. South Florida: Charlotte, Lee, Collier, Monroe, Dade, the Keys, Broward, Palm Beach, and Martin.

Comment: Ripe seeds easily drop off, hence the name "dropseed." One of the few salt-tolerant grasses that cattle and deer use as a pasture.

Synonym: *Sporobolus littoralis* (Lamarck) Kunth

344. Christmasberry or Matrimony Vine

Solanaceae (nightshade family)
Lycium carolinianum Walter

Description: Shrub to 6 ft tall with sprawling, spiny branches. Bark grayish. Leaves alternate, succulent, small, sessile, gray green. Margins entire. Flowers pale purple to whitish, single or clustered in axils of leaves. Calyx and corolla lobes 4 or 5. Berry bright red.

Flowering time: March–December.

Habitat: Beach dunes, salt flats, salt marshes, shell mounds, and hammocks.

Range: Coastal counties: Nassau, Duval, St. Johns, Volusia, Brevard, Indian River, St. Lucie, Dade, the Keys, Monroe, Collier, Lee, Sarasota, Manatee, Pinellas, Pasco, Hernando, Citrus, Levy, Taylor, Wakulla, Franklin, and Gulf. Inland county: Hillsborough.

345. Sand Cherry or Ground Cherry

Solanaceae (nightshade family)
Physalis walteri Nuttall

Description: Herb with slender stems. Plant usually sticky. Leaves alternate, petioled, ovate to spatulate. Lower leaf surface with star-shaped hairs (magnification needed). Flowers solitary, nodding, bell-shaped. Petals fused, greenish yellow with a dark center. Mature berry surrounded by a papery calyx.

Flowering time: January–December.

Habitat: Beach dunes, coastal grasslands, and coastal and inland disturbed sites.

Range: Panhandle: Escambia, Santa Rosa, Holmes, Jackson, Wakulla, Franklin, and Leon. North Florida: Taylor, Lafayette, Dixie, Levy, Marion, Flagler, St. Johns, Clay, Duval, and Nassau. Central Florida: Throughout, except Hardee and De Soto. South Florida: Throughout, except Monroe. In the Keys.

Comment: A common sand cherry (*Physalis arenicola*) occurs in both coastal and inland ruderal areas. This similar species with bell-shaped yellow flowers lacks the star-shaped hairs.

Synonym: *Physalis viscosa* Linnaeus

346. Bay Cedar or Tassel Plant

Surianaceae (bay cedar family)
Suriana maritima Linnaeus

Description: Shrub or small tree to 10 ft tall or more. Foliage dense, clustered at the ends of branches. Leaves alternate, sessile, grayish or pale green. Blades linear to spatulate, succulent. Flowers small, solitary or clustered among the leaves. Sepals 5, green. Petals 5, yellow. Fertile stamens 5. Fruit dry, 5 nutlets.

Flowering time: All year.

Habitat: Beach dunes, coastal grasslands, coastal strand, and rocky exposures.

Range: Coastal counties: Brevard south through the Keys. Monroe north to Pasco.

Comment: Endangered in Florida. Crushed leaves smell like cedar. Herbal baths for rheumatism have been made from the plant's leaves and bark. A tea from twigs has been used for toothaches and mouth sores. One of the first plants to colonize new beaches. Seeds tolerate salt water. Can be used as a landscape plant.

347. Coastal Vervain or Beach Verbena

Verbenaceae (vervain or verbena family)
Glandularia maritima (Small) Small

Description: Herb with angled, branched stems that are prostrate or ascending. Leaves opposite, petioled, ovate. Margins lobed, toothed. Flowers rose purple, hairy, in slender spikes. Calyx glandular, 5-lobed, tips pointed. Petals 5-lobed. Stamens 4. Fruits of 4 nutlets.

Flowering time: January–December.

Habitat: Beach dunes, coastal grasslands, coastal strand, oak scrubs, pinelands, and ruderal.

Range: Coastal counties: Flagler south through the Keys. Collier and Levy. Inland county: Hendry.

Comment: Threatened and endemic to Florida.

Synonym: *Verbena maritima* Small

Coastal Strands

348. Coastal Strand at Playalinda Beach, Canaveral National Seashore, Brevard County, Florida. April 22, 1996. Note the edge of the dune, seagrapes (*Coccoloba uvifera*), saw palmetto (*Serenoa repens*), and the partially dead Florida privet (*Forestiera segregata*) near the center of the picture.

349. Spanish Dagger or Spanish Bayonet

Agavaceae (century plant family)
Yucca aloifolia Linnaeus

Description: Woody evergreen plant with a distinct trunk to 5 ft tall or more. Leaves large, tough, overlapping, sharp-tipped. Inflorescence dense, terminal, above the leaves. Flowering stem leafless. Flowers bell-shaped, drooping, white, with 6 tepals. Berries reddish, with black seeds.

Flowering time: April–October; sporadically at other times.

Habitat: Coastal strand, coastal grasslands, maritime hammocks, sandhills, and disturbed sites.

Range: Coastal counties: Nassau south to Flagler; Volusia south to Broward; Dade and the Keys. Monroe north to Pasco; Hernando to Dixie. Wakulla and Escambia. Inland county: Suwannee.

Comment: Native to West Indies and Mexico. Used in coastal and inland landscapes. The sharp-pointed leaves can be dangerous. A related species of sandhills, scrubs, and pine flatwoods is Adam's needle (*Yucca filamentosa*). A trunk is lacking and the firm leaves have margins that fray into threads.

350. Natal Plum

Apocynaceae (dogbane family)
Carissa macrocarpa (Ecklon) Alph. de Candolle

Description: Evergreen shrub with milky sap and forked thorns on the branches. Leaves opposite, leathery, oval, dark green above. Margins entire. Flowers fragrant, white, star-shaped. Petals narrow. The scarlet, egg-shaped, fleshy fruit tastes like cranberry.

Flowering time: June–October.

Habitat: Coastal strand and ruderal.

Range: Coastal counties: Flagler, Brevard, Palm Beach, Dade, the Keys, Lee, and Sarasota.

Comment: Native to southern Africa. Used in ornamental plantings.

Synonym: *Carissa grandiflora* (E. Meyer) Alph. de Candolle

351. Yellow-top

Asteraceae or Compositae (daisy or sunflower family)
Flaveria linearis Lagasca y Segura

Description: Perennial herb to 3 ft tall; bases somewhat woody. Stems branched, glabrous, often reddish. Leaves opposite, linear, sessile, with 1 prominent vein. Margins entire. Inflorescence somewhat flat-topped and terminal. Heads yellow, with 1 ray floret. Fruit an achene.

Flowering time: March–December.

Habitat: Coastal strand, coastal marshes, coastal flats, and ruderal.

Range: Panhandle: Wakulla. North Florida: Taylor, Levy, and Flagler. Central Florida: Citrus, Hernando, Pinellas, Hillsborough, Manatee, Sarasota, Lake, Orange, Seminole, Volusia, Brevard, Indian River, and St. Lucie. South Florida: Martin south to the Keys. Monroe north to Charlotte, Hendry, and Glades.

Synonym: *Flaveria latifolia* (J. R. Johnston) Rydberg

352. Prickly-pear Cactus or Indian Fig

Cactaceae (cactus family)
Opuntia stricta (Haworth) Haworth

Description: Stems erect, branched to 6 ft. Joints thick, glabrous, green. Spines, if present, yellow at maturity. Flowers large, bright yellow to reddish yellow. Stamens many, shorter than the petals. Berry pear-shaped, purplish, edible.

Flowering time: May.

Habitat: Coastal strand, shell middens, beach dunes, coastal hammocks, and disturbed coastal sites.

Range: Coastal counties: Nassau south to Martin. Palm Beach, Dade, and the Keys. Monroe north to Pasco. Citrus, Levy, Taylor, Wakulla, Franklin, and Walton. Inland county: Okeechobee.

Synonyms: *Opuntia atrocapensis* Small; *Opuntia dillenii* (Ker-Gawler) Haworth

353. Snake Cactus

Cactaceae (cactus family)
Selenicereus pteranthus (Link & Otto) Britton & Rose

Description: Viny cactus with stems and branches clambering over objects and forming serpentlike masses. Branches usually 4-angled and the branchlets 4–6-angled or ridged. Spines conic, very short, inconspicuous. Leaves obsolete. Flowers showy, nocturnal. Petals white, broader than the pale green sepals. Base of flower has scales, long, stiff white hairs, and clusters of long, slender spines. Berry globose, red.

Flowering time: All year.

Habitat: Coastal strand, hammocks, and ruderal.

Range: Central Florida: Seminole, Brevard, and St. Lucie. South Florida: Palm Beach, Lee, and Collier.

Comment: Native to Mexico; apparently introduced by settlers during the Seminole War.

Synonym: *Cereus pteranthus* Link & Otto

354. Glades Morning-glory

Convolvulaceae (morning-glory family)
Ipomoea sagittata Poiret

Description: Twining or trailing perennial vine. Stems glabrous. Leaves alternate, smooth, long-petioled. Blades arrow-shaped. Flowers showy, funnel-shaped, usually solitary, in axils of leaves. Sepals 5, glabrous. Petals 5, fused, rose purplish with 5 stripes. Stamens 5. Capsule globose, with 4 large seeds.

Flowering time: April–October.

Habitat: Coastal strand, coastal marshes, flatwoods, and wet, disturbed coastal sites.

Range: Panhandle: Escambia, Santa Rosa, Okaloosa, Walton, Franklin, and Wakulla. North Florida: Taylor, Dixie, Levy, Nassau, Duval, St. Johns, and Flagler. Central Florida: Throughout, except Sumter, Seminole, Osceola, Okeechobee, Hardee, and Manatee. South Florida: Throughout.

355. Beach Star

Cyperaceae (sedge family)
Cyperus pedunculatus (R. Brown) Kern

Description: Perennial creeping herb to 1 ft tall or more. Spreads by underground rhizomes. Leaves many, more or less two-ranked, stiff, tips sharp. Inflorescence spike-like, terminal, scaly. Flowers inconspicuous. Sepals and petals lacking. Stamens 3. Fruit an achene.

Flowering time: July–November.

Habitat: Coastal strand and beach dunes.

Range: Coastal counties: Brevard to Broward; Dade.

Comment: One of the first invaders of open beach sands. An important dune stabilizer. Endangered in Florida.

Synonym: *Remirea maritima* Aublet

356. Sweet Acacia

Fabaceae or Leguminosae (bean or pea family)
Acacia farnesiana (Linnaeus) Willdenow

Description: Branched evergreen shrub or small tree to 15 ft tall or more. Plant richly supplied with paired, pale gray spines to 1.5 inches long. Leaves alternate, twice-compound, leaflets over 10 pairs. Flowers small, yellow, in globose clusters. Fragrant. Legume cylindric, glabrous, reddish brown.

Flowering time: November–February.

Habitat: Coastal strand, shell middens, coastal hammocks, and pinelands.

Range: Panhandle: Escambia, Bay, and Franklin. North Florida: Marion. Central Florida: Volusia, Brevard, Polk, Pinellas, Hillsborough, Manatee, and Sarasota. South Florida: Lee, Hendry, Collier, Monroe, Broward, and the Keys.

Comment: Name honors Cardinal Odoardo Farnese, who cultivated the plant in Italy in the early 1600s.

Synonyms: *Acacia smallii* Isely; *Vachellia farnesiana* (Linnaeus) Wight & Arnott

357. Gray Nicker or Nickerbean

Fabaceae or Leguminosae (bean or pea family)
Caesalpinia bonduc (Linnaeus) Roxburgh

Description: Robust shrub with vinelike
branches covered with sharp thorns. Leaves
opposite, twice-compound. Leaflets oblong or
ovate, shiny green. Flowers yellow orange. Petals 5. Legume flat, spiny, reddish brown. Seeds
hard, gray, smooth.

Flowering time: April–October.

Habitat: Coastal strand.

Range: North Florida: Levy. Central Florida:
Volusia, Brevard, Indian River, St. Lucie,
Manatee, Pinellas, and Hillsborough. South
Florida: Martin, Palm Beach, Broward, Dade,
the Keys, Monroe, Collier, Lee, and Charlotte.

Comment: Plant often scrambles over nearby
vegetation. Native to the West Indies, where
the poisonous seeds are called "warry stones"
or "pet rocks." The bark was used for treating
malaria. A similar species, the yellow nicker
(*Caesalpinia major*), has yellow seeds.

358. Coin-vine or Fish Poison Vine

Fabaceae or Leguminosae (bean or pea family)
Dalbergia ecastophyllum (Linnaeus) Taubert

Description: Shrub or small tree to 12 ft tall
with sprawling or reclining branches. Older
branches lack spines. Leaves alternate, petioled, leathery, ovate or elliptic. Flowers pea-
shaped, clustered in the leaf axils. Petals white
or pinkish, glabrous. Legume flat to kidney-
shaped, mostly 1-seeded.

Flowering time: May–June.

Habitat: Coastal strand, beach dunes, coastal
grasslands, and coastal hammocks.

Range: Coastal counties: Brevard south
through the Keys. Monroe north to Pasco. Inland county: Seminole.

Comment: Leaves and bark contain rotenone,
which blocks oxygen uptake of gills in fishes.
The coppery, coinlike pod gives the plant its
common name. The genus honors Nil and Carl
Dalberg, 18th-century botanical colleagues of
Carolus Linnaeus. A related native species is
Dalbergia brownii, found in hammocks of the
Keys. This species differs in the above species
in having longer leaf petioles and 2-seeded le-
gumes.

Synonym: *Ecastophyllum ecastophyllum*
(Linnaeus) Britton

359. Blackbead

Fabaceae or Leguminosae (bean or pea family)
Pithecellobium keyense Britton ex Britton & Rose

Description: Spineless shrub or small tree to 20 ft tall. Bark gray. Leaves evergreen, leathery, alternate, twice-compound. Leaflets paired. Leaf stalk with a circular gland. Flowers small, fragrant, in creamy or pink clusters. Calyx 5-lobed. Corolla 5-lobed. Legume brown, twisted. Seeds black with red appendages (arils).

Flowering time: January–April; September–December.

Habitat: Coastal strand and coastal hammocks.

Range: South Florida: Martin, Palm Beach, Broward, Dade, Monroe, and the Keys.

Comment: The seeds are used for necklaces and eaten by birds and other animals.

Synonym: *Pithecellobium guadalupense* sensu Small 1933, non (Persoon) Chapman

360. Necklace Pod

Fabaceae or Leguminosae (bean or pea family)
Sophora tomentosa Linnaeus

Description: Woody shrub to 9 ft tall or more. Plant covered with whitish to grayish hairs. Leaves opposite, compound. Young leaflets covered with fuzz; mature leaflets green, leathery. Calyx 5-lobed. Flowers pea-shaped, yellow, in a terminal inflorescence. Legume constricted between seeds, resembling a necklace. Seeds are poisonous.

Flowering time: March–September.

Habitat: Coastal strand, beach dunes, coastal grasslands, coastal scrubs, and coastal hammocks.

Range: Coastal counties: Brevard south through the Keys. Collier north to Citrus. Levy.

361. Narrow-leaved Hoary Pea or Devil's Shoestring

Fabaceae or Leguminosae (bean or pea family)
Tephrosia angustissima Shuttleworth

Description: Perennial shrub to 2 ft tall. Base woody, leafy toward the tips. Leaves alternate, compound. Leaflets about ½ inch long, linear, tips sharp. Flowers pea-shaped, purple, in long clusters. Legume straight, about 1½ inches long.

Flowering time: April–October.

Habitat: Coastal strand.

Range: Central Florida: Volusia, Brevard, and Hillsborough. South Florida: Palm Beach, Dade, and Hendry.

Comment: Endangered and endemic to Florida.

Synonym: *Cracca curtissii* Small

362. Inkberry or Beachberry

Goodeniaceae (goodenia family)
Scaevola plumieri (Linnaeus) Vahl

Description: Perennial succulent shrub to 5 ft tall. Leaves alternate, fleshy, glabrous, broadly spatulate. Margins entire. Leaves 1–2.5 inches long, crowded near the ends of branches. Sepals yellow, attached to the petals. Flowers in leaf axils, white or pink white, with 5 or 6 fused lobes. Flowers hairy inside, fanlike. Stamens 5, free. Drupe ovoid, black, bitter.

Flowering time: April–November.

Habitat: Coastal strand, beach dunes, and coastal grasslands.

Range: Coastal counties: Brevard south through the Keys. Collier north to Hernando.

Comment: Plant endangered in Florida. Colonies may arise from underground stems. Inkberry was named for the French monk Charles Plumier (1647–1704). The introduced relative, half-flower (*Scaevola sericea*), has invaded the dune areas of south Florida. The leaves are longer (3–6 inches), lighter green, and ovate. Flower is similar to that of the above species. Drupe white.

363. Poorman's Patch or Poorman's Patches

Loasaceae (loasa family)
Mentzelia floridana Nuttall

Description: Branched perennial herb to 3 ft tall. Stems and leaves brittle, covered with minute hooked hairs (magnification needed). Leaves alternate, short-petioled, 3-lobed, toothed. Flowers mostly solitary, sessile, in axils of upper leaves. Sepals 5. Petals 5, yellow orange. Fruit a capsule with calyx lobes remaining attached.

Flowering time: January–December, mostly January–March.

Habitat: Coastal strand, coastal hammocks, and beach dunes.

Range: Coastal counties: Levy south to (including) Monroe, except Hernando, Pasco, and Pinellas. Duval south through the Keys.

Comment: Endemic to Florida. Only representative of this tropical genus. Leaves and other parts readily adhere to clothing, making "patches," hence the common name. Christian Mentzel (1622–1701) was a German botanist.

364. Mahoe or Sea Hibiscus

Malvaceae (mallow family)
Hibiscus tiliaceus Linnaeus

Description: Large evergreen shrub or tree to 30 ft high. Leaves alternate, petioles long. Blades broadly heart-shaped, leathery, apex tipped. Lower leaf surface with white hairs. Flowers large, solitary, funnel-shaped. Calyx 5-lobed. Petals 5, yellow with red center. Fruit a hairy capsule.

Flowering time: All year.

Habitat: Coastal strand, margins of mangroves, and disturbed coastal sites.

Range: Central Florida: Manatee, Brevard, Indian River, and St. Lucie. South Florida: Martin, Palm Beach, Broward, Dade, the Keys, Collier, Hendry, and Lee.

Comment: Native to tropical Asia. Flowers and young leaves are edible. Flowers turn reddish in the late afternoon.

Synonyms: *Pariti grande* Britton; *Pariti tiliaceum* (Linnaeus) Jussieu

365. Twinberry, Nakedwood, or Simpson's Stopper

Myrtaceae (myrtle family)
Myrcianthes fragrans (Swartz) McVaugh

Description: Evergreen shrub or tree to 25 ft tall or more. Bark smooth, flaking, reddish brown. Leaves opposite, petioles short. Blades dark green above, paler below, tips sharp. Black dots may occur on the leaves and leaves pellucid dotted if held to the light. Flowers stalked, clustered in leaf axils, fragrant. Calyx lobes 4, unequal. Petals 4, white. Stamens many. Berry globose or ellipsoidal, red or orangish.

Flowering time: March–June.

Habitat: Coastal strand, coastal hammocks, coastal scrubs, shell mounds, and rocky flats.

Range: North Florida: St. Johns. Central Florida: Volusia, Seminole, Orange, Brevard, Indian River, St. Lucie, and Osceola. South Florida: Martin, south through the Keys. Monroe, Collier, Hendry, and Lee.

Comment: Often used as an ornamental plant.

Synonyms: *Anamomis simpsonii* Small; *Myrcianthes fragrans* (Swartz) McVaugh var. *simpsonii* (Small) R. W. Long

366. Sea Lavender

Plumbaginaceae (leadwort family)
Limonium carolinianum (Walter) Britton

Description: Perennial herb to 2 ft tall. Stems erect, nearly leafless. Basal leaves variable in shape. Stem leaves alternate, scalelike. Inflorescence branched, bearing small, lavender flowers. Calyx white, 5-lobed. Corolla 5-lobed. Stamens 5. Fruit a capsule.

Flowering time: March; August–November.

Habitat: Coastal strand, brackish marshes, and salt flats.

Range: Nassau to Flagler. Volusia, Brevard, Indian River, St. Lucie, Martin, Dade, the Keys, Collier, and Lee. Sarasota north to Citrus. Levy to Walton.

Synonyms: *Limonium angustatum* (A. Gray) Small; *Limonium nashii* Small; *Limonium obtusilobum* S. F. Blake

367. Standing Cypress or Spanish Larkspur

Polemoniaceae (phlox family)
Ipomopsis rubra (Linnaeus) Wherry

Description: Stout biennial with leafy, pubescent stems 5 ft tall or more. Leaves alternate, sessile, divided into threadlike segments. Leaves crowded. Flowers showy, in a terminal inflorescence. Calyx tubular, 5-lobed. Corolla 5-lobed, trumpet-shaped, red to reddish orange. Stamens 5. Fruit a capsule.

Flowering time: June–November.

Habitat: Coastal strand, beach dunes, dry pinelands, and ruderal.

Range: Panhandle: Escambia. North Florida: Suwannee, Lafayette, Dixie, Levy, Marion, Alachua, Putnam, Clay, Nassau, Duval, St. Johns, and Flagler. Central Florida: Volusia, Brevard, Indian River, Lake, Sumter, and Pasco.

Comment: Excellent plant to attract butterflies.

Synonym: *Gilia rubra* (Linnaeus) A. Heller

368. Seagrape

Polygonaceae (buckwheat or knotweed family)
Coccoloba uvifera (Linnaeus) Linnaeus

Description: Evergreen shrub or small tree with stout, spreading branches. Leaves alternate, round, often with red veins. Leaves leathery, petioles stout, associated with sheathing ocrea. Inflorescence enlongated, spikelike. Male flowers clustered, female flowers solitary. Perianth 5-lobed, whitish. Stamens 8. Ripe fruit reddish to purple, in grapelike clusters.

Flowering time: April–July.

Habitat: Coastal strand, coastal hammocks, beach dunes, and coastal grasslands.

Range: Coastal counties: Volusia south through the Keys. Monroe north to Pasco.

Comment: Fruits edible raw or used in making jellies and wines. Teas made from the roots, leaves, and bark have been used to treat diarrhea, hemorrhages, and asthma. Seeds are salt tolerant. The other member of this genus in Florida is the pigeon plum (*Coccoloba diversifolia*). This evergreen tree with smooth, peeling bark is common in hammocks of South Florida and the Keys. The simple, alternate leaves are leathery, bright green, rounded at the base, and with entire margins. Flowers small, white, in long racemes. Ripe fleshy fruit black.

369. Water Pimpernel

Primulaceae (pimpernel family)
Samolus ebracteatus Kunth

Description: Herb with a glabrous stem to 15 inches tall. Basal leaves broadened upward. Stem leaves alternate, succulent, broadened upward. Stem leaves extend into the inflorescence. Flowers small, terminal. Calyx 5-lobed. Corolla 5-lobed, white or tinged with pink. Stamens 5.

Flowering time: January–April.

Habitat: Coastal strand, salt marshes, and freshwater areas.

Range: Coastal counties: Brevard south through the Keys. Monroe north to (except Dixie) Bay.

Comment: The pineland pimpernel (*Samolus valerandi*) occurs nearly throughout the state. The flowers are small, white, and 5-lobed. Stem leaves extend into the inflorescence.

Synonym: *Samodia ebracteata* (Kunth) Baudo

370. Tough Bumelia or Buckthorn

Sapotaceae (sapodilla or sapote family)
Sideroxylon tenax Linnaeus

Description: Woody evergreen shrub or small tree to 25 ft or more with milky sap. Stems zigzag, thorny, hairy. Leaves alternate, often clustered. Lower leaf surfaces silvery or coppery. Flowers small, clustered in axils of leaves. Calyx 5-lobed. Corolla white, 5-lobed. Berry black, ovoid, 1-seeded.

Flowering time: April–August.

Habitat: Coastal strand, coastal hammocks, coastal grasslands, dry pinelands, and coastal and inland scrubs.

Range: North Florida: Levy, Marion, Alachua, Putnam, Clay, Duval, Nassau, St. Johns, and Flagler. Central Florida: Throughout, except Seminole, Pinellas, Sarasota, Hardee, De Soto, and Okeechobee. South Florida: Martin, Palm Beach, Dade, and Collier.

Synonyms: *Bumelia lacuum* Small; *Bumelia tenax* (Linnaeus) Willdenow

371. False Foxglove

Scrophulariaceae (figwort family)
Agalinis maritima (Rafinesque) Rafinesque

Description: Annual with glabrous, branched stems to 2 ft. Somewhat succulent, leafy-branched below. Leaves opposite, sessile, linear. Inflorescence with 5 or more flowers per branch. Flowers tubular, pink purple. Calyx 5-lobed. Corolla 5-lobed, edges fringed. Stamens 4. Fruit a capsule.

Flowering time: March–November.

Habitat: Coastal strand, salt marshes, and coastal flats.

Range: Coastal counties: St. Johns, Brevard, Indian River, Dade, the Keys, Monroe, Collier, Lee, Charlotte, Manatee, Pinellas, Hernando, Citrus, Levy, Taylor, Wakulla, Franklin, and Gulf. Inland counties: Seminole and Hillsborough.

Comment: A related but taller (to 2 ft tall or more) false foxglove that occurs in coastal and inland sites is *Agalinis fasciculata*. It has similar pink, tubular flowers, usually 1 per branch. Clusters of small leaves occur in the leaf axils.

Synonyms: *Gerardia maritima* Rafinesque; *Gerardia spiciflora* Engelmann

372. Wild Sage or Wild Lantana

Verbenaceae (vervain or verbena family)
Lantana involucrata Linnaeus

Description: Aromatic branched shrub to 16 ft tall or more. Bark yellowish. Leaves opposite, pale green, upper surfaces rough to the touch. Blades ovate or elliptic. Margins scalloped. Flowers small, in terminal clusters. Corolla tubular white or light purple with a yellow throat. Drupe 1-seeded, purple or blue.

Flowering time: February–October; sporadically at other times.

Habitat: Coastal strand, coastal hammocks, coastal grasslands, beach dunes, coastal scrubs, and ruderal.

Range: Coastal counties: Brevard south through the Keys. Monroe north to Pasco.

Comment: Plant attracts butterflies. Teas from wild sage are consumed to treat colic and topically used to treat eruptions from measles and chickenpox. Plant often forms thickets in full sun. The shrub verbena (*Lantana camara*) is a common, widespread species along the coast and in most dry habitats throughout the state. It can be identified by orange and pink flowers and spiny stems.

Coastal Grasslands

373. A Coastal Grassland at Playalinda Beach, Canaveral National Seashore, Brevard County, Florida. April 22, 1996. Grasses are mostly sea oats (*Uniola paniculata*) and bitter panicum (*Panicum amarum*). Note the reddish-colored seagrapes (*Coccoloba uvifera*) and saw palmetto (*Serenoa repens*) along the dune.

374. Sand Bean

Fabaceae or Leguminosae (bean or pea family)
Strophostyles helvula (Linnaeus) Elliott

Description: Annual twining or trailing herbaceous vine. Leaves alternate, long-stalked, often 3-lobed. Margins entire. Flowers stalked, in leaf axils. Flowers pea-shaped, pink to rose fading to greenish. Calyx 2-lipped, tube short. Lower petals (keel) united, purple-tipped, strongly incurved. Legume slender, pubescent.

Flowering time: July–September.

Habitat: Coastal grasslands, beach dunes, salt marshes, pond margins, open woods, and disturbed sites.

Range: Panhandle: Escambia, Santa Rosa, Okaloosa, Walton, Bay, Jackson, Liberty, and Franklin. North Florida: Madison, Nassau, Duval, and St. Johns. Central Florida: Volusia.

Comment: Species name often spelled *helvola*.

375. Bushy Bluestem or Beardgrass

Poaceae or Gramineae (grass family)
Andropogon glomeratus (Walter) Britton et al.

Description: Stems (culms) stout, compressed, to 3 ft tall or more. Often in large clumps. Inflorescence bushy, dense, feathery, silvery. Leaf margins rough. Leaf sheaths compressed, keeled, wider than the blade. Stalked spikelet shorter than the sessile, awn-tipped spikelet (magnification needed). Fruit a grain or caryopsis.

Flowering time: July–November.

Habitat: Coastal grasslands, scrubs, pine flatwoods, savannas, and ruderal.

Range: Panhandle: Throughout, except Okaloosa, Walton, Holmes, and Gadsden. North Florida: Levy, Gilchrist, Hamilton, Columbia, Baker, Alachua, Putnam, Clay, Nassau, Duval, St. Johns, and Flagler. Central Florida: Volusia, Brevard, St. Lucie, Orange, Seminole, Lake, Polk, and Highlands. South Florida: Collier, Martin, Palm Beach, and Broward.

376. Hairgrass
or Hairawn Muhly

Poaceae or Gramineae (grass family)
Muhlenbergia capillaris (Lamarck) Trinius
var. *trichopodes* (Elliott) Vasey

Description: Perennial grass to 3 ft tall or
more. Stems (culms) slender, nearly glabrous.
Stem branches flexible. Leaf blades flat, becoming inturned toward the tips. Inflorescence may occupy about one-half the length
of the culm. Flowers purple. Seedheads
(spikelets) terminate the thin, elongated
branches, hence the name "hairgrass." Fruit a
grain or caryopsis.

Flowering time: October–November.

Habitat: Coastal grasslands, coastal hammocks, sandhills, pine flatwoods, beach
dunes, coastal strand, and disturbed sites.

Range: Panhandle: Escambia, Gadsden, Leon,
Wakulla, and Franklin. North Florida: Madison, Taylor, Dixie, Suwannee, Columbia,
Alachua, Nassau, Duval, and St. Johns. West
coastal counties from Hernando south
through Monroe. East coastal counties:
Brevard, Palm Beach, Dade, and the Keys.

Comment: An attractive grass often used in
landscaping.

377. Bitter Panicum, Beachgrass,
or Dune Panic Grass

Poaceae or Gramineae (grass family)
Panicum amarum Elliott

Description: Perennial grass with stout, glabrous stems (culms). Foliage bluish green.
Plant grows in clumps to 5 ft tall. Leaves alternate, blades flat, leathery. Margins smooth,
turned down at the tips. Inflorescence compact, branching, erect to nodding. Seedheads
(spikelets) ovate, glabrous, over $^2/_{16}$ inch long.
Fruit a grain or caryopsis.

Flowering time: August–October.

Habitat: Coastal grasslands, beach dunes,
coastal swales, salt marshes, and disturbed
sites.

Range: Throughout coastal counties, except
Indian River, Charlotte, Sarasota, Pasco and
north to Wakulla, Gulf, and Walton.

Comment: An important dune builder.

Synonym: *Panicum amarulum* Hitchcock &
Chase

378. Sea Oats

Poaceae or Gramineae (grass family)
Uniola paniculata Linnaeus

Description: Glabrous perennial, often in clumps. Root system extensive. Leaves flat, becoming inturned at the flexous tips. Stem (culm) rigid, to 6 ft tall or more. Branches arching, terminating in a drooping inflorescence. Seedheads (spikelets) flat, straw-colored or purplish, about 1 inch long. Fruit a grain or caryopsis.

Flowering time: June–September.

Habitat: Coastal grasslands, coastal strand, and beach dunes.

Range: Coastal counties, except north of Hillsborough to Wakulla; Gulf, Flagler, and Broward.

Comment: Sea oats are important dune builders and are protected throughout Florida. Several species of grasses called sandspurs (*Cenchrus*) occur in Florida. Most people who have walked in sandy soils have felt the sharp spines on the burs. *Cenchrus incertus* occurs in coastal sites, sandhills, and ruderal areas. Stems are often purplish at the base. Spines number 25 or fewer.

Coastal Scrubs

379. Coastal Scrub at Cape Canaveral Air Station, Brevard County, Florida. July 3, 1996. The low-growing trees are scrub live oak (*Quercus geminata*).

380. Yaupon Holly or Yaupon

Aquifoliaceae (holly family)
Ilex vomitoria Aiton

Description: Usually a woody shrub, but may reach 25 ft tall. Leaves evergreen, alternate, leathery, dark green above, paler below. Blades 1 inch long or less. Margins scalloped. Male and female flowers in the leaf axils of separate plants. Corolla 4-lobed, white. Drupe red, with 4 seeds.

Flowering time: March–May.

Habitat: Coastal and inland scrubs, coastal strand, coastal grasslands, coastal hammocks, coastal pine flatwoods, upland mixed forests, and river swamps.

Range: Panhandle: Throughout, except Calhoun. North Florida: Throughout, except Madison, Union, Bradford, Lafayette, Gilchrist, and Putnam. Central Florida: Coastal counties from Citrus south to Charlotte; Volusia, Brevard, St. Lucie, Polk, and Highlands.

Comment: Used as a landscape plant. Leaves and twigs contain caffeine. Male southern Indians made an emetic decoction called "black drink" from its leaves. Large quantities were swallowed but usually not retained, hence the name "vomitoria."

381. Woody Goldenrod or Bush Goldenrod

Asteraceae or Compositae (daisy or sunflower family)
Chrysoma pauciflosculosa (Michaux) Greene

Description: Bushy-branched evergreen shrub. Stems glabrous, round in cross section, to 3 ft tall or more. Leaves alternate, sessile, grayish green. Margins entire. Heads sticky, in clusters of yellow flowers. Achenes with numerous bristles.

Flowering time: November.

Habitat: Coastal scrubs, beach dunes, coastal grasslands, and sandhills.

Range: Panhandle: Liberty, Franklin, Gulf, Bay, Washington, Walton, Okaloosa, Santa Rosa, and Escambia.

Synonym: *Solidago pauciflosculosa* Michaux

382. Love Vine or Dodder

Convolvulaceae (morning-glory family)
Cuscuta pentagona Engelmann

Description: Twining vine with slender, yellowish brown stems. Plant often matted. Leaves scalelike. Flowers tiny, whitish yellow in loose clusters. Corolla 5-lobed, lobes triangular (magnification needed). Fruit a capsule.

Flowering time: May–October.

Habitat: Coastal scrubs, coastal dunes, brackish marshes, open woods, thickets, and ruderal.

Range: Panhandle: Leon, Gadsden, Franklin, Bay, Walton, Okaloosa, Santa Rosa, and Escambia. North Florida: Columbia, Bradford, Alachua, Levy, Marion, Putnam, Flagler, St. Johns, Duval, and Nassau. Central Florida: Citrus, Pasco, Pinellas, Hillsborough, Highlands, Polk, Lake, Orange, Seminole, Volusia, and Brevard. South Florida: Charlotte, Lee, Collier, Glades, Palm Beach, and Dade.

Comment: Parasitic on a variety of plants. Heavy growth may be destructive to the host.

Synonym: *Cuscuta campestris* Yuncker

383. Feay's Prairie-clover

Fabaceae or Leguminosae (bean or pea family)
Dalea feayi (Chapman) Barneby

Description: Branched herb to 2 ft tall. Leaves alternate, gland-dotted. Leaflets 3–9, narrow, short. Margins turned down. Flowers many, pink to rose purple, in globular terminal spikes. Stamens 5. Legume straight.

Flowering time: May–July.

Habitat: Coastal and inland scrubs and sandhills.

Range: Panhandle: Wakulla and Franklin. North Florida: Putnam, Alachua, and Marion. Central Florida: Throughout, except Pinellas, Manatee, Sarasota, Hardee, De Soto, Okeechobee, Indian River, Osceola, and Seminole. South Florida: Martin and Palm Beach.

Synonym: *Petalostemon feayi* Chapman

384. Love Vine or Woevine

Lauraceae (laurel family)
Cassytha filiformis Linnaeus

Description: Parasitic or hemiparasitic herbaceous vine. Stems yellowish or pale green, glabrous, often forming dense tangles. Leaves absent or scale-like. Flowers inconspicuous, sessile, in small spikes. Sepals 6, whitish. Petals lacking. Fertile stamens 9, infertile stamens 3. Drupe globose, white when ripe.

Flowering time: January–November.

Habitat: Coastal scrubs, coastal strand, and hammocks.

Range: Coastal counties: Pinellas south through Monroe; Brevard south through the Keys. Inland counties: Hillsborough, Polk, and Highlands.

Comment: Plant has a spicy odor. Resembles dodder (*Cuscuta* spp.) of the morning-glory family. Lovevine attaches to various host plants by root-like structures, but rarely kills the hosts. The related silk bay (*Persea humilis*) occurs in scrubs. This aromatic evergreen shrub or small tree has rusty hairs on the lower leaf surface.

Temperate Coastal Hammocks

385. A Coastal Hammock, Castle Windy, Canaveral National Seashore, Volusia County, Florida. April 8, 1995. Note the saw palmettos (*Serenoa repens*) in the foreground and resurrection ferns (*Polypodium polypodioides*) on the Virginia live oak (*Quercus virginiana*).

386. False Mint

Acanthaceae (acanthus family)
Dicliptera sexangularis (Linnaeus) Jussieu

Description: Perennial branched herb to 3 ft
tall. Leaves opposite, entire, elliptic-lanceolate
to ovate. Flowers in terminal or axillary
spikes. Calyx 5-lobed. Corolla 2-lipped, red.
Stamens 2. Fruit a capsule.

Flowering time: April–October.

Habitat: Coastal hammocks, shell mounds,
and ruderal.

Range: Panhandle: Calhoun. North Florida:
Levy. Central Florida: Citrus, Brevard, Polk,
Hardee, De Soto. South Florida: Martin,
Broward, Dade, Monroe, Collier, Lee, and the
Keys.

Synonym: *Dicliptera assurgens* (Linnaeus)
Jussieu

387. Rubber Vine

Apocynaceae (dogbane family)
Rhabdadenia biflora (Jacquin) Muller
Argoviensis

Description: Erect, viny shrub or twining vine
with smooth stems. Sap milky. Leaves opposite, oblong or widest at the base, petioles
pinkish orange. Venation feathery, conspicuous. Margins entire. Flowers funnellike, about
2 inches across, in leaf axils. Calyx 5-lobed.
Corolla 5-lobed, white with a yellow throat.
Seedpod elongated.

Flowering time: January–December.

Habitat: Coastal hammocks, coastal strand,
and mangrove swamps.

Range: East Coast: Brevard south through the
Keys. South Florida: Lee and Collier.

388. Coastal Cynanchum

Asclepiadaceae (milkweed family)
Cynanchum angustifolium Persoon

Description: Glabrous vine with twining or trailing stems. Leaves mostly opposite, narrow, sessile, drooping. Flowers in stalked clusters. Calyx 5-lobed. Corolla 5-lobed, greenish white to purplish. Seedpods glabrous, narrow.

Flowering time: April–October.

Habitat: Coastal hammocks, coastal swales, and coastal marshes.

Range: Coastal counties, except Flagler, Martin to Dade, Manatee, and Santa Rosa. Inland county: Polk.

Synonym: *Cynanchum palustre* (Pursh) A. Heller

389. Scorpion-tail

Boraginaceae (borage family)
Heliotropium angiospermum Murray

Description: Annual to 3 ft tall. Stems branched, haired, ascending. Leaves veiny, entire, broadest at the middle. Flowers small, tubular, paired, in 1 or 2 curved spikes. Calyx 5-lobed. Corolla 5-lobed, white. Fruit a schizocarp covered with minute scales, forming 4 mericarps.

Flowering time: January–December.

Habitat: Coastal hammocks, shell mounds, and ruderal.

Range: Coastal counties: Volusia south through the Keys. Monroe north to Pasco.

Synonym: *Schobera angiosperma* (Murray) Britton

390. Coco-plum

Chrysobalanaceae (chrysobalanus family)
Chrysobalanus icaco Linnaeus

Description: Usually a branched evergreen shrub, but can be a small tree to 15 ft tall. Leaves alternate, leathery. Blades rounded. Margins entire. Flowers bell-shaped, pubescent, fragrant, in axillary clusters. Calyx 5-lobed. Petals 5, white. Stamens many. Drupe spherical, creamy to purple.

Flowering time: February–April; sporadically at other times.

Habitat: Coastal hammocks, beach dunes, coastal strand, swamps, and bayheads.

Range: Coastal counties: Brevard south through the Keys. Monroe north to Manatee. Inland county: Glades.

Comment: Fruit can be eaten raw or made into jellies. The edible seeds taste like almonds. Important food for Seminole Indians. Used as a landscape plant.

Synonym: *Chrysobalanus interior* Small

391. Buttonwood

Combretaceae (Indian-almond or white mangrove family)
Conocarpus erectus Linnaeus

Description: Evergreen shrub or tree to 60 ft tall or more (usually less). Leaves alternate, glabrous, light green or silvery. Blades elliptic, margins entire. Two salt glands occur at the base of the leathery blades. Flowers small, whitish green, in buttonlike terminal heads. Sepals 5. Petals lacking. Fruit small, reddish green, buttonlike cones.

Flowering time: March–September; sporadically at other times.

Habitat: Coastal hammocks, coastal dunes, coastal strand, coastal grasslands, and coastal swamps.

Range: Coastal counties: Volusia south through the Keys. Monroe north to Dixie.

Comment: The hard wood is used to make charcoal to smoke meats and fish. The silver buttonwood (*Conocarpus erectus* var. *sericeus*) of South Florida, with silvery gray branches and leaves, was once considered a separate species.

392. Leadtree or Jumbie Bean

Fabaceae or Leguminosae (bean or pea family)
Leucaena leucocephala (Lamarck) de Wit

Description: Spineless shrub or small tree to 30 ft tall. Leaves alternate, twice compound with many opposite leaflets. Flowers in a round, white to yellowish, globular head. Petals 5. Stamens 10, white to pinkish. Legumes reddish brown, flat, often clustered.

Flowering time: January–May.

Habitat: Coastal hammocks, coastal strands, and ruderal.

Range: North Florida: Alachua. Central Florida: Hernando, Pinellas, Hillsborough, Manatee, Lake, Seminole, Volusia, Brevard, St. Lucie, and Highlands. South Florida: Lee, Collier, Dade, Palm Beach, and the Keys.

Comment: Introduced from the American tropics. Can be a pest plant. Roasted seeds were used as a coffee substitute.

Synonym: *Leucaena glauca* Bentham

393. Red Bay

Lauraceae (laurel family)
Persea borbonia (Linnaeus) Sprengel

Description: Evergreen, aromatic, large shrub or tree to 60 ft tall or more. Leaves alternate, glossy green above, grayish below, ends often tapered. Flowers yellowish green, clustered in leaf axils or terminal. Perianth bell-shaped, with 6 tepals. Drupe dark blue or black.

Flowering time: April–October; December–February.

Habitat: Coastal hammocks, coastal strand, oak scrubs, and upland mixed forests.

Range: Panhandle: Santa Rosa, Walton, and Bay. North Florida: Throughout, except Madison, Taylor, Lafayette, Baker, Union, and Bradford. Central Florida: Throughout, except Lake, Osceola, Hardee, and De Soto. South Florida: Collier and Lee; coastal counties from Martin south through the Keys.

Comment: Wood from this bay has been used for making cabinets. Leaves used for teas and for flavoring meats and soups. Can be a substitute for store-bought bay leaf.

394. Bladder Mallow

Malvaceae (mallow family)
Herissantia crispa (Linnaeus) Brizicky

Description: Viny herb, erect or prostrate. Leaves alternate, heart-shaped, toothed. Flowers small, delicate, solitary. Calyx 5-lobed, hairy. Petals 5, pale yellow to whitish. Fruit white or light green, papery, becoming inflated.

Flowering time: May.

Habitat: Coastal hammocks, pinelands, and ruderal.

Range: Central Florida: Brevard. South Florida: Lee, Collier, Monroe, Dade, and the Keys.

Synonym: *Gayoides crispum* (Linnaeus) Small

395. Pavonia

Malvaceae (mallow family)
Pavonia spinifex (Linnaeus) Cavanilles

Description: Low-growing herb or shrub to 9 ft tall. Branches hairy, often trailing. Leaves alternate, ovate, toothed, hairy. Flowers in axils of leaves. Calyx 5-lobed. Petals 5, yellow, reddish, or white. Five bracts below the calyx. Fruit a capsule, with spiny projections.

Flowering time: August–October.

Habitat: Coastal hammocks and ruderal.

Range: North Florida: Duval and Flagler. Central Florida: Volusia, Brevard, Citrus, Polk, and Alachua. A relative found in coastal hammocks is the seaside mahoe (*Thespesia populnea*). This tree has heart-shaped leaves with conspicuous veins, entire margins, and long petioles. The solitary, tubular flowers are yellow, changing to purple in the afternoon. Capsules hard, 5-parted, somewhat flattened on all sides.

Comment: Native to South America.

396. Florida Privet

Oleaceae (olive family)
Forestiera segregata (Jacquin) Krug & Urban

Description: Shrub or small tree to 10 ft tall.
Bark grayish, smooth. Leaves opposite, tapered at the base, dark green and shiny
above, paler and veiny below. Margins entire.
Male and female flowers separate. Flowers
clustered on the branches. Tepals small,
greenish yellow. Drupe blue purple.

Flowering time: January–November.

Habitat: Coastal hammocks, coastal strand,
coastal scrubs, pinelands, and marshes.

Range: Coastal counties: Duval south
through the Keys; Dixie south through the
Keys. Inland county: Glades.

Synonyms: *Forestiera globularis* Small;
Forestiera porulosa (Michaux) Poiret

397. Rouge Plant or Bloodberry

Phytolaccaceae (pokeweed family)
Rivina humilis Linnaeus

Description: Erect herb or woody-base shrub
to 3 ft tall. Branches viny. Leaves alternate,
tapered toward apex. Flowers in short, terminal clusters, pink and white. Tepals 4. Stamens 4. Mature fruit a bright red berry.

Flowering time: January–December.

Habitat: Coastal hammocks, coastal dunes,
and disturbed sites.

Range: North Florida: Levy, Marion,
Alachua, and Duval. Central Florida:
Throughout, except Okeechobee. South Flor-
ida: Throughout.

398. Wild Plumbago

Plumbaginaceae (leadwort family)
Plumbago scandens Linnaeus

Description: Perennial with brittle, viny, partially woody stems that climb, recline, or are erect. Leaves alternate, entire, clasping. Flowers terminal, short-stalked, in spikelike clusters. Calyx 5-lobed, glandular. Corolla white, 5-lobed, tubular. Stamens 5, anthers black.

Flowering time: April–November.

Habitat: Coastal hammocks, shell mounds, and disturbed sites.

Range: Coastal counties: Volusia south through the Keys; Monroe, Collier, Lee, Manatee, and Levy.

399. Rattan Vine or Supplejack

Rhamnaceae (buckthorn family)
Berchemia scandens (Hill) K. Koch

Description: Vigorous climbing or clambering vine with glabrous, round stems. Leaves alternate, glabrous, elliptic, darker green above. Margins entire or wavy. Featherlike veins prominent on leaves. Flowers mostly in a terminal, elongated inflorescence. Flowers small, greenish white. Petals 5. Stamens 5. Mature drupe dark purple, ellipsoid.

Flowering time: March–April; September.

Habitat: Coastal hammocks, pine flatwoods, creek swamps, floodplains, and ruderal.

Range: Panhandle: Throughout, except Okaloosa, Holmes, Bay, and Jefferson. North Florida: Taylor, Dixie, Levy, Marion, Alachua, Columbia, Suwannee, Putnam, Clay, Duval, and Nassau. Central Florida: Throughout, except Manatee, Sarasota, Hardee, De Soto, Polk, Okeechobee, and St. Lucie. South Florida: Martin, Palm Beach, Dade, Monroe (except the Keys), Collier, and Lee.

400. Seven-year Apple

Rubiaceae (madder family)
Genipa clusiifolia (Jacquin) Grisbach

Description: Evergreen shrub or tree to 10 ft
tall or more. Leaves opposite, glossy green
above, petioled, leathery. Leaves tend to cluster near ends of branches. Flowers clustered
in leaf axils near ends of branches. Flowers
fragrant, star-shaped, white, fleshy. Calyx and
petals 5-lobed. Berry large, pulpy.

Flowering time: All year.

Habitat: Coastal hammocks and coastal
strand.

Range: Coastal counties: Broward, Dade, the
Keys, Collier, and Lee.

Comment: The yellow brown, hard wood has
been used to make tool handles. Used in ornamental plantings. Pear-shaped fruit tastes
like dried apples. A relative, the beach creeper
(*Ernodea littoralis*), occurs in coastal hammocks and dune crests lacking a shrub community. This woody shrub has narrow, fleshy-
leathery, 1-inch-long leaves that are often
clustered at the branch tips. Flowers small,
pinkish to white. Drupe small, ovoid, yellow.

Synonym: *Casasia clusiifolia* (Jacquin) Urban

401. Wild Coffee

Rubiaceae (madder family)
Psychotria nervosa Swartz

Description: Woody evergreen shrub to 6 ft
tall or more. Stems glabrous. Leaves opposite,
entire. Blades glossy green above, paler below, strongly veined. Flowers greenish white,
clustered in the leaf axils or terminal. Calyx
and corolla 4- or 5-lobed. Drupe usually red,
oval.

Flowering time: March–August; sporadically
at other times.

Habitat: Coastal hammocks, swampy woods,
tropical hardwood hammocks, and pinelands.

Range: North Florida: Duval, Flagler,
Marion, Alachua, and Levy. Central Florida:
Throughout, except Sumter and Okeechobee.
South Florida: Throughout, except Glades.

Comment: Roasted seeds have been used as a
coffee substitute. Teas from the leaves have
been consumed for colds and stomach ailments.

Synonym: *Psychotria undata* Jacquin

402. Sulzner's Wild Coffee

Rubiaceae (madder family)
Psychotria sulzneri Small

Description: Evergreen shrub to 6 ft tall. Stems pubescent. Leaves opposite, entire, strongly veined. Leaf surfaces dull bluish green. Flowers greenish white, sessile, in the leaf axils or terminal. Calyx and corolla 4- or 5-lobed. Drupe red, yellow or orange, oval.

Flowering time: Spring-summer.

Habitat: Coastal hammocks, tropical hardwood hammocks, and swampy woods.

Range: Central Florida: Throughout, except Hernando, Pinellas, Hardee, Orange, and Seminole. South Florida: Throughout, except Charlotte, Glades, Hendry, and the Keys.

403. Indigo-berry or White Indigo-berry

Rubiaceae (madder family)
Randia aculeata Linnaeus

Description: Usually an evergreen shrub with paired spines and opposite branches. Leaves opposite, shiny above, glabrous, widest at or above the middle. Leaves often clustered at the ends of branches. Flowers fragrant, white, 5-lobed, in the leaf axils. Berry white to greenish white.

Flowering time: January–July; sporadically at other times.

Habitat: Coastal hammocks, beach dunes, coastal grasslands, coastal strand, scrubs, and pinelands.

Range: Coastal counties: Brevard south through the Keys. Monroe to Manatee; Hillsborough.

Comment: Fruit has been used to treat dysentery. The hard wood is used to make cooking tools and fishing poles. Used as a Christmas tree in Puerto Rico and may be cultivated as an ornamental.

404. Wild Lime

Rutaceae (rue or citrus family)
Zanthoxylum fagara (Linnaeus) Sargent

Description: Spiny evergreen shrub or tree to 30 ft tall. Leaves alternate, compound. Leaflets 7–9, oval. Leaf stem (rachis) between leaflets winged. Male and female flowers on separate plants, clustered in axils of leaves. Sepals 4. Petals 4, greenish yellow. Stamens 4. Fruit red to yellow brown. Seeds shiny black cling to the open, brownish husk.

Flowering time: January–August.

Habitat: Coastal hammocks and coastal strand.

Range: North Florida: Marion. Central Florida: Citrus, Sumter, Osceola, Volusia, Brevard, Indian River, St. Lucie, Highlands, Polk, Hardee, De Soto, Sarasota, Manatee, Pinellas, and Hillsborough. South Florida: Throughout, except Glades.

Comment: Plant smells like lemon. Wood is prized for cabinetry.

405. Marine Vine or Sorrel Vine

Vitaceae (grape family)
Cissus trifoliata (Linnaeus) Linnaeus

Description: Deciduous climbing vine with unbranched tendrils. Stems warty, producing aerial roots. Leaves alternate, fleshy. Leaflets 3. Blades wedge-shaped, toothed. Flowers small, greenish yellow, in clusters. Sepals 4. Petals 4. Mature berry bluish black, inedible.

Flowering time: May–October.

Habitat: Coastal hammocks, dunes, and shell mounds.

Range: Panhandle: Escambia, Gulf, Wakulla, and Leon. North Florida: Flagler. Central Florida: Volusia, Brevard, St. Lucie, Pinellas, Hillsborough, and Manatee. South Florida: Martin, Dade, the Keys, Monroe, Collier, and Lee.

Synonym: *Cissus incisa* (Nuttall ex Torrey & A. Gray) Des Moulins

406. Summer Grape

Vitaceae (grape family)
Vitis aestivalis Michaux

Description: Woody vine that climbs using forked tendrils opposite the leaves. Leaves heart-shaped, often with 3–5 lobes. Margins toothed. Mature leaves with rusty hairs below. Sepals lacking lobes. Petals 5, greenish. Berries in leaf axils, purple when ripe.

Flowering time: May–July.

Habitat: Coastal hammocks, coastal strand, upland mixed forests, and thickets.

Range: Panhandle: Throughout, except Escambia, Santa Rosa, Holmes, Bay, Gulf, and Gadsden. North Florida: Madison, Suwannee, Columbia, Baker, Bradford, Alachua, Clay, Putnam, Nassau, Duval, and Flagler. Central Florida: Throughout, except Manatee, Hardee, De Soto, Okeechobee, Indian River, and St. Lucie. South Florida: Martin, Palm Beach, Broward, Dade, Monroe, Collier, Hendry, and Lee.

Synonym: *Vitis rufotomentosa* Small

Shell Mounds

407. Turtle Mound is one of Florida's oldest and largest shell mounds. The mound is composed largely of oyster shells and supports both tropical and temperate plants. It is located south of New Smyrna on north Canaveral National Seashore in Volusia County, Florida.

Rockland Pinelands

Above: 408. Rockland Pineland, Everglades National Park, Dade County, Florida. March 8, 1994. Effects of Hurricane Andrew can be seen in this photograph.

Right: 409. Solution hole in the limestone floor of a Rockland Pineland, Everglades National Park, Dade County, Florida. March 9, 1994. The sharp-edged holes can damage a leg.

410. Rockland Ruellia

Acanthaceae (acanthus family)
Ruellia succulenta Small

Description: Perennial herb with stiff, succulent stems to 20 inches long. Leaves opposite, petioled, mostly entire, deep purplish blue. Flowers tubular, purplish blue, sessile in the leaf axils. Calyx lobes 5, narrow. Corolla 5-lobed. Stamens 4. Fruit a cylindrical capsule.

Flowering time: All year.

Habitat: Rockland pinelands.

Range: South Florida: Lee, Collier, Monroe, Dade, and the Keys.

Comment: Endemic to Florida.

Synonyms: *Ruellia caroliniensis* (J. F. Gmelin) Steudel var. *succulenta* (Small) R. W. Long; *Ruellia heteromorpha* Fernald

411. Rubber Vine
or Devil's Potato

Apocynaceae (dogbane family)
Echites umbellata Jacquin

Description: Evergreen twining or climbing vine. Stems glabrous, with milky sap. Leaves opposite, petioled. Blades oval, margins entire. Flowers stalked, white or greenish, clustered in axils of leaves. Calyx short, glandular inside. Flowers tubular, 5-lobed, lobes twisted. Seedpods paired, narrow, elongated.

Flowering time: June–October; sporadically at other times.

Habitat: Rockland pinelands, coastal strand, and margins of hammocks.

Range: Coastal counties from Brevard south to the Keys; Monroe and Lee.

Comment: This plant, like its widely introduced relative the oleander (*Nerium oleander*), is very toxic and should be avoided. The wild allamanda (*Pentalinon luteum*) of south Florida pinelands and hammocks is another related species. This vine or scrambling shrub has clusters of bright yellow flowers about 2 inches across.

Synonym: *Echites echites* (Linnaeus) Britton

412. Silver Thatch Palm, Silver Palm, or Biscayne Palm

Arecaceae (palm family)
Coccothrinax argentata (Jacquin) L. H. Bailey

Description: Shrub or tree to 20 ft tall or more. Trunk unbranched, smooth, grayish to brown, terminated by a crown of leaves. Leaves fan-shaped, green above, silvery below. Petioles unarmed, midrib orangish. Flowers whitish, fragrant, in a 2-ft cluster. Stamens 11 or 12. Mature berrylike fruit round, purple or black, 1-seeded.

Flowering time: Spring.

Habitat: Rockland pinelands and coastal dunes.

Range: South Florida: Palm Beach south to the Keys; Monroe.

Comment: Commercially exploited in Florida. Uncommon within Everglades National Park, but common in limestone pinelands outside the park. Terminal buds edible. Leaves used in making hats, baskets, and mats.

413. Blodgett's Cynanchum

Asclepiadaceae (milkweed family)
Cynanchum blodgettii (A. Gray) Shinners

Description: Twining vine, leaves usually persistent on older branches. Leaves opposite, linear. Flowers small, in stalked axillary clusters. Calyx 5-lobed, lobes ovate. Corolla 5-lobed, white, hairy inside. Seedpods linear.

Flowering time: Spring–fall.

Habitat: Pinelands, tropical hammocks, and sandy soils.

Range: Dade and the Keys.

Synonym: *Metastelma blodgettii* A. Gray

414. Pineland Heliotrope

Boraginaceae (borage family)
Heliotropium polyphyllum Lehmann

Description: Perennial herb. Stems hairy to 30 inches tall. Leaves alternate, numerous, sessile or nearly so. Blades narrow, lower surfaces densely pubescent. Margins entire. Flowers in curved, usually paired, spikes. Calyx 5-lobed. Corolla 5-lobed, yellow or white. Stamens 5. Fruit a schizocarp, producing 4 mericarps.

Flowering time: All year.

Habitat: Pinelands, brackish shores, prairies, pond margins, and ruderal.

Range: Coastal counties: Flagler south through the Keys. Monroe north to Taylor. Escambia. Inland counties: Gilchrist, Sumter, Polk, Osceola, Highlands, Okeechobee, De Soto, Glades, and Hendry.

Synonym: *Heliotropium polyphyllum* Lehmann var. *horizontale* (Small) R. W. Long

415. Pineland Clustervine or Pineland Jacquemontia

Convolvulaceae (morning-glory family)
Jacquemontia curtissii Peter ex Hallier f.

Description: Prostrate or erect perennial vine. Stems semiwoody, to 3 ft long. Vine glabrous or pubescent. Leaves alternate, elliptic or spatulate. Flowers white, clustered in the leaf axils. Calyx and petals 5-lobed. Stamens 5. Stigmas 2. Fruit a capsule, producing 4 seeds.

Flowering time: January–December.

Habitat: Rockland pinelands and ruderal.

Range: South Florida: Glades, Dade, Monroe, and the Keys.

Comment: Endemic to and endangered in Florida. The genus was named for the French botanical explorer Victor Jacquemont (1801–1832). A related species of south Florida pinelands and hammocks is *Jacquemontia pentantha*. It has twining and trailing stems and the small flowers are blue.

416. Rockland Spurge

Euphorbiaceae (spurge family)
Chamaesyce conferta Small

Description: Prostrate or decumbent herb with hairy, reddish stems. Leaves opposite, elliptic to ovate. Margins finely toothed. Leaves of the flowering branch reduced in size. Flowers small, in a cup-shaped structure called a cyathium. Cyathia congested, bearing loose hairs. Petaloid appendages red or magenta, unequal in size, toothed. Capsule minutely pubescent.

Flowering time: All year.

Habitat: Rockland pinelands.

Range: South Florida: Broward, Dade, Monroe, and the Keys.

Comment: Endemic to South Florida. Occurs in the Everglades National Park and near Homestead. A related species of south Florida is *Chamaesyce deltoidea*. The stems are prostrate and wiry, and form dense mats. Capsule is glabrous.

417. Pineland Croton

Euphorbiaceae (spurge family)
Croton linearis Jacquin

Description: Evergreen shrub to 6 ft tall. Leaves alternate, narrow, short-petioled. Blades glabrous above, with yellow or silvery hairs below. Male flowers with about 15 stamens, petals, and triangular sepals. Female flowers lack petals and are shorter than the male cluster. Capsule globose, with yellowish pubescence.

Flowering time: January–December.

Habitat: Rockland pinelands, scrubs, and coastal sites.

Range: South Florida: Martin, Palm Beach, Dade, and the Keys.

Comment: Leaves have been used for a tea.

Synonym: *Croton fergusonii* Small ex A. M. Ferguson

418. Rhynchosia

Fabaceae or Leguminosae (bean or pea family)
Rhynchosia parvifolia de Candolle

Description: Low-growing, prostrate or twining herb with velvety grayish hairs. Leaves alternate, long-petioled, leaflets 3. Blades broad, thickish. Calyx 2-lipped, hairy, shorter than the corolla. Flowers pea-shaped, yellow. Legume elliptic, pubescent, glandular.

Flowering time: January–March.

Habitat: Rockland pinelands.

Range: South Florida: Dade and the Keys.

Synonym: *Leucopterum parvifolium* (de Candolle) Small

419. Bahama Senna

Fabaceae or Leguminosae (bean or pea family)
Senna mexicana (Jacquin) Irwin & Barneby var. *chapmanii* (Isely) Irwin & Barneby

Description: Shrub upright or sprawling. Stems glabrous, to 3 ft tall or more. Leaves alternate, leaflets 5 pairs or fewer. Flowers clustered, stalked in upper leaf axils or terminal. Calyx 5-lobed, yellowish. Petals 5, unequal, yellow orange with red veins. Stamens 7, anther reddish. Legume flat, brown; seeds shiny, brown.

Flowering time: March–May.

Habitat: Rockland pinelands, edges of hammocks, and coastal strand.

Range: South Florida: Dade and the Keys.

Comment: Plant apparently is salt tolerant.

Synonyms: *Cassia bahamensis* sensu R. W. Long & Lakela 1971, non Miller; *Cassia chapmanii* Isely

420. Locust-berry

Malpighiaceae (malpighia family)
Byrsonima lucida (Miller) de Candolle

Description: Multitrunked evergreen shrub or tree to 15 ft tall or more. Bark pale, smooth. Terminal twigs jointed. Leaves opposite, broadened upward. Blades entire, leathery, dark green above, paler below. Flowers in terminal clusters, white or pink turning rose. Sepals 5, bearing paired oil glands. Petals 5. Stamens 10. Mature fruit fleshy, red brownish, edible.

Flowering time: March–May.

Habitat: Rockland pinelands and hammocks.

Range: South Florida: Dade and the Keys.

Comment: A very attractive native shrub. Endangered in Florida.

Synonym: *Byrsonima cuneata* (Turczaninow) P. Wilson

421. Spanish Leather or Florida Tetrazygia

Melastomataceae (meadow beauty or melastoma family)
Tetrazygia bicolor (Miller) Cogniaux

Description: Woody shrub usually, but may grow to 20 ft tall or more. Leaves opposite, broadest near the base, dark green above and silvery below. Venation distinct. Flowers in a terminal cluster, white yellow. Petals 4–6. Stamens 8. Berry purplish black, globose.

Flowering time: March–August.

Habitat: Rockland pinelands, scrubs, and hammocks.

Range: South Florida: Dade and Monroe (except the Keys).

Comment: Plant sometimes called "jewel of the Everglades" because of its attractiveness. Threatened in Florida.

422. Myrsine or Guiana Rapanea

Myrsinaceae (myrsine family)
Myrsine floridana Alph. de Candolle

Description: Evergreen shrub or small tree to 25 ft tall. Bark pale gray. Leaves alternate, leathery, often clustered at ends of branches. Leaf margins often curled under. Male and female flowers separate. Flowers small, white with some purple. Flowers and fruit clustered tightly on the branches. Drupe dark blue or black.

Flowering time: November–March.

Habitat: Rockland pinelands, coastal hammocks, and coastal strand.

Range: North Florida: Dixie and Levy. Central Florida: Throughout, except Hernando, Pasco, Sumter, Orange, Okeechobee, and De Soto. South Florida: Throughout.

Comment: The long-stalked stopper (*Psidium longipes*) of the family Myrtaceae is also found in the pinelands. This scrub has glossy opposite leaves and white flowers and fruits on very long stalks. Fruit fleshy, red turning black.

Synonyms: *Myrsine guianensis* sensu R. K. Godfrey & Wooten 1982, non (Aublet) Kuntze; *Rapanea guianensis* sensu Small 1933, non Aublet; *Rapanea punctata* (Lamarck) Lundell

423. Pine-pink

Orchidaceae (orchid family)
Bletia purpurea (Lamarck) de Candolle

Description: Mainly terrestrial to 3 ft tall or more. Flowering stem leafless, arising to the sides of the leaves. Leaves basal, grasslike, narrowing at the base. Flowers many, stalked, pink to rose purple. Lower lip recurved, 3-lobed, with reddish purple veins and yellowish ridges. Fruit a cylindrical capsule.

Flowering time: February–April.

Habitat: Rockland pinelands and scrubs.

Range: Central Florida: Polk and Highlands. South Florida: Palm Beach, Broward, Dade, the Keys, Monroe, Collier, and Lee.

Comment: Threatened in Florida.

424. Corky-stemmed Passion-flower

Passifloraceae (passion-flower family)
Passiflora suberosa Linnaeus

Description: Vine with smooth branches and axillary tendrils. Leaves alternate, entire or 3-lobed. Gland on leaf stalk. Flowers usually solitary in the leaf axils, greenish with yellow and purple. Corona filamentous, greenish. Petals lacking. Mature berry purplish black.

Flowering time: January–December.

Habitat: Rockland pinelands, hammocks, pinelands, coastal strand, and ruderal.

Range: North Florida: Dixie, Levy, Suwannee, and Columbia. Central Florida: Throughout, except Pasco, Sumter, Manatee, De Soto, Hardee, Highlands, Okeechobee, Osceola, and Seminole. South Florida: Martin, Palm Beach, Broward, Dade, the Keys, Monroe, Collier, Lee, Charlotte, and Hendry.

Comment: The raw fruit is edible. The zebra butterfly (Heliconidae) lays its eggs on this and other passion-flowers.

Synonym: *Passiflora pallida* Linnaeus

425. Boykin's Polygala

Polygalaceae (milkwort family)
Polygala boykinii Nuttall

Description: Herb with erect, slender stems to 25 inches tall. Leaves whorled; lower ones reduced, upper ones linear to elliptic. Inflorescence cylindrical, spikelike, terminal. Sepals 5; outer 3 small, inner 2 large (wings). Petals 3, fused, greenish white or white. Lower petal fringed. Capsule spheroid.

Flowering time: March–July

Habitat: Rockland pinelands, prairies, secondary woods, and ruderal.

Range: Panhandle: Jackson, Gadsden, and Leon. West coastal counties: Taylor south to (including) Dade, the Keys.

Synonyms: *Polygala flagellaris* Small; *Polygala praetervisa* Chodat

426. Snowberry

Rubiaceae (madder family)
Chiococca alba (Linnaeus) Hitchcock

Description: Evergreen shrub to 10 ft tall (usually less). Bark yellowish gray. Branches slender, glabrous, may be viny. Leaves opposite, ovate, leathery. Margins entire. Flowers fragrant, bell-shaped, creamy white. Sepals 5. Corolla lobes 5, short. Stamens 5. Drupe white, oblong.

Flowering time: March; June–November.

Habitat: Rockland pinelands, edges of hammocks, coastal strand, oak scrubs, and shell mounds.

Range: Coastal counties: Duval south through the Keys. Monroe north to Taylor. Inland county: Polk.

Comment: Two other woody members of the family found in the pinelands are the velvetseed (*Guettarda scabra*) and Indian mulberry (*Morinda royoc*). Flowers are small and white or reddish in both species. The elliptic to ovate leaves of the velvetseed are thick, rough to the touch, deeply veined, and with stiff tips that turn down. Blades of the mulberry become narrow at the base. The drupe of the velvetseed is red, velvety, and edible; the mulberry's drupe is yellowish and edible.

Synonyms: *Chiococca parvifolia* Wullschlaegel ex Grisebach; *Chiococca pinetorum* Britton

427. Varnish Leaf

Sapindaceae (soapberry family)
Dodonaea viscosa (Linnaeus) Jacquin

Description: Evergreen shrub or tree to 10 ft tall or more. Leaves alternate, simple, broadest at the ends. Upper leaf surface scaly, appearing varnished. Margins curled down. Flowers small, sticky, greenish yellow, in clusters. Petals lacking. Fruit a 3-winged capsule, yellow green turning to reddish brown.

Flowering time: October–May.

Habitat: Rockland pinelands, hammocks, and coastal strand.

Range: Coastal counties: St. Johns, Volusia south to Broward; Dade, the Keys, Monroe, Collier, Lee, Sarasota, Pinellas, and Hernando (introduced). Inland counties: Hillsborough and Highlands.

Comment: Resin coats and protects the leaves. Becomes more treelike in hammocks.

428. Willow Bustic or Bustic

Sapotaceae (sapodilla or sapote family)
Sideroxylon salicifolium (Linnaeus) Lamarck

Description: Evergreen woody shrub or tree to 30 ft tall. Bark grayish, milky sap, scaly, thornless. Leaves alternate, glabrous, widest near the middle, shiny above and dull green below. Midveins and petioles yellowish. Flowers fragrant, whitish, clustered on the stems. Corolla and calyx 5-lobed. Fertile stamens 5, infertile stamens 5. Berry black, ovoid.

Flowering time: February–June.

Habitat: Edges of rockland pinelands and tropical hammocks.

Range: South Florida: Martin, Palm Beach, Broward, Dade, Monroe, Collier, and the Keys.

Comment: Fruit and flowers produced on older branches. The fern in the background is bracken (*Pteridium aquilinum*).

Synonyms: *Bumelia salicifolia* (Linnaeus) Swartz; *Dipholis salicifolia* (Linnaeus) Alph. de Candolle

429. Mexican Alvaradoa

Simaroubaceae (alianthus or quassia family)
Alvaradoa amorphoides Liebmann

Description: Deciduous woody shrub or small tree to 30 ft tall (usually less). Leaves alternate, odd-pinnate. Leaflets about 1 inch long, usually more than 19. Male and female flowers on separate plants. Flowers tiny, greenish or yellowish white, in elongated drooping spikes. Female inflorescence plumelike. The 1-seeded, winged fruit is hairy and reddish with fringed margins.

Flowering time: February; September–October.

Habitat: Rockland pinelands and hammocks.

Range: South Florida: Dade.

Comment: Endangered in Florida. Species rare and local in the Everglades National Park and in remnant pinelands and hammock margins north of Homestead.

430. Ground Cherry
Solanaceae (nightshade family)
Physalis angustifolia Nuttall

Description: Herb with diffuse-branching stems. Older plants glabrous. Leaves alternate, linear, longer than wide, tapering into the petiole. Margins entire, blade thickish. Flowers solitary, nodding, bell-shaped, yellow with a purplish center. Stamens 5, inserted at the base of the corolla.

Flowering time: March–December.

Habitat: Rockland pinelands, beach dunes, and ruderal.

Range: Panhandle: Wakulla, Franklin, Gulf, Bay, Walton, Okaloosa, Santa Rosa, and Escambia. Southwest coastal counties from Pinellas and Hillsborough south to Monroe; the Keys.

Rockland Hardwood Hammocks

Above: 431. Edge of Mahogany Hammock, Everglades National Park, Dade County, Florida. March 13, 1996. The tallest tree is a West Indian mahogany (*Swietenia mahagoni*).

Right: 432. Royal palm (*Roystonea elata*) in the Fakahatchee Strand State Preserve, Collier County, Florida. April 24, 1993.

433. Poisonwood

Anacardiaceae (cashew or sumac family)
Metopium toxiferum (Linnaeus) Krug &
Urban

Description: Shrub or tree to 35 ft tall or
more. Leaves alternate, entire. Leaflets usually
3 to 7, leathery, petioled. Blades shiny green,
often black-spotted. Petioles and midveins yellowish. Male and female flowers on separate
plants. Flowers greenish yellow, in clusters
near the ends of branches. Petals, sepals, and
stamens 5. Mature drupe yellow orange.

Flowering time: March–June.

Habitat: Tropical and maritime hammocks,
rockland pinelands, coastal strand, and
coastal beach dunes.

Range: South Florida: Martin south to the
Keys; Monroe.

Comment: Often a shrub in the pinelands and
a tree in hammocks. Alkaloids in the plant's
sap may irritate the skin as with its relative,
poison ivy. White-crowned pigeons favor the
fruit.

434. Bushy Fleabane
or Sour-bush

Asteraceae or Compositae (daisy or sunflower
family)
Pluchea carolinensis (Jacquin) G. Don

Description: Shrub to about 10 ft tall,
branched, densely covered with grayish hairs.
Leaves alternate, petioled, elliptic to lanceolate. Margins entire or slightly toothed.
Flower clusters supported by a long, stout peduncle that arises from the upper leaf axils or
terminally. Florets tubular, pink, pale purple,
or white. Ray florets lacking. Fruit an achene.

Flowering time: February–June.

Habitat: In openings or edges of tropical hammocks and ruderal.

Range: Central Florida: Pinellas and
Hillsborough. South Florida: Collier,
Broward, Dade, and the Keys.

Comment: Plant odiferous.

Synonym: *Pluchea symphytifolia* (Mill.) Gillis

435. Hairy Tournefort

Boraginaceae (borage family)
Tournefortia hirsutissima Linnaeus

Description: Partly woody vine or viny shrub to about 7 ft tall. Stems stout, pubescent. Leaves alternate, petioled, pubescent. Margins entire, tapered at the ends. Flowers white, fragrant, in a curved spikelike inflorescence. Corolla and calyx lobes 5. Stamens 5. Drupes ovoid, unlobed, white.

Flowering time: February–March.

Habitat: Tropical hammocks.

Range: South Florida: Hendry, Collier, Monroe, Dade, and the Keys.

Comment: A related species that may be found in south Florida and along the southern coasts is *Tournefortia volubilis*. This slender, woody vine is less hairy than the above species. The flowers are greenish white and the drupes are lobed. The woody geiger tree (*Cordia sebestena*) of South Florida hammocks is another relative that has 5-lobed orange flowers and rough leaves that are broadest near the base. This plant is used as an ornamental.

436. Wild Pine

Bromeliaceae (pineapple or bromeliad family)
Tillandsia balbisiana Schultes & Schultes f.

Description: Erect or pendent epiphyte on trees and scrubs. Basal leaf sheaths inflated. Leaf blades recurved, narrowed to involuted tips. Flowers in spikelike inflorescence. Stem and floral bracts reddish, glabrous. Petals blue purple. Fruit a capsule that splits along the septa.

Flowering time: April.

Habitat: Tropical hammocks, rockland pinelands, cypress swamps, and scrubs.

Range: Central Florida: Hillsborough, Polk, Osceola, Indian River, Okeechobee, Highlands, De Soto. South Florida: Throughout.

Comment: Threatened in Florida. A more widespread relative is *Tillandsia setacea* of central and south Florida. The plant forms reddish clumps on tree trunks and branches. The needlelike, slender leaves become abruptly dilated at the bases. Flower spike consists of reddish bracts and purple flowers that are often shorter than the leaves.

437. Wild Pine

Bromeliaceae (pineapple or bromeliad family)
Tillandsia fasciculata Swartz

Description: Epiphyte on a variety of trees and shrubs. Leaves grayish green, stiff, recurved, in rosettes. Flower stalk covered with numerous bracts of green, yellow, white, or rose purple. Flower stalk equal to or shorter than the leaves. Flowers in narrow spikes. Petals 3, tubular, purplish. Stamens 3. Fruit a capsule that splits along the septa.

Flowering time: January–June.

Habitat: Tropical hammocks and cypress swamps.

Range: Central Florida: Throughout, except Manatee, Citrus, Hernando, Sumter, Lake, and Indian River. South Florida: Throughout.

Comment: Commercially exploited in Florida. A very large relative of central and south Florida is *Tillandsia utriculata*. It can be identified by the large, urn-shaped rosette of erect leaves and the long (to 3 ft or more) spike that bears the flowers with ivory white petals.

Synonym: *Tillandsia hystricina* Small

438. Gumbo-limbo

Burseraceae (bursera or torchwood family)
Bursera simaruba (Linnaeus) Sargent

Description: Deciduous tree to 60 ft tall. Bark thin, smooth. In older plants the bark becomes reddish and sheds in thin, papery strips. Leaves alternate, compound. Leaflets 3–9, glossy green, pointed, clustered near the ends of branches. Flowers tiny, greenish white. Male flowers 5-parted. Female flowers 3-parted. Fruit dark red, 3-angled.

Flowering time: March.

Habitat: Tropical hammocks, maritime hammocks, coastal strand, and shell middens.

Range: Coastal counties: Brevard south through the Keys. Monroe to Charlotte. Manatee, Pinellas, and Hillsborough. Inland county: Hendry.

Comment: Crushed leaves smell like turpentine. Rosin used as a cement for manufacturing varnish, treating gout, and mending glass and china.

Synonym: *Elaphrium simaruba* (Linnaeus) Rose

439. Wild Tamarind

Fabaceae or Leguminosae (bean and pea family)
Lysiloma latisiliquum (Linnaeus) Bentham

Description: Often a small tree, but may reach 60 ft tall. Bark pale gray. Leaves alternate, light green, twice-compound. Leaflets many, small. Flowers small, greenish white, in globular clusters. Legumes to 6 inches long, flat, papery. Legumes may remain on the plant for a long time.

Flowering time: April–May; August–October.

Habitat: Tropical hammocks and ruderal.

Range: South Florida: Dade, the Keys, Monroe, Collier, and Lee.

Comment: Salt tolerant. The hard wood is used to make boats. The related Jamaica dogwood (*Piscidia piscipula*) is a tree of South Florida, with compound leaves usually of 7 leaflets. The pink purple, pea-shaped flowers are in stalked clusters. Legume has 4 thin, papery wings.

Synonym: *Lysiloma bahamense* Bentham

440. Lancewood

Lauraceae (laurel family)
Nectandra coriacea (Swartz) Grisebach

Description: Evergreen shrub or small tree to 30 ft tall or more. Aromatic. Bark smooth, reddish or light gray. Leaves alternate, glossy green above, petioled. Margins entire. Midvein yellow. Flower clusters in leaf axils and terminal. Perianth of 6 tepals, creamy white, hairy within. Drupe ovoid, dark blue or black.

Flowering time: January–July.

Habitat: Tropical and coastal hammocks, pinelands, and coastal strand.

Range: Coastal counties: Volusia south through the Keys; Monroe and Collier. Inland county: Highlands.

Comment: The brown wood is used for cabinet work. Crushed leaves smell like the culinary herb bay leaf.

Synonym: *Ocotea coriacea* (Swartz) Britton

441. West Indian Mahogany

Meliaceae (mahogany family)
Swietenia mahagoni (Linnaeus) Jacquin

Description: Tree to 60 ft tall. Bark brown, scaly, deeply furrowed in older plants. Leaves alternate. Leaflets 4–8, dark green above, yellowish brownish below. Bases of leaflets unequal. Margins entire. Flowers fragrant, small, in the leaf axils. Petals 5, greenish or white. Stamens filaments fused, anthers 10. Capsule erect, woody gray with an orangish interior. Seeds winged.

Flowering time: May–June.

Habitat: Tropical hammocks.

Range: South Florida: Lee, Broward, Dade, the Keys, and Monroe.

Comment: The hard red brown wood is valued for furniture and for shipbuilding. Bark has been used as a substitute for quinine. A dominant canopy tree in the hammocks and commonly used as an ornamental. Endangered in Florida. The other member of this family in Florida is the introduced, naturalized, and widespread Chinaberry (*Melia azedarach*). This tree, native to Asia, is commonly used as an ornamental. The compound leaves, fragrant purple flowers, and globose, smooth, yellow drupes are characteristic of the species.

442. Strangler Fig or Golden Fig

Moraceae (mulberry family)
Ficus aurea Nuttall

Description: Tree to 50 ft tall or more, often with aerial roots. Bark smooth, gray to brownish. Sap milky. Leaves alternate, leathery, glabrous. Blades widest at the middle. Bases of leaves tapered. Midvein yellow, margins entire. Male and female flowers separate. Flowers small, inside a fleshy, globose receptacle in the leaf axils. Red purple or yellow fig sessile on the branch.

Flowering time: March–May.

Habitat: Tropical and coastal hammocks, coastal strand, and shell mounds.

Range: Central Florida: Volusia, Brevard, Indian River, St. Lucie, Okeechobee, Highlands, Sarasota, Manatee, Hillsborough, and Pinellas. South Florida: Throughout.

Comment: Plant wraps aerial roots around its host, which the fig eventually kills, hence the name "strangler" fig. Some botanists include this family under Urticaceae (nettle family). A naturalized relative of south Florida is the weeping fig (*Ficus benjamina*). The slender branches droop, hence the common name. Aerial roots are produced. Leaves alternate, thin, shiny, strongly veined, and pointed at the tips. Fleshy fruit is yellowish to reddish.

443. Shortleaf Fig or Wild Banyan Tree

Moraceae (mulberry family)
Ficus citrifolia Miller

Description: Tree to 35 ft tall or more. Bark pale gray. Sap milky. Aerial roots may be present. Leaves alternate, broad, leathery, glabrous. Blades dark green above, bases broad. Petioles and midveins yellow. Male and female flowers separate. Flowers small, inside a fleshy globose receptacle. Mature fig red, with a short stem.

Flowering time: March–May.

Habitat: Tropical hammocks.

Range: Central Florida: Hillsborough. South Florida: Palm Beach, Broward, Dade, the Keys, Monroe, Collier, and Lee.

Synonym: *Ficus brevifolia* Nuttall

444. Marlberry

Myrsinaceae (myrsine family)
Ardisia escallonioides Schiede & Deppe ex Schlechtendal & Chamisso

Description: Evergreen shrub or rarely small tree to 12 ft tall or more. Bark smooth. Leaves alternate, petioled, thick, dark green and glossy above. Margins entire. Flowers white in a large, terminal cluster. Calyx 5-lobed. Petals 5, recurved. Stamens 5. Mature drupe black, shiny.

Flowering time: August–December.

Habitat: Tropical and coastal hammocks, coastal strand, and pinelands.

Range: North Florida: Flagler. Central Florida: Coastal counties from St. Johns to Martin; Pinellas, Hillsborough, Manatee, Sarasota, Polk, De Soto, Highlands, and Okeechobee. South Florida: Throughout, except Charlotte, Glades, and Hendry.

Comment: Grows in the shade or sun; used in ornamental plantings. The acid, tart fruit is edible when ripe. A related species is *Ardisia crenata* of central and north Florida and the Panhandle. This introduced plant is becoming a troublesome escapee from cultivation and has invaded moist woods. The plant does well in total shade. The bright red drupes are characteristic of the species.

Synonym: *Icacorea paniculata* (Nuttall) Sudworth

445. White Stopper

Myrtaceae (myrtle family)
Eugenia axillaris (Swartz) Willdenow

Description: Evergreen shrub or tree to 20 ft tall or more. Bark smooth, grayish. Leaves opposite, broadest near the middle, leathery. Petioles reddish. Blades dark green above, paler below with black dots that are pellucid when held to the light. Margins entire, tips pointed. Flowers fragrant, small, in the leaf axils. Petals 4, white, wider than long. Stamens many. Reddish berry turns black when ripe; edible.

Flowering time: June–October.

Habitat: Tropical and coastal hammocks, coastal strand, and shell mounds.

Range: North Florida: Levy. Central Florida: Citrus, Pinellas, Hillsborough, Manatee, Sarasota, Osceola, Volusia, Brevard, Indian River, and St. Lucie. South Florida: Throughout, except Glades.

Comment: Leaves used to treat diarrhea, hence the name "stopper." Leaves smell like a skunk to some people. Three other native stoppers occur in Florida. The red stopper (*Eugenia rhombea*) of Dade County and the Keys and the Spanish stopper (*Eugenia foetida*) of South Florida and coastal sites are close relatives. Both species have similar leaves, white flowers, and red to black drupes. Flower pedicels of the red stopper are longer than the flowers, leaf margins are faintly outlined in yellow, and the leaf apices lack narrowed tips. Spanish stopper is a small tree to 15 ft tall or more whose bark may be mottled with lichens. The elliptic, leathery leaves are pale below, with margins curled down and white flowers in the leaf axils. Drupe globose, dark red to black. The redberry stopper (*Eugenia confusa*) has longer leaves with downward-pointed tips, margins curled under, and red fruits.

Synonym: *Eugenia anthera* Small

446. Devil's-claws, Cockspur, or Pull-and-hold Back

Nyctaginaceae (four-o'clock family)
Pisonia aculeata Linnaeus

Description: Sprawling, climbing, woody vine with recurved spines at the leaf axils. Bark blackish. Leaves opposite, broadest near the middle, pale green, soft. Inflorescence terminal and axillary. Male and female flowers separate. Petals lacking. Male flowers yellow green with 5 stamens. Fruit club-shaped, angled, with rows of viscid glands.

Flowering time: January–April.

Habitat: Hammocks, pinelands, moist thickets, and ruderal.

Range: Central Florida: Hillsborough and St. Lucie. South Florida: Martin, Palm Beach, Broward, Dade, the Keys, Collier, and Lee.

Comment: The cockspur (*Pisonia rotundata*), found in hammocks and pinelands of South Florida, is similar to the above species, except it is a shrub or small tree with erect, unarmed stems. Another relative found in hammocks and pinelands of southern Florida is the blolly (*Guapira discolor*). This shrub or small tree has pale, smooth bark. The opposite or alternate leaves are often crowded and variable in shape. Leaf petiole is slender. Flowers are small, greenish yellow, and the oblong, fleshy, juicy fruits are red.

447. Clam Shell Orchid

Orchidaceae (orchid family)
Anacheilium cochleatum (Linnaeus) Hoffmannsegg

Description: Erect epiphyte to 2 ft tall. Primary stem short, stout. Secondary stem modified into compressed pseudobulbs from which emerge 1–3 leaves. Leaves strap-shaped. Inflorescence terminal. Lip of flower uppermost, shell-shaped, green or greenish yellow with purple and purple veins. Other petals and sepals narrow, greenish yellow, twisted, tapered. Stamens 3. Fruit a winged capsule.

Flowering time: Fall–spring.

Habitat: Tropical hammocks.

Range: South Florida: Lee, Collier, Monroe (except the Keys), Dade, and Martin.

Comment: Threatened in Florida. The endangered dollar orchid (*Encyclia boothiana*) of South Florida hammocks is an epiphyte with round, flattened pseudobulbs. The flowers are greenish yellow, with each sepal and lateral petals heavily blotched with red purple. Lip is pale yellow to white. The thickroot orchid (*Campylocentrum pachyrrhizum*) is limited to the Fakahatchee Strand of Collier County. Leaves are few and fleshy. The yellowish brown flowers occur in a small pendulous spike less than 2 inches long. Another orchid limited to the Fakahatchee Strand is the rat-tail orchid (*Bulbophyllum pachyrhachis*). This epiphyte has short pseudobulbs scattered along a creeping rhizome. The green blotched with purple flowering axis may reach 8 inches long or more. Flowers numerous, sessile, and greenish yellow with red purple specks. The tonguelike lip is red.

Synonym: *Encyclia cochleata* (Linnaeus) Dressler

448. Wild Coco

Orchidaceae (orchid family)
Eulophia alta (Linnaeus) Fawcett & Rendle

Description: Terrestrial orchid. Flowering stalk arises separately from but near the basal leaves. Leaves grasslike, to 4 ft long. Flowers terminal, greenish or bronze. Lip purplish, crinkled. Fruit a capsule.

Flowering time: September.

Habitat: Hammocks, wet pine flatwoods, cypress hardwood swamps, and marshes.

Range: Central Florida: Throughout, except Citrus, Hernando, Pinellas, Hardee, Sumter, Lake, Seminole, Volusia, Brevard, St. Lucie, Osceola, and Okeechobee. South Florida: Throughout, except Charlotte and the Keys.

Comment: Threatened in Florida. The delicate ionopsis (*Ionopsis utricularioides*) is an uncommon epiphyte on trees of the hammocks of South Florida. The leafless, slender flowering stalk may grow to 20 inches tall or more. One or several delicate pinkish lavender flowers with a broad lip may occur on the stalk.

Synonym: *Platypus altus* (Linnaeus) Small

449. Dingy-flowered Oncidium or Mule-ear Orchid

Orchidaceae (orchid family)
Oncidium undulatum (Swartz) Salisbury

Description: Epiphytic orchid, growing on trees and rocks. Leaf single, elliptic or lanceolate, growing from a pseudobulb. Flowering inflorescence 6 ft long or more arising from the base of the pseudobulb. Flowers orangish mottled with reddish brown marks. Petals shorter than the sepals. Lip wider than long; lateral lip lobes knoblike.

Flowering time: March–June.

Habitat: Tropical hardwood hammocks.

Range: Monroe (except the Keys) and Dade.

Comment: Several species of orchids of the genus Epidendrum occur in hammocks of southern Florida, and most have very restricted ranges. The dingy epidendrum (*Epidendrum anceps*) has leafy stems that may reach 3 ft long. The greenish yellow flowers are less than 1 inch across. The rigid epidendrum (*Epidendrum rigidum*) is an epiphyte, with small greenish flowers less than a half inch long.

Synonym: *Oncidium luridum* Lindley

450. Coffee Colubrina or Snake-bark

Rhamnaceae (buckthorn family)
Colubrina arborescens (Miller) Sargent

Description: Woody evergreen shrub or small tree to 20 ft or more. Young stems rusty tomentose. Leaves alternate, leathery, dark green and glabrous above. Lower surfaces with rusty hairs and scattered black glands. Margins entire. Flowers clustered in the leaf axils. Flowers small, greenish yellow or white covered with rusty hairs. Petals 5. Capsule purplish to black.

Flowering time: January; September–October.

Habitat: Rockland hammocks and pinelands.

Range: South Florida: Collier, Monroe, and the Keys.

Comment: Limited to Long Pine Key in Everglades National Park. Plant smells like manure. Another relative is *Colubrina asiatica* of South Florida and the Keys. This introduced and naturalized species occurs in coastal hammocks and beach dunes. The 3-ft shrub has smooth sprawling viny branches. The alternate leaves are strongly 3-veined at the base and the leaf margins are toothed. The small flowers are greenish.

Synonym: *Colubrina colubrina* (Jacquin) Millspaugh

451. Coffee Colubrina, Cuban Colubrina, or Snake-bark

Rhamnaceae (buckthorn family)
Colubrina cubensis (Jacquin) Brongniart

Description: Woody evergreen shrub or small tree to 15 ft tall or more. Stems and leaves pubescent. Leaves alternate, narrow, leathery, veins distinct. Flowers small, yellow, hairy, clustered in the leaf axils. Petals 5. Fruit a round capsule.

Flowering time: Nearly all year.

Habitat: Rockland hammocks and pinelands.

Range: South Florida: Dade and the Keys.

Comment: Uncommon on Miami Rock Ridge, where it occurs in the pinelands and at hammock margins; limited in Everglades National Park to Long Pine Key. Endangered in Florida. A widespread relative along the coast and in hammocks and sandy sites is the buckthorn (*Sageretia minutiflora*). This shrub has a pubescent, spiny stem. Leaves are opposite, leathery, ovate. Flowers small, fragrant, in spikes at the ends of branches. Drupe globose, reddish black.

452. Torchwood or Sea Amyris

Rutaceae (rue or citrus family)
Amyris elemifera Linnaeus

Description: Evergreen, aromatic shrub or tree to 15 ft tall or more. Bark gray brown. Leaves opposite, compound, petioled. Leaflets usually 3, broadest near the middle, drooping with tapered apices. Margins entire or finely toothed. Flowers fragrant, in terminal or axillary clusters. Petals 4, white. Stamens 8. Drupe gland-dotted, purple or black.

Flowering time: October–February.

Habitat: Tropical and coastal hammocks.

Range: Coastal counties: Flagler south through the Keys.

Comment: Fruit edible. Wood contains oils and resins used for fuel and torches, hence the name "torchwood."

453. Inkwood or Butterbough

Sapindaceae (soapberry family)
Exothea paniculata (Jussieu) Radlkofer ex Durand

Description: Evergreen shrub or tree to 30 ft tall or more. Bark gray, branches smooth. Leaves alternate, compound, clustered near ends of branches. Leaflets 2, 4, or 6. Flowers fragrant, clustered terminally or in the axils of branches. Calyx 5-lobed. Petals 5, white. Fruit berrylike, orange red turning dark purple.

Flowering time: February–April.

Habitat: Tropical and coastal hammocks, shell mounds, and calcareous soils.

Range: Coastal counties: Volusia south through the Keys. Collier.

Comment: The strong wood is used in boatbuilding and for making tool handles. Sap of plant turns black when exposed to air.

454. Satinleaf

Sapotaceae (sapodilla or sapote family)
Chrysophyllum oliviforme Linnaeus

Description: Evergreen shrub or small tree to 30 ft tall with milky sap. Bark scaly, reddish brown. Branchlets with milky sap. Leaves alternate, leathery, shiny and dark green above. Lower leaf surface usually reddish brown, velvety. Flowers fragrant, small, white to greenish yellow. Corolla and calyx 5-lobed. Stamens 5. Berry globose, dark purple, with large seeds.

Flowering time: June–September.

Habitat: Tropical hammocks, coastal hammocks, thickets, and pinelands.

Range: Central Florida: Brevard, Indian River, and St. Lucie. South Florida: Martin, Palm Beach, Broward, Dade, the Keys, Monroe, Collier, and Hendry.

Comment: Sweet fruit eaten by birds and other animals. Used in making jellies or eaten raw. Endangered in Florida. The wild dilly (*Manilkara jaimiqui*) of south Florida hammocks is a relative. The alternate, evergreen, elliptic to oblong leaves often have slightly notched tips. The small, clustered flowers are pale yellow. Fruit fleshy, round, brown, about an inch wide. Another relative found in the hammocks of south Florida and scattered along the east coast to about Volusia County is the mastic (*Sideroxylon foetidissimum*). This tree (to 100 ft tall) has alternate, evergreen leaves that are long-stalked and margins that are wavy in mature individuals. The bark is reddish brown and scaly. Flowers tiny, yellow, clustered. Drupe yellow.

455. Paradise Tree or Bitter-wood

Simaroubaceae (ailanthus or quassia family)
Simarouba glauca de Candolle

Description: Tree with a straight, single trunk to 50 ft tall. Bark brown, scaly. Leaves alternate. Leaflets 6 or more, dark green above, grayish below. Male and female flowers on separate plants. Flower clusters terminal or axillary. Calyx usually 5-lobed. Petals 4 or usually 5, whitish yellow. Stamens usually 10. Fruit bright red turning purplish, in clusters.

Flowering time: February–May.

Habitat: Tropical and coastal hammocks.

Range: Coastal counties: Brevard, St. Lucie south through the Keys. Monroe, Collier, and Lee.

Comment: Branches, bark, and leaves bitter. One of the tallest canopy trees of hammocks.

456. Potato Tree or Blodgett's Nightshade

Solanaceae (nightshade family)
Solanum donianum Walpers

Description: Spineless, erect shrub to 4 ft tall or more. Grayish pubescence covers the plant. Leaves alternate, simple, leathery, margins entire and wavy. Flowers white or bluish, star-shaped, in terminal clusters. Stamens 5. Red berries occur in terminal clusters.

Flowering time: All year.

Habitat: Edges of hammocks, pinelands, and ruderal.

Range: Collier, Monroe, the Keys, and Dade.

Comment: John Loomis Blodgett (1809–1853) was an important figure in South Florida's botanical explorations. He was a druggist and physician and settled at Key West in 1838. Another potato tree, *Solanum erianthum*, occurs in edges of hammocks, pinelands, and ruderal of South Florida. The leaves are gray green, velvety, and aromatic when crushed. Flowers white, star-shaped. Berries yellow.

Synonym: *Solanum blodgettii* Chapman

457. Joewood

Theophrastaceae (theophrasta or joewood family)
Jacquinia keyensis Mez

Description: Evergreen shrub or small tree to 20 ft tall. Stems brittle with small brown dots. Bark smooth, pale gray. Leaves alternate, yellow green, leathery. Blades wedge-shaped. Margins curved down. Leaves crowded near ends of branches. Flowers fragrant, yellowish or white, in loose clusters terminating the branches. Calyx 5-lobed. Corolla 5-lobed, trumpet-shaped. Mature fruit orange red.

Flowering time: Summer–fall.

Habitat: Tropical hammocks, rockland pinelands, coastal strand, coastal grasslands, and coastal scrubs.

Range: South Florida: Lee, Dade, and the Keys.

Comment: Threatened in Florida. Fruit is said to be poisonous.

458. Florida Trema or Nettle Tree

Ulmaceae (elm family)
Trema micranthum (Linnaeus) Blume

Description: Usually an evergreen, sprawling shrub; may grow to 30 ft tall. Twigs pubescent. Leaves alternate, dull green, white woolly below. Margins finely toothed. Upper leaf surface rough to the touch. Male and female flowers separate, in axillary clusters on the branches. Tepals 5, greenish yellow. Drupe yellow orange, surrounded by persisting perianth.

Flowering time: February–April.

Habitat: Edges of tropical hammocks and thickets.

Range: South Florida: Martin south through the Keys. Monroe, Collier, Hendry, Sarasota, and Pinellas.

Comment: One of the first shrubs to appear after a fire or hurricane. Some botanists place this species in Celtidaceae.

Synonym: *Trema floridanum* Britton ex Small

459. Possum Grape

Vitaceae (grape family)
Cissus verticillata (Linnaeus) Nicolson & C. E. Jarvis

Description: Woody vine with thick, usually hairy stems. Often climbs in trees. Leaves alternate, simple, toothed. Petioles 2½ inches long. Flowers green or yellow green. Sepals and petals 4. Berry bluish black, 1-seeded.

Flowering time: February.

Habitat: Hammocks and low ground.

Range: South Florida: Martin south through the Keys. Monroe, Collier, and Lee.

Comment: A related species, the pepper vine (*Ampelopsis arborea*), can be found in hammocks as well as other habitats. It is common in ruderal areas. This climbing vine has compound leaves; leaflets are toothed and ovate. Flowers small, greenish. Mature berry dark purple. Other viny, climbing plants that occur in south Florida hammocks and disturbed sites include several species of jasmines (*Jasminum*), all introduced and naturalized. They have tubular, white, fragrant flowers that open at night, and the berry is often 2-lobed. The Gold Coast jasmine (*Jasminum dichotomum*) from Africa has a glabrous calyx with very short lobes. The berry is black. The Arabian jasmine (*Jasminum sambac*) has a pubescent calyx with 7 to 12 lobes.

Synonym: *Cissus sicyoides* Linnaeus.

Ruderal Sites

460. Annual garden phlox (*Phlox drummondii*), dye flowers (*Coreopsis basalis*), and other spring wildflowers along highway 41, Alachua County. May 17, 1997.

461. Small Queen Anne's-lace

Apiaceae or Umbelliferae (carrot or parsley family)
Daucus pusillus Michaux

Description: Annual to 32 inches tall. Stems hairy, ribbed. Leaves alternate, petioled, segments ferny. Inflorescence a terminal umbel. Leaflike bracts extend beyond the umbel. Flowers small, numerous, white greenish. Petals, sepals, and stamens 5. Fruit with barbed spines.

Flowering time: May.

Habitat: Roadsides and other ruderal sites.

Range: Panhandle: Throughout, except Gulf, Bay, and Washington. North Florida: Marion, Alachua, Union, Columbia, Suwannee, Gilchrist, Lafayette, Madison, and Duval. Central Florida: St. Lucie.

Comment: Differs from Queen Anne's-lace (*Daucus carota*), which occurs in the Panhandle, in having smaller flowering heads and fruit with barbed spines.

462. Dog Fennel

Asteraceae or Compositae (daisy or sunflower family)
Eupatorium capillifolium (Lamarck) Small

Description: Stout herb with pubescent stems to 3 ft tall or more. Odoriferous. Leaves mostly alternate, finely dissected less than [2/10] inch wide. Flowers small, creamy white, on diffuse branches appearing feathery. Fruit a black achene.

Flowering time: September–November.

Habitat: Ruderal, pine flatwoods, and marshes.

Range: Panhandle: Throughout, except Holmes, Calhoun, Gulf, and Bay. North Florida: Lafayette, Gilchrist, Hamilton, Suwannee, Baker, Union, Bradford, Alachua, Marion, Putnam, Clay, Duval, St. Johns, and Flagler. Central Florida: Throughout. South Florida: Throughout.

Comment: *Eupatorium serotinum*, a relative found in moist disturbed sites, grows to 9 ft tall or more. Leaves alternate, long-petioled. Blades broadest at the base, tips pointed. Inflorescence large, terminal, white.

463. Joe-pye-weed or Queen-of-the-meadow

Asteraceae or Compositae (daisy or sunflower family)
Eupatorium fistulosum Barratt

Description: Stout perennial to 10 ft tall or more. Stems smooth, purplish green, hollow. Leaves whorled, petioled, 4–7 leaves per node. Blades veiny, margins toothed. Flowers in a large, round-topped pink to purplish terminal clump. Showy. Ray florets absent. Stamens 5. Fruit a black achene.

Flowering time: May–July.

Habitat: Moist meadows, pastures, roadsides, borders of woods, and other ruderal sites.

Range: Panhandle: Throughout, except Gulf and Bay. North Florida: Putnam. Central Florida: Lake, Orange, Seminole, Polk, and Osceola.

Synonym: *Eupatoriadelphus purpureus* (Linnaeus) R. M. King & H. Robinson

464. Flat-topped Goldenrod

Asteraceae or Compositae (daisy or sunflower family)
Euthamia caroliniana (Linnaeus) Greene ex Porter & Britton

Description: Perennial herb to 3 ft tall or more. Stems becoming woody, branched above. Leaves alternate, numerous, grasslike. Flowers many, yellow, arranged in a flat-topped cluster. Ray florets more numerous than disk florets. Fruit an achene.

Flowering time: October–December.

Habitat: Vacated fields, roadsides, pine flatwoods, and coastal sites.

Range: Panhandle: Throughout. North Florida: Throughout, except Dixie, Lafayette, Suwannee, Baker, and Flagler. Central Florida: Throughout. South Florida: Throughout, except Hendry, Monroe, and the Keys.

Comment: True goldenrods belong to the genus *Solidago*. The bright yellow, tubular flowers are commonly seen in late summer and fall. *Solidago fistulosa*, found throughout the state, grows to 6 ft tall or more and has rough stems and sessile, rough leaves. A similar, tall species found in north Florida and the Panhandle is *Solidago canadensis*. Stems pubescent; lower leaves short-petioled, upper ones sessile. Leaf blades have rough upper surfaces, toothed margins, and prominent lateral veins.

Synonyms: *Euthamia minor* (Michaux) Green; *Euthamia tenuifolia* (Pursh) Green

465. Spanish Daisy or Bitterweed

Asteraceae or Compositae (daisy or sunflower family)
Helenium amarum (Rafinesque) H. Rock

Description: Odoriferous annual herb to 20 inches tall. Stems glabrous, branched. Leaves alternate, threadlike, glandular. Lower leaves absent at flowering time. Flowers terminal, small. Heads yellow, ray florets 3-lobed, drooping. Fruit a brown, hairy achene.

Flowering time: April–November.

Habitat: Roadsides, pastures, and vacated fields.

Range: Panhandle: Throughout, except Bay. North Florida: Throughout, except Lafayette. Central Florida: Throughout, except Sumter, Orange, Hardee, and St. Lucie. South Florida: Throughout, except Glades, Hendry, Monroe, and the Keys.

Comment: Milk from cows that have eaten this plant is bitter. Horses and mules have been poisoned by eating Spanish daisy. A related sneezeweed (*Helenium flexuosum*) grows to about 3 ft tall and has a brownish purple center. The species may be seen along roadsides as well as in mesic pinelands and bluffs of north-central Florida and the Panhandle.

Synonym: *Helenium tenuifolium* Nuttall

466. Sneezeweed

Asteraceae or Compositae (daisy or sunflower family)
Helenium pinnatifidum (Nuttall) Rydberg

Description: Erect herb to 3 ft tall or more. Stems pubescent or glabrous. Basal leaves in a rosette, entire or shallowly toothed. Stem leaves alternate, sessile, reduced upward. Single flower terminates the flowering stalk. Heads of disk and ray florets yellow. Fruit a brown, hairy achene.

Flowering time: February–July.

Habitat: Roadsides, wet pinelands, and swamps.

Range: Panhandle: Walton, Bay, Gulf, Franklin, Wakulla, Liberty, Jefferson, and Jackson. North Florida: Throughout, except Madison, Hamilton, Suwannee, Columbia, Gilchrist, and Clay. Central Florida: Throughout, except De Soto and Indian River. South Florida: Throughout, except Glades and the Keys.

Comment: Plant similar to the sneezeweed (*Helenium vernale*), which has smooth fruits instead of pubescent ones (magnification needed). Plant mainly occurs in wet areas in the Panhandle.

467. Camphorweed or Telegraphweed

Asteraceae or Compositae (daisy or sunflower family)
Heterotheca subaxillaris (Lamarck) Britton & Rusby

Description: Odoriferous variable annual or biennal herb to 3 ft tall or more. Stems branched, rough, sticky. Stem leaves reduced, alternate, toothed. Flower heads of ray and disk florets yellow. Fruit an achene.

Flowering time: January–December.

Habitat: Vacated lots, roadsides, pastures, pine flatwoods, and coastal scrubs and dunes.

Range: Panhandle: Throughout, except Jefferson, Calhoun, Washington, Holmes, and Santa Rosa. North Florida: Throughout, except Baker, Union, Bradford, Lafayette, and Dixie. Central Florida: Throughout, except Manatee. South Florida: Throughout, except Monroe and the Keys.

Synonym: *Heterotheca latifolia* Buckley

468. Blue Lettuce or Michaux's Lettuce

Asteraceae or Compositae (daisy or sunflower family)
Lactuca graminifolia Michaux

Description: Stems to 3 ft tall or more, branched, glabrous, greenish reddish. Sap milky. Upper leaves reduced or absent. Lower leaves narrow, lobed or entire. Inflorescence terminal, branched, of cylindrical glabrous heads. Flowers bluish purple or white. Disk florets lacking. Fruit an achene. Fruiting heads form a puffball of achenes with their attached pappus.

Flowering time: February–December.

Habitat: Roadsides, vacated fields, and dry woods.

Range: Panhandle: Throughout, except Holmes, Washington, Bay, Gulf, Calhoun, and Jefferson. North Florida: Throughout. Central Florida: Throughout. South Florida: Throughout, except Okeechobee, Palm Beach, Glades, Charlotte, Monroe, and the Keys.

Comment: Another lettuce seen along roadsides and in other ruderal sites is the wood-lettuce or wild lettuce (*Lactuca canadensis*). This larger and taller species occurs mainly in North Florida and the Panhandle. It has orange yellow flowers. Like the two species of lettuce, the false dandelion (*Pyrrhopappus carolinianus*) lacks disk florets and has milky sap. This ruderal species is about 24 inches tall and has large lemon yellow flowers. Each flower terminates at the end of a nearly leafless stem. Most leaves are basal like those of the common dandelion (*Taraxacum officinale*).

469. Hempweed

Asteraceae or Compositae (daisy or sunflower family)
Mikania scandens (Linnaeus) Willedenow

Description: Herbaceous climbing, glabrous vine. Leaves opposite, petioled, somewhat heart-shaped. Blades mainly glabrous, margins entire or sparsely toothed. Inflorescence axillary, stalked, of clusters of white to pinkish florets. Ray florets lacking. Fruit a black achene.

Flowering time: January–December.

Habitat: Roadsides, fencerows, thickets, and other ruderal areas.

Range: Panhandle: Throughout, except Santa Rosa, Gulf, and Gadsden. North Florida: Throughout, except Madison, Hamilton, Lafayette, Baker, and Bradford. Central Florida: Throughout. South Florida: Throughout.

Comment: A similar species of drier areas is *Mikania cordifolia*. This hempweed differs from the above species in having hairy stems, inflorescence, and leaves.

Synonym: *Mikania batatifolia* de Candolle

470. Pucoon or Puccoon

Boraginaceae (borage family)
Lithospermum incisum Lehmann

Description: Perennial herb with hairy stems to 20 ft tall. Stem leaves alternate, many, reduced upwards. Blades linear. Flowers yellow, in terminal clusters. Calyx 5-lobed, lobes narrow. Corolla 5-lobed, tubular. Fruit of 4 nutlets.

Flowering time: March–April.

Habitat: Roadsides, grassy areas, and other ruderal sites.

Range: Panhandle: Jackson and Leon. North Florida: Dixie, Alachua, and Duval. Central Florida: Citrus, Hernando, Lake, Seminole, and Hillsborough.

Comment: Roots have a reddish purple sap that was used as a dye. A related species of sandhills is *Lithospermum caroliniense*. This pucoon has yellow flowers, softer hairs, and wider leaves at midstem.

Synonym: *Batschia linearifolia* (Goldie) Small

471. Little White Lobelia

Campanulaceae (bellflower or lobelia family)
Lobelia homophylla Wimmer

Description: Annual to 2 ft tall. Stems glabrous or finely pubescent. Leaves alternate, ovate, petioled, clustered at the base. Margins toothed. Corolla 2-lipped, white, pedicels nearly [1/2] inch long. Fruit a capsule.

Flowering time: March–May

Habitat: Ruderal and pinelands.

Range: North Florida: St. Johns. Central Florida: Coastal counties from Citrus south to Charlotte; Brevard to Martin. Inland counties: Sumter, Lake, and Highlands. South Florida: Lee and Collier.

Comment: The bay lobelia (*Lobelia feayana*) commonly occurs along roadsides and other moist grassy areas. This low-growing species with small, blue flowers is endemic to Florida. The corolla tube is less than a half inch long. Lower leaves are small and roundish with entire or toothed margins.

472. Manroot, Wild Potato Vine, or Man-of-the-Earth

Convolvulaceae (morning-glory family)
Ipomoea pandurata (Linnaeus) G. Meyer

Description: Twining or climbing perennial vine. Stem sparsely pubescent, growing from an enlarged root. Leaves alternate, heart-shaped, widest at the base. Leaf margins entire. Flowers large, funnel-shaped, white with a purple red throat. Sepals 5, unequal, essentially glabrous. Stamens 5. Fruit a capsule.

Flowering time: May–October.

Habitat: Roadsides, abandoned fields, sandhills, margins of upland mixed forests, and riverbanks.

Range: Panhandle: Throughout, except Washington, Bay, Gulf, and Calhoun. North Florida: Throughout, except Hamilton, Lafayette, Dixie, Bradford, Putnam, Clay, and St. Johns. Central Florida: Throughout, except Seminole, Hardee, De Soto, and Okeechobee. South Florida: Lee.

Comment: American Indians used the tuberous root for rheumatism. A root tea was taken as a laxative and also for coughs and asthma. Two other common large-flowered, white morning-glories seen along roadsides and other disturbed areas are the Alamo vine (*Merremia dissecta*) and hedge bindweed (*Calystegia sepium*). The former has a purple or rose throat and deeply dissected or lobed (7–9 lobes) leaves. The bindweed has triangular or arrow-shaped leaves and two large bracts covering the sepals.

473. Common Morning-glory

Convolvulaceae (morning-glory family)
Ipomoea purpurea (Linnaeus) Roth

Description: Herbaceous twining vine with pubescent stems. Leaves alternate, heart-shaped, base round. Flowers funnel-shaped, axillary, purple, pink, or white. Sepals 5, glabrous, except at the margins and base. Stamens 5. Fruit a capsule.

Flowering time: December–January; April–September.

Habitat: Roadsides, vacated fields, and other ruderal sites.

Range: Panhandle: Jackson, Gadsden, and Liberty. North Florida: Columbia, Suwannee, Hamilton, Baker, and Duval. Central Florida: Orange and Brevard.

Comment: Several large species of purple-flowered morning-glories occur along roadsides and in other ruderal areas. *Ipomoea cairica* has 5–7 segments to the leaves, *Ipomoea cordatotriloba* has hairy leaves that are ovate, unlobed or with 2 basal lobes, and the island morning-glory (*Ipomoea indica*) has hairy leaves that are unlobed or 3-lobed. The latter's flowers are deep purple or pink purple. All are twining and climbing vines.

Synonym: *Pharbitis purpurea* (Linnaeus) Voigt

474. Painted-leaf or Wild Poinsettia

Euphorbiaceae (spurge family)
Poinsettia cyathophora (Murray) Bartling

Description: Glabrous annual to 3 ft tall or more. Stems solitary, greenish. Sap milky. Lower branches opposite, upper ones alternate. Leaves opposite, thin, linear to fiddle-shaped. Upper bracts with red blotches at the base. Flowers small, greenish. Petals absent. Stamen 1. Capsule 3-lobed.

Flowering time: January–December.

Habitat: Roadsides, hammocks, and coastal sites.

Range: Panhandle: Escambia, Okaloosa, Walton, Jackson, Gadsden, Leon, Bay, and Franklin. North Florida: Hamilton, Suwannee, Columbia, Baker, Dixie, Levy, Alachua, Clay, Duval, Nassau, and St. Johns. Central Florida: Throughout. South Florida: Throughout, except Glades.

Comment: The ruderal fiddler's spurge (*Poinsettia heterophylla*) is related to the above species, but differs in having green or purplish floral bracts. Red never occurs at the bases of the bracts.

Synonym: *Euphorbia cyathophora* Murray

475. Crab's-eye or Rosary Pea

Fabaceae or Leguminosae (bean or pea family)
Abrus precatorius Linnaeus

Description: Perennial vine, branching and twining. Base woody, terminal ends herbaceous. Leaves alternate, leaflets many, small. Flowers pea-shaped, pale pink or lavender, in dense axillary clusters. Stamens 9. Legumes broad. Seeds bright red, each with a black base.

Flowering time: Summer.

Habitat: Roadsides and other ruderal sites.

Range: North Florida: Marion, Suwannee, Hamilton, Columbia, Baker, and Union. Central Florida: Throughout, except Citrus and Sumter. South Florida: Throughout, except Glades, Broward, and Monroe.

Comment: Seeds are poisonous. Necklaces have been made from the seeds. In India the seeds were used as a standard of weight.

Synonym: *Abrus abrus* (Linnaeus) W. Wight

476. Shy-leaf

Fabaceae or Leguminosae (bean or pea family)
Aeschynomene americana Linnaeus

Description: Annual to 3 ft tall or more. Stems hairy. Leaves alternate, leaflets many. Corolla pea-shaped, yellow with purple lines. Seedpod jointed (loment).

Flowering time: September–December.

Habitat: Ruderal and pine flatwoods.

Range: Panhandle: Escambia, Calhoun, Jackson, Liberty, Gadsden, Gulf, Wakulla, Leon, and Jefferson. North Florida: Levy, Gilchrist, Union, Bradford, Alachua, Marion, Putnam, and Flagler. Central Florida: Throughout, except Citrus. South Florida: Throughout, except Charlotte, Glades, Monroe, and the Keys.

Comment: Beggarweeds, beggar's lice, or beggar's ticks (*Desmodium*) also have jointed seedpods (loments). Many species occur in ruderal areas as well as in pinelands, upland mixed forests, and other communities. The small pea-shaped flowers are purple. The Florida beggarweed (*Desmodium tortuosum*) has tall stems with slender, spreading branches and trifoliate leaves that are rough on both surfaces. *Desmodium viridiflorum* is similar, but the lower surfaces of the leaflets are velvety to the touch. *Desmodium incanum* usually grows less than 3 ft tall. The leaflets are glabrous above with whitish blotches and hairs below. Unlike the former two species, loments of the latter have straight upper surfaces.

477. Partridge-pea

Fabaceae or Leguminosae (bean or pea family)
Chamaecrista fasciculata (Michaux) Greene

Description: Annual with erect or diffuse stems
to 3 ft tall or more. Leaves alternate, compound,
leaflets many. Leaf petiole near the middle, bearing a round gland. Calyx 5-lobed, lobes narrow.
Petals 5, yellow often with reddish spots at the
base. Stamens 10, unequal in size. Legume narrow, few to many hairs.

Flowering times: January–December.

Habitat: Ruderal, pine flatwoods, and sandhills.

Range: Panhandle: Throughout. North Florida:
Throughout. Central Florida: Throughout.
South Florida: Throughout.

Comment: A related species of south Florida is
Chamaecrista lineata. This species with yellow
flowers and reddish anthers has rough, gray
hairs throughout and grayish legumes. Leaflets
are not sensitive.

Synonyms: *Cassia deeringiana* Small & Pennell;
Cassia fasciculata Michaux; *Chamaecrista
brachiata* Pollard

478. Wild Sensitive Plant

Fabaceae or Leguminosae (bean or pea family)
Chamaecrista nictitans Linnaeus

Description: Annual to 2 ft tall. Stems smooth or
with incurved hairs. Leaf petiole with a gland
just below the lowest leaflet. Leaflets many, closing when touched. Flowers in leaf axils, [1/2]
inch long or less. Calyx 5-lobed. Petals 5, yellow. Stamens 5. Legume hairy.

Flowering time: August–December.

Habitat: Ruderal, pine flatwoods, sandhills,
bluffs, and upland mixed forests.

Range: Panhandle: Throughout, except Holmes.
North Florida: Throughout, except Lafayette,
Gilchrist, Nassau, and Flagler. Central Florida:
Throughout, except Indian River. South Florida:
Throughout.

Comment: Cherokees made a tea from this plant
for fatigue. Two related ruderal species with yellow, pea-shaped flowers are the sicklepod (*Senna
obtusifolia*) and coffee senna (*Senna
occidentalis*). The sicklepod has 2 or 3 pairs of
leaflets whose ends are broad and round. Legume is sickle-shaped and about 8 inches long.
The coffee senna has 6–12 leaflets with pointed
tips. Legume linear, compressed.

Synonyms: *Cassia nictitans* Linnaeus;
Chamaecrista procumbens (Linnaeus) Greene

479. Rabbit-bells

Fabaceae or Leguminosae (bean or pea family)
Crotalaria rotundifolia J. F. Gmelin

Description: Trailing and erect herb with hairy stems. Leaves alternate, oval to elliptic. Flowers pea-shaped, yellow, at the ends of long stalks. Legume inflated, glabrous, to about 1 inch long.

Flowering time: January–December.

Habitat: Roadsides, vacated lots, pine flatwoods, and dry woods.

Range: Panhandle: Throughout, except Holmes and Gulf. North Florida: Throughout. Central Florida: Throughout. South Florida: Throughout, except Hendry.

Comment: Plant poisonous. Other weedy Florida species of *Crotalaria*, often called rattlebox, include *Crotalaria spectabilis*, *Crotalaria lanceolata*, and *Crotalaria pallida*. All have yellow, pea-shaped flowers in a long, terminal inflorescence. They can be separated by their leaves. The former has large, unifoliate leaves, whereas the last two have trifoliate leaves. Those of *C. lanceolata* are narrower than those of *C. pallida*. *Crotalaria retusa*, naturalized in south Florida, has unifoliate leaves and red and yellow flowers.

Synonyms: *Crotalaria linaria* Small; *Crotalaria maritima* Chapman

480. Hairy Indigo

Fabaceae or Leguminosae (bean or pea family)
Indigofera hirsuta Linnaeus

Description: Annual to 3 ft tall or more. Stems hairy, branched. Leaves alternate, compound. Leaflets 5–9. Inflorescence spikelike. Flowers pea-shaped, red. Legumes hairy, reflexed.

Flowering time: January–April; June; September–December.

Habitat: Roadsides, vacated fields and lots, and floodplains.

Range: Panhandle: Escambia, Santa Rosa, Jackson, Franklin, Liberty, Gadsden, Leon, Jefferson, and Wakulla. North Florida: Madison, Hamilton, Columbia, Baker, Levy, Gilchrist, Suwannee, Alachua, Union, Putnam, Clay, Nassau, and Duval. Central Florida: Throughout. South Florida: Throughout, except Hendry, Monroe, and the Keys.

Comment: Native to Africa. Plant escaped from cultivation. *Indigofera spicata* is a low-growing or prostrate species that is somewhat cloverlike. The species can be found in lawns and other ruderal areas. Flowers pea-shaped, pinkish, clustered in spikelike racemes. Leaflets hairy, legumes hairy, clustered and pointed downward.

481. Phasey Bean

Fabaceae or Leguminosae (bean or pea family)
Macroptilium lathyroides (Linnaeus) Urban

Description: Perennial to 3 ft tall. Stems branched. Leaves petioled; leaflets 3. Flowers showy, pink to reddish purple, in spikelike inflorescence. Legume elongated, narrow.

Flowering time: January–December.

Habitat: Roadsides and vacated fields and lots.

Range: Panhandle: Escambia, Washington, Bay, and Leon. North Florida: Absent. Central Florida: Throughout, except Glades. South Florida: Throughout, except Monroe. Found in the Keys.

Comment: Native to tropical America.

Synonym: *Phaseolus lathyroides* Linnaeus

482. Bladderpod

Fabaceae or Leguminosae (bean or pea family)
Sesbania vesicaria (Jacquin) Elliott

Description: Annual to 3 ft tall or more. Leaves alternate. Leaflets many, corolla pea-shaped, reddish yellow with reddish markings. Legume flat, usually 2-seeded.

Flowering time: August–October.

Habitat: Roadsides and vacated fields and lots.

Range: Panhandle: Throughout, except Washington and Jefferson. North Florida: Throughout, except Madison, Hamilton, Taylor, Lafayette, Dixie, Union, Bradford, Nassau, and Flagler. Central Florida: Throughout, except Hardee and Sarasota. South Florida: Martin, Palm Beach, Dade, Collier, and Lee.

Comment: Dead plants can be readily identified by the persisting legumes. Chickens, goats, hogs, sheep, and cattle have been poisoned, especially by eating the green or mature seeds. Related species that occur in Florida's ruderal areas are the bequilla (*Sesbania herbacea*) and purple sesbania (*Sesbania punicea*). The bequilla has linear legumes and yellow flowers mottled with red purple. The purple sesbania is a woody shrub with orange red flowers and legumes with 4 wings.

Synonym: *Glottidium vesicarium* (Jacquin) C. Mohr

483. Rabbit-foot Clover

Fabaceae or Leguminosae (bean or pea family)
Trifolium arvense Linnaeus

Description: Annual to 16 inches tall. Stems with soft hairs. Leaves 3, covered with soft hairs. Margins entire, finely toothed at the tips. Heads oblong, grayish. Flowers numerous, sessile, pale rose, pinkish, or white. Calyx grayish, densely haired. Legume broadly ovoid, enclosed by the calyx tube.

Flowering time: April.

Habitat: Roadsides, pastures, and other ruderal sites.

Range: Panhandle: Escambia, Okaloosa, Walton, Holmes, Gadsden, Leon, and Jefferson. North Florida: Alachua. Central Florida: Hillsborough and De Soto.

Comment: White clover (*Trifolium repens*) is a common species in lawns and other ruderal sites. The small pedicellate flowers are clustered in a terminal, globose head. Leaves usually have 3 leaflets that are widely elliptic and toothed. *Trifolium resupinatum* is less common and occurs in fields and along roadsides. Flowers are nearly sessile, rose to purplish, in terminal heads. A common species of much of North Florida and the Panhandle is the low hop clover (*Trifolium campestre*). The yellow heads grow to about ¼ inch wide.

484. Crimson Clover

Fabaceae or Leguminosae (bean or pea family)
Trifolium incarnatum Linnaeus

Description: Annual herb to 16 inches tall. Stems erect, pubescent. Leaves of 3 leaflets, rough, upper margins toothed. Heads cylindric. Flowers many, sessile, bright red (rarely white). Calyx 5-lobed, hairy. Legume ovoid, sessile.

Flowering time: March–May.

Habitat: Roadsides, pastures, and other ruderal sites.

Range: Panhandle: Throughout, except Holmes, Washington, Bay, and Calhoun. North Florida: Madison, Suwannee, Bradford, and Alachua. Central Florida: Hillsborough.

Comment: Introduced from Europe. Commonly planted along I-10 and other roads.

485. Cowpea

Fabaceae or Leguminosae (bean or pea family)
Vigna luteola (Jacquin) Bentham

Description: Perennial trailing vine with glabrous stems. Leaves alternate. Leaves 3, ovate to lanceolate. Leaf surface sparsely haired. Flowers large, pea-shaped, bright yellow. Calyx 2-lipped, sparsely haired. Legume hairy, about 2½ inches long.

Flowering time: January–December.

Habitat: Roadsides, thickets, and coastal sites.

Range: Panhandle: Escambia, Okaloosa, Bay, Gulf, and Franklin. North Florida: Levy, Suwannee, Hamilton, Columbia, Baker, Union, Duval, St. Johns, Clay, Putnam, and Flagler. Central Florida: Throughout, except Hernando, Sumter, Polk, and Hardee. South Florida: Throughout.

Synonym: *Vigna repens* (Linnaeus) Kuntze

486. Harlequin or Slender Fumeroot

Fumariaceae (fumitory family)
Corydalis micrantha (Engelmann ex A. Gray) A. Gray

Description: Weedy annual herb usually less than 16 inches tall. Stems contain bitter, watery juices. Leaves alternate, short-stalked or sessile. Blades finely divided. Flowers yellow, elongated with a straight, saclike spur. Petals 4. Sepals 2. Capsule cylindrical.

Flowering time: January–April.

Habitat: Roadsides and other ruderal areas.

Range: Panhandle: Throughout, except Walton, Holmes, Washington, Bay, and Gulf. North Florida: Throughout, except Taylor, Lafayette, Dixie, Levy, Baker, Union, Bradford, Clay, and Flagler. Central Florida: Citrus, Hernando, Sumter, Lake, Orange, Hillsborough, and Pinellas.

Comment: A related species of ruderal sites is the earthsmoke or common fumitory (*Fumaria officinalis*). This annual is glabrous with terminal, dark pink flowers with purplish tips.

Synonym: *Capnoides halei* Small

487. Blue-eyed Grass

Iridaceae (iris family)
Sisyrinchium angustifolium Miller

Description: Grasslike herb to 20 inches tall. Leaves resemble blades of grasses, shorter than or equal to the flower stems. Flowers star-shaped, bluish purple with a yellow center. Flower stalk swollen below the perianth. Fruit a small capsule.

Flowering time: January–June; September–November.

Habitat: Lawns, grassy fields, marshes, and pine flatwoods.

Range: Panhandle: Throughout, except Escambia and Holmes. North Florida: Throughout, except Lafayette, Baker, and Bradford. Central Florida: Throughout, except Indian River, Okeechobee, and De Soto. South Florida: Throughout.

Comment: A root tea made from the plant was given to American Indian children for diarrhea. A smaller species (6 inches tall or less) with perianth rose lavender and a rose purple eye is *Sisyrinchium rosulatum*. It is common in moist grassy areas. *Sisyrinchium exile* also is a small plant, but the perianth is yellow with a brownish or purplish eye. This species occurs in lawns and other ruderal sites.

Synonym: *Sisyrinchium atlanticum* E. P. Bicknell

488. Lion's-ear

Lamiaceae or Labiatae (mint family)
Leonotis nepetifolia (Linnaeus) R. Brown

Description: Erect, stout annual to 8 ft tall or more. Stems angled, hairy. Leaves opposite, petioled. Blades broad, margins toothed. Flowers in a dense, prickly, round cluster encircling the stem. Calyx 2-lipped, hairy. Corolla yellow orange, 2-lipped. Upper lip hoodlike. Stamens 4. Fruit of 4 nutlets.

Flowering time: June–January.

Habitat: Pastures, vacated fields, roadsides, and floodplains.

Range: Panhandle: Escambia, Jackson, Calhoun, Liberty, Gadsden, Leon, Wakulla, and Franklin. North Florida: Lafayette, Gilchrist, Suwannee, Hamilton, Columbia, Baker, Alachua, and Marion. Central Florida: Throughout, except Hernando, Manatee, Sarasota, St. Lucie, Osceola, Brevard, and Volusia. South Florida: Collier.

Comment: Introduced from Africa.

489. Horsemint or Spotted Beebalm

Lamiaceae or Labiatae (mint family)
Monarda punctata Linnaeus

Description: Aromatic perennial to 4 ft tall. Often clumped. Stems hairy, 4-angled. Leaves opposite, petioled. Blades hairy, margins toothed. Flowers small in dense clusters above the conspicuous, colored leaflike bracts. Bracts yellowish or purplish tinged. Corolla 2-lipped, yellow with purplish spots. Stamens 2. Fruit of 4 nutlets.

Flowering time: May–December.

Habitat: Roadsides, meadows, floodplains, and coastal sites.

Range: Panhandle: Throughout, except Okaloosa, Holmes, Washington, Calhoun, Gulf, and Wakulla. North Florida: Throughout, except Taylor, Union, Bradford, and Nassau. Central Florida: Throughout, except Osceola, Hardee, Highlands, and Okeechobee. South Florida: Throughout, except Glades, Hendry, Broward, Dade, Monroe, and the Keys.

Comment: Oil of this mint is high in thymol, used to expel worms. A leaf tea was used by American Indians for flu, fevers, colds, and stomach cramps.

490. Lyre-leaved Sage

Lamiaceae or Labiatae (mint family)
Salvia lyrata Linnaeus

Description: Herb to 2 ft tall. Stem square, hairy. Leaves mostly basal, broad, petioled, often mixed green with purple. Stem leaves opposite, reduced, lobed or unlobed, sessile. Calyx 2-lipped, hairy, bluish purple. Corolla 2-lipped, purple, whorled on the stem. Fertile stamens 2. Fruit of 4 nutlets.

Flowering time: January–December, especially the spring.

Habitat: Roadsides, wooded areas, and thickets.

Range: Panhandle: Throughout, except Bay. North Florida: Throughout. Central Florida: Throughout, except Okeechobee and St. Lucie. South Florida: Throughout, except Glades, Hendry, Palm Beach, Broward, Monroe, Dade, and the Keys.

Comment: Folk remedies using this plant include treating cancer and warts. Teas made by American Indians were taken for colds, coughs, and asthma. Other ruderal mints with 2-lipped, purplish flowers are henbit (*Lamium amplexicaule*), hedge nettle (*Stachys floridana*), and buttermint (*Hyptis mutabilis*). Henbit is a low-growing annual with sessile leaves below the whorls of flowers. Corolla reddish purple with deeper spots on the lower lip. The whorled flowers of hedge nettle are pink or pale purple with dark dots. Leaves stalked, lanceolate, toothed. Buttermint grows to 6 ft tall or more. Stem is woody below, hairy, rough. Flowers are small, pale lavender to purple to whitish, in sessile clusters. Leaves ovate, toothed.

491. Red Spiderling or Wineflower

Nyctaginaceae (four-o'clock family)
Boerhavia diffusa Linnaeus

Description: Perennial sprawling or ascending herb to 3 ft tall or more. Stems many, radiating out from a crown. Leaves opposite, ovoid. Margins undulate. Flowers small, pink or purplish, on thin stalks. Calyx tube glandular, 5-lobed. Petals lacking. Stamens 3.

Flowering time: April–November.

Habitat: Lawns, vacated fields, and other ruderal sites.

Range: Panhandle: Escambia, Gadsden, Leon, Gulf, and Franklin. North Florida: Columbia, Gilchrist, Alachua, Levy, Marion, St. Johns, and Duval. Central Florida: Volusia, Brevard, Seminole, Orange, Lake, Hernando, Pinellas, Hillsborough, Manatee, Sarasota, Highlands, Indian River, St. Lucie. South Florida: Throughout, except Charlotte, Glades, and Broward.

Synonym: *Boerhavia coccinea* Miller

492. Weedy Evening Primrose

Onagraceae (evening primrose family)
Oenothera biennis Linnaeus

Description: Biennial to 6 ft tall or more. Stems leafy, usually branched above, hairy or smooth. Stem leaves alternate, narrow at the base, upper ones sessile. Margins entire or toothed. Flowers yellow, terminal, few to many. Calyx 4-lobed, bent downward. Petals 4, stigma X-shaped. Stamens 8. Capsule cylindric, in leaf axils.

Flowering time: March; June–December.

Habitat: Lawns, vacated fields, and other ruderal sites.

Range: Panhandle: Throughout, except Santa Rosa, Calhoun, Bay, and Gulf. North Florida: Madison, Columbia, Gilchrist, Levy, Alachua, Marion, Clay, Nassau, Duval, and St. Johns. Central Florida: Volusia, Brevard, Seminole, Lake, Sumter, Citrus, Hernando, Pasco, and Polk. South Florida: Broward.

Comment: Oil from the plant's seeds is a natural source of gamma-linolenic acid, which may be useful for eczema, migraines, and alcholism. Related weedy species are the cut-leaved evening primrose (*Oenothera laciniata*), primrose willow (*Ludwigia peruviana*), and southern gaura (*Gaura angustifolia*). The evening primrose has 4-petaled flowers with lobed, hairy leaves. It is a low-growing species that branches near the base. The primrose willow is shrubby, herbaceous, hairy, and 5 ft tall or more. The 4 or 5 petals are large, separate, and yellow. Southern gaura is slender, branched, and grows to 6 ft tall. Flowers small, on or near the ends of wandlike spikes. Petals 3 or 4, pinkish white.

493. Showy Primrose

Onagraceae (evening primrose family)
Oenothera speciosa Nuttall

Description: Spreading or erect perennial to 2 ft tall. Stems usually branched, with short hairs. Leaves alternate, sessile or petioled. Margins toothed, wavy or lobed near the base. Sepals 4, narrow. Petals 4, large, white to pink marked with reddish veins. Stamens 8. Capsule ribbed.

Flowering time: March–May.

Habitat: Roadsides and other ruderal sites.

Range: Panhandle: Throughout, except Holmes, Bay, Gulf, Calhoun, and Jefferson. North Florida: Madison, Columbia, Gilchrist, Taylor, Dixie, Levy, Marion, Alachua, Bradford, Clay, and Duval. Central Florida: Citrus, Lake, and Manatee. South Florida: Dade.

Comment: Commonly planted in lawns and gardens.

Synonym: *Hartmannia speciosa* (Nuttall) Small

494. Annual Garden Phlox

Polemoniaceae (phlox family)
Phlox drummondii Hooker

Description: Annual herb to 20 inches tall. Stems glandular, hairy, usually branched. Upper leaves alternate, lower ones opposite. Leaf surfaces hairy. Flowers in terminal clusters, pink, lavender, magenta, red, white. Calyx 5-lobed, lobes hairy. Corolla tubular, 5-lobed. Stamens 5. Fruit a 3-valved capsule.

Flowering time: January–July.

Habitat: Roadsides, pastures, fields, and lawns.

Range: Panhandle: Throughout, except Okaloosa, Holmes, Washington, Jackson, Bay, and Gadsden. North Florida: Throughout, except Bradford and Flagler. Central Florida: Citrus, Hernando, Polk, Pasco, Pinellas, Hillsborough, Sumter, Lake, Orange, Seminole, Volusia, Brevard, and Osceola.

Comment: Native to Texas. Escaped from cultivation, often in masses along roadsides and in fields. Plant name honors Thomas Drummond (1780–1835), who collected from Florida to Texas from 1831 to 1835. Drummond also was a part of the team looking for the Northwest Passage, and he collected extensively in the Mackenzie River region.

495. Mock Strawberry

Rosaceae (rose family)
Duchesnea indica (Andrews) Focke

Description: Low-growing, colony-forming perennial with runners above the ground. Leaves compound, long-petioled. Leaflets 3, toothed. Flowers solitary, on long stalks. Calyx 5-lobed. Petals 5, yellow. Stamens 20. Fruit a red, tasteless strawberry.

Flowering time: March–April.

Habitat: Ruderal sites and calcareous hammocks.

Range: Panhandle: Escambia, Santa Rosa, Jackson, Liberty, Gadsden, Leon, and Jefferson. North Florida: Madison and Marion. Central Florida: Seminole and Hillsborough.

Comment: Plant naturalized from Asia, where it is used for boils, eczema, ringworm, and burns. A tea from the flowers has been used to stimulate blood circulation.

496. Dewberry

Rosaceae (rose family)
Rubus trivialis Michaux

Description: Trailing or semierect perennial. Canes slender, with stout, curved prickles. Leaves alternate, compound. Leaflets 3 or 5, toothed. Flowers showy, solitary or clustered, stalked. Sepals 5. Petals 5, white, pink, or rose. Ripe fruit black, juicy, edible.

Flowering time: January–May.

Habitat: Roadsides, thickets, secondary woods, and pine flatwoods.

Range: Panhandle: Throughout, except Santa Rosa. North Florida: Throughout, except Madison, Hamilton, Suwannee, and Dixie. Central Florida: Throughout, except Osceola, Hardee, Highlands, Okeechobee, and St. Lucie. South Florida: Charlotte, Lee, Collier, Glades, Palm Beach, and Martin.

Comment: The highbush blackberry (*Rubus argutus*) occurs in the central and northern parts of the peninsula and in the Panhandle. It has flowers similar to those of above species, but can be identified by the tall, arching or scrambling thorny stems. Leaves are green on both surfaces.

Synonyms: *Rubus continentalis* (Focke) L. H. Bailey; *Rubus ictus* L. H. Bailey

497. Innocence

Rubiaceae (madder family)
Hedyotis procumbens (J. F. Gmelin) Fosberg

Description: Perennial with prostrate, creeping stems. Leaves opposite, round. Flowers solitary, white. Calyx 4-lobed, lobes soundish. Corolla 4-lobed. Sepals roundish, small. Stamens 4. Fruit a small capsule.

Flowering time: December–May.

Habitat: Ruderal, pine flatwoods, sandhills, scrubs, bluffs, and secondary woods.

Range: Panhandle: Throughout, except Santa Rosa, Holmes, Washington, and Gulf. North Florida: Throughout, except Bradford. Central Florida: Throughout, except De Soto. South Florida: Throughout, except Glades, Monroe, and the Keys.

Comment: A related species of the Panhandle is the star-violet (*Hedyotis crassifolia*). It can be found blooming in the spring along roadsides and in other grassy areas. This low-growing species has solitary blue flowers borne on long pedicels. The elliptic or ovate leaves are near the base of the slender stem. The related bedstraws or cleavers (*Galium*), with their small, white flowers and whorled leaves, occur in vacated areas, along grassy roadsides, and in other disturbed sites. *Galium aparine* has prostrate or trailing branched stems that are angled and rough, and form mats. There are usually 8 rough leaves at each node. *Galium hispidulum* has 4 leaves per node.

Synonym: *Houstonia procumbens* (J. F. Gmelin) Standley

498. Indian Paintbrush

Scrophulariaceae (figwort family)
Castilleja indivisa Engelmann

Description: Erect, hairy annual to 16 inches tall. Leaves alternate, sessile, hairy. Blades linear, entire or lobed. Flowers small, 2-lipped, white or greenish. Flowers surrounded by showy, reddish-tipped, leaflike bracts in a terminal spike. Capsule ellipsoid.

Flowering time: March–May.

Habitat: Roadsides and other ruderal areas.

Range: Panhandle: Leon. North Florida: Madison, Taylor, and Levy. Central Florida: Citrus and Hillsborough.

Comment: Plant parasitic on grasses and herbs. Recent molecular data indicate that all of the parasitic members of Scrophulariaceae should be transferred to Orobanchaceae (broomrape family).

499. Mullein

Scrophulariaceae (figwort family)
Verbascum virgatum Stokes

Description: Perennial or biennial herb with a stout stem to 3 ft tall or more. Basal leaves long, veiny. Stem leaves alternate, sessile, reduced above. Flowers yellow in elongated, showy spikes. Calyx 5-lobed. Corolla 5-lobed. Stamens 5. Ripe fruit a hard, brown capsule.

Flowering time: November–August.

Habitat: Roadsides, fields, and sandhills.

Range: Panhandle: Escambia, Santa Rosa, Okaloosa, Gulf, Franklin, and Liberty. North Florida: Taylor, Dixie, Levy, Marion, Alachua, Bradford, Clay, Putnam, and Nassau. Central Florida: Citrus, Hernando, Pasco, Sumter, Pinellas, Polk, and Brevard.

Comment: Recent molecular data indicate that *Verbascum* is not closely related to Scrophulariaceae. A related species occurring in North Florida and the Panhandle is the wooly mullein (*Verbascum thapsus*). This tall, robust, hairy plant has yellow flowers in stout, elongated spikes.

500. Caltrop

Zygophyllaceae (caltrop family)
Kallstroemia maxima (Linnaeus) Hooker & Arnott

Description: Branching annual with prostrate, hairy stems. Leaves of 3 or 4 pairs of leaflets. Flowers solitary, in leaf axils. Sepals 5, hairy. Petals greenish yellow. Fruit smooth.

Flowering time: October.

Habitat: Open ruderal areas.

Range: North Florida: St. Johns and Marion. Central Florida: Seminole, Lake, Pinellas, Hillsborough, De Soto, Highlands, and Indian River. South Florida, Lee, Dade, the Keys, and Martin.

Comment: A showy, weedy relative of central and south Florida is the burnut or puncture weed (*Tribulus cistoides*). This low-growing plant has 5 bright yellow flowers and hairy, compound leaves. Leaflets many, spine-tipped. Fruit a spiny capsule.

Places to Visit

Despite Florida's rapid population growth and concomitant development of the land in the past 50 years, sites representing all terrestrial communities described in this book can be visited. Most of these places are Florida Conservation Lands that are publicly owned.

In the listing of selected sites that follows, I have arranged the places to visit by community type and by county. Large sites, such as the Apalachicola National Forest, are listed more than once because they occur in two or more counties or have more than one community type. I have not described each place because of the large amount of space needed to do so. Published sourcebooks that do describe in detail many of the sites mentioned are available and can be purchased at nominal costs. Selected books that may be of interest are listed in the Reference section. There are publications that can be obtained at no cost. "Florida State Parks . . . the Real Florida" is a must for those interested in visiting Florida's state parks and recreational areas. This free booklet can be obtained by asking at most parks or by writing to the Department of Natural Resources, Division of Recreation and Parks, MS#535, 3900 Commonwealth Blvd., Tallahassee, Florida 32399–3000. Florida's water management districts have published "Recreational Guides" that describe district-owned lands that can be visited. These booklets are also free. Up-to-date, "Recreational Guides" from the Southwest (January 1994) and St. Johns River (Spring 1995) Water Management District can be obtained by writing to the appropriate district's Division of Public Information. "Florida Conservation Lands," a March 1997 publication from the Florida Natural Areas Inventory, and "Florida Trails" (undated) from the Division of Tourism, Department of Commerce, are useful guides that can be obtained from the cited agencies in Tallahassee.

In addition to these publications, an indispensable tool for locating the places mentioned below is the "Florida Atlas & Gazetteer," fourth edition, ISBN 0–89933–209–9. This gazetteer shows each county in detail and lists nearly all state parks, reserves, preserves, recreation areas, wildlife refuges, seashores, and national forests. I never leave for a trip without my Florida atlas. This atlas can be purchased at most large bookstores or map stores or by writing to DeLorme Mapping, P.O. Box 298, Freeport, Maine 04032, by calling (207) 865–4171, or by visiting their website at http://www.delorme.com.

Some sites listed below and designated "TNC" are under the jurisdiction of the Nature Conservancy. Most are limited-access sites and require permission before they can be visited. One should contact the Nature Conservancy Florida Chapter, 222 S. Westmonte Drive, Suite 300, Altamonte Springs, Florida 32714. To visit Eglin Air Force Base, a permit is required from Eglin's Natural Resources Office on U.S. 98 north of Niceville.

Pine Flatwoods

Alachua County
Morningside Nature Center, east of Gainesville
Paynes Prairie State Preserve, south of Gainesville

Baker County
Olustee Battlefield State Historic Site, 2 miles east of Olustee
Osceola National Forest, east of Lake City
Osceola Wildlife Management Area, south of Taylor

Bay County
Camp Helen, west of Hollywood Beach near the Walton County line

Brevard County
St. Sebastian River Buffer Preserve, south of Palm Bay
Enchanted Forest Nature Sanctuary, south of Indian River City

Clay County
Bayard Point Conservation Area, southeast of Green Cove Springs

Citrus County
Potts Preserve (formerly Dee River Ranch), north of Inverness, off County Road 581

Collier County
Corkscrew Swamp Sanctuary, northeast of Bonita Springs off 846

Columbia County
Osceola National Forest, northeast of Lake City

Escambia County
Big Lagoon State Recreation Area, east of Gulf Islands National Seashore

Franklin County
Apalachicola National Forest, south of Sumatra
St. George Island State Park (St. George Island), south of Eastpoint

Hernando County
Janet Butterfield Brooks Preserve (TNC), near Bailey Hill

Highlands County
Highlands Hammock State Park, near Sebring

Indian River County
Fort Drum Marsh Conservation Area, west of Vero Beach

Lake County
Lake Louisa State Park, south of Clermont

Levy County

Cedar Key Scrub State Reserve, northeast of Cedar Key

Goethe State Forest, southeast and northeast of Lebanon

Liberty County

Apalachicola National Forest, south of Bristol

Manatee County

Lake Manatee State Recreation Area, east of Bradenton

Martin County

Jonathan Dickinson State Park, south of Hobe Sound

Orange County

Hal Scott Regional Preserve and Park, north of SR 528 and west of SR 520

Rock Springs Run State Reserve, west of Sanford

Tosohatchee State Reserve, south of Christmas off Taylor Creek Road

Wekiwa Springs State Park, near Apopka

Osceola County

Disney Wilderness Preserve, south of Kissimmee (TNC)

Palm Beach County

Frenchman's Forest, Palm Beach Gardens, west of Prosperity Farms Road

Juno Hills Natural Area, south of Jupiter Inlet

Okeeheelee Nature Center, West Palm Beach

Patch Reef Park, Boca Raton

Royal Palm Beach Pines, north of Okeechobee Boulevard, Palm Beach

Pinellas County

Caladesi Island State Park, west of Dunedin

Honeymoon Island State Recreation Area, northwest of Dunedin

Polk County

Disney Wilderness Preserve, south of Kissimmee (TNC)

Lake Kissimmee State Park, east of Lake Wales

North of Avon Park Air Force Range and west of Kicco Wildlife Management Area (bounded by SRs 60 and 630 and the Kissimmee River)

Saddle Blanket Lakes Preserve, near Frostproof (TNC)

Tiger Creek Preserve, southeast of Lake Wales (TNC)

Putnam County

Welaka State Forest, south of Welaka

Santa Rosa County

Blackwater River State Forest, northeast of Milton

Sarasota County

Myakka River State Park, east of Sarasota

Myakka State Forest, Sarasota

Oscar Scherer State Park, south of Osprey

Seminole County

Lower Wekiva River State Preserve, west of Sanford

St. Johns County

Faver-Dykes State Park, southwest of Ft. Matanzas

Guana River State Park, north of St. Augustine

Sumter County

Withlacoochee State Forest, off SR 471

Taylor County

Econfina River State Park, on hwy 14, south of U.S. 98

Volusia County

Lake George Conservation Area, west of Crescent City, Seville, and Pierson

Wakulla County

Ochlockonee River State Park, south of Sopchoppy

St. Marks National Wildlife Refuge, near St. Marks

Walton County

Grayton Beach State Recreation Area, Grayton Beach

Topsail, near Destin

Scrubby Flatwoods

Alachua County

O'Leno State Park, north of High Springs

Columbia County

O'Leno State Park, north of High Springs

De Soto County
Western edge of county, north and south of SR 72

Highlands County
Archbold Biological Station, south of Lake Placid
Highlands Hammock State Park, near Sebring

Hillsborough County
Balm-Boyette Scrub, north of 674 near Balm

Levy County
Cedar Key Scrub State Reserve, on the north side of SR 24, northeast of Cedar Key

Osceola County
Disney Wilderness Preserve, south of Kissimmee (TNC)

Palm Beach County
Frenchman's Forest, north of West Palm Beach
Yamato Scrub, near Boca Raton (TNC)

Polk County
Disney Wilderness Preserve, south of Kissimmee (TNC)

Sarasota County
Oscar Scherer State Park, south of Osprey

St. Lucie County
Savannas State Preserve, south of Ft. Pierce

Walton County
Point Washington State Forest, south of Choctawhatchee Bay

Dry Prairies

De Soto County
Southwestern edge of county, south of SR 70
Western edge of county, north and south of SR 72

Duval County
Big Talbot Island State Park, northeast of Jacksonville

Hernando County
Janet Butterfield Brooks Preserve (TNC), near Bailey Hill

Highlands County
Southwestern area of county, south of SR 70

Indian River County
Fort Drum Marsh Conservation Area, west of Vero Beach

Okeechobee County
Kissimmee Prairie, bordering the east bank of the Kissimmee River, south of Osceola and Okeechobee county lines, and north of Eagle Island Road (724)
Ordway-Whittell Kissimmee Prairie Sanctuary, east of the Kissimmee Prairie

Osceola County
Three Lakes Wildlife Management Area, near Yeehaw Junction

Palm Beach County
Yamato Scrub, near Boca Raton (TNC)

Pasco County
Southwest area of County, west of U.S. 41

Polk County
Disney Wilderness Preserve, south of Kissimmee (TNC)
North of Avon Park Air Force Range and west of Kicco Wildlife Management Area (bounded by SRs 60 and 630 and the Kissimmee River)

Sarasota County
Myakka River State Park, east of Sarasota

St. Lucie County
Savannas State Preserve, south of Ft. Pierce

Sandhills

Alachua County
Katharine Ordway Preserve, east of Gainesville (Univ. of Florida)
O'Leno State Park, north of High Springs
San Felasco Hammock State Preserve, northwest of Gainesville

Calhoun County
Area in and around Chipola Experimental Forest

Citrus County
Fort Cooper State Park, southeast of Inverness

Withlacoochee State Forest, north of 480 and south and west of Inverness

Clay County

Bayard Point Conservation Area, southeast of Green Cove Springs

Gold Head Branch State Park, northeast of Keystone Heights

Jennings State Forest, near Middleburg

Columbia County

Ichetucknee Springs State Park, near Fort White

O'Leno State Park, north of High Springs

Hernando County

Annutteliga Hammock, northwest of Brooksville, off U.S. 98

Chassahowitzka Wildlife Management Area, south of the border of Citrus and Hernando counties, along the west side of U.S. 19

Janet Butterfield Brooks Preserve (TNC), near Bailey Hill

Lake County

Lake Griffin State Recreation Area, near Fruitland Park

Lake Louisa State Park, south of Clermont

Rock Springs Run State Reserve (BMK Ranch), west of Sanford

Leon County

Southeast of Tallahassee

Levy County

Andrews Wildlife Management Area, west of junction of U.S. 19 and County Road 211

Manatee Springs State Park, west of Chiefland

South and east of Chassahowitzka National Wildlife Refuge, east of U.S. 98

South of Williston Highlands (from County Road 316 south, east, and west of 121)

Liberty County

Apalachicola Bluffs and Ravines Preserve, east bank of Apalachicola River (TNC)

Torreya State Park, north of Bristol

Manatee County

Lake Manatee State Recreation Area, east of Bradenton

Marion County

Riverside Island, northwest of Salt Springs, Ocala National Forest

Romeo and surrounding area

Ross Prairie State Forest, south of junction of 484 and 200

Salt Spring Island, northwest of Salt Springs, Ocala National Forest

Martin County

Hobe Sound Sandhills (TNC), west bank of Hobe Sound

Nassau County

St. Mary's River State Forest, northeast of Boulogne

Okaloosa County

Eglin Air Force Base, north of I-10 and east of Dorcas

Orange County

Wekiwa Springs State Park, near Apopka

Pasco County

Northwest part of county, defined by county line and SRs 52, 55, and 45

Polk County

Allan David Broussard Catfish Creek State Preserve, southeast of Haines City

Tiger Creek Preserve, southeast of Lake Wales (TNC)

Putnam County

Along SR 19, north of Marion County line

Welaka State Forest, south of Welaka

Santa Rosa County

Blackwater River State Forest, northeast of Milton

Eglin Air Force Base

Seminole County

Lower Wekiva River State Preserve, west of Sanford

Suwannee County

Ichetucknee Springs State Park, near Fort White

Suwannee River State Park, northwest of Live Oak

Wakulla County

East half of Apalachicola National Forest

Walton County

Eglin Air Force Base

Point Washington State Forest, south of
Choctawhatchee Bay

Washington County
Falling Waters State Recreation Area,
south of Chipley
Rock Hill Preserve (TNC), south of
Chipley

Sand Pine Scrubs

Bay County
Camp Helen, west of Hollywood Beach
near the Walton County line

Citrus County
Withlacoochee State Forest, north of 480
and south and west of Inverness

Clay County
Gold Head Branch State Park, northeast
of Keystone Heights

Escambia County
Big Lagoon State Recreation Area, east of
Gulf Islands National Seashore

Hernando County
Chassahowitzka Wildlife Management
Area, south of the border of Citrus and
Hernando counties, along the west side
of U.S. 19
Withlacoochee State Forest

Highlands County
Archbold Biological Station, south of Lake
Placid
Highlands Hammock State Park, near
Sebring

Lake County
Rock Springs Run State Reserve (BMK
Ranch), west of Sanford

Levy County
Cedar Key Scrub State Reserve, on the
north side of SR 24, northeast of Cedar
Key

Manatee County
Lake Manatee State Recreation Area, east
of Bradenton

Marion County
"Big Scrub" and surrounding areas, Ocala
National Forest

Martin County
Jonathan Dickinson State Park, south of
Hobe Sound
Seabranch Reserve, near Port Salerno

Okaloosa County
Fred Gannon Rocky Bayou State Recreation Area, east of Niceville
Henderson Beach State Recreation Area,
near Destin

Orange County
Rock Springs Run State Reserve, west of
Sanford
Wekiwa Springs State Park, near Apopka

Palm Beach County
Jupiter Ridge, south of Indiantown Road,
Jupiter
Patch Reef Park, Boca Raton
Yamato Scrub, near Boca Raton (TNC)

Pasco County
Northwest part of county, defined by
county line and SRs 52, 55, and 45

Polk County
Lake Wales Ridge State Forest, east of
Frostproof
Tiger Creek Preserve, southeast of Lake
Wales (TNC)

Sumter County
North of SR 44

Walton County
Grayton Beach State Recreation Area,
Grayton Beach

Oak Scrubs

Alachua County
O'Leno State Park, north of High Springs

Brevard County
Melbourne Beach, south of Indialantic
Merritt Island National Wildlife Refuge,
near Titusville

Columbia County
O'Leno State Park, north of High Springs

Highlands County
Archbold Biological Station, south of Lake
Placid
Carter Creek (TNC)

Fishing Creek near Old Venus (TNC)
Holmes Avenue Scrub Wildlife and Environmental Area, near Lake Placid
Lake Glenda Scrub (TNC)
Lake Jackson Scrub (TNC)

Lake County
Rock Springs Run State Reserve, west of Sanford

Orange County
Wekiwa Springs State Park, near Apopka

Osceola County
Disney Wilderness Preserve, south of Kissimmee (TNC)

Palm Beach County
Juno Hills Natural Area, south of Jupiter Inlet

Polk County
Allan David Broussard Catfish Creek State Preserve, southeast of Haines City
Avon Park Air Force Range and west of Kicco Wildlife Management Area
Disney Wilderness Preserve, south of Kissimmee (TNC)
Lake Arbuckle State Forest, northeast of Avon Park
Lake Wales Ridge State Forest, east of Frostproof
Saddle Blanket Lakes Preserve, near Frostproof (TNC)
Tiger Creek Preserve, southeast of Lake Wales (TNC)

Seminole County
Lower Wekiva River State Preserve, west of Sanford

St. Lucie County
Savannas State Preserve, south of Fort Pierce

Upland Hardwood Forests

Hernando County
Annutteliga Hammock, northwest of Brooksville, off U.S. 98

Jackson County
Florida Caverns State Park, north of Marianna
Three Rivers State Recreation Area, north of Sneads

Jefferson County
Northern part of county

Leon County
Woodyard Hammock, Tall Timbers Research Station

Levy County
Along Suwannee River (areas east of County Road 347)
Andrews Wildlife Management Area, west of junction of U.S. 19 and County Road 211
South and east of Chassahowitzka National Wildlife Refuge (east of U.S. 98)

Liberty County
Torreya State Park, north of Bristol
West half of Apalachicola National Forest

Marion County
West of Ocala National Forest, north of Ft. McCoy

Suwannee County
Suwannee River State Park, northwest of Live Oak

Wakulla County
Wakulla Springs State Park, near Wakulla Springs

Washington County
Falling Waters State Recreation Area, south of Chipley

Slope Forests

Gadsden County
Chattahoochee Nature Park, Chattahoochee

Jackson County
Florida Caverns State Park, north of Marianna
Three Rivers State Recreation Area, north of Sneads

Leon County
Alfred B. Maclay State Gardens, north of Tallahassee

Liberty County
Apalachicola Bluffs and Ravines Preserve, east bank of Apalachicola River (TNC)
Torreya State Park, north of Bristol

Bluffs

Bay County
Econfina Creek Water Management Area, along Econfina Creek

Columbia County
Ichetucknee Springs State Park, near Fort White

Liberty County
Apalachicola Bluffs and Ravines Preserve, east bank of Apalachicola River (TNC)
Torreya State Park, north of Bristol

Suwannee County
Ichetucknee Springs State Park, near Fort White
Suwannee River State Park, northwest of Live Oak

Washington County
Econfina Creek Water Management Area, along Econfina Creek

Floodplain Forests

Alachua County
O'Leno State Park, north of High Springs

Clay County
Bayard Point Conservation Area, southeast of Green Cove Springs

Columbia County
Deep Creek Conservation Area, north of Lake City
Ichetucknee Springs State Park, near Fort White
O'Leno State Park, north of High Springs

Hamilton County
Belmont Conservation Area, east of Jasper and near the border of Columbia County

Jackson County
Florida Caverns State Park, north of Marianna
Ocheesee Pond and west floodplain of Apalachicola River

Lafayette County
Allen Mill Pond Conservation Area, north of Blue Spring along the border of Lafayette and Suwannee counties

Levy County
Andrews Wildlife Management Area, west of junction of U.S. 19 and County Road 211

Liberty County
Apalachicola Bluffs and Ravines Preserve, east bank of Apalachicola River (TNC), 2 miles north of Bristol
Torreya State Park, north of Bristol

Osceola County
Disney Wilderness Preserve, south of Kissimmee (TNC)

Polk County
Disney Wilderness Preserve, south of Kissimmee (TNC)

Putnam County
Dunns Creek Conservation Area, south of Palatka
Welaka State Forest, south of Welaka

Seminole County
Wekiva River Buffers Conservation Area, west of Sanford

St. Johns County
Deep Creek Conservation Area, north of Hastings

Suwannee County
Suwannee River State Park, northwest of Live Oak

Volusia County
Kratzert Conservation Area, south of Osteen

Mixed Hardwood Forests

Alachua County
Devil's Millhopper State Geological Site, northwest of Gainesville
O'Leno State Park, north of High Springs
Paynes Prairie State Preserve, south of Gainesville
San Felasco Hammock State Preserve, northwest of Gainesville

Citrus County
Fort Cooper State Park, southeast of Inverness
Withlacoochee State Forest, north of 480 and south and west of Inverness

Clay County

Gold Head Branch State Park, northeast of Keystone Heights

Columbia County

Ichetucknee Springs State Park, near Fort White

O'Leno State Park, north of High Springs

Hernando County

Chassahowitzka Wildlife Management Area, south of the border of Citrus and Hernando counties, along the west side of U.S. 19

Janet Butterfield Brooks Preserve, near Bailey Hill (TNC)

Highlands County

Archbold Biological Station, south of Lake Placid

Hillsborough County

Hillsborough River State Park, south of Zephyrhills

Jackson County

Three Rivers State Recreation Area, north of Sneads

Levy County

Andrews Wildlife Management Area, west of junction of U.S. 19 and County Road 211

Manatee Springs State Park, west of Chiefland

Marion County

Ocala National Forest

Orange County

Tosohatchee State Reserve, south of Christmas off Taylor Creek Road

Wekiwa Springs State Park, near Apopka

Suwannee County

Ichetucknee Springs State Park, near Fort White

Suwannee River State Park, northwest of Live Oak

Coastal Beach Dunes

Bay County

Camp Helen, west of Hollywood Beach near the Walton County line

St. Andrews State Recreation Area, south of Panama City

Brevard County

Archie Carr National Wildlife Refuge, Melbourne Beach and south

Canaveral National Seashore (south end), east of Titusville

Sebastian Inlet State Recreation Area, south of Melbourne Beach

Broward County

John U. Lloyd Beach State Recreation Area, northeast of Dania

Dade County

Bill Baggs Cape Florida State Recreation Area, southwest of Biscayne Bay Aquatic Preserve

Duval County

Big Talbot Island State Park, northeast of Jacksonville

Little Talbot Island State Park, northeast of Mayport

Escambia County

Big Lagoon State Recreation Area, east of Gulf Islands National Seashore

Perdido Key State Recreation Area, southwest of Pensacola

Santa Rosa Island National Seashore, south of Pensacola

Flagler County

Gamble Rogers Memorial State Recreation Area, south of Flagler Beach

Franklin County

St. George Island State Park (St. George Island), south of Eastpoint

St. Vincent's National Wildlife Refuge (St. Vincent's Island), southwest of Apalachicola

Gulf County

St. Joseph Peninsula State Park, Port St. Joe

Indian River County

Archie Carr National Wildlife Refuge

Martin County
Blowing Rock Preserve, north of Jupiter Inlet (TNC)

Monroe County
Bahia Honda State Park, south of Marathon

Nassau County
Amelia Island State Recreation Area, Amelia Island
Fort Clinch State Park, north of Fernandina Beach

Okaloosa County
Fred Gannon Rocky Bayou State Recreation Area, east of Niceville
Henderson Beach State Recreation Area, east of Destin

Palm Beach County
John D. MacArthur Beach State Park, North Palm Beach
Red Reef and Gumbo Limbo Parks, Boca Raton

Pasco County
Anclote Key State Preserve, Anclote Keys, west of Holiday

St. Lucie County
Avalon State Recreation Area, northeast of Fort Pierce
Fort Pierce Inlet State Recreation Area, east of Fort Pierce
Pepper Beach State Park, north of Fort Pierce Inlet Recreation Area
St. Lucie Inlet State Preserve, east of Port Salerno

Volusia County
Canaveral National Seashore (north end), south of New Smyrna

Walton County
Grayton Beach State Recreation Area, Grayton Beach
Topsail, near Destin

Coastal Strands

Bay County
St. Andrews State Recreation Area, south of Panama City

Brevard County
Archie Carr National Wildlife Refuge, Melbourne Beach and south
Canaveral National Seashore (south end), east of Titusville

Collier County
Marco Island, south of Belle Meade

Flagler County
Gamble Rogers Memorial State Recreation Area, south of Flagler Beach
Washington Oaks State Gardens, south of Marineland

Franklin County
St. George Island State Park (St. George Island), south of Eastpoint
St. Vincent's National Wildlife Refuge (St. Vincent's Island), southwest of Apalachicola

Gulf County
St. Joseph Peninsula State Park, Port St. Joe

Martin County
Blowing Rock Preserve, north of Jupiter Inlet (TNC)

Palm Beach County
Red Reef and Gumbo Limbo Parks, Boca Raton

St. Johns County
Guana River State Park, north of St. Augustine

St. Lucie County
Savannas State Preserve, south of Fort Pierce

Volusia County
Canaveral National Seashore (north end), south of New Smyrna
North Peninsula State Recreation Area, southeast of Bulow Plantation Ruins State Historic Site

Coastal Scrubs

Bay County
Camp Helen, west of Hollywood Beach near the Walton County line
St. Andrews State Recreation Area, south of Panama City

Brevard County

Archie Carr National Wildlife Refuge, Melbourne Beach and south

Canaveral National Seashore (south end), east of Titusville

Coconut Point, south of Melbourne Beach

Enchanted Forest Nature Sanctuary, south of Indian River City

Merritt Island National Wildlife Refuge, near Titusville

Collier County

Marco Island, south of Belle Meade

Duval County

Big Talbot Island State Park, northeast of Jacksonville

Escambia County

Fort Pickens State Park, west end of Santa Rosa Island

Flagler County

Gamble Rogers Memorial State Recreation Area, south of Flagler Beach

Washington Oaks State Gardens, south of Marineland

Franklin County

St. George Island State Park (St. George Island), south of Eastpoint

St. Vincent's National Wildlife Refuge (St. Vincent's Island), southwest of Apalachicola

Gulf County

St. Joseph Peninsula State Park, Port St. Joe

Indian River County

Archie Carr National Wildlife Refuge

Martin County

Hobe Sound National Wildlife Refuge, Hobe Sound

Seabranch Reserve, near Port Salerno

Palm Beach County

Juno Hills Natural Area, south of Jupiter Inlet

Jupiter Inlet, northeast of Jupiter

St. Johns County

Guana River State Park, north of St. Augustine

Volusia County

Canaveral National Seashore (north end), south of New Smyrna

North Peninsula State Recreation Area, southeast of Bulow Plantation Ruins State Historic Site

Walton County

Grayton Beach State Recreation Area, Grayton Beach

Topsail, near Destin

Coastal Grasslands

Bay County

Camp Helen, west of Hollywood Beach near the Walton County line

Brevard County

Canaveral National Seashore (south end), near Titusville

Cape Canaveral, near Titusville

Sebastian Inlet State Recreation Area, south of Melbourne Beach

Escambia County

Fort Pickens State Park, west end of Santa Rosa Island

Gulf Islands National Seashore, west of Santa Rosa Island

Franklin County

St. George Island State Park (St. George Island), south of Eastpoint

St. Vincent's National Wildlife Refuge (St. Vincent's Island), southwest of Apalachicola

Gulf County

St. Joseph Peninsula State Park, Port St. Joe

Lee County

Cayo Costa Island State Park, Boca Grande

Pasco County

Anclote Key State Preserve, Anclote Keys, west of Holiday

Pinellas County

Caladesi Island State Park, west of Dunedin

Coastal Hammocks

Bay County

Camp Helen, west of Hollywood Beach near the Walton County line

Brevard County

Archie Carr National Wildlife Refuge, near Melbourne Beach

Canaveral National Seashore (south end), east of Titusville

Cape Canaveral, near Titusville

Coconut Point, south of Melbourne Beach

Enchanted Forest Nature Sanctuary, south of Indian River City

Sebastian Inlet State Recreation area, south of Melbourne Beach

Broward County

Hugh Taylor Birch State Recreation Area, Fort Lauderdale

John U. Lloyd Beach State Recreation Area, northeast of Dania

Duval County

Big Talbot Island State Park, northeast of Jacksonville

Little Talbot Island State Park, northeast of Mayport

Escambia County

Gulf Islands National Seashore, west of Santa Rosa Island

Flagler County

Washington Oaks State Gardens south of Marineland

Martin County

Blowing Rock Preserve, north of Jupiter Inlet (TNC)

Monroe County

Bahia Honda State Park, south of Marathon

Nassau County

Amelia Island State Recreation Area, south end of Amelia Island

Fort Clinch State Park, north of Fernandina Beach

Palm Beach County

John D. MacArthur Beach State Park, North Palm Beach

Red Reef and Gumbo Limbo Parks, Boca Raton

Pasco County

Anclote Key State Preserve, Anclote Keys, west of Holiday

Pinellas County

Caladesi Island State Park, west of Dunedin

St. Johns County

Anastasia State Recreation Area, on Anastasia Island, south of St. Augustine

Fort Matanzas National Monument (south end), south of Crescent Beach

Guana River State Park, north of St. Augustine

St. Lucie County

Avalon State Recreation Area, northeast of Fort Pierce

Fort Pierce Inlet State Recreation Area, east of Fort Pierce

St. Lucie Inlet State Preserve, near Port Salerno

Volusia County

Canaveral National Seashore (north end), south of New Smyrna

Tomoka State Park, west of Ormond-by-the-Sea

Walton County

Grayton Beach State Recreation Area, Grayton Beach

Rockland Pinelands

Dade County

Deering Estate Park, Miami

Long Pine Key, Everglades National Park

Monroe County

Big Pine Key, west of Marathon

Cudjoe Key, west of Big Pine Key

Key Largo Hammock State Botanical Site, Key Largo

Tropical Hardwood Hammocks

Collier County

Collier-Seminole State Park, northeast of Marco Island

Corkscrew Swamp Sanctuary, northeast of Bonita Springs off 846

Fakahatchee Strand State Preserve, east of Copeland

Dade County

Deering Estate Park, Miami

Elliott Key, north of Key Largo

Mahogany Hammock, Everglades National Park

Matheson Hammock County Park, east of Kendall

Martin County

Blowing Rock Preserve, north of Jupiter Inlet (TNC)

Monroe County

Bahia Honda State Park, south of Marathon

Cudjoe Key, west of Big Pine Key

John Pennekamp Coral Reef State Park, Key Largo

Key Largo Hammock State Botanical Site, Key Largo

Lignumvitae Key State Botanical Site, Islamorada

Long Key State Recreation Area, Long Key

No Name Key, east of Big Pine Key (TNC)

Royal Palm Hammock (Paradise Key), Everglades National Park

Sugarloaf Key, west of Cudjoe Key

Summerland Key, west of Big Pine Key (TNC)

Torchwood Hammock Preserve, Little Torch Key, west of Big Pine Key (TNC)

Palm Beach County

John D. MacArthur Beach State Park, North Palm Beach

Glossary

Achene (akene). A one-seeded, nonsplitting hard fruit.

Aerial root. A root that grows from the stem anchoring the plant to a substrate. Usually several aerial roots are produced, as in poison ivy.

Alternate. Not opposite, but appearing on one side of an axis and then on the other side.

Annual. A plant whose life cycle from seed sprouting through seed production and death occurs in one year.

Anther. Pollen-producing part of the male reproductive organ (stamen).

Awn. A bristlelike structure that is often stiff.

Axil. Angle formed between two structures.

Axillary. In or arising from an axil, such as a leaf joined to a stem.

Basal leaf. Leaves growing at the base of the stem and flush with the ground.

Berry. A fleshy fruit lacking a stone, but usually with many seeds in the pulp.

Biennial. A plant whose life cycle from seed sprouting through seed production and death occurs during a two-year period.

Bilabiate. Being two-lipped, such as a flower of a snapdragon.

Blade. Expanded part of a leaf or other organ.

Bract. Reduced leaf located below the inflorescence, flower, or flower part.

Bracteate. Having bracts.

Bulb. A short, often roundish, underground stem that is surrounded by fleshy leaves.

Calyx. Collectively the sepals.

Capsule. Dry fruit that splits along definite lines.

Caryopsis. A one-seeded, nonsplitting fruit.

Catkin. Spikelike inflorescence or ament that is unisexual, lacks petals, and is often pendulous.

Clasping. Reaching around or hugging the stem, such as a clasping leaf.

Compound leaf. A leaf composed of two or more leaflets.

Corolla. Collectively the petals.

Culm. Stem of a grass or sedge.

Cyathium. A cuplike structure enclosing the reduced flowers in certain members of the spurge family (Euphorbiaceae).

Deciduous. A plant that loses its leaves essentially at the same time every year.

Decumbent. Lying flat or nearly so on the ground.

Disk (Disc). An enlarged outgrowth of the receptacle. The central part of the head of a composite flower that contains tubular or disk florets.

Disk floret. Tubular flowers that comprise the disk of the head of certain members of the daisy family (Asteraceae).

Dissected. Divided into smaller, finer parts.

Drupe. A fleshy fruit, usually with one seed (pit) that is surrounded by a hard covering.

Drupelet. A small drupe.

Elliptic. Widest at the middle, tapering to both ends.

Endemic. Limited to a particular geographic region.

Entire margin. Toothless or smooth-edged, as in certain leaves.

Epiphyte. A plant, such as certain bromeliads (Bromeliaceae) and certain orchids (Orchidaceae), that uses another plant or other substrate for an anchor rather than the soil. Nonparasitic.

Evergreen. A plant that retains green leaves throughout the year. Term not limited to cedars, spruce, and other gymnosperms.

Falcate. Sickle-shaped.

Filament. Stalk of a stamen to which an anther is attached.

Filiform. Threadlike.

Floret. A small flower, as found in members of the aster family (Asteraceae) or grass family (Poaceae).

Foliate. Bearing leaves.

Glabrous. Smooth or lacking hairs.

Gland-dotted. Having glands that resemble dots or circles.

Grain. A one-seeded, nonsplitting fruit.

Herb. Typically a nonwoody plant, such as an annual, that dies to ground level during the dormant season.

Herbaceous. Not woody.

Hood. A structure that extends over some other part, as in certain pitcher-plants. Segment of the corona of milkweeds.

Infertile stamen or staminode. Sterile stamen with nonfunctional anthers.

Inflorescence. Arrangement of flowers on a plant. Flower cluster. Common types of inflorescences are spike, raceme, panicle, corymb, umbel, and cyme.

Internode. Region of a stem between nodes.

Involucre. A series of bracts surrounding a single flower or flower cluster. *See* Phyllary.

Lanceolate. A narrow shape that is broader at the base, gradually tapering to the tip.

Leaf axil. The angle between the leaf petiole and stem or stalk.

Leaflet. A blade or secondary leaf of a compound leaf.

Legume. Fruit of certain members of the bean family (Fabaceae) that usually opens along two sutures. Commonly called a pod or seedpod.

Linear. Narrow and much longer than wide.

Lip. The upper or lower part of the corolla or calyx that is parted. The odd petal (labellum) of an orchid that often is the largest.

Loment. Fruit of certain members of the bean family (Fabaceae), where constrictions occur between the seeds.

Margin. Outer edge of a flattened structure such as a leaf or leaflet. The edge may be smooth (entire) or variously toothed.

Midrib. Main vein of a leaf or leaflet.

Node. The place on a stem where branches, leaves, or the flowering stalk are attached. A joint.

Nut. A hard, one-seeded and one-celled fruit.

Nutlet. A small, one-seeded nut.

Oblong. Longer than broad, and with the sides nearly parallel most of their length.

Ocrea. A nodal sheath, having or lacking spines as in the Polygonaceae, that is formed by the fusion of two stipules.

Ovate. With an outline that is widest toward the base.

Palmate. Arising and radiating from a common point.

Panicle. A type of inflorescence that is a branching raceme.

Pappus. Bristles, scales, or awns that represent modifications of the calyx, as found in members of the aster family (Asteraceae). These modifications can be best seen in mature fruits.

Parallel veins. Veins that run lengthwise and parallel to each other.

Pedicel. Stalk of an individual flower in a cluster of several flowers.

Peduncle. Stalk of a flower cluster or a solitary flower.

Perennial. A plant that survives the winter or a dormant period for two or more years.

Perianth. Collectively the petals and sepals. Often the parts are of similar color, as in many lilies.

Petal. A single, usually colored, component of the corolla. Petals form the innermost whorl of nonreproductive flower parts.

Petaloid. Resembling a petal.

Petiole. Stalk of a leaf.

Petioled. Having a petiole.

Phyllary. An involucral bract, as found in members of the aster family (Asteraceae). *See* Involucre.

Pinnate. Feather-formed; with the leaflets of a compound leaf placed on either side of the rachis.

Plumose. Featherlike.

Pseudobulb. Solid, bulblike stem of certain orchids.

Pubescent. Covering of soft hairs.

Raceme. Spikelike inflorescence with single-stalked flowers.

Rachis. That part of the petiole between the leaflets of a compound leaf.

Ray floret. Flower with a strap-shaped petal (ray or ligule), as in certain members of the daisy family (Asteraceae). Contrasting flower is the disk or tubular floret that lacks the ray.

Receptacle. The terminal part of a pedicel or peduncle, to which the flower parts are attached, or the expanded axis of a flower-head, as in Asteraceae.

Reflexed. Bent downward or backward.

Reticulate. Netlike, as in the veins of many leaves.

Rhizome. Rootlike, horizontal stem; often underground.

Rosette. Leaves in a circular cluster at the base of a plant.

Scape. Stalk of a plant having few or no leaves.

Schizocarp. A dry fruit that splits into two one-seeded halves called mericarps.

Secondary woods. Any forested land that was once in cultivation or disturbed and has been allowed to become reforested.

Seed. A mature ovule.

Seedpod. Podlike fruit containing seeds.

Sepal. A segment of the calyx. Sepals form the outermost whorl of nonreproductive flower parts.

Sessile. Lacking a stalk, petiole, pedicel, or peduncle.

Silique. A narrow, elongated, podlike capsule of certain members of the mustard (Brassicaceae) family and caper (Capparaceae) family. Siliques of capers lack the false septum.

Simple. Undivided or single; not compound.

Spadix. Fleshy spike that bears tiny flowers, as in members of the arum family (Araceae).

Spathe. Leafy bract.

Spatulate. Spoon-shaped.

Spike. An elongated, unbranched inflorescence with sessile flowers.

Spikelet. Basic floral unit of the inflorescence of grasses (Poaceae) and sedges (Cyperaceae).

Spur. A tubular projection of a petal or sepal.

Stamen. Male reproductive organ consisting of a stalk (the filament) and a pollen-producing part (the anther).

Staminode. A sterile stamen. *See* Infertile stamen.

Stem. The main axis of a plant that bears the leaves and flowers.

Style. Stalklike extension above the ovary, terminating at the stigma.

Succulent. Being thick, fleshy, and juicy.

Tendril. Usually a slender, coiling or twining appendage used for support in climbing plants such as members of the grape family (Vitaceae). Tendrils may be branched or unbranched.

Tepal. A unit of the perianth when it is not clearly differentiated into a sepal and a petal.

Tomentose. Pubescence of dense, matted, soft hairs. Velvety.

Umbel. An inflorescence whose flower stalks (pedicels) meet at a common point, like the ribs of an umbrella. Many members of the carrot family (Apiaceae) and milkweed family (Asclepiadiaceae) have umbels.

Unifoliate. Having one leaf or leaflet.

Utricle. A bladderlike achene.

Viscid. Sticky.

Wildflower. A flowering plant growing in a natural state.

Whorl. Arrangement of three or more structures arising from the same location.

Selected References

Abrahamson, W. G., and D. C. Hartnett. "Pine Flatwoods and Dry Prairies." In *Ecosystems of Florida*, ed. R. L. Myers and J. J. Ewel, 103–49. Orlando: University of Central Florida Press, 1990.

Ajilvsgi, G. *Wild Flowers of the Big Thicket: East Texas, and Western Louisiana*. College Station: Texas A & M University Press, 1979.

Amoroso, J. L., and W. S. Judd. "A Floristic Study of the Cedar Key Scrub Reserve, Levy County, Florida." *Castanea* 60, no. 3 (September 1995): 210–32.

Anderson, L. C. "Noteworthy Plants from North Florida." *Sida* 10, (1984): 295–97.

———. "Noteworthy Plants from North Florida II." *Sida* 11, no. 4 (1986): 379–84.

———. "Noteworthy Plants from North Florida III." *Sida* 13, no. 1 (1988): 93–100.

———. "Noteworthy Plants from North Florida IV." *Sida* 13, no. 4 (1989): 497–504.

———. "Noteworthy Plants from North Florida V." *Sida* 14, no. 4 (1991): 467–74.

———. "Noteworthy Plants from North Florida VI." *Sida* 16, no. 3 (1995): 581–87.

Anonymous. "Recreational Guide to Southwest Florida Water Management District Lands." Southwest Florida Water Management District, Land Resources Department, January 1994.

Anonymous. "Recreation Guide to District Lands." 1st ed. St. Johns River Water Management District, Division of Public Information, and the Division of Land Management, Spring 1995.

Austin, D. F. "Vegetation of Southeastern Florida, USA. Part 1. Pine Jog." *Florida Scientist* 39, no. 4 (Fall 1976): 230–35.

Austin, D. F., K. Coleman-Marois, and D. R. Richardson. "Vegetation of Southeastern Florida II–V." *Florida Scientist* 40, no. 4 (Fall 1977): 331–61.

Austin, D. F. "Studies of the Florida Convolvulaceae—III. Cuscuta." *Florida Scientist* 43, no. 4 (Fall 1980): 294–302.

Austin, D. F., P. N. Honychurch, and S. C. Bass. *Coastal Park Plant Guide.* Boca Raton, Fla.: City of Boca Raton, 1989.

———. *Coastal Dune Plants. A Pocket Guide to the Common Plants of Southeast Florida's Ocean-side Communities.* Boca Raton, Fla.: City of Boca Raton, 1991.

———. *Scrub Plant Guide. A Pocket Guide to the Common Plants of Southern Florida's Scrub Community.* Boca Raton, Fla.: Gumbo Limbo Nature Center of South Palm Beach County, Inc. 1993.

———. *Coastal Hammock and Mangrove Guide. A Pocket Guide to the Common Trees, Shrubs, and Vines of S.E. Florida's Hammock and Mangrove Communities.* Boca Raton, Fla.: Gumbo Limbo Nature Center of South Palm Beach County, Inc. 1997.

Avery, G. N., and L. L. Loope. "Plants of Everglades National Park: A Preliminary Checklist of Vascular Plants." Report T–574. U.S. Natl. Park Service, South Florida Research Center, Everglades National Park, Homestead, Fla., 1980.

Baker, M. F. *Florida Wild Flowers: An Introduction to the Florida Flora.* New York: Macmillan, 1959.

Bartram, W. *Travels Through North and South Carolina, Georgia, East and West Florida, the Cherokee Country, the Extensive Territories of the Muscogulges, or Creek Confederacy, and the Country of the Chactaws.* Introduction by James Dickey. New York: Viking Penguin, 1988.

Bell, C. R., and B. J. Taylor. *Florida Wild Flowers and Roadside Plants.* Chapel Hill, N.C.: Laurel Hill Press, 1982.

Bergh, C., and J. Wisby. "Fire History of Lower Keys Pine Rocklands." The Nature Conservancy, Florida Keys Initiative, Key West, Fla., May 1996.

Berkeley, E., and D. S. Berkeley. *The Life and Travels of John Bartram.* Tallahassee: University Presses of Florida, 1982.

Blanchard, J., and S. Jue. "Florida Conservation Lands." Florida Natural Areas Inventory, Tallahassee, Fla., March 1997.

Bullard, L. F., and J. B. Harrell. "Coastal Plants of Florida: A Key to Good Land Management." Florida Department of Agriculture and Consumer Services, Division of Forestry, Tallahassee, Fla., 1979.

Buswell, W. M. "Native Orchids of South Florida." *Bulletin of University of Miami* 19, no. 3 (February 1945): 1–29.

Cerulean, S., and A. Morrow. "Florida Trails." Florida Department of Commerce, Division of Tourism, Tallahassee, Fla. (no date).

Chapman, A. W. *Flora of the Southern United States.* 3rd ed. New York: American Book Co., 1897.

Chen, E., and J. F. Gerber. "Climate." In *Ecosystems of Florida,* ed. R. L. Myers and J. J. Ewel, 11–34. Orlando: University of Central Florida Press, 1990.

Christman, S. P. "The Florida Scrub: Our Oldest and Most Rapidly Disappearing Plant Communities." Florida Defenders of the Environment, Bulletin 28, Nov.–Dec. 1988.

Christman, S. P., and W. S. Judd. "Notes on Plants Endemic to Florida Scrub." *Florida Scientist* 53, no. 1 (Winter 1990): 52–73.

Clewell, A. F. *Guide to the Vascular Plants of the Florida Panhandle.* Tallahassee: Florida State University Press, 1985.

———. "Natural Setting and Vegetation of the Florida Panhandle."COESAM/ PDEI-86/001, Contract No. DACW O1–77-C- 0104. U.S. Army Corps Engr., Mobile, Ala., 1986.

Coile, N. C. "Notes on Florida's Endangered and Threatened Plants." Florida Department of Agriculture and Consumer Services, Division of Plant Industry, Bureau of Entomology, Nematology and Plant Pathology, Botany Section, Gainesville, Contribution No. 38, 1996.

Cox, J., R. Kautz, M. MacLaughlin, and T. Gilbert. "Closing the Gaps in Florida's Wildlife Habitat Conservation System." Office of Environmental Services, Florida Game and Fresh Water Fish Commission, 620 South Meridian Street, Tallahassee, Fla., 1994.

Craig, R. M. "Woody Vegetation for Coastal Dune Areas." *Proceedings of the Florida State Horticultural Society* 88, (4–6 November 1975): 428–34.

Davis, J. H. "General Map of Natural Vegetation of Florida." Institute of Food and Agricultural Sciences, Florida Agricultural Experimental Station, Circular S-178. Gainesville: University of Florida, 1967.

deHart, A. *Adventuring in Florida.* Revised ed. Westminster, Maryland: Random House, 1995.

Delaney, K. R., and R. P. Wunderlin. "A New Species of *Crotalaria* (Fabaceae) from the Florida Central Ridge." *Sida* 13, no. 3 (1989): 315–24.

Doing, H. "Coastal Fore-dune Zonation and Succession in Various Parts of the World." In *Ecology of Coastal Vegetation,* ed. W. G. Beeftink, J. Rozema, and A. H. L. Huiskies, 65–77. The Hague: Junk, 1981.

Duncan, W. H., and L. E. Foote. *Wildflowers of the Southeastern United States.* Athens: University of Georgia Press, 1975.

Easley, M. C., and W. S. Judd. "Vascular Flora of the Southern Upland Property of Paynes Prairie State Preserve, Alachua County, Florida." *Castanea* 55, no. 3 (September 1990): 142–86.

———. "Vascular Flora of Little Talbot Island, Duval County, Florida." *Castanea* 58, no. 3 (September 1993): 162–77.

Easterday, J. C. "A Flora of Paynes Prairie Basin and Alachua Sink Hammock." M.S. thesis, University of Florida, Gainesville.

Ewan, J., ed. *A Short History of Botany in the United States.* New York: Hafner Publishing Company, 1969.

Florida Natural Areas Inventory and Department of Natural Resources. "Guide to the Natural Communities of Florida." Tallahassee, Fla., February 1990.

Foster, S., and J. A. Duke. *A Field Guide to Medicinal Plants: Eastern and Central North America.* New York: Houghton Mifflin Co., 1990.

Franz, R., and D. W. Hall. "Vegetative Communities and Annotated Plant Lists for the Katharine Ordway Preserve–Swisher Memorial Sanctuary, Putnam County, Florida." Ordway Preserve Res. Series, Rept. No. 3, Florida Museum of Natural History, University of Florida, Gainesville, January 1991.

Gleasner, B., and D. Gleasner. *Florida Off the Beaten Path.* 4th ed. Old Saybrook, Conn.: Globe Pequot Press, 1993.

Godfrey, R. K. *Trees, Shrubs, and Woody Vines of Northern Florida and Adjacent Georgia and Alabama.* Athens: University of Georgia Press, 1988.

Godfrey, R. K., and J. W. Wooten. *Aquatic and Wetland Plants of Southeastern United States: Monocotyledons.* Athens: University of Georgia Press, 1979.

———. *Aquatic and Wetland Plants of Southeastern United States: Dicotyledons.* Athens: University of Georgia Press, 1981.

Greene, W. F., and H. L. Blomquist. *Flowers of the South: Native Exotic.* Chapel Hill: University of North Carolina Press, 1953.

Greller, A. M. "Correlation of Some Climatic Statistics with Distribution of Broadleaved Forest Zones in Florida, U.S.A." *Bull. Torrey Botanical Club* 107, no. 2 (April–June 1980): 189–219.

Gunderson, L., D. Taylor, and J. Craig. "Fire Effects on Flowering and Fruiting Patterns of Understory Plants in Pinelands of Everglades National Park." Report SFRC-83/04. U.S. Natl. Park Service, South Florida Research Center, Everglades National Park, Homestead, Fla., 1983.

Hall, D. W. *Illustrated Plants of Florida and the Coastal Plain.* Gainesville, Fla.: Maupin House, 1993.

Hanna, A. J., and K. A. Hanna. *Florida's Golden Sands.* Indianapolis: Bobb-Merrill Co., 1950.

Harper, R. M. "Geography and Vegetation of Northern Florida." *Sixth Annual Report Florida State Geological Survey,* 1914, 163–437.

———. "A Preliminary List of the Endemic Flowering Plants of Florida." *Journal of Florida Academy of Sciences* 11, no. 1 (March 1948): 25–35.

Herring, B. J., and W. S. Judd. "A Floristic Study of Ichetucknee Springs State Park, Suwannee and Columbia Counties, Florida." *Castanea* 60, no. 4 (December 1995): 318–69.

Hitchcock, A. S. *Manual of the Grasses of the United States.* 2nd ed. Revised by Agnes Chase. USDA Misc. Publ. 200. Washington, D.C.: U. S. Government Printing Office, 1950.

Huck, R. B., W. S. Judd, W. M. Whitten, J. D. Skean, Jr., R. P. Wunderlin, and K. R. Delaney. "A New *Dicerandra* (Labiatae) from the Lake Wales Ridge of Florida, with a Cladistic Analysis and Discussion of Endemism." *Systematic Botany* 14, no. 2 (1989): 197–213.

Hume, H. H. "Advancing Knowledge of Florida's Vast Plant Life." *Proceedings of the Florida Academy of Sciences for 1937* 2 (1938): 5–12.

———. "Botanical Explorers of the Southeastern United States." *Florida Historical Quarterly* 21, no. 4 (April 1943): 289–304.

Johnson, A. F., and M. G. Barbour. "Dunes and Maritime Forests." In *Ecosystems of Florida,* ed. R. L. Myers and J. J. Ewel, 429–80. Orlando: University of Central Florida Press, 1990.

Johnson, A. F., and J. W. Muller. "An Assessment of Florida's Remaining Coastal Upland Natural Communities: Southwest Florida." Florida Natural Areas Inventory, Tallahassee, Fla., 1992.

———. "An Assessment of Florida's Remaining Coastal Upland Natural Communities: Northeast Florida." Florida Natural Areas Inventory, Tallahassee, Fla., 1992.

————. "An Assessment of Florida's Remaining Coastal Upland Natural Communities: Final Summary Report." Florida Natural Areas Inventory, Tallahassee, Fla., 1993.

Johnson, A. F., J. W. Muller, and K. A. Bettinger. "An Assessment of Florida's Remaining Coastal Upland Natural Communities: Panhandle." Florida Natural Areas Inventory, Tallahassee, Fla., 1992.

Klinkenberg, M., and E. Leach. *Natural Wonders of Florida: A Guide to Parks, Preserves, and Wild Places.* Castine, Maine: Country Roads Press, 1996.

Kurz, H., and R. K. Godfrey. *The Trees of Northern Florida.* Gainesville: University of Florida Press, 1962.

Lamson-Scribner, F. "Southern Botanists." *Bull. Torrey Botanical Club* 20, no. 7 (1893): 315–34.

Laudonniere, R. *Three Voyages.* Translated and an introduction and notes by Charles E. Bennett. Gainesville: University Presses of Florida, 1975.

Lins, H. F., Jr. "Patterns and Trends of Land Use and Land Cover on Atlantic and Gulf Coast Barrier Islands." Geological Survey Professional Paper 1156, U.S. Geological Survey. Washington, D.C.: U.S. Government Printing Office, 1980.

Lippold, W., and M. L. Lippold. *Florida State and National Parks.* St. Augustine, Fla.: CWS Publications, 1994.

Long, R. W., and O. Lakela. *A Flora of Tropical Florida.* Coral Gables, Fla.: University of Miami Press, 1976.

Loope, L. L. "Phenology of Flowering and Fruiting in Plant Communities of Everglades National Park and Biscayne National Monument, Florida." Report T-593. U.S. Natl. Park Service, South Florida Research Center, Everglades National Park, Homestead, Fla., 1980.

Loope, L. L., D. W. Black, S. Black, and G. N. Avery. "Distribution and Abundance of Flora in Limestone Rockland Pine Forests of Southeastern Florida." Report T-547. U.S. Natl. Park Service, South Florida Research Center, Everglades National Park, Homestead, Fla., 1979.

McMillon, B. *Country Roads of Florida.* Castine, Maine: Country Roads Press, 1994.

Michaux, A. "Journal de André Michaux." Cahier 2, 1787-Cahier 10, 1796. Introduction and explanatory notes by C. S. Sargent. *Proceedings of the American Philosophical Society* 36, no. 129 (January to July 1889): 1–145.

Mitchell, R. S. "Phytogeography and Floristic Survey of a Relic Area in the Marianna Lowlands, Florida." *American Midland Naturalist* 69, no. 2 (1963): 328–66.

Monk, C. D. "Southern Mixed Hardwood Forests of Northcentral Florida." *Ecological Monographs* 35, no. 4 (1965): 335–54.

Myers, R. L. "Scrub and High Pine." In *Ecosystems of Florida,* ed. R. L. Myers and J. J. Ewel, 150–93. Orlando: University of Central Florida Press, 1990.

Nellis, D. W. *Seashore Plants of South Florida and the Caribbean: A Guide to Identification and Propagation of Xeriscape Plants.* Sarasota, Fla.: Pineapple Press, 1994.

Nelson, G. *The Trees of Florida: A Reference and Field Guide.* Sarasota, Fla.: Pineapple Press, 1994.

————. *The Shrubs and Woody Vines of Florida: A Reference and Field Guide.* Sarasota, Fla.: Pineapple Press, 1996.

Norman, E. M. "An Analysis of the Vegetation at Turtle Mound." *Florida Scientist* 39, no. 1 (Winter 1976): 19–31.

Norman, E. M., and S. S. Hawley. "An Analysis of the Vegetation at Turtle Mound, Volusia County, Florida: Twenty Years Later." *Florida Scientist* 58, no. 3 (Summer 1995): 258–69.

Oostings, H. J., and W. D. Billings. "Factors Affecting Vegetational Zonation on Coastal Dunes." *Ecology* 23, (1942): 131–42.

Peet, R. K. "A Taxonomic Study of *Aristida stricta* and *A. beyrichiana*." *Rhodora* 95, no. 881 (1993): 25–37.

Perry, J., and J. G. Perry. *The Sierra Club Guide to the Natural Areas of Florida.* San Francisco: Sierra Club Books, 1992.

Platt, W. J., and M. W. Schwartz. "Temperate Hardwood Forests." In *Ecosystems of Florida*, ed. R. L. Myers and J. J. Ewel, 194–229. Orlando: University of Central Florida Press, 1990.

Poppleton, J. E., A. G. Shuey, and H. C. Sweet. "Vegetation of Central Florida's East Coast: A Checklist of the Vascular Plants." *Florida Scientist* 40, no. 4 (Fall 1977): 362–89.

Porcher, R.D. *Wildflowers of the Carolina Lowcountry and Lower Pee Dee.* Columbia: University of South Carolina Press, 1995.

Pritchard, P. C. H., and H. W. Kale. "Saving What's Left." Florida Audubon Society, Altamonte Springs, Florida, 1994.

Radford, A. E., H. E. Ahles, and C. R. Bell. *Manual of the Vascular Flora of the Carolinas.* 10th Printing. Chapel Hill: University of North Carolina Press, 1987.

Richardson, D. R. "Vegetation of the Atlantic Coastal Ridge of Palm Beach County, Florida." *Florida Scientist* 40, no. 4 (Fall 1977): 281–330.

Rickett, H. W. *Wildflowers of the United States: The Southeastern States.* Vol. 2 (Parts 1 and 2). New York: McGraw-Hill Book Company, 1967.

Romans, B. *A Concise Natural History of East and West Florida: A Facsimile Reproduction of the 1775 Edition.* Gainesville: University of Florida Press, 1962.

Scalpone, J. L. *Florida Super Parks.* 2nd Printing. Punta Gorda, Fla.: Chris the Printer. 1990.

Schmalzer, P. A., and C. R. Hinkle. "Flora and Threatened and Endangered Plants of John F. Kennedy Space Center, Florida." NASA Technical Memorandum 102791, John F. Kennedy Space Center, August 1990.

Scurlock, J. P. *Native Trees and Shrubs of the Florida Keys: A Field Guide.* Bethel Park, Penn.: Laurel Press, 1987.

Slaughter, T. P. *William Bartram: Travels and Other Writings.* New York: Literary Classics of the United States, 1996.

Small, J. K. *Manual of the Southeastern Flora.* Part 1. New York: Hafner Publishing Co., 1972.

————. *Manual of the Southeastern Flora.* Part 2. New York: Hafner Publishing Co., 1972.

Snyder, J. R., A. Herndon, W. B. Robertson, Jr. "South Florida Rockland." In *Ecosystems of Florida*, ed. R. L. Myers and J. J. Ewel, 230–74. Orlando: University of Central Florida Press, 1990.

Stevenson, G. B. "Trees of Everglades National Park and the Florida Keys." Distributed by Florida National Parks and Monuments Association, P.O. 279, Homestead, Fla., 1992.

Stout, I. J., and W. R. Marion. "Pine Flatwoods and Xeric Pine Forests of the Southern (Lower) Coast Plain." In *Biodiversity of the Southeastern United States: Lowland Terrestrial Communities*, ed. William H. Martin, Stephen G. Boyce, and Arthur C. Echternacht, 373–446. New York: John Wiley and Sons, 1993.

Tan, B. H., and W. S. Judd. "A Floristic Inventory of O'Leno State Park and Northeast River Rise State Preserve, Alachua and Columbia Counties, Florida." *Castanea* 60, no. 2 (June 1995): 141–63.

Taylor, W. K. *The Guide to Florida Wildflowers*. Dallas, Tex.: Taylor Publishing Co., 1992.

Ward, D. B. *Plants*. Vol. 5 of *Rare and Endangered Biota of Florida*, ed. P. C. H. Pritchard. Gainesville: University Presses of Florida, 1979.

Webb, S. D. "Historical Biogeography." In *Ecosystems of Florida*, ed. R. L. Myers and J. J. Ewel, 70–100. Orlando: University of Central Florida Press, 1990.

West, E., and M. W. Emmel. "Plants That Poison Farm Animals." Institute of Food and Agricultural Sciences, University of Florida, Gainesville: Bulletin 510A (1987): 3–55.

White, D. L., and W. S. Judd. "A Flora of Gold Head Branch Ravine and Adjacent Uplands, Clay County, Florida." *Castanea* 50, no. 4 (December 1985): 250–61.

Windler, D. R. "A Systematic Treatment of the Native Unifoliolate Crotalarias of North America (Leguminosae)." *Rhodora* 76, no. 806 (1974): 151–204.

Wood, D. A. "Florida's Endangered Species, Threatened Species and Species of Special Concern." Official Lists. Florida Game and Fresh Water Fish Commission. Tallahassee, Fla.: Bureau of Nongame Wildlife, Division of Wildlife, 1996.

Wunderlin, R. P. *Guide to the Vascular Plants of Central Florida*. Tampa: University Presses of Florida, 1982.

———. *Guide to the Vascular Plants of Florida*. Gainesville: University Press of Florida, 1998.

Wunderlin, R. P., and B. F. Hansen. "Preliminary Checklist of the Vascular Flora of Florida with Major Synonyms: Atlas Version." Unpublished checklist, Department of Biology, Tampa: University of South Florida, 1996.

Wunderlin, R. P., B. F. Hansen, and D. W. Hall. "The Vascular Flora of Central Florida: Taxonomic and Nomenclatural Changes, Additional Taxa." *Sida* 11 (1985): 232–44.

Index to People and Places

Bold indicates a page with a photograph.

Index to Species and Families

Bold indicates a page with a line drawing or a photograph.

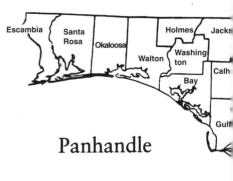

Panhandle